The Intelligence Test Desk Reference (ITDR)

The Intelligence Test Desk Reference (ITDR)

Gf-Gc Cross-Battery Assessment

Kevin S. McGrew
St. Cloud State University

Dawn P. Flanagan
St. John's University, New York

Foreword by
John B. Carroll

Allyn and Bacon
Boston • London • Toronto • Sydney • Tokyo • Singapore

Series Editor: Carla F. Daves
Series Editorial Assistant: Susan Hutchinson
Manufacturing Buyer: Suzanne Lareau

Library of Congress Cataloging-in-Publication Data

McGrew, Kevin S.
    The intelligence test desk reference (ITDR) : *Gf-Gc* cross-battery
assessment / Kevin S. McGrew, Dawn P. Flanagan.
        p.   cm.
    Includes bibliographical references and index.
    ISBN 0-205-19857-0
    1. Intelligence tests. 2. Intellect. I. Flanagan, Dawn P.
II. Title.
BF431.M3514 1998
153.9′3—dc21
97-27414
        CIP

Printed in the United States of America

10 9 8 7 6 5 4 3 2 1   02 01 00 99 98

To our mentors

Richard Woodcock
KSM

Judy Genshaft
DPF

For teaching us, guiding us, challenging us, and helping us to develop important skills in our profession. Through your expertise, encouragement, and support we have benefited professionally and personally. Thank you for enabling us to make a contribution to our profession.

Contents

PART III   The Gf-Gc Cross-Battery Approach to Assessing and Interpreting Cognitive Abilities

Foreword

This is a remarkable book. It covers or touches on just about everything that can now be stated about the structures of intellectual abilities as measured by currently available individual intelligence and cognitive ability tests. It is based on a sagaciously integrated version of so-called *Gf-Gc* (fluid and crystallized intelligence) theory. It draws mainly on the work of two current investigators of cognitive abilities, John Horn and myself, but it considers the work of many others in this field. It also treats special abilities that are not necessarily covered by *Gf-Gc* theory, but that need to be taken account of in assessing subjects' capabilities and possible deficiencies. It gives information on the possible limitations of the intelligence test theories on which it is based.

Further, it presents an impressively broad and up-to-date survey of the relations between individual intelligence test performances and the success of children, adolescents, and adults in their school studies and in their eventual occupations.

For the practitioner of intelligence testing, it makes easily available an enormous amount of information about eight widely used batteries of individual intelligence tests—information that would be hard for an individual tester to compile from test manuals. It gives guidance on how a practitioner can best select and use the components of these batteries, either singly or in combination. For this purpose, it describes a "*Gf-Gc* cross-battery approach" that can be used to develop the most appropriate information about an individual in a given testing situation. It gives advice on what kinds of information need to be considered beyond what can be obtained from tests, and presents a sample case study to illustrate wise procedures.

The audience for this book is mainly school psychologists who need to give individual intelligence tests to guide educational selection, placement, and treatment, but the book would be valuable for anyone involved in the use of individual intelligence tests in other settings, such as governmental organizations, industry, the courts, correctional institutions, etc. (It should be understood that an "individual intelligence test" is any test of intelligence that is designed to be administered on a one-on-one basis, as opposed to tests that can be administered to groups, such as various paper-and-pencil tests of ability.)

The authors have obviously devoted an enormous amount of work and professional experience to producing this book. In the past there have been problems in training psychologists to use proper procedures and judgment in administrating individual intelligence tests, with the result that, undoubtedly, many mistakes have been made. This book has every chance of assisting in the training and proper guidance of those who use individual intelligence and cognitive ability tests.

John B. Carroll

Preface

*Respect the past in the full measure of its deserts,
but do not make the mistake of confusing it with
the present nor seek in it the ideals of the future.*
—JOSE INGENIEROS, Proposiciones Relativas al
Porvenir de la Filosofia (1918)

Intelligence testing is a serious business. Professionals who administer and interpret intelligence tests are engaged in activities that often have significant implications (e.g., diagnostic, treatment, eligibility, placement) for the individuals who are evaluated. Just as we expect a medical specialist to use the most current and research-based medical technology to assist us in making important decisions about our health, individuals who are assessed with an intelligence test should expect intelligence test professionals to use tools that are based on the best evidence of current science and to make interpretations of the testing data that are supported by contemporary theory and research.

Unfortunately, much of current intellectual assessment practice does not live up to this expectation. Few would argue against the idea that the Wechsler intelligence batteries dominate the field of individual intelligence testing. Despite the significant contributions that these batteries have made to research and practice in psychology and special education, they are based on a relatively old and narrow concept of intelligence. All versions of the Wechsler batteries, including the most recent WISC-III and WAIS-III, maintain a strong link with their ancestral parent (the 1939 Wechsler-Bellevue). However, we have come a long way in our understanding of the construct of intelligence since 1939. Furthermore, based on a review of recent factor analytic research, we know that no single intelligence battery adequately measures the broad construct of intelligence. Does this mean that we should abandon some of our tried and true instruments? No. Intelligence batteries such as the Wechslers need not be discarded. Rather, they need to be *modern-*

ized by supplementing them with other tests to more fully approximate the measurement of the major known cognitive abilities. Additionally, they need to be interpreted within the context of a more contemporary and empirically supported theoretical model of intelligence.

Research in cognitive science, particularly that focused on the factor analysis of a wide variety of cognitive variables, has converged on a structure of intelligence that is much more complex and differentiated than that measured by the Wechslers or Stanford-Binet. In particular, scholars working in the psychometric tradition of intelligence have converged on the hierarchical *Gf-Gc* theory of intelligence, a theory best represented by the Horn-Cattell *Gf-Gc* and Carroll *Three-Stratum* models. Most intelligence batteries measure approximately 3 to 5 of the 10 broad cognitive abilities that are represented in these models, and they therefore lag considerably behind contemporary theory. As a result, it is time that professionals involved in the applied practice of intelligence test development, use, and interpretation begin to narrow the intelligence testing theory–practice gap. Intelligence testing professionals must begin to meet consumers' expectations of theoretically sound and empirically supported intelligence testing practices. To do any less will significantly retard progress in the field of intelligence testing.

Purpose

The overriding purpose of this book is to provide information and procedures that will aid in narrowing the gap that currently exists between contemporary research and theory on the structure of intelligence and the applied practice of intelligence testing. We attempt to fulfill this purpose through three major objectives.

First, we seek to update the intelligence theory knowledge base of professionals by describing the most comprehensive and empirically supported psychometric theories of intelligence and providing a framework based on the integration of these theories that can be used to evaluate the abilities measured by all intelligence batteries. Second, we offer a "Desk Reference" to help practitioners better understand the characteristics of the tools they use.

Practitioners need to understand the quantitative (i.e., psychometric) and qualitative (e.g., variables that influence test performance) characteristics of each of their instruments. Unfortunately, as noted by Matarrazzo (1990), "published information on the psychometric properties of the tests is . . . too infrequently used by some practitioners" (p. 1004). We believe that this lapse is due in part to the difficulty of tracking down the quantitative and qualitative test characteristic information for different tests in a myriad of different manuals, books, and journal articles. Many practitioners simply do not have the time or the access to all relevant sources to enable them to "know" their tools better. The desk reference section of this book provides technical test information for all the major intelligence batteries via a common format that uses common terms and evaluative criteria. Considering the often arduous task of sifting through tables upon tables of numbers in technical manuals and reports, we have removed this potential barrier to better practice by presenting technical test information in an easy-to-read, "consumer's report," visual-graphic format.

In addition to including quantitative and qualitative test characteristic information of all the major intelligence batteries, the desk reference provides *a common theoretical nomenclature* for understanding the constructs that underlie these instruments through the classification of all cognitive ability tests according to *Gf-Gc* theory. These empirical and logical classifications will help facilitate and improve communication between and among professionals and aid in grounding intelligence test interpretation in contemporary theory and research.

Third, we outline an approach to assessment that we refer to as the *Gf-Gc cross-battery approach*. This method of assessing intelligence addresses Carroll's (1997) conclusion that the breadth of the *Gf-Gc* taxonomy of human cognitive abilities "appears to prescribe that individuals should be assessed with regard to the *total range* of abilities the theory specifies" (p. 129). The *Gf-Gc* cross-battery approach is presented as a means to "spell out" how practitioners can conduct assessments that more adequately approximate the total range of broad cognitive abilities than that assessed by any single intelligence battery. Specifically, *the Gf-Gc cross-battery approach is a time-efficient method of intellectual assessment that allows practitioners to measure validly a wider range (or a more in-depth but selective range) of cognitive abilities than that represented by any one intelligence battery in a manner consistent with contemporary psychometric theory and research on the structure of intelligence.*

It is our belief that the information presented in this book—information that should expand and update the knowledge base and skill level of intelligence testing professionals in the areas of intelligence theory, testing, and interpretation—will provide a bridge between contemporary theory and research and the practice of intellectual assessment. Intelligence testing practice needs to "catch up" with theory and research. It is our hope that this book will contribute to this process.

Organization

The book is organized in three sections. Part I (Intelligence Tests and *Gf-Gc* Theory) consists of two chapters. Chapter 1 gives an overview (via a continuum) of the progress that has been made in the development of psychometric theories and measures of intelligence. Contemporary *Gf-Gc* theory is presented as the most empirically supported and comprehensive theoretical framework from which to understand the structure of human intelligence. An integrated *Gf-Gc* model, a model based on the Horn-Cattell *Gf-Gc* and Carroll Three-Stratum models, is presented and defined. Other popular and contemporary theories or conceptions of intelligence (e.g., verbal/nonverbal, Luria–Das, Gardner's multiple intelligences) are then compared to the *Gf-Gc* model. Chapter 2 presents information regarding the supporting evidence for *Gf-Gc* theory. Specifically, it gives information about the relations between *Gf-Gc* abilities and academic achievement, occupational success, and personality and interest traits. Limitations of the theory are also discussed. Together, chapters 1 and 2 provide the foundational knowledge upon which the "Desk Reference" and "Cross-Battery Assessment" sections of the book are based.

Part II (The Intelligence Test Desk Reference [ITDR]: Psychometric, Theoretical, and Qualitative Descriptions and Evaluations) is the "Desk Reference" portion of the book. Chapter 3 sets the stage for the eight subsequent chapters in this section (chapters 4 through 11), each of which is devoted to a major individually administered intelligence battery. In Chapter 3, a "big picture" framework and guide to understanding the broad categories of information that describe every subtest in every intelligence battery is presented. These broad categories include Basic Psychometric Characteristics, *Gf-Gc* Test Classifications, and Other Variables That Influence Test Performance. The various quantitative and qualitative concepts and terms (e.g., specificity, *g* loadings, test floors and ceilings, degree of cultural content, and so forth) as well as evaluative criteria that are used throughout the ITDR are defined and discussed in Chapter 3. The rationale for a cross-battery approach to evaluating the abilities measured by all intelligence tests, as well as assessing and interpreting cognitive abilities, is presented.

Immediately following the eight ITDR chapters is a brief chapter (Chapter 12) that describes commonly used and new "special purpose" tests and/or batteries in terms of the *Gf-Gc* abilities they measure. This information is presented so that practitioners can, when appropriate and necessary, supplement the major intelligence batteries in pursuit of broader measurement of abilities or more in-depth measurement of a select set of abilities via cross-battery procedures.

Finally, Part III (The *Gf-Gc* Cross-Battery Approach to Assessing and Interpreting Cognitive Abilities) consists of two chapters that define and operationalize the *Gf-Gc* cross-battery approach to intellectual assessment and interpretation. Chapter 13 defines the cross-battery approach and highlights the importance of this approach for improving the state of the art of assessing cognitive abilities. The rationale, definition, and guiding principles of the cross-battery approach are presented. In addition, a step-by-step approach to conducting cross-battery assessments is presented using a case study. The necessary procedures and worksheets (which are reproduced in the appendices of the book for use by practitioners) for conducting cross-battery assessments are presented.

The book's final chapter (Chapter 14) offers practitioners a set of guiding principles for conducting "selective" cross-battery assessments. Guidelines are presented for tailoring cross-battery assessments to adequately address specific referral concerns and questions. This chapter ends with an analysis of the extent to which the various *Gf-Gc* abilities that underlie the major intelligence batteries differ in their relative emphasis on process, content, and manner of response. Results of this analysis were used to understand the degree to which the cultural content of intelligence batteries is likely to influence test performance. This information coupled with knowledge of the receptive/expressive language demands of the various cognitive ability tests is presented as a "blue print" to guide practitioners in selecting tests that may be more valid for use with culturally and linguistically diverse populations.

Intended Audience

This book is intended for scholars, researchers, and practitioners who seek to narrow the intelligence theory–practice gap in their work. It is intended for practitioners, university trainers, researchers, students, and other professionals in school, clinical, counseling, and educational psychology who are involved in the development and/or use and interpretation of individually administered intelligence batteries. This book would be appropriate for a graduate course in beginning or advanced intelligence testing, particularly if combined with a more general text on psychological or intellectual assessment that addresses the topics of test administration, scoring, basic interpretation, recommendations, and report writing. This book can either serve as the primary text in a course on intelligence testing when supplemented by lecture and other materials, or it could be combined with a more general assessment text. This book will be a particularly valuable resource to the many practitioners who use intelligence tests on a frequent basis in applied settings.

Acknowledgments

We are deeply grateful to a number of individuals who facilitated the preparation of this book. We wish to extend our deepest gratitude to Nya Ittai who spent countless hours doing library research, preparing tables, organizing materials, and performing numerous other book preparation tasks. We also wish to thank Donna Boyce, Bhupin Butaney, Lisa DeFelice, Theresa Huettl, Meredyth Otlin, and Evan Schermer for their assistance in locating articles, entering literature in our reference database, editing earlier drafts of this manuscript, and doing many tasks related to data analysis for the ITDR. The diligence of Syed Raza is also recognized for the countless hours he spent completing the ITDR computer files for each intelligence battery. In addition, we are grateful to Vincent Alfonso and Amy Zgodny for providing us with *Gf-Gc* cross-battery data for the case study presented in this text.

Our appreciation also goes to the following reviewers for their valuable thoughts and comments on the manuscript: Vincent C. Alfonso, Fordham University; James M. Creed, Educational Specialist; Judith A. Friedman, Educational Specialist; Michael E. Gerner, Consulting Psychologists; Steven K. Kaplan, Lesley College; Ruben Lopez, Moreno Valley Unified School District; Samuel O. Ortiz, San Diego University; and Brian Stone, Wichita State University.

Finally, the contributions of Carla Daves, Mylan Jaixen, and Susan Hutchinson and the rest of the staff at Allyn and Bacon as well as the staff at Michael Bass Associates and Solar Script Inc. are gratefully acknowledged. Their expertise and pleasant and cooperative working style made this project an enjoyable and productive endeavor.

KSM
DPF

The Intelligence Test Desk Reference (ITDR)

A Continuum of Progress in Psychometric Theories and Measures of Intelligence

From Spearman's g to Contemporary Gf-Gc Theory

Minds differ still more than faces.
—VOLTAIRE, "WIT, SPIRIT, INTELLECT,"
PHILOSOPHICAL DICTIONARY (1746).

There is only one irrefutable law or truth in psychology—the law of individual differences. That is, no two individuals, not even identical twins, are exactly alike. Considerable variability exists on all human traits such as weight, height, temperament, social skills, and facial characteristics, to name but a few. Accordingly, "individuals differ from one another in their ability to understand complex ideas, to adapt effectively to the environment, to learn from experience, to engage in various forms of reasoning, to overcome obstacles by taking thought" (Neisser et al., 1996; p.77). The construct of *intelligence* has been offered to explain and clarify the complex set of phenomena that account for individual differences in intellectual functioning.

Attempts to define the construct of intelligence and to explain individual differences in intellectual functioning, attempts which have spanned decades (Carroll, 1993; Gustafsson & Undheim, 1996; Kamphaus, 1993; Thorndike, 1997; Thorndike & Lohman, 1991; Sattler, 1988), have been characterized by much variability. The significant differences between theories of intelligence is exemplified by the various multiple intelligences models that have been offered and revised recently to explain the structure of intelligence, namely, Carroll's Three-Stratum Theory of Cognitive Abilities, Gardner's Theory of Multiple Intelligences, the Horn-Cattell Fluid-Crystallized *Gf-Gc* theory, Feuerstein's theory of structural cognitive modifiability (SCM), the Luria-Das Model of Information Processing, and Sternberg's Triarchic Theory of Intelligence (see Flanagan, Genshaft, & Harrison, 1997, for a comprehensive description of these theories). Each of these theories provides a framework from which to understand the multidifferentiated structure of cognitive abilities and the interrelations among them.

Theories of Intelligence: Three Research Traditions

To a large extent the variability between theories of intelligence can be accounted for by differences in underlying research traditions in psychological measurement that have developed largely independently of one another. Taylor (1993) suggests that the psychometric, information processing, and cognitive modifiability theories are the most prominent approaches used to conceptualize the measurement of intelligence. The *psychometric* or structural approach "attempts to measure performance along dimensions which are purported to constitute the fundamental structure of the psychological domain" (Taylor, 1994; p. 185). The psychometric approach relies on psychological tests that yield scores on quantitative scales that may be analyzed by correlative and factor-analytic methods to identify ability dimensions that form the structure of individual diferences in cognitive ability (Gustafsson & Undheim, 1996).

Information processing theories are more recent in origin (largely since the 1960s) and, in general, have taken a cognitive-rational view of human intellectual functioning using the computer analogy of humans as information processors. In general, information processing theories are "limited capacity theories of cognitive competence" (Taylor, 1994, p. 185) that are concerned with how information is processed efficiently during problem solving and everyday tasks. Information processing research typically uses fine-grained computer-administered chronometric measures of human performance (e.g., response latency).

Cognitive modifiability theories have focused on the "capacity of humans to adapt to circumstantial demands—in other words to learn to function effectively in their environment" (Taylor, 1993, p. 187). The key component of such models is that intelligence is dynamic, modifiable, and changeable. Dynamic assessment evolved from cognitive modifiability theories (Lidz, 1987, 1991) and "refers to approaches to the development of decision-specific information that most characteristically involve interaction between the examiner and examinee, focus on learner metacognitive processes and responsiveness to intervention, and follow a pretest-intervene-posttest administration format" (Lidz, 1997, p. 281).

Of the three theoretical perspectives, the psychometric approach is the oldest and most research based and has produced the most economically efficient and practical measures for measuring intelligence in applied settings (Gustafsson & Undheim, 1996; Neisser et al., 1996; Taylor, 1993). Space limitations preclude the presentation of a detailed summary of the history and evolution of the dominant psychometric theories of intelligence. Instead, the reader is referred to Carroll (1993); Gustafsson and Undheim (1996); Ittenbach, Esters, and Wainer (1997), Kamphaus (1993), Sattler (1988), and Thorndike and Lohman (1990) for historical information on the development of psychometric theories of intelligence.

In lieu of a detailed discussion of the evolution of research on psychometric theories and measures of intelligence, which have primarily been concerned with specifying a "complete" taxonomy of human cognitive abilities, an adaptation and extension of Woodcock's (1994) "continuum of progress in theories of multiple intelligences" is presented to summarize the "that was then–this is now" perspective of psychometric theories of intelligence. Figure 1–1 depicts a continuum in psychometric theories of intelligence, a continuum of prominent approaches to the applied measurement of intelligence, and the relation between the respective theoretical "benchmarks" and intelligence measures. It is important to note that the two continua presented in Figure 1–1 do not portray linear timelines; rather, they portray continua of progress in understanding and measuring the structure of human intelligence. Also, the specific theories listed under the theory contin-

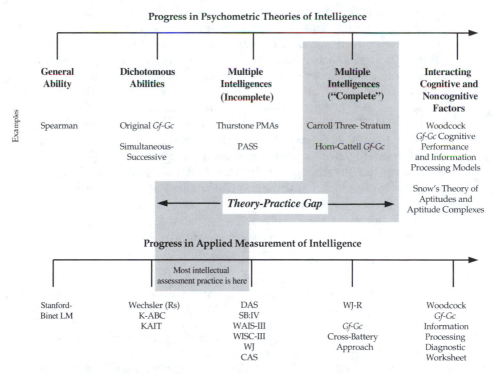

FIGURE 1–1   Continua of Progress in Psychometric Theories and Applied Measurement of Intelligence

uum are illustrative examples and are not intended to represent a complete list of theories.

Progress in Psychometric Theories and Measures of Intelligence

Spearman's (1904, 1927) presentation of the *general factor* or *g theory of intelligence* is considered the birth of the psychometric research tradition. As shown in Figure 1–1, the most notable applied measure of intelligence that reflected the single or *g* model of intelligence was the omnibus Stanford-Binet Intelligence Scale (Terman, 1916; Terman & Merrill, 1937, 1960, 1972).[1] The marriage of psychometric theory and measurement evolved next into dichotomous models such as the original *Gf-Gc* (Cattell, 1941, 1957) and Wechsler-based verbal/nonverbal frameworks. Cattell's original *Gf-Gc* dichotomous theory did not result in any widely used practical assessment battery and Wechsler's framework represented (and continues to represent) modalities through which intelligence can be expressed rather than a theoretical model (this issue is discussed later in this chapter).

As can be seen in Figure 1–1, the Kaufman Adolescent and Adult Intelligence Test (KAIT; Kaufman & Kaufman, 1993), although one of the newest intelligence batteries in the field, is organized around the *dichotomous Gf-Gc* model; hence, it is placed at the "older" end of the progress-in-theories continuum. The most widely recognized applied measures of dichotomous abilities are the versions of the Wechsler batteries that were grounded exclusively in the verbal/performance (or verbal/nonverbal) conception of intelligence (i.e., Wechsler Adult Intelligence Scale [WAIS; Wechsler, 1955], Wechsler Adult Intelligence Scale—Revised [WAIS-R; Wechsler, 1981], Wechsler Adult Intelligence Scale—Third Edition [WAIS-III; Wechsler, 1997], Wechsler Intelligence Scale for Children [WISC; Wechsler, 1949], Wechsler Intelligence Scale for Children—Revised [WISC-R; Wechsler, 1974], Wechsler Intelligence Scale for Children—Third Edition [WISC-III; Wechsler, 1991], Wechsler Preschool and Primary Scale of Intelligence [WPPSI; Wechsler, 1967], and Wechsler Preschool and Primary Scale of Intelligence—Revised [WPPSI-R; Wechsler, 1991]).

Finally, although the simultaneous/successive processing theories of intellectual functioning evolved largely from the information processing research tradi-

---

[1] It is important to note that although Spearman's *g* theory is most often considered to be a single-factor theory (as portrayed in Figure 1–1), this characterization is not entirely accurate. Spearman's model included both a large general (*g*) factor and smaller specific (*s*) factors. Spearman became increasingly interested in the specific factors and together with Karl Holziner developed a "bi-factor" model. According to Carroll (1993a), if Spearman had lived beyond 1945, he probably would have converged on a multiple abilities model similar to others' (e.g., Thurstone's primary mental abilities).

tion and cerebral specialization research (e.g., Bogen, 1969; Luria, 1966; Sperry, 1968, 1974), they are listed as dichotomous psychometric theories to reflect the fact that attempts to measure the two processing components of this theory have utilized the tools and procedures of psychometrics. As reflected in the applied measurement continuum in Figure 1–1, the Kaufman Assessment Battery for Children (K-ABC; Kaufman & Kaufman, 1983) is the only major intelligence battery that operationalized the *dichotomous* simultaneous/successive model.

The earliest recognizable attempt to identify "multiple" intelligences was Thurstone's factor analysis–based efforts to identify *primary mental abilities* (*PMAs*) (Thurstone, 1938; Thurstone & Thurstone, 1941). The PMA theory suggested that performance on tests was not a function of *g*, but rather was due to a number of primary mental abilities or faculties such as Space, Perceptual Speed, Number, Verbal Meaning, Word Fluency, Memory, and Inductive Reasoning (Kamphaus, 1993). Thurstone's PMA model is significant, as most modern test construction tends to be based on it (Taylor, 1994). Other examples of factor-analytically based models are in the works of Burt (1949); French, Ekstrom, and Price (1963); Guilford (1967); and Vernon (1961). Given the benefit of hindsight, this generation of multiple intelligences theories can be seen as "incomplete."

Other intelligence batteries that reflect the incomplete measurement of multiple cognitive abilities include the Differential Abilities Scales (DAS; Elliott, 1990), Stanford-Binet Intelligence Scale: Fourth Edition (SB:IV; Thorndike, Hagen, & Sattler, 1986), the original Woodcock-Johnson Psycho-Educational Battery (WJ; Woodcock & Johnson, 1977), WISC-III (Wechsler, 1991), and the WAIS-III (Wechsler, 1997). These intelligence batteries are considered to be incomplete because they measure between three and five cognitive abilities, reflecting only a *subset* of known broad cognitive abilities. Finally, the previously discussed simultaneous/successive processing model has evolved recently into a four-construct Planning, Attention, Simultaneous, and Successive model (PASS; Naglieri, 1997) based on the work of A. R. Luria (1966, 1973, 1976, 1980, 1982). The Cognitive Assessment System (CAS; Das & Naglieri, 1997) is the psychometric intelligence battery that purports to operationalize the PASS model. This instrument too is considered an incomplete measure of intelligence when evaluated against contemporary psychometric theory, as it assesses only a subset of *Gf-Gc* broad cognitive abilities.

As portrayed in Figure 1–1, psychometric intelligence theories have converged recently on the more "complete" (in a relative sense, no theory is ever complete) *Gf-Gc* multiple intelligences taxonomy, reflecting a review of the extant factor-analytic research conducted over the past 50 or 60 years. For example, this taxonomy serves as the organizational framework for both the Carroll and Horn-Cattell models (Carroll, 1983, 1989, 1993, 1997; Gustafsson, 1984, 1988; Horn, 1988, 1991, 1994; Horn & Noll, 1997; Lohman, 1989; Snow, 1986). Following in the footsteps of Cattell (1941), Horn's systematic program of *Gf-Gc* research has resulted in the identification of nine broad cognitive abilities: Fluid Intelligence (*Gf*), Crystallized Intelligence (*Gc*), Short-Term Acquisition and Retrieval (*Gsm*), Visual Intelligence (*Gv*), Auditory Intelligence (*Ga*), Long-Term Storage and Retrieval (*Glr*), Cognitive

Processing Speed (*Gs*), Correct Decision Speed (*CDS*), and Quantitative Knowledge (*Gq*) (see Horn, 1991, 1994; Horn & Noll, 1997).

Following an extensive review and reanalysis of most of the theoretical and empirical research on human cognitive abilities and their measurement since the late 1900s, Carroll (1993, 1997) recently proposed a "Three-Stratum Theory of Cognitive Abilities" that, according to a number of scholars, is a benchmark and the most ambitious attempt to provide a psychometric taxonomy of intelligence abilities (Gustafsson & Undheim, 1996). For example, Snow (1993) stated that Carroll's model "defines the taxonomy of cognitive differential psychology for many years to come." Burns (1994) also considered Carroll's three-stratum model to be an important landmark work, predicting that it is "destined to be the classic study and reference work on human abilities for decades to come" (p. 35). Carroll's model organizes cognitive ability at three strata that differ as a function of breadth or generalizability of abilities. *General* cognitive ability or *g* is located at *stratum III* and subsumes eight *broad* cognitive abilities that are located at *stratum II*, which, in turn, subsumes approximately 70 *narrow* abilities that are located at *stratum I*. The broad abilities identified by Carroll are very similar to those reported by Horn and include Fluid Intelligence (*Gf*), Crystallized Intelligence (*Gc*), General Memory and Learning (*Gy*), Broad Visual Perception (*Gv*), Broad Auditory Perception (*Gu*), Broad Retrieval Ability (*Gr*), Broad Cognitive Speediness (*Gs*), and Processing Speed/Reaction Time Decision Speed (*Gt*).

Currently only one intelligence battery, the Woodcock-Johnson Psycho-Educational Battery—Revised (WJ-R;Woodcock & Johnson, 1989), comes close to measuring the broad abilities specified in the more "complete" psychometrically based *Gf-Gc* multiple intelligences theories. The WJ-R was designed specifically to measure eight broad *Gf-Gc* abilities. However, recent joint or cross-battery factor analyses of the WJ-R and most other major intelligence batteries (e.g., Flanagan & McGrew, in press; McGhee, 1993; McGrew, 1997; Woodcock, 1990) indicate that none of the current intelligence batteries, including the WJ-R, adequately assesses the complete range of *Gf-Gc* abilities that are included in either Horn's (1991, 1994) or Carroll's (1993, 1997) models of the structure of intelligence (see Chapter 3 for a summary of the *Gf-Gc* abilities measured by the major intelligence batteries).

Narrowing the Theory–Practice Gap

As depicted in Figure 1–1, there currently exists a significant "theory–practice gap" in the field of intellectual assessment due to the dominant use of the Wechsler batteries in practice (see Flanagan & Genshaft, 1997; Harrison, Flanagan, & Genshaft, 1997; Harrison, Kaufman, et al., 1988; Stinnett, Havey, & Oehler-Stinnett, 1994; Wilson & Reschly, 1996). In terms of a single battery, the WJ-R comes closest to narrowing the gap between practice and contemporary *Gf-Gc* theory. However, as will be highlighted in Chapter 3, even the WJ-R does not provide adequate breadth and depth of coverage of all broad *Gf-Gc* abilities. Thus, the practice of conducting an incomplete assessment of intelligence via the use of any single battery may significantly impact the accuracy and appropriateness of diagnostic, classification, and placement decisions. All major intelligence batteries need to be supplemented with other measures in order to broaden assessments and, in turn, narrow the theory–practice gap. To achieve this goal, a contemporary *Gf-Gc*–organized cross-battery approach to intellectual assessment is presented in Part III of this book.

Finally, while research continues to focus on the identification of the major abilities in the multiple intelligences taxonomy (Carroll, 1993a), a number of researchers are attempting to push the far end of the intelligence theory continuum through the specification of models that describe and explain cognitive performance as the integration of both cognitive and noncognitive variables within an information processing framework (see Figure 1–1). For example, Woodcock (1993, 1997) presented a *Gf-Gc* Cognitive Performance Model (CPM) that suggests that *Gf-Gc* abilities can be organized into four interacting but functionally distinct categories. Briefly, *Acquired Knowledge* includes stores of acquired declarative and procedural knowledge that is represented by the *Gc*, *Gq*, and *Grw* abilities. These stores of information are available to short-term memory and for subsequent processing (Woodcock, 1993). *Thinking abilities* (viz., *Gv*, *Ga*, *Glr*, *Gf*) are involved in the cognitive processing of information that is placed in *Short-Term Memory* (*Gsm*) but cannot be processed automatically. Finally, *Facilitators-Inhibitors* are internal (e.g., *Gs*, health, emotional state) and external (e.g., distracting stimuli) variables that can modify cognitive performance either positively or negatively. The collective participation of these functional cognitive and noncognitive components aids in explaining complex cognitive activities. Woodcock (1993, 1997) has extended the CPM model into a more complex *Gf-Gc* Information Processing Model (IPM) that portrays the relations between *Gf-Gc* abilities and other aspects of cognition within an information processing framework. Woodcock's grounding of his CPM and IPM models in the Horn-Cattell *Gf-Gc* theory is consistent with Taylor's (1994) conclusion that a "positive feature of the Cattell model is that it is amenable to dynamic, learning, or developmental interpretations" (p. 185).

Another notable effort along these lines is Snow's (1989) attempt to use new forms of psychometric theory to measure information processing constructs such as declarative knowledge acquisition, proceduralization, and automatization (Anderson, 1985). Snow suggested that cognitive constructs need to be combined with affective and conative (i.e., noncognitive) constructs to measure fully an individual's "aptitudes" for learning (Snow, Corno, & Jackson, 1996). According to Snow (1989), learners come to tasks with previously developed *conceptual structures* and *procedural skills* (i.e., initial states) that subsume *Gf-Gc* type cognitive constructs (e.g., *Gc*, *Gv*, *Gsm*). In addition, conative personal characteristics in the broad domains of *learning strategies, self-regulatory functions,* and *motivational orientation* are viewed as interacting with the cognitive constructs during cognitive performance. Woodcock and Snow, then, both articulate dynamic models that include cognitive and noncognitive constructs in an attempt to explain cognitive performance. It is beyond the scope of this book to treat their models in detail. Furthermore, neither has produced assessment batteries that operationalize their respective theoretical models, and both need a long-term program of research

(Snow, 1989). However, as indicated in Figure 1–1, Woodcock (1997) has presented a *Gf-Gc* Diagnostic Worksheet that allows practitioners to organize measures of *Gf-Gc* abilities into an information processing interpretive model.

As just described, *Gf-Gc* theory is the most comprehensive and empirically supported psychometric theory of intelligence. Therefore, the *Gf-Gc* theory should serve as a foundation for the development and interpretation of intelligence batteries. In order to develop and implement a *Gf-Gc*–based approach to assessing and interpreting cognitive abilities (as described in chapters 13 and 14), it is necessary to understand the major components of the theory and its relations to other theoretical frameworks. The remainder of this chapter addresses these topics.

What Is Gf-Gc Theory?

The Evolution of Gf-Gc Theory

Gf-Gc theory was first postulated by Cattell (1941, 1957) to consist of two major types of cognitive abilities. Cattell considered fluid intelligence (*Gf*) to include inductive and deductive reasoning, abilities that were thought to be influenced primarily by biological and neurological factors, as well as by incidental learning through interaction with the environment (Taylor, 1994). In contrast, crystallized intelligence (*Gc*) was postulated to consist primarily of abilities (especially knowledge) that reflected individual differences due to the influences of acculturation (viz., verbal-conceptual and knowledge) (Gustafsson, 1994; Taylor, 1994). Thus, the original *Gf-Gc* theory was a dichotomous conceptualization of human cognitive ability. Unfortunately (or fortunately, depending on one's belief in maintaining the historical integrity of a theory), the *Gf-Gc* theory label has been retained as the acronym for this theory despite the fact that the theory has not been conceived of as a dichotomy since the 1960s (Gustafsson & Undheim, 1996; Horn & Noll, 1997; Woodcock, 1990). As a result, *Gf-Gc* theory is often misunderstood as being a two-factor model of the structure of intelligence.

As early as the mid-1960s, Horn (1965) expanded the *Gf-Gc* model to include four additional cognitive abilities in the domains of visual perception or processing (*Gv*), short-term memory (Short-term Acquisition and Retrieval—SAR or *Gsm*), long-term storage and retrieval (Tertiary Storage and Retrieval—TSR or *Glr*), and speed of processing (*Gs*). Horn (1968) next refined the definition of *Gv*, *Gs*, and *Glr*, and added an auditory processing ability (*Ga*). More recently, factors representing a person's quantitative ability or knowledge (*Gq*) and facility with reading and writing (*Grw*) (Horn, 1985, 1988, 1991; Woodcock, 1994) were added to the model, resulting in a 10-factor ability structure.

It is clear that a dichotomous *Gf-Gc* model has not been the view of Horn or Cattell for nearly 30 years and is inconsistent with the recent writings of Carroll (1989, 1993) and Horn (1985; 1988; 1989; 1991), as well as other researchers (Gustafsson, 1984; Lohman, 1989). *Contemporary or modern Gf-Gc theory, which is best represented by the Horn-Cattell Gf-Gc and the Carroll Three-Stratum models of cog-*

nitive abilities, is a multiple intelligences model of the structure of human cognitive abilities.

The Hierarchical Structure of Gf-Gc Theory

Most assessment-related discussions of the *Gf-Gc* theory tend to focus on the 10 broad cognitive abilities. However, this does not accurately represent the number of abilities included in the complete model. To fully appreciate the richness of the *Gf-Gc* model of intelligence, one must understand the hierarchical differentiation of abilities by levels of generality or breadth (Gustafsson & Undheim, 1996).

In his review of the extant factor-analytic research literature, Carroll (1997) differentiated factors or abilities by three strata that varied according to the "relative variety and diversity of variables" (p. 124) included at each level. The various "G" abilities (i.e., the most prominent and recognized abilities of the model at the middle stratum—*Gf, Gc,* etc.) are classified as broad or stratum II abilities. Broad abilities represent "basic constitutional and long standing characteristics of individuals that can govern or influence a great variety of behaviors in a given domain" (Carroll, 1993a, p. 634). The broad abilities vary in differing degrees of relative emphasis on process, content, and manner of response. What is often not immediately clear when discussing *Gf-Gc* theory is that the broad abilities subsume a large number of narrow or stratum I abilities (currently approximately 70 have been identified) (Carroll, 1993a, 1997). Narrow abilities "represent greater specializations of abilities, often in quite specific ways that reflect the effects of experience and learning, or the adoption of particular strategies of performance" (Carroll, 1993a, p .634). The hierarchical structure of *Gf-Gc* theory is demonstrated for the domain of visual processing (*Gv*) in Figure 1–2.

Figure 1–2 shows that *Gv* is a very broad ability. That is, 10 different narrow cognitive abilities are subsumed by *Gv* (the broad and narrow *Gv* abilities, as well

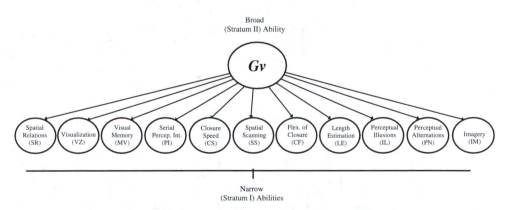

FIGURE 1–2   A *Gv* Example of the Hierarchical Structure of *Gf-Gc*Theory

as the other *Gf-Gc* broad and narrow abilities, are defined later in this chapter). When extended to 9 other broad cognitive domains, each subsuming several narrow abilities, it is clear that the complete hierarchical *Gf-Gc* theory is extremely comprehensive.

The broadest or most general level of ability is represented by Carroll's (1993a) stratum III, located at the apex of the hierarchy. This single cognitive ability subsumes the broad (stratum II) and narrow (stratum I) abilities. Carroll interpreted this general intelligence, or *g*, as involving complex higher-order cognitive processes (Gustafsson & Undheim, 1996).

Finally, it is important to recognize that the abilities within each level of the hierarchical *Gf-Gc* model typically display non-zero positive intercorrelations (Carroll, 1993a; Gustafsson & Undheim, 1996). For example, although it is not readily apparent from a review of Figure 1–2, the 10 different stratum I (narrow) *Gv* abilities presented in this figure are positively correlated to varying degrees. These intercorrelations give rise to, and allow for the estimation of, the stratum II (broad) *Gv* factor. Likewise, the positive non-zero correlations among the stratum II (broad) *Gf-Gc* abilities allow for the estimation of the stratum III (general) *g* factor (see Figure 1–3). The practical implication of the positive factor intercorrelations

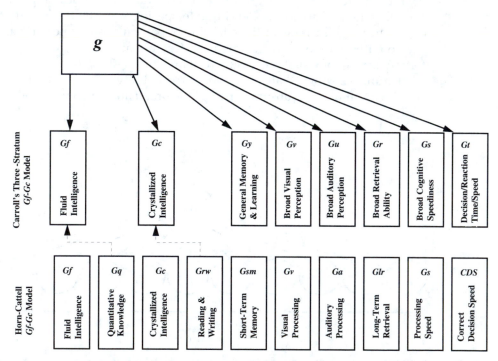

FIGURE 1–3   A Comparison of the Carroll and Horn-Cattell *Gf-Gc* **Models**

within each level of the *Gf-Gc* hierarchy is the recognition that measures of different *Gf-Gc* abilities do not reflect independent (uncorrelated) traits.

The Carroll and Horn-Cattell Gf-Gc Models

Model Similarities and Differences

The broad and general strata of the Horn-Cattell and Carroll *Gf-Gc* models are presented together in Figure 1–3. A review of Figure 1–3 reveals many similarities, as well as a number of notable differences between the two models.

Although there are differences in terms and *G* notations, in general the models are similar in that they both include some form of fluid (*Gf*), crystallized (*Gc*), short-term memory and/or learning (*Gsm* or *Gy*), visual (*Gv*), auditory (*Ga* or *Gu*), retrieval (*Glr* or *Gr*), processing speed (*Gs*), and decision and/or reaction time speed (*CDS* or *Gt*) abilities. Although there are some minor differences in broad ability definitions and the narrow abilities subsumed by the respective broad *Gf-Gc* abilities, the major differences between the two models are primarily four-fold (McGrew, 1997).

First, the Carroll and Horn-Cattell models differ in their inclusion of *g* at stratum III. According to Carroll (1993), the general intelligence factor at the apex of his three-stratum theory (see Figure 1–3) is analogous to Spearman's *g*. The off-center placement (to the left side of the figure) of *g* in the Carroll model is intended to reflect the strength of the relations between the respective broad *Gf-Gc* abilities and *g*. As represented in the Carroll model portion of Figure 1–3 (i.e., the top half of the figure), *Gf* has been reported to have the strongest association with *g*, followed next by *Gc*, and continuing on through the remaining abilities to the two broad abilities that are weakest in association with *g* (i.e., *Gs* and *Gt*). In contrast, Horn disagrees that there is a large general intelligence ability that subsumes the broad *Gf-Gc* abilities (Horn, 1991; Horn & Noll, 1997). Arguments about the nature and existence of *g* have waxed and waned over decades and have been some of the liveliest debates in differential psychology (Gustafsson & Undheim, 1996; Jensen, 1997). Much of the debate has been theoretical (e.g., what is *g*?). A thorough treatment of the " *g* or not to *g*" theoretical issues is beyond the scope of this book. The debate will continue to fuel discussion in the years to come. Interested readers are directed to the writings of Carroll (1993a, 1997), Horn (1991), Horn and Noll (1997), and Jensen (1997) for further information. The meaning of a large general intellectual ability in *Gf-Gc* cross-battery assessment will be discussed in Chapter 13.

Second, in the Horn-Cattell model, quantitative knowledge is a distinct broad ability, as represented by the inclusion of the *Gq* rectangle in the bottom half of Figure 1–3. In contrast, Carroll (1993a) considers quantitative ability to be "an inexact, unanalyzed popular concept that has no scientific meaning unless it is referred to the structure of abilities that compose it. It cannot be expected to constitute a higher-level ability" (p. 627). Therefore, Carroll considers quantitative reasoning to be a narrow ability subsumed by *Gf*, as indicated by the arrow leading from the *Gq* rectangle in the Horn-Cattell model to the *Gf* rectangle in the Carroll model in Figure 1–3. Furthermore, Carroll included mathematics achievement and mathematics knowledge factors in a separate chapter in his book that described a variety of knowledge and achievement abilities (e.g., technical and mechanical knowledge; knowledge of behavioral content) that are not included in his theoretical model.

Third, recent versions of the Horn-Cattell model have included a separate broad, English-language reading and writing ability (*Grw*), as depicted in the bottom half of Figure 1–3 (McGrew, 1997; Woodcock, 1993). Carroll considers narrow reading and writing abilities to be part of the broad ability of *Gc*, as reflected by the arrow leading from the *Grw* rectangle in the Horn-Cattell model to the *Gc* rectangle in the Carroll model in Figure 1–3. Finally, the Carroll and Horn-Cattell models differ in their treatment of certain narrow memory abilities. Carroll includes short-term memory abilities and the narrow abilities of associative, meaningful, and free recall memory (these abilities are defined later in this chapter) together with learning abilities under his General Memory and Learning factor (*Gu*). Horn (1991) makes a distinction between immediate apprehension (e.g., short-term memory span) and storage and retrieval abilities, while Carroll includes both of these classes of memory abilities in a single broad ability (*Gu*). However, Horn (1988) indicated that it is often difficult to distinguish short-term memory and storage and retrieval abilities. For example, in some of his writings, Horn (1991) referred to associative memory as a narrow ability subsumed by short-term memory. Alternatively, Horn (1988) has also listed the Delayed Recall tests of the Woodcock-Johnson Tests of Cognitive Ability—Revised (Woodcock & Johnson, 1989), tests that are clear measures of associative memory (McGrew, 1997), under the broad long-term storage and retrieval (*Glr*) ability.

An Integrated Carroll and Horn-Cattell Gf-Gc Model
Notwithstanding the important differences between the Carroll and Horn-Cattell models, in order to classify all intelligence batteries from the perspective of *Gf-Gc* theory and to operationalize a *Gf-Gc* cross-battery approach to assessment, it is necessary to settle on a single model. Based on a comparison of the two models within the context of a set of confirmatory factor analyses and a review of other non—factor-analytic validity evidence (e.g., *Gf-Gc* ability growth curves), McGrew (1997) presented a synthesized *Gf-Gc* model for use in the evaluation and interpretation of intelligence test batteries. This model was most similar (at the broad level) to the Horn-Cattell model presented in Figure 1–3, as it included separate broad *Grw* and *Gq* abilities. The *Gq* ability in his model subsumed all narrow quantitative reasoning and mathematics achievement abilities. In McGrew's integrated model, auditory and visual short-term memory narrow abilities were subsumed by *Gsm* and long-term storage and retrieval memory (e.g., associative memory) narrow abilities were subsumed by *Glr*, together with various fluency abilities.

The integrated Carroll and Horn-Cattell model proposed by McGrew (1997) was further examined and refined for the purpose of this book. A series of confirmatory factor analyses (McGrew & Flanagan, 1997) were designed to examine whether (1) quantitative reasoning, achievement, and knowledge narrow abilities are subsumed by *Gf* or whether they compose a separate broad *Gq* ability; (2) the narrow visual memory ability is subsumed by *Gsm* or *Gv;* and (3) the narrow associative memory ability is subsumed by *Gsm* or *Glr*. The results of these analyses are discussed below.

Quantitative and Mathematical Abilities. In a sample of 124 school-age subjects who had been administered the WJ-R mathematics, fluid reasoning, and comprehension-knowledge tests and the SB:IV reasoning tests (see description of the grade 3/4 and 10/11 validity samples in McGrew et al., 1991), confirmatory factor analysis procedures were used to compare a series of models that included (in various combinations); (1) separate *Gc*, quantitative reasoning, mathematics achievement, and *Gf* factors; (2) a second-order *Gq* (quantitative reasoning and mathematics achievement) factor; (3) a combined *Gf/Gq* factor; (4) a *Gf* factor that also included quantitative reasoning; (5) a second-order *Gf/Gq* factor; and (6) a single second-order factor that subsumed first-order mathematics achievement, quantitative reasoning, and a *Gf* factor. A comparison of model fit statistics found that all models were equally plausible.

However, when the processes involved in the quantitative reasoning tasks (viz., SB:IV Number Series and Equation Building tests) were carefully examined, they were judged to be very similar to the reasoning demands of other tasks that Carroll (1993a) considered to be measures of *Gf* (viz., inductive and deductive reasoning). Thus, we modified McGrew's (1997) model to include quantitative reasoning (defined below) as a narrow ability subsumed by *Gf* rather than *Gq*. Furthermore, given the significant differences between the growth curves reported for the WJ-R Broad Mathematics achievement and Fluid Reasoning (*Gf*) clusters (McGrew et al., 1991), evidence that suggests that these clusters represent different constructs, we retained a broad *Gq* factor that subsumed the narrow mathematics knowledge and achievement abilities discussed in Carroll (1993a, ch. 12).

***Gsm* and General Memory.** In a sample of 114 elementary-age students who had been administered the WJ-R and KAIT (Flanagan & McGrew, in press), confirmatory factor analyses were completed to investigate the relations between visual memory, memory span, and associative memory factors. Models were compared that included (in various combinations) factors made up of measures of (1) memory span and associative memory; (2) visual memory and visual closure speed; and (3) memory span, associative memory, and visual memory. The results did not clarify whether associative memory together with memory span are subsumed by *Glr* or *Gsm*. Thus, as in McGrew's (1997) model, we retained associative memory (as well as other types of long-term memory abilities) as a narrow ability subsumed by *Glr*, which is consistent with some (but not all) of Horn's writings (e.g., Horn, 1988). However, a consistent finding in these analyses was that the visual memory factor did not combine with the memory span factor to form a strong *Gsm* factor. Rather, consistent with other factor analyses (McGrew et al., 1991; Woodcock, 1990) that have reported measures of visual memory to load on a *Gv* factor, as well as Carroll's (1993a) comments about the unclear nature of a visual memory factor and Lohman's (1979) classification of visual memory as a *Gv* ability, we modified the integrated Carroll and Horn-Cattell model proposed by McGrew (1997) to include visual memory as a narrow ability subsumed by *Gv*—not *Gsm*.

The Final Model.   The final integrated Carroll and Horn-Cattell *Gf-Gc* model that was used to guide the classifications of the abilities measured by intelligence batteries in the ITDR (chapters 3 through 12) and which served as the foundation for the cross-battery assessment approach (chapters 13 and 14), included the 10 Horn-Cattell *Gf-Gc* abilities and excluded *g*. The exclusion of *g* does not mean that the integrated model does not subscribe to a separate general human ability or that *g* does not exist. Rather, it was omitted by McGrew (1997) (and is similarly omitted in the current integrated model) since it has little practical relevance to cross-battery assessment and interpretation. That is, the cross-battery approach was designed to improve psychoeducational assessment practice by describing the unique *Gf-Gc pattern of abilities* of individuals that in turn can be related to important occupational and achievement outcomes and other human traits (see last section of this chapter). The definition of the broad and narrow *Gf-Gc* abilities included in the integrated Carroll and Horn-Cattell model (hereafter called the *Gf-Gc* model) are presented next.

Broad and Narrow **Gf-Gc** *Ability Definitions*

In this section the definitions of the broad and narrow abilities included in the *Gf-Gc* model are presented. These definitions draw from the work of Carroll (1993), Gustafsson and Undheim (1996), Horn (1991), McGrew (1997), McGrew and colleagues (1991), and Woodcock (1993). The narrow ability definitions are presented in Table 1–1. The two-letter narrow ability codes are drawn from the coding system reported in Carroll's (1993) cognitive ability taxonomy.

Fluid Intelligence (Gf)

Fluid Intelligence refers to mental operations that an individual may use when faced with a relatively novel task that cannot be performed automatically. These mental operations may include forming and recognizing concepts, identifying relations, perceiving relationships among patterns, drawing inferences, comprehending implications, problem solving, extrapolating, and reorganizing or transforming information. The narrow abilities of inductive and deductive reasoning are generally considered to be the hallmark narrow ability indicators of *Gf*. The definition for these two abilities, as well as three other narrow abilities subsumed by *Gf*, are presented in Table 1–1.

Crystallized Intelligence (Gc)

Crystallized Intelligence refers to the breadth and depth of a person's acquired knowledge of a culture and the effective application of this knowledge. This store

TABLE 1-1   Narrow *Gf-Gc* Stratum Ability Definitions

Gf-Gc Broad Stratum II Ability	
Narrow Stratum I Name (Code)	Definition

FLUID INTELLIGENCE (*Gf*)

General Sequential Reasoning (RG)	Ability to start with stated rules, premises, or conditions and to engage in one or more steps to reach a solution to a problem.
Induction (I)	Ability to discover the underlying characteristic (e.g., rule, concept, process, trend, class membership) that governs a problem or a set of materials.
Quantitative Reasoning (RQ)	Ability to inductively and deductively reason with concepts involving mathematical relations and properties.
Piagetian Reasoning (RP)	Seriation, conservation, classification and other cognitive abilities as defined by Piaget.
Speed of Reasoning (RE)	(Not clearly defined by existing research.)

QUANTITATIVE KNOWLEDGE (*Gq*)

Mathematical Knowledge (KM)	Range of general knowledge about mathematics.
Mathematical Achievement (A3)	Measured mathematics achievement.

CRYSTALLIZED INTELLIGENCE (*Gc*)

Language Development (LD)	General development, or the understanding of words, sentences, and paragraphs (*not* requiring reading) in spoken native language skills.
Lexical Knowledge (VL)	Extent of vocabulary that can be understood in terms of correct word meanings.
Listening Ability (LS)	Ability to listen and comprehend oral communications.
General (verbal) Information (KO)	Range of general knowledge.
Information about Culture (K2)	Range of cultural knowledge (e.g., music, art).
General Science Information (K1)	Range of scientific knowledge (e.g., biology, physics, engineering, mechanics, electronics).
Geography Achievement (A5)	Range of geography knowledge.
Communication Ability (CM)	Ability to speak in "real- life" situations (e.g., lecture, group participation) in an adult manner.
Oral Production and Fluency (OP)	More specific or narrow oral communication skills than reflected by Communication Ability (CM).
Grammatical Sensitivity (MY)	Knowledge or awareness of the grammatical features of the native language.

Continued

TABLE 1-1   *Continued*

Gf-Gc Broad Stratum II Ability

Narrow Stratum I Name (Code)	Definition
Foreign Language Proficiency (KL)	Similar to Language Development (LD) but for a foreign language.
Foreign Language Aptitude (LA)	Rate and ease of learning a new language.

READING/WRITING (*Grw*)

Reading Decoding (RD)	Ability to recognize and decode words or pseudowords in reading.
Reading Comprehension (RC)	Ability to comprehend connected discourse during reading.
Verbal (printed) Language Comprehension (V)	General development, or the understanding of words, sentences, and paragraphs in native language, as measured by *reading* vocabulary and *reading* comprehension tests.
Cloze Ability (CZ)	Ability to supply words deleted from prose passages.
Spelling Ability (SG)	Ability to spell. (Not clearly defined by existing research.)
Writing Ability (WA)	Ability to write with clarity of thought, organization, and good sentence structure. (Not clearly defined by existing research.)
English Usage Knowledge (EU)	Knowledge of writing in the English language with respect to capitalization, punctuation, usage, and spelling.
Reading Speed (RS)	Time required to silently read a passage as quickly as possible.

SHORT-TERM MEMORY (*Gsm*)

Memory Span (MS)	Ability to attend to and immediately recall temporally ordered elements in the correct order after a single presentation.
Learning Abilities (L1)	[Also listed under *Glr* (Not clearly defined by existing research.)]

VISUAL PROCESSING (*Gv*)

Visualization (VZ)	Ability to mentally manipulate objects or visual patterns and to "see" how they would appear under altered conditions.
Spatial Relations (SR)	Ability to rapidly perceive and manipulate visual patterns or to maintain orientation with respect to objects in space.

TABLE 1-1   *Continued*

Gf-Gc Broad Stratum II Ability	
Narrow Stratum I Name (Code)	Definition
Visual Memory (MV)	Ability to form and store a mental representation or image of a visual stimulus and then recognize or recall it later.
Closure Speed (CS)	Ability to quickly combine disconnected, vague, or partially obscured visual stimuli or patterns into a meaningful whole, *without knowing in advance* what the pattern is.
Flexibility of Closure (CF)	Ability to identify a visual figure or pattern embedded in a complex visual array, *when knowing in advance* what the pattern is.
Spatial Scanning (SS)	Ability to accurately and quickly survey a spatial field or pattern and identify a path through the visual field or pattern.
Serial Perceptual Integration (PI)	Ability to identify a pictorial or visual pattern when parts of the pattern are presented rapidly in order.
Length Estimation (LE)	Ability to accurately estimate or compare visual lengths and distances without using measurement instruments.
Perceptual Illusions (IL)	Ability to resist being affected by perceptual illusions involving geometric figures.
Perceptual Alternations (PN)	Consistency in the rate of alternating between different visual perceptions.
Imagery (IM)	Ability to vividly mentally manipulate abstract spatial forms. (Not clearly defined by existing research.)

AUDITORY PROCESSING (*Ga*)

Phonetic Coding (PC)	Ability to process speech sounds, as in identifying, isolating, and blending sounds; phonological awareness.
Speech Sound Discrimination (US)	Ability to detect differences in speech sounds under conditions of little distraction or distortion.
Resistance to Auditory Stimulus Distortion (UR)	Ability to understand speech that has been distorted or masked in one or more ways.
Memory for Sound Patterns (UM)	Ability to retain on a short-term basis auditory events such as tones, tonal patterns, and voices.
General Sound Discrimination (U3)	Ability to discriminate tones, tone patterns, or musical materials with regard to pitch, intensity, duration, and rhythm.

Continued

TABLE 1-1   *Continued*

Gf-Gc Broad Stratum II Ability	
Narrow Stratum I Name (Code)	Definition
Temporal Tracking (UK)	Ability to track auditory temporal events so as to be able to count or rearrange them.
Musical Discrimination and Judgment (U1, U9)	Ability to discriminate and judge tonal patterns in music with respect to phrasing, tempo, and intensity variations.
Maintaining and Judging Rhythm (U8)	Ability to recognize and maintain a musical beat.
Sound-Intensity/Duration Discrimination (U6)	Ability to discriminate sound intensities and to be sensitive to the temporal/rhythmic aspects of tonal patterns.
Sound-Frequency Discrimination (U5)	Ability to discriminate frequency attributes (pitch and timbre) of tones.
Hearing and Speech Threshold factors (UA, UT, UU)	Ability to hear pitch and varying sound frequencies.
Absolute Pitch (UP)	Ability to perfectly identify the pitch of tones.
Sound Localization (UL)	Ability to localize heard sounds in space.

LONG-TERM STORAGE AND RETRIEVAL (*Glr*)

Associative Memory (MA)	Ability to recall one part of a previously learned but unrelated pair of items when the other part is presented (i.e., paired-associative learning).
Meaningful Memory (MM)	Ability to recall a set of items where there is a meaningful relation between items or the items create a meaningful story or connected discourse.
Free Recall Memory (M6)	Ability to recall as many unrelated items as possible, in any order, after a large collection of items is presented.
Ideational Fluency (FI)	Ability to rapidly produce a series of ideas, words, or phrases related to a specific condition or object.
Associational Fluency (FA)	Ability to rapidly produce words or phrases associated in meaning (semantically associated) with a given word or concept.
Expressional Fluency (FE)	Ability to rapidly think of and organize words or phrases into meaningful, complex ideas.
Naming Facility (NA)	Ability to rapidly produce names for concepts.
Word Fluency (FW)	Ability to rapidly produce words that have specific phonemic, structural, or orthographic characteristics.

TABLE 1-1 *Continued*

Gf-Gc Broad Stratum II Ability	
Narrow Stratum I Name (Code)	Definition
Figural Fluency (FF)	Ability to rapidly draw or sketch several examples or elaborations when given a starting visual stimulus.
Figural Flexibility (FX)	Ability to change set in order to generate new and different solutions to figural problems.
Sensitivity to Problems (SP)	Ability to rapidly think of solutions to practical problems.
Originality/Creativity (FO)	Ability to rapidly produce original, clever, or uncommon responses to specified tasks.
Learning Abilities (L1)	[Also listed under *Gsm*] (Not clearly defined by existing research.)
PROCESSING SPEED (*Gs*)	
Perceptual Speed (P)	Ability to rapidly search for and compare visual symbols presented side by side or separated in a visual field.
Rate-of-Test-Taking (R9)	Ability to rapidly perform tests that are relatively easy or that require very simple decisions.
Number Facility (N)	Ability to rapidly and accurately manipulate and deal with numbers, from elementary skills of counting and recognizing numbers to advanced skills of adding, subtracting, multiplying, and dividing numbers.
DECISION/REACTION TIME OR SPEED (*Gt*)	
Simple Reaction Time (R1)	Reaction time to the presentation of a single stimulus.
Choice Reaction Time (R2)	Reaction time to one of two or more alternative stimuli, depending on which alternative is signaled.
Semantic Processing Speed (R4)	Reaction time when the decision requires some encoding and mental manipulation of stimulus content.
Mental Comparison Speed (R7)	Reaction time when the stimuli must be compared for a particular attribute.

Note: Most definitions were derived from Carroll (1993a). Two-letter factor codes (e.g., RG) are from Carroll (1993a). The information in this table was reproduced with permission from Guilford Publishing Co. All rights reserved.

of primarily verbal or language-based knowledge represents those abilities that have been developed largely through the "investment" of other abilities during educational and general life experiences (Horn & Noll, 1997). Schematically, *Gc* might be represented by the interconnected nodes of a fishing net. Each node of the net represents an acquired piece of information, and the filaments between nodes (with many possible filaments leading to and from multiple nodes) representing links between different bits of stored information. A person high in *Gc* abilities would have a rich "fishing net" of information as represented by many nodes that are organized and interconnected meaningfully. Crystallized Intelligence is one of the abilities mentioned most often by lay persons when they are asked to describe an "intelligent" person (Horn, 1988). The image of a sage captures to a large extent the essence of *Gc*.

Gc includes both declarative and procedural knowledge—-a distinction between relatively static or dynamic knowledge, respectively. Declarative knowledge refers to knowledge "*that* something is the case, whereas procedural knowledge is knowledge of *how* to do something" (Gagné, 1985, p. 48). Declarative knowledge is held in long-term memory and is activated when related information is in short-term memory (*Gsm*). Declarative knowledge includes factual information, comprehension, concepts, rules, and relationships, especially when the information is verbal. Procedural knowledge refers to the process of reasoning with previously learned procedures to transform knowledge. A child's knowledge of his or her street address would reflect declarative knowledge, while demonstrating the ability to find his or her home from school would require procedural knowledge (Gagné, 1985). The breadth of *Gc* is apparent from the number (i.e., 12) of narrow abilities listed for this ability in Table 1–1.

A common misunderstanding about *Gc* abilities is their relationship to school achievement. As originally conceptualized by Cattell (1971), *Gc* is distinct from school achievement. McGrew and colleagues (1991) and Woodcock (1990) reported that in adequately designed factor analytic studies, measures of basic academic skills in reading, mathematics, and written language *do not* load together on a common factor with measures of verbal knowledge (e.g., vocabulary or information tests). Also, the observation that the growth curve for a measure of *Gc* differs from that of measures of reading and mathematics argues for the conceptual distinctness of the *Gc* construct (McGrew et al., 1991).

Furthermore, as noted by Carroll (1993a), "it is hard to draw the line between factors of cognitive abilities and factors of cognitive achievements. Some will argue that *all* cognitive abilities are in reality learned achievements of one kind or another" (p. 510). Horn (1988) made a similar point when he described the cognitive-achievement dichotomy as a popular *verbal*, rather than *empirical*, distinction. According to Horn (1988), "cognitive abilities are measures of achievements, and measures of achievements are just as surely measures of cognitive abilities" (p. 655). Most scholars of intelligence do not draw a hard and fast line between cognitive and achievement abilities but instead prefer to place abilities and achievements on a continuum ordered by the degree to which informal/indirect and formal/direct learning and instructional experiences influence the development of abilities (Carroll, 1993; Horn, 1988; Lohman, 1989). For example, *Gf* abilities would be placed at the informal/indirect end of the continuum, while *Grw* and *Gq* abilities would be placed at the formal/direct end of the continuum. Lying between these two extremes would be the other *Gf-Gc* abilities, with *Gc* being near (but not at) the formal/direct end of the continuum.

Quantitative Knowledge (Gq)

Quantitative Knowledge represents an individual's store of acquired quantitative declarative and procedural knowledge. This store of acquired knowledge is similar to *Gc*, with the difference being that the reservoir of knowledge associated with *Gq* relates to the ability to use quantitative information and to manipulate numeric symbols. It is important to understand the difference between *Gq* and the Quantitative Reasoning (RQ) ability that is subsumed by *Gf*. *Gq* represents an individual's store of acquired mathematical knowledge, while RQ represents the ability to reason inductively and deductively when solving quantitative problems. *Gq* would be evident when a task requires mathematical skills and general mathematical knowledge (e.g., knowing what the square root symbol means). RQ would be required to solve for a missing number in a number series task (e.g., 2 4 6 8 ___). Two narrow abilities are listed and defined under *Gq* in Table 1–1.

Reading/Writing Ability (Grw)

Reading/Writing Ability is an acquired store of knowledge that includes basic reading and writing skills required for the comprehension of written language and the expression of thought via writing. It includes both basic (e.g., reading decoding and spelling) and complex abilities (e.g., reading comprehension and the ability to write a story). Currently this ability domain is not well defined nor has it been extensively researched within the *Gf-Gc* framework. In Carroll's (1993a) three-stratum model, eight narrow reading and writing abilities are subsumed by *Gc* in addition to other abilities. In McGrew's (1997) model and in the present *Gf-Gc* model these eight narrow abilities define the broad *Grw* ability. These narrow abilities are defined in Table 1–1.

Short-Term Memory (Gsm)

Short-Term Memory is the ability to apprehend and hold information in immediate awareness and then use it within a few seconds. *Gsm* is a limited-capacity system, as most individuals can only retain seven "chunks" of information (plus or minus two chunks) in this system at one time. Real-world examples of tasks requiring *Gsm* would be the ability to remember a telephone number long enough to dial the phone or the ability to listen to and retain a sequence of spoken directions long enough to complete the tasks specified in the directions. Given the limited amount of information that can be held in short-term memory, information typically is retained for only a few seconds before it is lost. As most individuals have experienced, it is difficult to retain an unfamiliar telephone number for more than a few seconds unless one consciously uses a cognitive learning strategy (e.g., constantly repeating or rehearsing the numbers). Once a new task requires an individual to use *Gsm* abilities, the previous information is lost or is stored in the acquired stores of knowledge (i.e., *Gc*, *Gq*, *Grw*) through the use of *Glr*.

It is important to recognize two potentially confusing definitional issues regarding the broad *Gsm* ability. First, *Gsm* should not be confused with "working memory." *Gsm* is *part of* the broader construct of working memory, which is considered to be the "mechanism responsible for the temporary storage and processing of information" (Richardson, 1996, p. 23). In addition to a short-term buffer (i.e., memory span that is subsumed by *Gsm*), working memory has been described to include three other components—phonological loop, visuospatial sketchpad, and central executive (Logie, 1996; Richardson, 1996).

Second, in the integrated Horn-Cattell/Carroll *Gf-Gc* model, only two narrow abilities (Memory Span and Learning Abilities) are subsumed by *Gsm* (see Table 1–1). Given that Learning Abilities are not well defined by existing research (Carroll, 1993), this leaves Memory Span (MS) as the sole narrow ability subsumed by *Gsm*. This raises questions about the accuracy of the "broad" *Gsm* designation. Carroll's (1993a) broad Memory and Learning (*Gu*) factor is indeed broad given that it subsumes a larger array of narrow memory abilities (e.g., Memory Span, Visual Memory, Associative Memory, Meaningful Memory). However, as described previously, many of Carroll's narrow *Gu* abilities were placed under other broad abilities (e.g., *Gv*—Visual Memory; *Glr*—Associative Memory) in the integrated Horn-Cattell/Carroll *Gf-Gc* model. If these revisions to the Carroll model are correct, then Memory Span is essentially the sole narrow *Gsm* ability, a situation that raises a number of questions about the "broadness" of the construct:

- Is *Gsm* a broad or narrow ability, or is it an intermediate ability (Carroll, 1993a) that lies between the narrow and broad strata?
- How do Memory Span and working memory constructs relate to one another, and what are the implications of these relations for a broad short-term/working memory construct?
- Is Carroll's Memory and Learning (*Gu*) ability, an ability that subsumes a wider array of memory abilities, a more accurate representation of this domain?

In the absence of clear answers to these questions, in this book *Gsm* is retained as a broad ability that subsumes at least Memory Span and some of Carroll's (1993a) Learning Abilities. Additional research is needed to more accurately understand the relations between the various narrow memory abilities that have been identified. Moreover, practitioners need to recognize the somewhat tenuous nature of the *Gsm* domain used in the cross-battery assessment approach outlined in Chapter 13. As described in Chapter 13, the ambiguity present within the *Gsm* domain is reflected in alternative cross-battery assessment procedures. Procedures are outlined for operationalizing *Gsm* as either an ability that subsumes Memory Span only, or Memory Span and Visual Memory combined.

Visual Processing (Gv)

Visual Processing (*Gv*) is the ability to generate, perceive, analyze, synthesize, manipulate, transform, and think with visual patterns and stimuli. Frequently these abilities are measured by tasks that require the perception and manipulation of visual shapes and forms, usually figural or geometric. An individual who can effectively mentally reverse, rotate, and interpret how objects change as they move through space; manipulate and perceive spatial configurations; and maintain spatial orientation would be considered to be high in *Gv* abilities. The *Gv* domain includes a broad array of diverse visual abilities that emphasize "different aspects of the process of image generation, storage, retrieval, and transformation" (Lohman, 1994; p. 1000). The array of narrow abilities subsumed by *Gv* is listed and defined in Table 1–1.

Auditory Processing (Ga)

In the broadest sense, auditory abilities "are cognitive abilities that depend on sound as input and on the functioning of our hearing apparatus" (Stankov, 1994, p. 157) and reflect "the degree to which the individual can cognitively control the perception of auditory stimulus inputs" (Gustafsson & Undheim, 1996, p. 192). *Ga* includes the ability to perceive, analyze, and synthesize patterns among auditory stimuli, especially the ability to perceive and discriminate subtle nuances of patterns of sound (e.g., complex musical structure) and speech that may be presented under distorted conditions. *Ga* abilities do not require the comprehension of language (*Gc*) but may be very important in the development of such skills as language and music achievement. *Ga* subsumes most of those abilities referred to as "phonological awareness/processing." However, as can be seen from the list of narrow abilities subsumed by *Ga* (Table 1–1), this domain is very broad.

Long-Term Storage and Retrieval (Glr)

Long-Term Storage and Retrieval (*Glr*) refers to the ability to *store* information (e.g., concepts, ideas, items, names) in long-term memory and to fluently *retrieve* it later through association. *Glr* abilities have been prominent in research on creativity, where they have been referred to as idea production, ideational fluency, or associative fluency. It is important to not confuse *Glr* with a person's store of acquired knowledge. In the *Gf-Gc* framework the acquired stores of knowledge or information are *Gc*, *Gq*, and *Grw*. *Gc*, *Gq*, and *Grw* represent what is stored in long-term memory, while *Glr* is the efficiency by which this information is stored initially and later retrieved from long-term memory. Using the fishing net analogy presented earlier in the discussion of *Gc* (where the nodes and links of the net represent the knowledge that is stored in long-term memory), *Glr* can be considered to represent the process by which individuals add new nodes and links to, and later retrieve from, their "fishing net" of stored knowledge.

Different processes are involved in *Glr* and *Gsm*. Although the term "long-term" frequently carries with it the connotation of days, weeks, months, and years in the clinical literature, long-term storage processes can begin within a few *minutes* or hours of performing a task. The amount of time that lapses between the initial task performance and recall of information related to that task is not critically important in defining *Glr*. More important is the occurrence of an intervening task that engages short-term memory during the interim before recall of the stored information (e.g., *Gc*) is attempted (Woodcock, 1993). In the present *Gf-Gc* model, 13 narrow memory and fluency abilities are subsumed by *Glr* (see Table 1–1).

Processing Speed (Gs)

Mental quickness or processing speed is often mentioned when talking about intelligent behavior (Nettelbeck, 1994). Processing Speed is the ability to fluently perform cognitive tasks automatically, especially when under pressure to maintain focused attention and concentration. "Attentive speediness" encapsulates the essence of *Gs*. *Gs* is typically measured by fixed-interval timed tasks that require little in the way of complex thinking or mental processing.

Recent interest in information processing models of cognitive functioning has resulted in a renewed interest in *Gs* (Kail, 1991; Lohman, 1989). A central construct in information processing models is the idea of limited processing resources (e.g., the limited capacities of short-term or working memory). The essence of *Gs* is speed within limitations: "...many cognitive activities require a person's deliberate efforts and...people are limited in the amount of effort they can allocate. In the face of limited processing resources, the speed of processing is critical because it determines in part how rapidly limited resources can be reallocated to other cognitive tasks" (Kail, 1991, p. 152). Woodcock (1994) likens *Gs* to a valve in a water pipe. The rate of flow of the water in the pipe (i.e., *Gs*) is at a maximum when the valve is wide open and is reduced when the valve is partially closed. Three different narrow speed-of-processing abilities are subsumed by *Gs* in the present *Gf-Gc* model (Table 1–1).

Decision/Reaction Time or Speed (Gt)

In addition to *Gs*, both Carroll and Horn include a second broad speed ability in their respective *Gf-Gc* models. Carroll's ability is called "processing speed (reaction time and decision speed)" (*Gt*) and subsumes narrow abilities that reflect an individual's quickness in reacting (reaction time) or making decisions (decision speed). Horn's second speed ability is called Correct Decision Speed (*CDS*), and is typically measured by recording the time an individual needs to provide an answer to problems on a variety of tests (e.g., letter series, classifications, vocabulary) (Horn, 1988, 1991). *CDS* appears to be a much narrower ability than *Gt* and is thus subsumed by *Gt* in the *Gf-Gc* model used in this book.

Gt should not be confused with *Gs*. *Gt* abilities are those that reflect the *immediacy* with which an individual can react (typically measured in seconds or parts of seconds) to stimuli or a task. In contrast, *Gs* abilities have a more *sustained* quality in that they reflect the ability to work quickly over a longer period of time (typically measured in intervals of 2–3 minutes). Being asked to read the next five pages of this book (on a self-paced scrolling video screen) as quickly as possible and, in the process, touch the word "the" with a stylus pen each time it appears on the screen is an example of *Gs*. The individual's *Gs* score would reflect the number of correct responses (taking into account errors of omission and commission). In contrast, *Gt* may be measured by requiring a person to read the same text at their normal rate of reading and press the space bar as quickly as possible whenever a light is flashed on the screen. In this situation the individual's score is based on the average response latency (or the time interval between the onset of the stimulus and the individual's response).

The Relation Between Gf-Gc Theory and Other Select Theories of Intelligence

The history of psychology reports numerous endeavors to explicate theories of intelligence. As stated earlier, a thorough treatment of the various theories and their relations to the development and interpretation of intelligence tests is beyond the scope of this book. However, some comments about how certain popular theories of intelligence (including those that have been used to develop or interpret intelligence tests) relate to *Gf-Gc* theory are provided here.

Verbal/Nonverbal Conceptions

Given the historical dominance of the Wechsler series of intelligence batteries in psychological and psychoeducational assessment, it is understandable that many practitioners have come to view intelligence as consisting of verbal and nonverbal abilities. However, the Verbal and Performance (nonverbal) design of the original Wechsler scales was not based on an empirically supported theory of intelligence. Rather, Wechsler designed his first scale based on a combination of clinical, practical, and empirical considerations (Kaufman, 1990a; Zachary, 1990). Wechsler did not consider the Verbal–Performance dichotomy to represent two different types of intelligence. Rather, his intent was to organize the tests to reflect the two different ways (i.e., two different "languages") by which intelligence can be expressed (Kamphaus, 1993; Reynolds & Kamphaus, 1990; Zachary, 1990). Although verbal abilities represent a valid construct (i.e., *Gc*), *there is no such thing as "nonverbal" ability—only abilities that are expressed nonverbally.*

Given that the Wechsler verbal/nonverbal model was not based on an empirically derived theory of intelligence, the failure of a verbal/nonverbal model to emerge in comprehensive reviews of the extant factor analysis literature is not surprising. Carroll (1993a; 1993b) concluded that the Wechsler Verbal scale is an approximate measure of crystallized intelligence (*Gc*) and the Performance scale is an approximate measure of broad visual perception (*Gv*), and, somewhat less validly, fluid intelligence (*Gf*). Recent cross-battery factor analysis studies with the Wechsler's (WPPSI-R, WISC-III, WAIS-R) and other intelligence batteries (see Chapter 3) support Carroll's *Gf-Gc* analysis of the Wechsler scales, with the exception of the Wechsler Performance scale now being viewed as a measure of mainly *Gv*, but not *Gf*, abilities (Elliott, 1994; McGrew & Flanagan, 1996; Woodcock, 1990).[2]

Although the Wechsler verbal–nonverbal dichotomy may be clinically useful, it does not represent a valid theory of intelligence. Verbal/nonverbal intelligence test models are not developed according to the best available evidence of the theoretical structure of human cognitive abilities. From the perspective of *Gf-Gc* theory, the Wechsler-based verbal/nonverbal model measures only a small portion of the 10 empirically supported broad *Gf-Gc* abilities. According to Carroll (1993a), "presently available knowledge and technology would permit the development of tests and scales that would be much more adequate for their purpose than the Wechsler scales" (p. 702).

Luria-Based Theories

Since the early to mid 1980s there has been considerable interest in developing tests that have their roots in the neuropsychological model advanced by Soviet neuropsychologist A. R. Luria. The work of Luria (1966, 1970, 1973, 1980), plus related experimental and cognitive psychological research (Anokhin, 1969; Broadbent, 1958; Das, Kirby, & Jarman, 1979; Hunt & Lansman, 1986), has suggested a model of cognitive processing based on two to four mental operations (Kamphaus, 1990, 1993; Kamphaus & Reynolds, 1984; Kaufman, 1984; Kaufman & Kaufman, 1983; Naglieri, 1997; Naglieri & Das, 1990). The two-factor cognitive processing model consists of simultaneous and successive processes, whereas the four-factor model consists of these same processes together with planning and attention.

Currently there are two Luria-based intelligence batteries. The K-ABC was the first norm-referenced cognitive battery to operationalize the measurement of the simultaneous and successive processing dichotomy. Using the comprehensive *Gf-Gc* model as a guide, Carroll (1993) found that the K-ABC does not assess the total range of known mental abilities. Moreover, following a review of the K-ABC factor-analytic research, Carroll (1993a) concluded that "there is little if anything that is new in the K-ABC test" (p. 703). Both Carroll's (1993) and Woodcock's (1990) *Gf-Gc*– structured empirical analyses suggest that the K-ABC simultaneous and successive processing scales are primarily measures of visual processing (*Gv*) and short-term memory (*Gsm*), respectively (see Chapter 5).

The second Luria-based intelligence battery is the recently published Cognitive Assessment System (CAS; Das & Naglieri, 1997). The Luria-based conceptual-

---

[2] It should be noted that a logically based task analysis revealed that the new WAIS-III contains a measure of *Gf* (see Chapter 8).

ization that underlies the CAS is referred to as the Planning-Attention-Simultaneous-Successive (PASS) model (Naglieri & Das, 1990; Naglieri, 1997). Thus, in addition to measures of simultaneous and successive processing, the CAS includes tests of planning and attention processes.

Independent reviewers of the experimental versions of the CAS have raised questions about the construct validity of the battery (i.e., its underlying four-factor PASS model). Based on a confirmatory factor analysis of the experimental CAS measures, Kranzler and Weng (1995) did not find support for separate Planning and Attention factors. Instead, the measures of Planning and Attention formed a single factor that Kranzler and Weng interpreted as measuring speed of information processing, a factor very similar to the *Gs* factor in the *Gf-Gc* model. In another review of the experimental version of the CAS, Carroll (1995) used confirmatory factor analysis procedures with PASS datasets and concluded that

> Das, Naglieri, and Kirby have not yet arrived at a persuasive interpretable model of intellectual abilities that is supported adequately by empirical data...nor have they considered adequately the possibility that their PASS tests measure dimensions of ability, such as *g*, fluid intelligence, crystallized intelligence, spatial ability, perceptual speed, and many others, that have been recognized in the cognitive ability research. (p. 408)

In summary, when examined from the perspective of *Gf-Gc* theory, the Luria-based intelligence batteries have been suggested to measure nothing new beyond that already known from the abilities that make up the *Gf-Gc* framework. Empirical studies grounded in the modern *Gf-Gc* framework (Carroll, 1993a, 1995; Woodcock, 1990) suggest that the Luria-based simultaneous/successive and PASS assessment batteries only measure known *Gf-Gc* abilities, not new or unique processes. This does not necessarily mean that the underlying theory is not valid, only that the validity of the assessment batteries that have been developed to operationalize the theory has not been demonstrated convincingly. As described earlier in this chapter, the PASS theory is one attempt to harness the potential benefits of information processing theory for assessment and intervention. These potential benefits are described elsewhere by Das, Naglieri, and Kirby (1994) and by Naglieri (1997).

Gardner's Theory of Multiple Intelligences

The description of *Gf-Gc* theory as a multiple intelligences theory occasionally causes confusion when individuals try to reconcile this model with Gardner's multiple intelligences theory (Chen & Gardner, 1997; Gardner, 1983, 1993, 1994). Although Gardner's theory of multiple intelligences has yet to serve as the foundation for an individually administered norm-referenced battery of tests, the concepts have received considerable attention in the popular press.

Gardner described seven types of intelligence: logical-mathematical, linguistic, musical, spatial, bodily-kinesthetic, interpersonal, and intrapersonal. The terms Gardner uses to label his seven intelligences are dramatically different from the terminology of *Gf-Gc* theory. What are the differences and similarities between the *Gf-Gc* and Gardner multiple intelligences theories?

McGrew (1993, 1995) suggested that the fundamental differences between the two theories is that *Gf-Gc* theory is concerned with *describing the basic domains or building blocks of intelligent behavior* in the cognitive domain, while Gardner's theory focuses on *how these different domains or building blocks are combined,* together with other personal competencies (e.g., motor and social skills), in patterns representing different forms of aptitude or expertise (i.e., adult end-states valued by a culture) (Chen & Gardner, 1997). Using Greenspan's model of personal competence (Greenspan & Driscoll, 1997), a model that includes the broad domains of physical and emotional competence and conceptual, practical, and social intelligence, as an overarching framework, McGrew (1994) suggested that Gardner's seven intelligences represent unique combinations or patterns of human cognitive abilities across domains of personal competence. For example, Gardner's logical-mathematical intelligence reflects a sensitivity to and capacity for processing logical and/or numerical patterns and the ability to manage long sequences or chains of reasoning. Scientists and mathematicians would most likely be high on logical-mathematical intelligence. An individual who has high logical-mathematical intelligence may have high fluid reasoning (*Gf*), quantitative knowledge (*Gq*), and visual processing abilities (*Gv*). It is the specific combination of *Gf-Gc* strengths that a person exhibits that defines him or her as being high in logical-mathematical intelligence. As another example, individuals who are high in Gardner's bodily-kinesthetic intelligence may have specific *Gf-Gc* strengths (e.g., *Gv*), plus strengths in other personal competence domains such as physical competence.

In contrast to structural *Gf-Gc* theory, Gardner's theory of multiple intelligences focuses on a different aspect of human performance, namely, expertise or aptitude. Individuals with specific expertise or aptitudes likely have unique combinations of certain *Gf-Gc* abilities together with abilities in the other domains of personal competence. Gardner's theory is not an attempt to isolate the basic domains or elements of intelligence (a function performed by *Gf-Gc* theory); rather, it describes different patterns of expertise or aptitude based on specific combinations of *Gf-Gc* abilities *and other personal competencies.* In this regard, Gardner's different intelligences are conceptually similar to Snow's (1989, 1991, 1992) *aptitude complexes,* which define aptitudes in the broadest sense (i.e., including both cognitive and conative structures).

Although Gardner's theory has considerable appeal, it has been found wanting when subjected to empirical evaluation. In a review of Gardner's (1983) *Frames of Mind,* the book that describes his multiple intelligences (MI) theory, Lubinski and Benbow (1995) concluded that there is "little empirical support for or against the unique features of Gardner's ideas. Before MI theory can be taken seriously by the scientific community and policy makers, Gardner's (1983) bold theoretical skeleton is in need of empirical flesh" (p. 937). According to Carroll (1993a), Gardner "discounts multifactorial theories of intelligence...because, he claims, they fail to account for the full diversity of abilities that can be observed. Generally,

Gardner has neglected the evidence on the basis of which the present three-stratum theory has been constructed" (p. 641). Furthermore, in a review and comparison of structural *Gf-Gc* theory, Gardner's multiple intelligences theory, and Sternberg's Triarchic theory (Sternberg, 1985), Messick (1992) characterized Gardner's (as well as Sternberg's) theory as appealing selectively to factor-analytic research, ignoring or downplaying research that challenges his model. Thus, it seems clear that the descriptions of Gardner's seven multiple intelligences "do not derive from any consistent set of empirical data and can be tied to data only in piecemeal fashion, thereby being constantly threatened by the perverse human tendency to highlight results that are consonant with the theory's logic over findings that are dissonant" (Messick, 1992, p. 368). Bouchard (1984), Gustafsson and Undheim (1996), Scarr (1985), and Snow (1985) also questioned the empirical support for Gardner's theory.

Sternberg's Triarchic Theory

The Triarchic theory of intelligence (Sternberg, 1994, 1997) is an attempt to describe the processes that underlie intelligent thought by understanding the way in which intelligence relates to the internal and external world and experiences of individuals (Messick, 1992). Sternberg suggests that three major elements or "components" influence intelligent thought.

First, three sets of *processing components* (i.e., mental processes) allow individuals to solve problems (Sternberg, 1994, 1997). *Knowledge acquisition components* allow individuals to learn new information, while *performance* and *metacomponents* are involved in actually working with problems to produce solutions and executing and monitoring the problem-solving processes, respectively (Eggen & Kauchak, 1997). Second, *experiential components* are involved in relating new experiences and knowledge to old experiences and knowledge and recognizing and creating new patterns of information. Third, *contextual components* are concerned with adaptation—that is, explaining how a person's intelligence allows him or her to select new environments or adapt or modify existing environments (Eggen & Kauchak, 1997; Travers, Elliott, & Kratochwill, 1993).

According to Messick (1992), Sternberg's focus on culturally relevant conceptions of intelligence in relation to individual experiences results in a "focus on five critical aspects of intelligence—problem solving, verbal ability, social and practical competence, coping with novelty, and the automatization of performance" (p. 376). A consideration of these concepts suggests that the Triarchic theory includes parts of the *Gf-Gc* model, namely *Gf*, *Gc*, *Glr*, and *Gs*, respectively (Messick, 1992).

Like Gardner's theory, Sternberg's Triarchic theory has not fared well when evaluated against established standards of validity. Messick (1992) indicated that "several aspects of Sternberg's theory are simply nonfactual…the theory is construct dense . . . [I]n the process, he [Sternberg] forgoes relations of strict deductibility and tends to rely on metaphorical descriptions. . . . but they are not conducive to the derivation of empirical consequences instrumental to theory testing" (p.

379). Messick's less than positive treatment of Sternberg's Triarchic theory is echoed in Cronbach's (1986) response to some of Sternberg's claims:

> We don't have much theory, and I don't favor using the word loosely for almost any abstraction or point of view.... I would reserve the word *theory* for substantial, articulated, somewhat validated constructions. Rather than an emperor with no clothes, we have theory being used as an imperial cloak that has no emperor inside. (p. 23)

Cognitive Modifiability Theories

In contrast to the other theories just reviewed, cognitive modifiability theories are difficult to relate to *Gf-Gc* theory. Cognitive modifiability theories are associated with a number of different theorists, of which the most notable are Feuerstein (Feuerstein, Feuerstein, & Gross, 1997) and Vgotsky (1978, 1986). In general, cognitive modifiability theories are ecologically based theories that focus on the context and collaborative interaction between an individual and other persons in their environment. According to Vgotsky, the difference between a person's intelligence performance in isolation and one's performance when mediated by hints, guided instruction, and suggestions by another individual is the persons's *zone of proximal development* (ZPD). Translation of the ZPD concept into assessment practice has resulted in dynamic assessment approaches (see Feuerstein, Feuerstein, & Gross, 1997; Lidz, 1997).

An evaluation of cognitive modifiability theories and the resultant dynamic assessment approaches within the psychometric *Gf-Gc* framework is difficult. As noted by Lidz (1997), "dynamic assessment to a significant extent represents a clinician's dream and a psychometrician's nightmare. What is valid for one approach is invalid for the other" (p. 286). The relevance of traditional notions of reliability and validity has been questioned by cognitive modifiability theorists (see Lidz, 1997, for discussion). Although the process-oriented cognitive modifiability theories and dynamic assessment strategies appear to be qualitatively different from the other theories reviewed here, these theories have the potential to provide important information on the modifiability of different *Gf-Gc* abilities. For example, Carroll (1993a) concluded that abilities that are more specific and less general may be more malleable but that "there is yet inadequate information as to the limits, if any, to which these abilities may be improved, or as to the effects of different types of environments, training, and intervention" (p. 687). Cognitive modifiability theory could inform *Gf-Gc*–oriented researchers and practitioners about the malleability of different abilities and about potentially useful interventions. Much additional research in this area is needed.

Concluding Comments

In this chapter, *Gf-Gc* theory was described as the most comprehensive and empirically supported psychometric theory of intelligence and the theory around which intelligence tests should be interpreted. Therefore, determining how other popular theories of intelligence (viz., verbal/nonverbal, Luria-based processing models, Gardner's multiple intelligences theory, Sternberg's Triarchic theory) relate to *Gf-Gc* theory was considered important. From the perspective of *Gf-Gc* theory, the popular verbal/nonverbal or Wechsler model of intelligence was found wanting. The verbal/nonverbal (performance) model does not represent a theoretically or empirically supported model of the structure of intelligence. In contrast, the jury is still out on the usefulness of the Luria-based neuropsychological theory (viz., PASS) for applied intellectual assessment. Instruments based on the Luria model (e.g., CAS, K-ABC) have been said to measure nothing more than a restricted set of known *Gf-Gc* abilities (e.g., *Gsm, Gv, Gs*).

Gardner's multiple intelligences and Sternberg's Triarchic theories, although receiving much attention in the popular press, have been found to be theory-rich and data-poor. They both attend selectively to or ignore features of the extensive *Gf-Gc* research literature. Hence, if Sternberg (and Gardner) "had treated factorial theories and research on human abilities in more depth, their empirical and scholarly efforts might have systematically built upon (or undercut) these structural formulations and advanced the science of intellect in cumulative rather than idiosyncratic fashion" (Messick, 1992, p. 382).

As discussed in this chapter, the *Gf-Gc* and Gardner frameworks can be related to one another when both are evaluated within the confines of a comprehensive model of personal competence (e.g., Greenspan's Model of Personal Competence). A number of *Gf-Gc* abilities appear to underlie many of Gardner's multiple intelligences (e.g., *Gf, Gv,* and *Gq* likely underlie logical-mathematical intelligence; *Ga* likely underlies musical intelligence) *in combination* with other traits and aptitudes from other noncognitive domains (e.g., physical competence). Finally, portions of certain *Gf-Gc* abilities appear embedded in parts of Sternberg's Triarchic theory, a theory that (like Gardner's theory) has been found to rest on a weak foundation of validity evidence. In contrast, cognitive modifiability theories such as those advanced by Feuerstein or Vgotsky may prove useful in suggesting interventions related to the malleability of different *Gf-Gc* abilities.

The intent of these comparisons was not to provide a comprehensive analysis of the intricate features or strengths and limitations of each theory. (See Harrison, Flanagan, and Genshaft, [1997] for a comprehensive comparison of these and other intelligence theories.) Rather, the selective comparisons of theories presented in this chapter were made to determine how popular intelligence theories "fit" (or relate to) the *Gf-Gc* model. Thus, although not highlighted here, we recognize that other theories have important and unique features that, if held up against *Gf-Gc* theory, would illuminate its limitations. The reader is referred to Carroll (1997), Chen and Gardner (1997), Horn and Noll (1997), Naglieri (1997), and Sternberg (1997) for more in-depth discussions of the *Gf-Gc*, multiple intelligences, PASS, and Triarchic theories, respectively.

In conclusion, "all sciences need systems of description and classification" (Gustafsson & Undheim, 1996, p. 188). Contemporary *Gf-Gc* intelligence theory was described in this chapter as the most researched, empirically supported, and comprehensive psychometric descriptive hierarchical framework from which to organize thinking about intelligence test interpretation. According to Gustafsson and Undheim (1996), "the empirical evidence in favor of a hierarchical arrangement of abilities is overwhelming" (p. 204). An integrated Horn-Cattell/Carroll *Gf-Gc* model was presented as the taxonomic framework around which the practice of intelligence testing and interpretation should be organized. Supporting evidence for, and limitations of, the *Gf-Gc* model are presented next in Chapter 2. Subsequently, in Part II of this book (chapters 4 through 12), all subtests from the major intelligence batteries, as well as subtests from a number of "special purpose" tests/batteries, are classified according to the *Gf-Gc* model. Finally, given that no individual intelligence battery contains sufficient indicators all of the major *Gf-Gc* abilities (see Chapter 3), a cross-battery approach to intellectual assessment has been developed using the *Gf-Gc* classifications of cognitive ability tests from Part II as a foundation (and will be discussed further in chapters 13 and 14). This approach is offered as a way to bridge the current theory–practice gap in intellectual assessment.

Gf-Gc *Theory in Perspective*

Supporting Evidence, Relations to Academic Achievement, Occupational Outcomes and Other Traits, and Limitations

No way of thinking or doing, however ancient, can be trusted without proof.
— *THOREAU, "ECONOMY," WALDEN (1854)*

Placing trust in any psychological theory, no matter how venerable and steeped in tradition, is unwise unless significant evidence (proof) exists to support its validity. In Chapter 1, *Gf-Gc* theory was presented as the most comprehensive and empirically supported psychometric theory of intelligence. In addition, *Gf-Gc* theory was presented as the most promising framework for developing and interpreting intelligence batteries. In this chapter the empirical support for *Gf-Gc* theory is discussed. Furthermore, given that a primary goal of this book is to present an applied *Gf-Gc* cross-battery approach to intellectual assessment, this chapter reviews research that has investigated the relations between *Gf-Gc* abilities and academic achievement, occupational success, and other human traits. This information is important because it provides a context for interpreting and applying results from *Gf-Gc* cross-battery assessments. Finally, although *Gf-Gc* theory is well respected, it has limitations. These are discussed in the last section of this chapter.

Supporting Evidence for **Gf-Gc Theory**

As presented in Chapter 1, extensive and robust factor-analytic evidence supports the validity of the *Gf-Gc* theory of intelligence. Unfortunately, since the comprehensive factor-analytic literature on cognitive abilities is typically the only evidence cited in support of *Gf-Gc* theory, a common misconception is that *Gf-Gc* theory is only a factor-analytic–based theory. However, support for the hierarchical *Gf-Gc* theory has been documented through five major forms of validity evidence (Gustafsson & Undheim, 1996; Horn, 1994; Horn & Noll, 1997). Each is discussed briefly here.

Structural Evidence

First, *structural evidence,* or evidence based on the individual differences, factor-analytic research tradition, has been the most prominent evidential base for the *Gf-Gc* constructs (Taylor, 1994). This source of evidence is based on the principle of concomitant variation. That is, if measures covary repeatedly across studies that differ in sample characteristics, time, and place, then this covariation suggests the plausibility of a common underlying function (Horn & Noll, 1997). As presented in Chapter 1, the extant factor-analytic research over the past 50 to 60 years consistently has converged on models of intelligence similar to the *Gf-Gc* models presented in Figure 1–2. Furthermore, the *Gf-Gc* structure presented in Figure 1–2 has been found to be invariant across different gender, ethnic, and racial groups (Carroll, 1993a). Carroll (1993a) concluded that "with reference to the major types of cognitive ability, there is little evidence that factorial structure differs in any systematic way across male and female groups, different cultures, racial groups, and the like"(p. 687).

   Given the wide age range covered by the major intelligence batteries and the *Gf-Gc* cross-battery approach to intelligence test interpretation described in this book, it is important to know if the *Gf-Gc* model presented in Figure 1–3 is also invariant across ages. Historically both logical and theoretical considerations have suggested that cognitive abilities become more differentiated with age (the age-differentiation hypothesis) (Carroll, 1993a). Carroll's massive review of the cognitive ability factor-analytic research addressed the age-differentiation issue in that it included some studies with subjects from as young as 6 months to 70 years. Carroll (1993a) stated that "my general conclusion on age-differentiation of cognitive ability factors is that it is a phenomenon whose existence is hard to demonstrate.... [T]he question of age-differentiation is probably of little scientific interest except possibly at very young ages . . . the same factors are found throughout the life span" (p. 681). The apparent invariance of the *Gf-Gc* factors across ages, male and female groups, and different cultures and racial groups supports the application of the *Gf-Gc* cross-battery approach to intelligence test interpretation for most of the population. However, give the relatively small number of factor-analytic studies (viz., 13) that included subjects (less than 6 years of age) in Carroll's review, the extension of the cross-battery approach below age 6 should be approached cautiously.

   Some critics contend that because of the heavy emphasis on factor-analytic research, the *Gf-Gc* theory is "too data-driven and rather theory weak" (Taylor, 1994, p. 185). Furthermore, structural evidence is sometimes dismissed by critics who believe that it relies too heavily on a statistical method (i.e., factor analysis) that stimulates heated debate about the selection and implementation of different procedures. For example, Detterman (1979) jokingly stated that "even if it were possible to extract factors correctly, determining an acceptable rotation has never been accomplished by anyone in the history of Western civilization . . . [I]t is impossible to name factors and still have friends" (p. 169). Although the factors reported for individual studies or small groups of studies may be questioned legitimately on methodological grounds, the consistent emergence of the *Gf-Gc* factors across studies employing different procedural nuances and spanning many years cannot be ignored (Carroll, 1989, 1993a; Gustafsson, 1989; Hakistan & Cattell, 1978; Horn, 1968, 1976, 1988, 1989; Lohman, 1989; Thurstone, 1938, 1947; Vernon, 1961). In regard to *Gf-Gc* theory, Messick (1992) stated that the "convergent evidence about the nature of salient broad and narrow abilities and their hierarchical organization has emerged in spite of extensive study-to-study differences in task complexity, sample heterogeneity, method of factor extraction, and rotational procedures" (p. 371).

Developmental Evidence

The validity of the *Gf-Gc* constructs is supported also by differential *developmental* changes in the growth and decline of cognitive abilities across the lifespan (Carroll, 1993; Dixon, Kramer, & Baltes, 1985). This type of evidence typically takes the form of comparing *Gf-Gc* growth curves. Developmental evidence has shown that different *Gf-Gc* abilities follow divergent developmental trajectories with increasing age (Horn & Cattell, 1967; Horn, 1982, 1985; Schaie, 1979, 1983, 1994). For example, from young adulthood to old age, increases in *Gc* and *Glr* (maintained abilities) and decreases in *Gf*, *Gs*, and *Gsm* (vulnerable abilities) have been reported (Horn & Noll, 1997). The finding of maintained and vulnerable abilities and differential ability growth curves across the lifespan suggests that different mechanisms or determinants (e.g., education, genes, injuries, lifestyle factors) operate differentially in the development and decline of *Gf-Gc* abilities, evidence that supports the validity of the *Gf-Gc* constructs (Carroll, 1983; Horn & Noll, 1997).

Neurocognitive Evidence

Neurocognitive evidence exists in the form of empirical relations between measures of *Gf-Gc* abilities and physiological and neurological functioning (Horn & Noll, 1997). For example, the norepinephrine system of the brain has been associated with neurological arousal that is characteristic of *Gf* abilities (Iverson, 1979; Horn, 1982, 1985). The localization of specific cognitive abilities in certain regions of the brain (e.g., verbal or *Gc* type abilities are often reported to be localized mainly in the left hemisphere) is another example of neurocognitive evidence (Prohovnik, 1980). Differential declines in different *Gf-Gc* abilities that are associated with age-related central nervous system deterioration (e.g., due to reduced blood flow to the brain, strokes) suggest that different *Gf-Gc* abilities are supported by different underlying brain structures and functions—a finding that further supports the construct validity of the different abilities.

Heritability Evidence

Another form of support for the different *Gf-Gc* abilities is *heritability evidence.* Although at times controversial and theoretically and methodologically complex (see McArdle & Prescott, 1997), behavioral-genetic research has suggested that different sets of genes may determine different structures and functions of the brain. No clear conclusions have yet been reached(Gustafsson & Undheim, 1996); however, different heritability estimates (i.e., estimates of the proportion of variance in individual differences measurement due to genetics) (Plomin, DeFries, & McClearn, 1980; Plomin & Loehlin, 1989) have been reported for different cognitive abilities in some studies (Carroll, 1993a; McGue & Bouchard, 1989; Plomin, DeFries, & McClearn, 1990; Scarr & Carter-Saltzman, 1982; Vandenberg & Volger, 1985). For example, Vandenberg and Volger (1985) cite parent-offspring research that suggests that spatial (*Gv*—Spatial Relations) and verbal (*Gc*) abilities have higher heritabilities than visual memory (*Gv*—Visual Memory) and perceptual speed (*Gs*—Perceptual Speed). In studies of twins, McGue and Bouchard (1989) reported that genetic influences were largest for spatial (*Gv*—Spatial Relations) abilities and smallest for visual memory (*Gv*—Visual Memory) abilities. Recently, behavioral genetic research has provided preliminary support for the hierarchical model of general and specific cognitive abilities. Using DNA markers, Petrill and colleagues (1996) found that a "hierarchical model predicts that most genes associated with one cognitive ability will be associated with other cognitive abilities— that is, the association will be the result of general cognitive ability—although some genes will be specifically associated with a particular cognitive ability" (p. 201). Some behavioral genetic research has suggested that different *Gf-Gc* abilities may be influenced by separate genetic and environmental factors. When combined with research that has reported the differentiation of cognitive abilities at early ages (Carroll, 1993a), Horn and Noll (1997) concluded that "the outlines for different intelligences can be seen in early childhood" (p. 81).

Outcome-Criterion Evidence

Finally, differential *achievement* or *outcome-criterion evidence* supports the existence of separate *Gf-Gc* abilities. Supporting outcome-criterion evidence is found in research studies that have investigated the relations between *Gf-Gc* abilities and academic achievement, occupational success, and other human traits. Given the importance of achievement evidence for applied psychological testing (e.g., knowing whether performance on tests of certain *Gf-Gc* abilities is significantly related to reading performance), this evidence is summarized in greater detail in a separate section that follows.

This outcome-criterion evidence is important, as intellectual assessments that are grounded in *Gf-Gc* theory will be of little value to practitioners if they fail to produce valid interpretations of intellectual functioning that contribute to improved diagnostic and classification decisions, predictions about performance, and interventions. A first step on the road to using *Gf-Gc* theory to improve the practice of intellectual assessment is to understand the relations between *Gf-Gc* abilities and other variables. The following section summarizes research illuminating the relations between *Gf-Gc* abilities, academic achievement, occupational success, personality traits, and interests. The intent of this review was to highlight the consistent significant relations between *Gf-Gc* abilities and important outcome criteria, rather than to produce an exhaustive list of all investigations that included *Gf-Gc* abilities along with achievement and other outcome-criterion measures.

Academic Achievement

The number of research studies expressly designed to examine the relations between multiple *Gf-Gc* abilities and academic achievement is small. Although many studies have investigated the relations between a variety of cognitive constructs (e.g., short-term memory, phonological awareness, visual-spatial abilities) and school achievement, most studies have not conceptualized or classified the variables used in the studies according to the *Gf-Gc* taxonomy. For example, many recent research studies have investigated the relations between phonological awareness and reading performance (see studies listed under *Ga* in Table 2–1). A task analysis of the measures used in these studies found that many of the tasks can be classified at the narrow (stratum I) ability level of the *Gf-Gc* taxonomy. For example, Wagner, Torgesen, and Rashotte (1994) described a variety of phonological processing tasks that measure abilities approximating the definition of Phonetic Coding (PC), a narrow ability subsumed by *Ga* (see Table 1–1 for definition). Also included in this study were measures of Memory Span (MS), a narrow ability subsumed by *Gsm* (see Table 1–1) that the authors described as measures of "phonological coding in working memory." Finally, Wagner, Torgesen, and Rashotte (1994) used a number of rapid automatic naming tasks to measure "phonological code retrieval." The ability measured by rapid automatic naming appears to be very similar to the definition for Naming Facility (NA), a narrow ability subsumed by *Glr* (see Table 1–1).

Although many research studies have not used the terminology of *Gf-Gc* theory, it is still possible to examine the relations between *Gf-Gc* abilities and school achievement by "recasting" the variables used in research studies according to the *Gf-Gc* framework. To better understand the achievement literature, research studies that investigated the relations between cognitive constructs (regardless of their construct label in the original study) and reading and mathematics achievement were identified and (where possible and appropriate) translated into the terminology of *Gf-Gc* theory. The purpose of organizing the review of the literature this way was to provide a link between *Gf-Gc* constructs and achievement that can facilitate the appropriate design of cross-battery assessments that will address referral questions (see Chapter 14).

Studies were identified via five methods. First, research studies that investigated the relations between cognitive, reading, and mathematics achievement measures that were listed in a weekly social and behavioral sciences bibliographic software system (*Current Contents on Diskette*; Institute for Scientific Information; 1992) since 1994 were identified and reviewed. Second, an ancestral search strategy

TABLE 2–1 A Summary of Significant *Gf-Gc* Ability and Reading Achievement Relations from Select Research Studies

Type of Research	*Gf-Gc* Abilities		
	Fluid Intelligence (*Gf*)	Crystallized Intelligence (*Gc*)	Short-Term Memory (*Gsm*)[1]
Key *Gf-Gc* Studies	McGrew (1993)	McGrew (1993) McGrew, Vanderwood, et al. (1997)	McGrew (1993)
Reviews		Just & Carpenter (1992) Kintsch (1988) Lohman (1989)	Just & Carpenter (1992) Torgesen (1988)
Individual Studies	Santos (1989)	Badian (1988) Bowey et al. (1992) Bowey & Patel (1988) Bryant et al. (1989) Carnine et al. (1984) Das & Siu (1996) Engle et al. (1990) Griswold et al. (1987) Jackson et al. (1988) Leather & Henry (1994) MacDonald & Cornwall (1995) McGuinness et al. (1995) Snider & Tarver (1987) Snider (1989) Stanovich et al. (1984)	Bowey et al. (1992) Bowey & Patel (1988) Daneman & Carpenter (1980) Das & Siu (1982) Engle et al. (1990) Engle et al. (1992) Jackson et al. (1988) Mann & Liberman (1984) Shankweiler et al. (1979) Swanson & Berninger (1995) Turner & Engle (1989) Wagner et al. (1993) Wagner et al. (1994) Yuill et al. (1989)

Note: The studies listed in this table reported significant relations between reading achievement (decoding or comprehension) and at least one variable that was classified by the current authors as measuring a narrow (stratum I) *Gf-Gc* ability. *Gq* was excluded due to the achievement nature of the construct. None of the studies reviewed included measures of *Gt*. *Key Gf-Gc studies* are those that were designed specifically to investigate the relations between *Gf-Gc* measures and reading achievement in large, nationally representative samples across the lifespan. *Reviews* are either narrative or empirical (meta-analysis) summaries. *Individual studies* are single research studies. The majority of studies were conducted with elementary school-age subjects.

(i.e., locating key studies cited in other studies) was used to identify other potentially relevant studies. Third, the writings of Horn and Carroll were reviewed for studies that, according to these scholars, shed light on the relations between *Gf-Gc* abilities and academic achievement. Fourth, Mather's (1991) summary of *Gf-Gc*–related achievement research was reviewed for relevant studies.

Fifth, a series of studies that were designed expressly to examine the relations between multiple *Gf-Gc* abilities and school achievement across a wide age range were reviewed (Flanagan et al., 1997; McGrew, 1993; McGrew, Flanagan, et al., 1997; McGrew & Hessler, 1995; McGrew, Vanderwood, et al., 1997). These *key* studies investigated the relations between measures of seven *Gf-Gc* abilities and

TABLE 2–1   *Continued*

	Gf-Gc Abilities		
Visual Processing (*Gv*)	Auditory Processing (*Ga*)	Long-Term Storage & Retrieval (*Glr*)[2]	Processing Speed (*Gs*)
	McGrew (1993) McGrew, Vanderwood, et al. (1997)	McGrew (1993)	McGrew (1993) McGrew, Vanderwood, et al. (1997)
Kavale (1982)	Farmer & Klein (1995) Lyon (1995) McBride-Chang (1995) Torgesen et al. (1994) Wagner & Torgesen (1987)	Just & Carpenter (1992) Kavale (1982)	
Eden et al. (1996) Jackson et al. (1988)	Bowey et al. (1992) Bowey & Patel (1988) Brady et al. (1983) Bryant et al. (1989) Byrne et al. (1995) Leather & Henry (1994) MacDonald & Cronwall (1995) Mann & Liberman (1984) McGuinness et al. (1995) Shankweiler et al. (1979) Stahl & Murray (1994) Stanovich et al. (1984) Wagner et al. (1993) Wagner et al. (1994) Yopp (1988)	Das & Siu (1982) Jackson et al. (1988) McGuinness et al. (1995) Swanson (1982) Swanson (1986) Wagner et al. (1993) Wagner et al. (1994) Wolf (1991)	Baker et al. (1984) Decker & DeFries (1980) LaBada & DeFries (1988)

[1] Most studies have investigated the importance of working memory, which is a broad construct that subsumes *Gsm*.

[2] Most studies have investigated the importance of rapid automatic naming, which is classified as Naming Facility (NA), a narrow ability subsumed by *Glr*.

reading and mathematics achievement in large, nationally representative samples (i.e., the WJ-R norm data) from childhood to adulthood. Two of the key studies (McGrew, 1993; McGrew & Hessler, 1995) used multiple regression methodology to identify *Gf-Gc* abilities that had significant relations with reading and mathematics achievement. The remaining studies (Flanagan et al., 1997; McGrew, Flanagan, et al., 1997; McGrew, Vanderwood, et al., 1997) used the same samples as those used in the regression-based investigations but employed structural equation modeling methods to investigate the relations between a general intelligence (*g*) factor and seven *Gf-Gc* factors and broad and narrow aspects of reading and mathematics achievement. Summaries of the *Gf-Gc* reading and mathematics research literature are presented in Tables 2–1 and 2–2. Studies or reviews of studies listed in these tables reported significant relations between cognitive measures classified according to the *Gf-Gc* taxonomy and reading and mathematics achievement. These studies are listed under the respective *Gf-Gc* ability (or abilities) for which a significant relation was found with reading (Table 2–1) and/or mathematics (Table 2–2) achievement. The studies in these tables were classified according to whether they were *key Gf-Gc* studies (defined above), *reviews* (narrative or meta-analytic review of literature), or *individual investigations* (single research studies not considered to be "key" studies).

Although the original intent was to present the studies that showed significant relations between each *Gf-Gc* ability (or abilities) and reading or mathematics achievement for different age groups (e.g., childhood, adolescence, and adulthood), this was not necessary. Nearly all of the research on the relations between *Gf-Gc* abilities and reading achievement summarized here was conducted with elementary school-age subjects. With regard to the relations between *Gf-Gc* abilities and mathematics achievement, although studies were found at childhood, adolescent, and adult levels, the trends that emerged were generally consistent

TABLE 2–2   A Summary of Significant *Gf-Gc* Ability and Mathematics Achievement Relations from Select Research Studies

Type of Research	*Gf-Gc* Abilities		
	Fluid Intelligence (*Gf*)	Crystallized Intelligence (*Gc*)	Short-Term Memory (*Gsm*)[1]
Key *Gf-Gc* Studies	Flanagan et al. (1997) McGrew & Hessler (1995)	Flanagan et al. (1997) McGrew & Hessler (1995)	McGrew & Hessler (1995)
Reviews	Carroll & Maxwell (1979)	Carroll & Maxwell (1979) Friedman (1995)	Geary (1993) Snow & Swanson (1992)
Individual Studies	Hakstian & Bennet (1977) Manger & Eikeland (1996) Taylor et al. (1976)	Hale (1981) Marjoribanks (1976) Rasanen & Ahonen (1995) Taylor et al. (1976)	Cooney & Swanson (1990) Hitch (1978) Lemaire et al. (1996) Rasanen & Ahonen (1995) Swanson (1996) Webster (1979)

Note: The studies listed in this table reported significant relations between mathematics achievement and at least one variable that was classified by the current authors as measuring a narrow *Gf-Gc* ability. *Grw* was excluded due to the achievement nature of the construct. None of the studies reviewed included measures of *Ga* or *Gt*. *Key Gf-Gc studies* are those that were designed specifically to investigate the relations between *Gf-Gc* measures and mathematics achievement in large, nationally representative samples across the lifespan. *Reviews* are either narrative or empirical (meta-analysis). *Individual studies* are single research studies. With the exception of *Glr* (see footnote 2), the studies in this review reported significant results for each *Gf-Gc* ability from childhood to young adulthood.

across age groups. Thus, single tables for presenting information on the relations between *Gf-Gc* abilities and reading and mathematics achievement were developed. Interpretation of the *Gf-Gc* reading and mathematics research is presented below. The implications of this research for the design and interpretation of *Gf-Gc–*organized cross-battery assessments is discussed in Chapter 14.

Reading Achievement. A review of Table 2–1 suggests a number of conclusions regarding the relations between *Gf-Gc* abilities and reading achievement. First, narrow abilities subsumed by *Gc, Gsm,* and *Ga* displayed the most consistent significant relations with reading achievement. Measures of phonological processing or awareness (i.e., Phonetic Coding, which is subsumed by *Ga*) showed strong and consistent relations with reading achievement across many studies, especially during the early elementary school years (viz., kindergarten through third grade). *Gc* abilities, which were typically represented by measures of Language Development (LD), Lexical Knowledge (VL), or Listening Comprehension (LC), were also significantly related to reading achievement. As reported in some of the key *Gf-Gc* studies (McGrew, Flanagan, et al., 1997; McGrew, Vanderwood, et al., 1997), the significant effects of *Ga* and *Gc* on reading were present even after the powerful

TABLE 2–2 *Continued*

	Gf-Gc Abilities	
Visual Processing (*Gv*)	Long-Term Storage & Retrieval (*Glr*)[2]	Processing Speed (*Gs*)
		Flanagan et al. (1997) McGrew & Hessler (1995)
Bishop (1980) Carroll & Maxwell (1979) Friedman (1995) Geary (1993) Snow & Swanson (1992)	Geary (1993)	Carroll & Maxwell (1979) Geary (1993)
Hakstian & Bennet (1977) Marjoribanks (1976) Stevenson et al. (1976) Swanson (1996) Taylor et al. (1976)	Marjoribanks (1976) Rasanen & Ahonen (1995) Stevenson et al. (1976)	Ackerman et al. (1986) Hakstian & Bennet (1977) Kirby & Becker (1988) McGrew & Pehl (1988) Rasanen & Ahonen (1995) Stevenson et al. (1976)

[1]Most studies have investigated the importance of working memory, which is a broad construct that subsumes *Gsm*.

[2] Studies reported significant results for measures of *Glr* in elementary school-age adolescent samples only.

effect of *g* was accounted for in the analyses. That is, specific *Gf-Gc* abilities contributed significantly to the explanation of reading above and beyond the significant and large effect of *g*.

The importance of *Gsm* for reading achievement (as suggested by the number of studies listed under *Gsm*) needs qualification. Most of the studies listed under *Gsm* in Table 2–1 used measures of working memory, a broad construct that subsumes *Gsm* (see the definition of *Gsm* in Chapter 1). The studies that reported significant relations between measures of working memory and reading indicate that *Gsm* abilities most likely contribute to reading achievement through their involvement during the working memory processes. Support for a significant relation between *Gsm* and reading achievement independent of the working memory literature was present in the significant *Gsm* (Memory Span) and reading achievement relations reported in the key *Gf-Gc* study of McGrew (1993). Taken as a whole, the research studies listed in Table 2–1 suggest that *Gsm* contributes to the prediction of reaching achievement, particularly when embedded within the larger construct of working memory.

The significant studies listed under *Glr* in Table 2–1 are predominantly from investigations that examined the relations between rapid automatic naming (i.e., Naming Facility, or NA, which is subsumed by *Glr*) and reading achievement, especially during the early elementary school years. The key *Gf-Gc* study of McGrew (1993) reported significant relations between measures of Associative Memory (MA) (another narrow ability subsumed by *Glr*) and reading at only a small number of age levels (viz., age 6 with reading decoding, late adulthood with reading comprehension). Thus, the preponderance of the significant *Glr* literature reviewed suggests that the narrow ability of Naming Facility is an important predictor of early reading achievement.

Although no reviews and only a handful of individual studies were listed under *Gs* in Table 2–1, the strength of the *Gs* effects demonstrated in the key *Gf-Gc* studies cannot be ignored. In two studies (McGrew, 1993; McGrew, Vanderwood, et al., 1997), measures of the narrow *Gs* ability of Perceptual Speed (P) were related strongly to reading achievement throughout the elementary school years. The effect of *Gs* was even present in analyses in which the influence of *g* was present (McGrew, Vanderwood, et al., 1997). Thus, as with *Ga* and *Gc*, *Gs* adds significantly to the explanation of reading above and beyond that accounted for by *g*.

The small number of studies listed under *Gf* and *Gv* in Table 2–1 suggests that these two broad abilities are related less to reading achievement than are the other broad abilities. The significant *Gf* findings reported by McGrew (1993) were only for reading comprehension, not reading decoding. This suggests that the comprehension of text draws upon an individual's deductive and inductive reasoning abilities. In the case of *Gv* the fact that only two studies reported a significant relation between *Gv* and reading achievement and no key *Gf-Gc* studies or reviews were listed for *Gv* indicates that *Gv* abilities do not play a significant role in reading achievement. This does not mean that visual processing abilities are not involved during reading. The lack of significant *Gv*/reading research findings indicates that the contribution of *Gv* abilities to the explanation and prediction of reading achievement is so small that, when compared to other abilities (e.g., *Ga*), it is of little practical significance. However, it is important not to overgeneralize this conclusion to all visual abilities. As pointed out by Berninger (1990), visual perceptual abilities should not be confused with abilities that are related to the coding of visual information in printed words (i.e., orthographic code processing), visual processes that appear to be important during reading.

In summary, narrow abilities in five broad *Gf-Gc* domains appear to be associated with reading achievement. The literature reviewed here suggests that abilities subsumed by *Ga* (PC), *Gc* (LD, VL, K0), *Gsm* (MS—especially when part of working memory), *Gs* (P) and *Glr* (MA, NA) are related significantly to reading achievement. Furthermore, the developmental results reported in the key *Gf-Gc* studies suggests that the *Ga*, *Gs*, and *Glr* relations with reading are strongest during the early elementary school years, after which they systematically decrease in strength (e.g., McGrew, 1993). In contrast, the strength of the relations between *Gc* abilities and reading achievement increases with age. *Gf* abilities appear related primarily to reading comprehension from childhood to young adulthood. Finally, *Gv* abilities appear largely unrelated to reading achievement in school-age children. Given the importance of linking *Gf-Gc*–organized cross-battery assessments to academic outcomes, additional studies are needed that are designed to investigate specifically the relations between valid measures of *Gf-Gc* abilities and reading achievement. Such studies would elucidate the nature of the relations between broad and narrow *Gf-Gc* abilities and reading at different developmental periods.

Mathematics Achievement.   Although there were fewer research studies that investigated the relations between *Gf-Gc* abilities and mathematics achievement (see Table 2–2) than reading achievement (Table 2–1), the relatively equal distribution of studies listed under the respective *Gf-Gc* abilities for mathematics achievement suggests that a greater breadth of *Gf-Gc* abilities is related significantly to mathematics than to reading achievement. Similarly to reading, evidence from all three types of research (i.e., key *Gf-Gc* studies, reviews, and individual studies) suggests that *Gc*, *Gsm* (especially when part of the construct of working memory), and *Gs* are related significantly to mathematics achievement. In contrast to reading, evidence was also found for the importance of *Gf* and *Gv* abilities in predicting and explaining mathematics achievement.

In the key *Gf-Gc* study of McGrew and Hessler (1995), *Gf*, *Gc*, and *Gs* abilities were correlated consistently and significantly with mathematics achievement. However, there were developmental differences. The *Gc* relation with mathematics achievement increased monotonically with age, while the *Gs* relation was strongest during the elementary school years, after which it decreased (although the relationship remained significant well into adulthood). *Gf* was related consistently to mathematics achievement at levels higher than all other *Gf-Gc* abilities (except *Gc*) across all ages. As in the reading achievement research just mentioned, certain specific abilities (viz., *Gf*, *Gs*, *Gc*) were found to be related significantly to mathematics achievement above and beyond the contribution of *g* (Flanagan et al., 1997).

It is interesting to note that when the reading and mathematics achievement results are compared, *Gf* and *Ga* abilities appear to be differentially important for the prediction of each achievement domain. *Gf* abilities are related significantly to mathematics achievement and less so to reading achievement, while *Ga* abilities are related significantly to reading achievement but not to mathematics achievement. This finding has implications for the design of *selective* cross-battery assessments that address specific referral questions (see Chapter 14).

No significant findings are reported in Table 2–2 in the key *Gf-Gc* studies for *Gv* and *Glr*, and only one review reported significant findings for *Glr*. This suggests that, until further *Gf-Gc*–organized research demonstrates significant relations between *Glr* abilities and mathematics achievement, the importance of *Glr* for mathematics achievement must be viewed cautiously. In contrast, a review of the *Gv* studies suggests that *Gv* abilities are not significantly related to *basic* mathematics achievement (e.g., addition, subtraction) but, instead, may be related to performance on tasks that require advanced and higher-level mathematics skills and thinking (e.g., geometry, calculus). As is the case for reading, additional research is needed to clarify the nature of the relations between narrow and broad *Gf-Gc* abilities and mathematics achievement.

Occupational Success

An understanding of the relations between *Gf-Gc* abilities and occupational success is gained from a history of systematic programs of research that have investigated the relations between specific cognitive abilities and performance in industrial, personnel, and military settings (see Dawis, 1994; Hansen & Betsworth, 1994). This literature suggests that, in addition to educational settings, *Gf-Gc*–organized intellectual assessments may provide useful information in occupational and vocational contexts. Table 2–3 presents a summary of literature that highlights significant relations between certain *Gf-Gc* abilities and occupational success. Similarly to the previously discussed research on the relations between *Gf-Gc* abilities and reading and mathematics achievement, much of the original research cited in Table 2–3 did not classify the cognitive variables investigated within the *Gf-Gc* framework. Therefore, the present authors reclassified (where possible and appropriate) the relevant cognitive variables using *Gf-Gc* terminology (e.g., spatial abilities were classified as *Gv*, verbal abilities were classified as *Gc*, etc.).

Inspection of the information presented in Table 2–3 suggests a number of logical conclusions. First, *Gv* abilities appear to contribute to success in a wide variety of occupations. Most of the occupations listed under *Gv* (e.g., architect, artist, carpenter, engineer, photographer, pilot, sculptor) are positions that appear to require routine use of a number of narrow abilities subsumed by *Gv*—for example, Visualization (VZ), Spatial Relations (SR), and Visual Memory (MV). Second, success in occupations in the broad fields of science and mathematics (e.g., engineer, mathematician, scientist) may require high *Gf* and *Gq* abilities. Third, most of the occupations listed under *Gc* in Table 2–3 seem to be professions that require much formal education (e.g., accountant, lawyer, poet, scholar, scientist). Fourth, *Ga* abil-

TABLE 2–3 A Summary of Significant Relations Between *Gf-Gc* Abilities and Success in Various Occupations

Source	*Gf*	*Gc*	*Gq*	*Gv*	*Ga*	*Gs*
Davison & Torff (1994)					Musician	
Dawis (1994)		Accountant Leader (military) Soldier	Accountant Engineer Leader (military) Soldier	Carpenter Engineer Leader (military) Machinist Photographer Soldier Teacher		Accountant Leader (military) Soldier
Gardner (1994)	Mathematician Scientist	Lawyer Poet	Mathematician Scientist	Architect Artist Chess player Scientist Sculptor	Musical composer Musician	
Ghiselli (1966)			Repairman	Electrician		Clerk
Hansen & Betsworth (1994)				Architect Civil engineer		Typist Proofreader
Horn (1988)		Scholar Scientist		Navigator Pilot	Musician	
Lohman (1994)				Air traffic controller Architect Artist Cabinet maker Designer Draftsperson Mathematician Mechanic Pilot Scientist		
Mayer (1994)	Scientist					
Stankov (1994)					Musician Sonar operator	

ities appear to be related almost exclusively to performance in the music professions. Finally, the listing of clerk, typist, and proofreader under *Gs* in the table most likely reflects the need for individuals to make rapid visual perceptual discriminations (e.g., Perceptual Speed—P) when performing in these occupations.

The vast majority of the research literature investigating the relations between cognitive abilities and occupational success (e.g., the differential aptitude research literature) has suggested that, in general, global intelligence (*g*) typically accounts for the largest proportion of variance in occupational criterion variables (Cronbach & Snow, 1977; Jensen, 1984; McNemar, 1964). However, the research literature presented in Table 2–3 suggests that a number of interesting relations exist between *specific Gf-Gc* abilities and occupational success. Together, these findings suggest that, in addition to *g*, specific *Gf-Gc* cognitive abilities are important in predicting or explaining occupational success.

Personality and Interest Traits

Human behavior is complex and varied. The *Gf-Gc* theory, as described in Chapter 1, is a taxonomy that has the potential to contribute to a better understanding of the multidimensional nature of at least one of the domains of human behavior (i.e., intelligence). However, a thorough understanding of human behavior requires knowledge not only of a person's intellectual abilities, but also of other important variables (e.g., personality, interests, a person's immediate environment) (Gustafsson & Undheim, 1996). Now that an empirically validated taxonomy of human cognitive abilities (viz., *Gf-Gc* theory) is available, the potential exists for making additional progress in understanding human behavior via linkages with other theory-based trait taxonomies.

An attempt to bridge different human trait taxonomies was presented recently by Ackerman and Heggestad (1997). Through the use of meta-analysis and narrative literature review, they examined the relations between personality and interest traits and broad and narrow intellectual abilities. The meta-analytic component of their review synthesized over 2,000 intelligence-personality trait correlations from over 135 different studies. A comprehensive taxonomy of personality and interest traits was developed to organize the literature review. This taxonomy was derived from a synthesis of three trait-based personality theories (i.e., Eysenck's three-factor theory; the five-factor or "Big Five," approach; and Tellegen's 11-trait framework—Eysenck, 1991, 1992; Costa & McCrae, 1992a, 1992b; Tellegen, 1982; Tellegen & Waller, in press) and three interest frameworks (i.e., the Holland's themes, the Kuder Preference Record, and the Strong Vocational Interest—Adkins & Kuder, 1940; Campbell, 1971; Holland, 1973). Of particular interest to our inquiry was Ackerman and Heggestad's use of Carroll's three-stratum *Gf-Gc* model as the framework for classifying the cognitive variables in their review. This provides intriguing information on the relations between *Gf-Gc* abilities and personality and interest traits. The major findings from Ackerman and Heggestad's review are summarized in Tables 2–4 and 2–5.

A review of Table 2–4 indicates that the abilities of *Gf*, *Gc*, and *Gsm* displayed the largest number of significant positive and negative correlations with a num-

TABLE 2–4　Significant Relations Between *Gf-Gc* Abilities and Interests and Personality Traits (Ackerman & Heggestad, 1997)

Interest and Personality Trait Definitions	Gf[1]	Gc	Gq[2]	Gs	Gsm	Gv	Glr	Gs
Interest Traits:								
Realistic—prefers physical and motor activities and aggressive action	+	+			+			
Investigative—prefers to think and not act; a need to organize the world; task oriented	+	+						
Conventional—prefers structured activities and subordinate roles		−						+
Artistic—prefers indirect social relations and self-expression through artistic media		+						
Enterprising—prefers to use verbal skills to influence, sell, or lead others	−	−				−		
Personality Traits:								
Openness to Experiences—degree of preference for original and varied experiences	+		+		+			
Typical Intelligence Engagement—amount of intellectual effort likely to be exerted		+	+			+		
Test Anxiety—the degree of cognitive concern for, and autonomic (emotional) reaction to, test performance situations	−	−		−	−			
Alienation—the amount of perceived mistreatment and betrayal by others	−							

Note: A plus (+) indicates a significant positive correlation. A minus (−) indicates a significant negative correlation. The abilities reported by Ackerman and Heggestad were reclassified by the present authors into the *Gf-Gc* terminology used in this book. *Ga, Grw,* and *Gt* abilities were not included in the meta-analysis.

[1]*Gf* was represented by the narrow ability of quantitative reasoning (RQ).

[2]*Gq* was part of a broad "Knowledge/Achievement" ability.

ber of personality and interest traits. For example, the results summarized in Table 2–4 suggest that individuals who are high in *Gf* abilities may also display relatively high Realistic and Investigative interests together with low Enterprising interests. Furthermore, individuals who are high in *Gf* abilities may display a preference for new experiences (i.e., Openness to Experiences) and low Test Anxiety and Alienation. Of particular interest are the three intelligence-personality-interest "trait complexes" (see Table 2–5) identified by Ackerman and Heggestad (1997). For example, an "intellectual/cultural" trait complex is presented in Table 2–5 that suggests relations between and among the abilities of *Gc* and *Glr*; Artistic and Investigative interests; and the personality traits of Openness to Experiences,

TABLE 2–5   Significant *Gf-Gc* Ability-Interest-Personality Trait Complexes (Ackerman & Heggestad, 1997)

Trait Complex	Gf-Gc Abilities	Interest Traits/Definitions	Personality Traits/Definitions
Science/Math	Gv Gf (RQ)	*Realistic*—prefers physical and motor activities and aggressive action *Investigative*—prefers to think and not act; a need to organize the world; task-oriented	
Intellectual/ Cultural	Gc Glr	*Artistic*—prefers indirect social relations and self-expression through artistic media *Investigative*—prefers to think and not act; a need to organize the world; task-oriented	*Openness to Experiences*—preference for original and varied experiences *Absorption*—extent of responsiveness to sensory and imaginative stimuli and experiences *Typical Intellectual Engagement*—amount of intellectual effort likely to be exerted
Clerical/ Conventional	Gs		*Control*—degree of reflectivity and carefulness when working on a task; self-discipline *Traditionalism*—extent of belief in high moral and religious standards and institutions *Conscientiousness*—extent to which behavior is principled, careful, and deliberate

Absorption, and Typical Intellectual Engagement. These observations are intriguing, but additional research is necessary to determine the practical utility of this and other intelligence-personality-interest trait complexes.

Although the practical implications of Ackerman and Heggestad's (1997) intelligence-personality-interest trait complex research have yet to be demonstrated, this type of research has the potential to move the study of individual differences beyond the typical emphasis on single constructs in isolation to a more real-world emphasis on multivariate "aptitude complexes" (Snow, 1992). "Investigations of higher order interactions . . . and trait complexes . . . may provide for substantially improved understanding of the nature of individual differences in each of these traditionally separated domains of cognition, affect, and connotation (interests) and the development of intellect across the life span" (Ackerman & Heggestad, 1997, p. 239).

Moreover, Ackerman and Heggestad's (1997) use of the *Gf-Gc* taxonomy to organize the cognitive component of their review may represent the first of many attempts to organize and link *Gf-Gc* cognitive ability research to a wide array of other trait taxonomies. In contrast to the traditional practice of using a single intelligence test battery (e.g., Wechslers), *Gf-Gc*–organized cross-battery assessments (see chapters 13 and 14) have the potential to contribute to and benefit from research efforts that may identify meaningful relations between *Gf-Gc* abilities and other human traits and outcome variables. Researchers like Ackerman and Heggestad undoubtedly recognize the value of the empirically based *Gf-Gc* taxonomy.

Supporting Evidence: Concluding Comments

The *Gf-Gc* theory of intelligence is based on more than factor-analytic (i.e., structural) evidence. The validity of the *Gf-Gc* theory approximates the desired standard of validity evidence—a *network of different types of validity evidence* (viz., structural, developmental, neurocognitive, heritability, and achievement or outcome criteria). This conclusion is similar to that reached by Messick (1992), who, after comparing the validity evidence for the *Gf-Gc* theory and two other theories of multiple cognitive abilities (i.e., Gardner's and Sternberg's theories), concluded that the *Gf-Gc* theories of intelligence "fare somewhat better . . . because they reflect many decades of programmatic research" (p. 382). Messick went as far as to state that *Gf-Gc* "multifactor theory and measurement provide a partial standard of validity for both Gardner and Sternberg" (1992, p. 366). It seems clear that *Gf-Gc*– organized cross-battery assessments have the potential to contribute meaningfully to research studies and reviews on the relations between cognitive abilities and many different outcome criteria because they are organized within this well-articulated and well-researched theoretical framework.

Limitations of Gf-Gc Theory

Although there is considerable support for the *Gf-Gc* theory of intelligence, it should not be considered *the* definitive theory. *Gf-Gc* theory is not without limitations. Horn and Noll (1997) have summarized four major limitations of *Gf-Gc* theory. Carroll (1995b, 1997) also provided appropriate words of caution about the limits of *Gf-Gc* theory.

First, *Gf-Gc* theory is more a descriptive empirical generalization of research findings than a deductive explanation of these findings. A research tradition has evolved in which the *Gf-Gc* variables included in successive studies are based on the variables included in prior studies, a situation that does not include the requisite a priori theoretical basis for validating a theory. Horn and Noll (1997) acknowledge this limitation but point out that all scientific theory is the result of a research history and culture, and it "evolves out of a repetitive spiral of building on what is known (induction), which leads to deductions that generate empirical studies and more induction, which leads to further deductions, which spawn further induction, and so on" (p. 83).

Second, the structure implied in the *Gf-Gc* theory is a significant limitation. Although the statistical method of factor analysis can produce neat, hierarchically organized factors, these empirically based frameworks probably do not accurately represent the organization of actual human cognitive abilities. Similarly, a third limitation is the fact that the theory is largely a product of linear equations (viz., factor analysis). Natural phenomena most likely are nonlinear in nature. As Horn and Noll (1997) state:

> The equations that describe the outer structure and convolutions of brains must be parabolas, cycloids, cissoids, spirals, folliums, exponentials, hyperboles, and the like. It is likely that the equations that best describe the inner workings of brains—human capabilities—are of the same forms, not those that describe city blocks and buildings. (p. 84)

Fourth, *Gf-Gc* theory provides little information on how the *Gf-Gc* abilities develop or how the cognitive processes work together. The theory is largely product-oriented and provides little guidance on the dynamic interplay of variables (i.e., the processes) that occur in human cognitive processing (Gustafsson & Undheim, 1996). However, as described in Chapter 1, Woodcock (1993, 1997) has recently articulated a Cognitive Performance Model and a *Gf-Gc* Information Processing model of intellectual performance that specifies relations between and among *Gf-Gc* abilities, information processing constructs, and noncognitive variables. Currently these models are largely speculative and need further study.

Finally, Carroll (1997), one of the primary architects of the *Gf-Gc* taxonomy, humbly pointed out that additional work needs to be completed in the factor-analytic study of human cognitive abilities. "The map of abilities provided by the three-stratum theory undoubtedly has errors of commission and omission, with gaps to be filled in by further research" (Carroll, 1997, p. 128). Carroll (1995) stated that certain aspects of the hierarchical structure may need to be refined and/or revised, including the identification of additional narrow abilities, the clarification of already identified narrow abilities, and the clarification of the number and structure of broad abilities. Although Carroll's wise words should temper the tendency to believe that we have now discovered the "holy taxonomic grail" of human cognitive abilities, the *Gf-Gc* taxonomy is still the most comprehensive and empirically supported psychometric framework from which to understand the structure of intelligence.

Chapter 3

Understanding and Using the ITDR

*Whatever exists at all exists in some amount. To know it
thoroughly involves knowing its quantity as well as its quality*
—*E. L. THORNDIKE (1918)*

Purpose of the ITDR

Chapters 3 through 12 constitute the "Desk Reference" section of this book.
Because these chapters provide a comprehensive description of the critical features
of individually administered *intelligence* tests, it is called the *Intelligence Test Desk
Reference* (ITDR). Similarly to desk references in other fields (e.g., the *Physician's
Desk Reference* or PDR), the primary purpose of the ITDR is to provide (in one
place) important quantitative (i.e., psychometric) and qualitative (e.g., degree of
cultural content in cognitive ability tests) comparative information for the major
intelligence batteries. All tests included in the ITDR are evaluated according to
common criteria. Furthermore, the information pertaining to each test is presented
using a *standard nomenclature* and is displayed in a *uniform format*. In this respect,
the ITDR is like a "consumer's report" on intelligence tests.

The ITDR includes one chapter for each individually administered intelligence
battery that was available at the time this book was prepared. The following eight
intelligence batteries are included: Differential Ability Scales (DAS; Elliott, 1990);
Kaufman Assessment Battery for Children (K-ABC; Kaufman & Kaufman, 1983);
Kaufman Adolescent and Adult Intelligence Test (KAIT; Kaufman & Kaufman,
1993); Stanford-Binet Intelligence Scale: Fourth Edition (SB:IV; Thorndike, Hagen,
& Sattler, 1986); Wechsler Adult Intelligence Scale—Third Edition (WAIS-III;
Wechsler, 1997); Wechsler Intelligence Scale for Children—Third Edition (WISC-
III; Wechsler, 1991); Wechsler Preschool and Primary Scale—Revised (WPPSI-R;

Wechsler, 1989); and Woodcock-Johnson Psycho-Educational Battery—Revised (WJ-R; Woodcock & Johnson, 1989). The first pages of each chapter provide general test battery information (adapted from Flanagan, Genshaft, & Harrison, 1997) in the following broad categories:

- *General information*: Author(s); publisher; date of publication; age range of tests; and typical administration time
- *Composite measure information:* Number and type of broad and lower-order composite scores
- *Score information:* Type of peer comparison scores; range of standard scores; mean floor of subtests
- *Norming information*: Number of tests normed at each age; achievement battery conorming features; person and community variables in the norming plan; size of the norming sample; age blocks used in the norm tables
- *Reviews*: A bibliography of select published reviews of the intelligence battery

Immediately following the general battery summaries are pages that present quantitative and qualitative characteristics and evaluations of these characteristics for each individual test (i.e., subtest) in each intelligence battery. A unique feature of the ITDR is the use of a *visual-graphic* consumer's report format for presenting psychometric test information. According to Matarrazzo (1990), "published information on the psychometric properties of the tests is . . . too infrequently used by some practitioners" (p. 1004). This may be because psychometric test characteristics frequently are presented in tabular form and are often difficult to digest except by the most diligent of practitioners. The visual-graphic summaries of the ITDR replace the tables upon tables of numbers that are presented in most test manuals, books, and journal articles to describe the technical features of intelligence tests. By providing technical test information in an easy-to-read visual format, the ITDR allows practitioners to make important decisions about which tests can be used most effectively for a given purpose. Also, the ITDR's visual-graphic format allows practitioners to see similarities and differences in important test characteristics within and across batteries quickly and easily. In addition to the 8 major intelligence batteries, the ITDR includes a chapter that describes 18 "special purpose" tests and batteries. These instruments can be used to supplement the major intelligence batteries. The main goal of the ITDR is to provide a readily accessible bridge between the science and practice of intelligence test interpretation.

Understanding What Tests Measure: The "Big Picture"

A Conceptual Framework for the ITDR

Just as the skill of a carpenter is related to the carpenter's intimate familiarity with each of his or her tools, so is the interpretation of an intelligence battery dependent upon practitioners' familiarity with their "tools." Skillful interpretation of intelligence tests requires practitioners to "know thy instrument" (McGrew, 1994, p. 4). This requires knowledge of those important variables that may aid in understanding an individual's performance on a given test. Figure 3–1 presents a conceptual framework for understanding the different variables that account for a person's score on an individual cognitive test. The model serves as the overarching "big picture" framework by which the ITDR is organized. It is important to note that Figure 3–1 is intended to be a *conceptual* representation of psychometric concepts. It is not intended to be a perfect depiction of the relations between various psychometric concepts and the procedures used to calculate them. To illustrate how this framework can be used to interpret intelligence test scores, a single test (i.e., WJ-R Verbal Analogies) is presented as an example. Briefly, the WJ-R Verbal Analogies test consists of the familiar "this is to this as this is to ____?" analogies (e.g., mother is to father as sister is to [*brother*]).

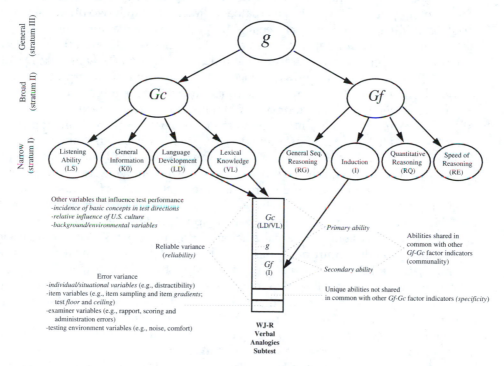

FIGURE 3–1   A Conceptual Model of the Variables That Need to Be Considered in Test Interpretation (WJ-R Verbal Analogies Example). There are additional narrow abilities in the domains of *Gc* and *Gf* that are not included in this figure; the rectangle represents the total score variance of the WJ-R Verbal Analogies test; the italicized terms represent the test characteristic information that is presented for each test in each intelligence battery in the ITDR summary pages.

Given that the *Gf-Gc* model of intelligence provides the most comprehensive and empirically supported model of the structure of human cognitive abilities (see chapters 1 and 2), it logically follows that the interpretation of intelligence batteries can be made most appropriately within this framework. The top portion of Figure 3–1 demonstrates that cognitive abilities that are located at different strata in the *Gf-Gc* model account for different proportions of the total test score variance of the Verbal Analogies test (which is represented by the rectangle in Figure 3–1). Understanding what an individual test measures requires an appreciation of which variables account for the total variance of a test score (i.e., the total area represented by the rectangle) and to what degree.

The Variables in the Big Picture

General, Broad, and Narrow Abilities

The most general (stratum III) influence on the Verbal Analogies test is that of general intelligence, or *g*, which is mediated indirectly through two broad (stratum II) *Gf-Gc* abilities (i.e., *Gf* and *Gc*) (see Figure 3–1). The broad abilities of *Gf* and *Gc* in turn influence performance on the Verbal Analogies test through their respective influences on the narrow (stratum I) abilities of Induction (I), Language Development (LD), and Lexical Knowledge (VL). Thus, appropriate interpretation of the Verbal Analogies test requires a practitioner to appreciate the degree to which the respective general, broad, and narrow abilities influence performance.

The extent to which *g* influences performance on a test is typically represented by the test's loading on a factorially derived *g* factor (these psychometric concepts and terms, as well as others, will be defined in greater detail later in this chapter). Moving down the cognitive ability hierarchy portrayed in Figure 3–1, the extent to which the different broad and narrow abilities influence performance on an individual test is typically estimated by examining the test's loadings on the respective ability factors (the ovals in Figure 3–1) in appropriately designed factor-analytic studies. In the case of the Verbal Analogies test, the *g* and *Gf-Gc* common factor loadings provide empirical estimates of the extent to which this test measures *g* and *Gf-Gc* abilities. Collectively, the amount of the Verbal Analogies test score variance that can be attributed to cognitive abilities within the *Gf-Gc* model (as represented by ovals with arrows that point directly, or indirectly in the case of *g*, to the Verbal Analogies rectangle) is referred to as *communality* or *common variance*. That is, this is what the Verbal Analogies test shares in common with all other indicators (or tests) comprising the *Gf-Gc* factors.

As visually portrayed in Figure 3-1, the *g*, *Gf* (I), and *Gc* (LD and VL) abilities account for the largest proportion of the Verbal Analogies test score variance. Thus, these abilities should receive priority consideration when interpreting a person's score on the Verbal Analogies test. The portion of the Verbal Analogies test score variance that may be attributable to the influence of *g* is represented by the dashed line within the rectangle. Tests such as Verbal Analogies that are highly related to *g* have proportionally more of their variance accounted for by the general factor.

The further division of the common variance of the Verbal Analogies test score into two portions signifies that Verbal Analogies is a *factorially complex* measure of more than one broad ability (viz., *Gf* and *Gc*). This means that the interpretation of an individual's score on the Verbal Analogies test should focus on both *Gf* and *Gc* abilities. Furthermore, in this example the influence of *Gc* on Verbal Analogies is depicted as being greater than *Gf* (i.e., it represents the larger area of the rectangle). Thus, *Gc* is the *primary* cognitive ability measured by the Verbal Analogies test. *Gf* is the *secondary* cognitive ability that should be considered when interpreting performance on this test. Furthermore, the narrow stratum I classifications suggest that the most likely *Gf* interpretation is that of Induction (I), whereas both Language Development (LD) and Lexical Knowledge (VL) account for the *Gc* influence on the Verbal Analogies test. The primary abilities—and in the case of factorially complex measures, primary and secondary abilities—of all the individual intelligence tests (i.e., subtests) included in the ITDR are listed.

What's Left Over? Unique Abilities and Error

As can be seen in Figure 3–1, the *Gf-Gc* general, broad, and narrow cognitive abilities account for the largest portion of the Verbal Analogies test score variance. However, two additional portions of test score variance need to be to considered in the interpretation process—unique abilities and error.

Unique abilities are the proportion of the Verbal Analogies test score variance attributed to abilities not represented in the *Gf-Gc* cognitive model. This test characteristic is typically referred to as *specificity*. As can be seen in Figure 3–1, the amount of the Verbal Analogies test score variance that is unique or specific to this test is proportionally much less than that attributable to *Gf-Gc* abilities (i.e., common variance or communality). Together the common *Gf* and *Gc* variance and specific variance represent the total reliable variance (i.e., *reliability*) of the Verbal Analogies test. In Figure 3–1 the combined *Gc*, *Gf*, and unique ability areas within the rectangle represent what is measured reliably by the Verbal Analogies test.

The abilities that account for reliable score variance should be the primary focus of interpretation of tests in intelligence batteries. Furthermore, the degree to which different abilities should be emphasized in the interpretation of a test is directly proportional to the amount of reliable score variance they explain. In the case of the Verbal Analogies test example, this means that *Gc* abilities should be the primary focus of interpretation, followed by *Gf* abilities and, to a much lesser extent, unique abilities.

The portion of Verbal Analogies test score variance that is not reliable (i.e., *error variance*) is that which is not accounted for by the common and unique abilities. In Figure 3–1 the Verbal Analogies error variance is represented by the area at the bottom of the rectangle. An inspection of the figure shows that the amount of the Verbal Analogies test score variance that is due to error (or unreliability) is relatively small when compared to the reliable variance. A test that has poor reliability would have a proportionally larger amount of error variance and less reliable variance to interpret. As summarized in Figure 3–1, a variety of variables can contribute to unreliability or error in a test, including examiner variables (e.g., rapport, administration and scoring errors) and variables related to the testing environment (e.g., noise, comfort level). Other variables (included in the ITDR) that can contribute to error in a test include *individual/situational* variables (e.g., *distractibility*) and item variables (e.g., *item gradients*, test *floors* and *ceilings*).

Contextual Variables

Finally, understanding an individual's test performance requires an appreciation of the contextual variables that influenced the development of the person's abilities measured by the test. For example, performance on the *Gc* (LD and VL) component of the Verbal Analogies test would most likely be related to variables that contribute to the development of an individual's language and vocabulary. These variables may include the extent of environmental stimulation, reading patterns, and level of acculturation, to name a few. In Figure 3–1 (and in the ITDR), contextual influences are referred to as *background/environmental variables* (e.g., language stimulation, intellectual curiosity).

Group-Versus Individually Centered Focus—A Caution

The preceding "big picture" conceptual explanation of intelligence test performance is based on group-centered statistical procedures that may not translate perfectly to a single individual. A statement about the proportion of a test's score variance that is accounted for by different *Gf-Gc* abilities "only has meaning as a statement that refers to a distribution of scores" (Gustafsson & Undheim, 1996, p. 217) and a value for the interpretation of ability factors. Because *Gf-Gc* test interpretations presented in this book are group-centered, the proportional *Gf-Gc* ability influences on test performance for *any single individual* may not be the same as those found in group data. For any individual the proportional relations between different *Gf-Gc* abilities, unique abilities, and error variance may well differ from that found across persons. Therefore, practitioners need to consider the *Gf-Gc* ability classifications presented in the ITDR as empirically grounded interpretative starting points that should be modified (if necessary) based on the individual nuances of a particular case.

"Focusing" the Big Picture: The Cross-Battery Perspective

As portrayed in Figure 3–1, factor analysis research indicates that the WJ-R Verbal Analogies test measures both *Gf* and *Gc* abilities. However, would this interpretation be the same if the factor analyses that included the Verbal Analogies test did not contain other tests of *Gf* or *Gc* abilities? Would the interpretation of the Verbal Analogies test change significantly? The answer is yes. To appreciate this answer, a rudimentary understanding of certain aspects of factor analysis methods is required.

Types of Factor-Analytic "Lenses"

One of the primary tools used to determine the construct validity of intelligence batteries is *factor analysis*, a statistical procedure that groups together measures (tests) that intercorrelate. In general, the use of factor-analytic methods in the study of the structure of intelligence batteries can be organized along two dimensions. The first dimension is the *method* of factor analysis that is employed, exploratory or confirmatory. *Exploratory* factor analysis lets the data "speak for themselves" since it identifies the factor structure of an intelligence battery with no a priori model in mind. In contrast, *confirmatory* factor analysis examines the extent to which a factor structure that is specified by an investigator in advance (i.e., the theoretical model) fits the data, and how the model might be modified to fit the data better. The second dimension is concerned with the *breadth* of test intelligence variables analyzed. *Within-battery* factor analysis is confined to the tests from a single intelligence battery (e.g., the 13 WISC-III tests). *Cross-battery* factor analysis, which is often referred to as *joint factor analysis,* includes tests from *more than one* intelligence battery (e.g., WISC-III and SB:IV).

In order to establish a link between what intelligence test batteries measure and the *Gf-Gc* taxonomy of cognitive abilities, the ideal research design is a *Gf-Gc*–conceptualized confirmatory cross-battery factor analysis study. The confirmatory procedures allow the *Gf-Gc* model to drive the analyses, and the cross-battery design ensures that sufficient breadth of indicators is present to represent adequately the major *Gf-Gc* abilities.

Using the Proper Lens: Gf-Gc Cross-Battery Confirmatory Factor Analysis Research

Identifying Gf-Gc Ability Test Characteristics

The importance of the cross-battery confirmatory research approach is demonstrated in Figures 3–2 and 3–3. Figure 3–2 is a visual representation of the robust within-battery exploratory factor analysis findings that have been reported for the WISC-R (Kaufman, 1979). Three factors, namely Verbal Comprehension (VC), Perceptual Organization (PO), and Freedom-From-Distractibility (FFD), typically have been reported for the WISC-R. When considered within the context of *Gf-Gc* theory, the VC and PO factors are interpreted as measuring mainly *Gc* and *Gv* abilities, respectively (Carroll, 1993a; McGrew & Flanagan, 1996). The dual placement of the Picture Completion and Picture Arrangement tests in the *Gc* and *Gv* factor domains reflects the consistent finding that these two tests are factorially complex or mixed tests of both abilities (Kaufman, 1979, 1994). A review of Figure 3–2 finds that the FFD factor has no analogous ability in the *Gf-Gc* taxonomy. Is the taxonomy "wrong," or is the FFD factor suspect?

A closer inspection of Figure 3–2 indicates (based on logical content analysis) that the three FFD tests (Arithmetic, Digit Span, Coding) are most likely "loner" indicators of *Gq*, *Gsm*, and *Gs*, respectively. This hypothesis has been confirmed in a *Gf-Gc*–based confirmatory cross-battery factor analysis of the WISC-R and WJ-R

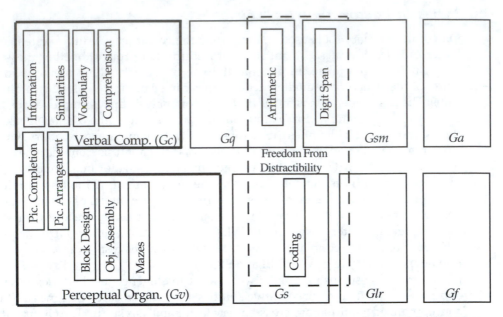

FIGURE 3–2   The Results of Within-Battery Factor Analysis of the WISC-R Subtests. All large rectangles (except the rectangle with dashed lines) represent the broad *Gf-Gc* abilities. The rectangles in bold (including the rectangle with dashed lines) represent the three WISC-R factors. The small rectangles represent the WISC-R subtests.

(Woodcock, 1990). When the WISC-R tests were analyzed together with 16 empirically validated indicators of eight *Gf-Gc* abilities from the WJ-R (Woodcock, 1990), the results summarized in Figure 3–3 were found. In the *Gf-Gc* cross-battery analysis the WISC-R FFD tests abandoned one another to "hang out" (i.e., correlate) with indicators of other *Gf-Gc* abilities with which they had more in common. Namely, Arithmetic, Digit Span, and Coding loaded strongly on the *Gq*, *Gsm*, and *Gs* factors, respectively. Thus, in within-battery factor analysis studies, the so-called FFD factor appears to be a "junk" factor that consists of three tests that have no other tests that measure similar cognitive ability constructs with which they could correlate to form valid factors. Because the FFD factor comprises three tests that are indicators of three *different Gf-Gc* abilities, it does not represent a valid theoretical cognitive construct. Given that three or more indicators are typically needed to define a factor in factor analysis (Zwick & Velicer, 1986), it is not surprising that these three WISC-R tests loaded together on the so-called FFD factor. There simply were not enough indicators present in the within-battery WISC-R factor analysis (i.e., at least two more tests each of *Gq*, *Gsm*, and *Gs*) to identify clearly the separate abilities measured by these three tests.

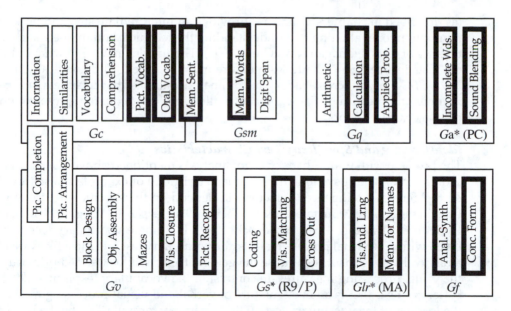

FIGURE 3–3   The Results of Cross-Battery Factor Analysis of the WISC-R and WJ-R Subtests. The large rectangles represent broad *Gf-Gc* abilities. The WISC-R subtests are represented by the small rectangles that are not in bold. The WJ-R subtests are indicated by bold-perimeter small rectangles. The asterisk (*) indicates factors that are "narrow" factors within the respective "broad" *Gf-Gc* factors. That is, the factors do not consist of indicators of two or more different narrow abilities under the respective *Gf-Gc* factors, but, rather, consist of subtests that measure only one narrow ability. The narrow ability is reported in parentheses.

The importance of the *Gf-Gc* confirmatory cross-battery factor analysis approach becomes even more apparent upon further inspection of Figure 3–3. A review of the figure shows that the WISC-R PO tests often interpreted as measuring *Gf* abilities (e.g., Kaufman, 1979, 1994) *do not load on the Gf factor* defined by the WJ-R Analysis-Synthesis and Concept Formation tests. These results, as well as other exploratory cross-battery analyses of the Wechslers with the DAS and KAIT (Elliott, 1994; Kaufman & Kaufman, 1993; Stone, 1992), call into question the traditional *Gf* interpretation of the Wechsler PO tests (see McGrew & Flanagan, 1996). The clarification of the abilities measured by the Wechsler PO and FFD tests was only possible through confirmatory cross-battery factor analyses that included a sufficient breadth of empirically validated indicators of each *Gf-Gc* broad ability.

Until test batteries with adequate indicators of most *Gf-Gc* broad abilities are developed, a cross-battery approach to intelligence test research and interpretation (as described in chapters 13 and 14) provides an intermediate step and necessary foundation for evaluating and understanding the technical and theoretical characteristics of tests (Flanagan & McGrew, 1997). The understanding of what individual tests in intelligence batteries measure must be based on theoretically driven (viz., *Gf-Gc* theory) cross-battery factor analytic studies that include a sufficient number and breadth of *Gf-Gc* indicators allowing for adequate representation of the major *Gf-Gc* factors.

Identifying g and Specificity Test Characteristics

The problem with within-battery factor analyses mentioned above also affects the estimation of other psychometric test characteristics. For example, a test's loading on the general intelligence (*g*) factor will depend on the specific mixture of tests used in the analysis (Gustafsson & Undheim, 1996; Jensen & Weng, 1994; McGrew, Untiedt, & Flanagan, 1996; Woodcock, 1990). If a single vocabulary test is combined with nine visual processing tests, the vocabulary test will most likely display a relatively low *g* loading because the general factor will be defined primarily by the visual processing measures. In contrast, if the vocabulary test is included in a battery of tests that is an even mixture of verbal and visual processing measures, the loading of the vocabulary test on the general factor will probably be higher. It is important to understand that test *g* loadings, as typically reported, only reflect each test's relation to the general factor *within a specific intelligence battery.* Although in many situations a test's *g* loading will not change dramatically when computed in the context of a different collection of diverse cognitive tests (Jensen & Weng, 1994), this will not always be the case.

Just as *g* loading estimates may change as a function of the diversity and complexity of tasks included in a single test battery, so too may the estimates of test specificity. Using the example just described, a single vocabulary test embedded within a battery with nine other visual processing tests would most likely have very high specificity because of its low common or shared variance with the visual processing tests. If the same vocabulary test is then examined in the context of a 10-test battery that has an even mixture of verbal and visual processing tests, the vocabulary test specificity values would probably drop appreciably because it shares abilities in common with four other verbal tests within the battery (which results in an increase in common variance and a proportional decrease in specific variance). Although the example of a test battery with a nine-to-one visual processing/verbal test mixture is extreme, it illustrates that traditionally computed test *g* and specificity estimates are interpretable primarily within the confines of a single specific intelligence battery.

A Within- and Cross-Battery WISC-R Example

When tests from different batteries are combined in the cross-battery approach, the battery-bound *g* and specificity estimates for some tests may be significantly altered. To illustrate this point, we calculated within- and cross-battery *g* and communality (which is the major variance component used to calculate specificity) estimates for the WISC-R. These estimates were derived from a sample of 128 subjects who were administered the WISC-R and WJ-R tests for a series of validity studies reported in the *WJ-R Technical Manual* (McGrew, Werder & Woodcock, 1991). Within-battery *g* estimates were calculated with the WISC-R data based on the first unrotated principal component and within-battery specificity estimates were based on squared multiple correlations. Consistent with the belief that contemporary *Gf-Gc* theory provides the most up-to-date and empirically supported psychometric theory from which to interpret intelligence tests, cross-battery *g* and specificity estimates were calculated in the same manner using the combined set of WISC-R and WJ-R tests. The cross-battery factor analysis allowed for an examination of the *g* and specificity characteristics of the WISC-R tests vis à vis the comprehensive *Gf-Gc* model underlying the WJ-R. The WISC-R results are summarized in Table 3–1.

A review of Table 3–1 shows that the within- and cross-battery WISC-R *g* loadings are similar for many of the individual tests. For example, the within- and cross-battery test *g* loadings are almost identical for the Information (.71 vs .70), Arithmetic (.72 vs .74), and Coding (.30 vs .29) tests. These three WISC-R tests appear to have the same *g* characteristics when examined from the perspective of either the WISC-R or *Gf-Gc* frameworks. However, the cross-battery *g* loadings are noticeably lower for Picture Completion (.64 vs .54), Block Design (.72 vs .62), and Object Assembly (.68 vs .59). These results suggest that the latter three WISC-R tests are relatively weaker *g* indicators than is suggested by within-battery WISC-R *g* analysis.

TABLE 3–1 **Example of Within- and Cross-Battery *g* Loading and Communality Estimates for the WISC-R Subtests**

Subtest	*g* loadings		Communality	
	Within-Battery	Cross-Battery	Within-Battery	Cross-Battery
Information	.71	.70	.45	.46
Similarities	.81	.76	.64	.56
Arithmetic	.72	.74	.47	.54
Vocabulary	.83	.76	.69	.57
Comprehension	.77	.69	.55	.46
Digit Span	.51	.58	.21	.31
Picture Completion	.64	.54	.35	.27
Picture Arrangement	.55	.47	.25	.20
Block Design	.72	.62	.47	.35
Object Assembly	.68	.59	.40	.32
Coding	.30	.29	.07	.07
Mazes	.50	.43	.20	.16

Note: Estimates are based on 128 subjects who had been administered the WISC-R and the WJ-R cognitive tests for the validity studies reported in the WJ-R technical manual (McGrew et al., 1991). *g* loading estimates are based on the first unrotated principal component. Communality estimates are squared multiple correlations.

As was the case with the WISC-R *g* loadings, the within- and cross-battery communality estimates were similar for some tests. For example, the respective communality estimates were very similar for the Information test (.45 vs .46) and identical for the Coding test (.07 vs .07). As a result, the specificities for these two tests are the same when interpreted from the perspective of either the WISC-R or *Gf-Gc* frameworks. In contrast, the cross-battery communality estimates were lower (approximately 10% less common variance) for the Vocabulary (.69 vs .57), Comprehension (.55 vs .46), and Block Design (.47 vs .35) tests. The lower communality estimates indicate that these three tests have *higher* specificities when examined within the *Gf-Gc* framework. This is because the WISC-R is predominantly a mixture of verbal (*Gc*) and visual-spatial (*Gv*) tests; thus, these three tests have many other similar *Gc* and *Gv* tests with which they share common variance in the WISC-R. However, when analyzed together with a collection of tests that assess a broader array of *Gf-Gc* abilities, the proportional amount of shared variance attributable to *Gc* and *Gv* abilities is less. Thus, the Vocabulary, Comprehension, and Block Design tests have less in common with the other tests and, as a result, have more uniqueness (i.e., higher specificities in appropriately designed *Gf-Gc* cross-battery factor analyses).

A review of the communality results for the Arithmetic and Digit Span tests revealed the opposite finding. Since both of these tests are the lone indicators within the WISC-R of quantitative (*Gq*) and short-term memory (*Gsm*) abilities, respectively, they have relatively low shared variance with the other WISC-R measures (and, therefore, high specificity). However, when analyzed together with the WJ-R *Gf-Gc* tests that include tests of *Gq* and *Gsm*, the communality estimates increased for Arithmetic (.47 to .54) and Digit Span (.21 to .31), and, therefore, the specificity estimates decreased. The presence of other indicators of *Gq* and *Gsm* in the *Gf-Gc*–organized cross-battery analyses resulted in Arithmetic and Digit Span no longer being considered the "loner" tests they were in the within-battery WISC-R analyses. The cross-battery analyses demonstrated that Arithmetic and Digit Span share something in common with other *Gq* and *Gsm* tests, respectively. As a result, the Arithmetic and Digit Span tests are actually less unique (i.e., have lower specificities) than the within-battery WISC-R values revealed.

This example demonstrates that test *g* and specificity estimates that are calculated within the confines of individual intelligence batteries may not be the same as those calculated within the comprehensive *Gf-Gc* model (via cross-battery analyses). Thus, when practitioners combine tests across different batteries according to the *Gf-Gc* cross-battery approach (as described in chapters 13 and 14), it is important to understand the impact this approach has on the psychometric characteristics of *g* and specificity. Although the ITDR provides both within- and cross-battery *g* and specificity estimates for the tests in the major intelligence batteries, the most appropriate values are those estimated from the cross-battery perspective. Since the central tenet of this book is that all intelligence tests should be interpreted within the context of the best and most current evidence of the structure of intelligence from cognitive psychology research (viz., contemporary *Gf-Gc* theory), it logically follows that the characteristics of each individual test in each intelligence battery should be estimated and evaluated within this larger *Gf-Gc* framework. Selective attention to certain within-battery psychometric test characteristics—characteristics that for most intelligence batteries are based typically on incomplete theoretical models of the structure of cognitive abilities—may result in erroneous and inappropriate test interpretation.

Psychometric Characteristics Presented in the ITDR

Psychometrics is the specialty within psychology that uses a set of agreed-upon measurement procedures to operationalize the concepts of reliability and validity. Given that the individual tests in intelligence test batteries provide the foundation for interpretation either at the individual test or composite score level, it is essential that practitioners understand the psychometric characteristics of each test. According to Reynolds and Kaufman (1990): "The clinical evaluation of test performance must be directed by careful analyses of the statistical properties of the test scores, the internal psychometric characteristics of the test, and the data regarding its relationship to external factors" (p. 131). Otherwise, interpretation of tests may become an idiosyncratic enterprise dependent on the individual skills and whims of different practitioners.

The psychometric characteristics presented for every test in the ITDR are reliability, *g* loadings, specificity, test floors and ceilings, item gradients, and construct validity (i.e., *Gf-Gc* broad and narrow ability classifications). (See Figure 3–1 and the related discussion for information on the relations between these different psychometric characteristics.) Sources that were used to establish the ITDR evaluative psychometric criteria included the *Standards for Educational and Psychological Testing* (APA, 1985); *A Consumer's Guide to Tests in Print* (Hammill, Brown, & Bryant, 1992); and a review of recent literature that focused on the evaluation of the major intelligence batteries (e.g., Alfonso & Flanagan, in press; Bracken, 1986, 1987; Flanagan & Alfonso, 1995; Flanagan et al., 1995; Harrison, Flanagan, & Genshaft, 1997). Based on these sources, a set of ITDR criteria was compiled and used to evaluate the technical adequacy of the tests included in the major intelligence batteries.

Only the *subtests* of the major intelligence batteries are included and evaluated in the ITDR. Intelligence battery composites (or clusters) are not included and evaluated because they are generally not consistent with the *Gf-Gc* broad abilities specified in contemporary *Gf-Gc* theory and research (i.e., most are confounded or mixed measures). Furthermore, the technical characteristics of intelligence test composites are typically adequate according to most standards (e.g., most composites are highly reliable). Since the primary purpose of this book is to aid practitioners in selecting the most technically adequate and theoretically pure tests for inclusion in *Gf-Gc* cross-battery assessment, subtest information is considered most critical. That is, based on the information provided in the ITDR, relatively pure *Gf-Gc* broad ability clusters can be constructed that more adequately represent the cognitive abilities specified in contemporary theory than the composites (or clusters) of most intelligence batteries.

The next section of this chapter describes each quantitative and qualitative test characteristic that is used to describe the major intelligence batteries in the ITDR. Specifically, the importance of each test characteristic is highlighted, the procedures for reporting technical and descriptive data are described, and the way the various test characteristics were evaluated is presented. The definitions of the quantitative and qualitative test characteristics and evaluative criteria included in the ITDR are also presented in Table 3–2.

TABLE 3–2   Definition of Quantitative and Qualitative Test Characteristics and Evaluative Criteria Included in the ITDR

Characteristic	Definition
Reliability	The degree to which a test score is free from errors of measurement.
High	Coefficients of .90 or above
Medium	Coefficients from .80 to .89 inclusive
Low	Coefficients below .80
Within-Battery *g* Loading	Each test's loading on the first unrotated factor or component in principal factor or component analysis with all other tests from a specific intelligence battery.
Cross-Battery *g* Loading	A test's loading on the first unrotated factor or component in principal joint factor or component analysis with all other tests from a specific intelligence battery together with the WJ-R.[1]
Good	General factor or *g* loading of .70 or higher
Fair	A loading of .51 to .69
Poor	A loading of .50 or lower
Within-Battery Specificity	The portion of a test's variance that is reliable and unique to the test. Within-battery specificity is calculated by subtracting the communality estimate of the test (the squared multiple correlation between each test and all other tests within the battery) from the total reliable variance (a value obtained by subtracting a test's reliability coefficient from unity).
Cross-Battery Specificity	The portion of a test's variance that is reliable and unique to the test. Cross-battery specificity is calculated by subtracting the communality estimate of the test (the squared multiple correlation between each test and all other tests within the battery together with the WJ-R[1]) from the total reliable variance (a value obtained by subtracting a test's reliability coefficient from unity).

TABLE 3–2 *Continued*

Characteristic	Definition
Cross-Battery Specificity (cont'd)	
Ample	A test's unique reliable variance is equal to or above 25% of the total test variance and it exceeds error variance (1-reliability).
Adequate	When a test meets only one of the criteria for Ample.
Inadequate	When a test does not meet either of the criteria for Ample.
Test Floor	The test contains a sufficient number of easy items to distinguish adequately between individuals functioning in the average, low average, and borderline ranges of ability.
Adequate	The maximum raw score for the test is associated with a standard score that is more than 2 standard deviations below the normative mean of the test.
Inadequate	The maximum raw score for the test is associated with a standard score that is *not* more than 2 standard deviations below the normative mean of the test.
Test Ceiling	The test contains a sufficient number of difficult items to distinguish between individuals functioning in the average, high average, and superior ranges of ability.
Adequate	The maximum raw score for the test is associated with a standard score that is more than 2 standard deviations above the normative mean of the test.
Inadequate	The maximum raw score for the test is associated with a standard score that is *not* more than 2 standard deviations above the normative mean of the test.
Gf-Gc Broad (stratum II) Classification	A description of the broad abilities that underlie intelligence tests based on an examination of the extant *Gf-Gc* confirmatory cross-battery factor analysis research.
Empirical: strong	A test having a substantial factor loading (>.50) on a primary factor and a secondary factor loading (if present) that is equal to or less than 1/2 of its loading on the primary factor.
Empirical: moderate	A test having a primary factor loading of <.50 and a secondary factor loading (if present) that is less than 1/2 of the primary loading, or any primary factor loading and secondary loading between 1/2 and 7/10 of the primary loading.
Empirical: mixed	A test having a factor loading on a secondary factor that is greater than 7/10 of its loading on the primary factor.
Gf-Gc Narrow (stratum I) Classification[2]	A description of the narrow abilities that underlie intelligence tests based on expert consensus.

Continued

TABLE 3–2   *Continued*

Characteristic	Definition
Gf-Gc Narrow (stratum I) Classification (cont'd)	
Probable	Classifications in which there was a clear correspondence between the content and task demands of a test and a particular *Gf-Gc* narrow ability definition according to expert opinion.
Possible	Classifications in which there was a moderate degree of correspondence between the content and task demands of a test and a particular *Gf-Gc* narrow ability definition according to expert opinion.
Incidence of Basic Concepts in Test Directions	The degree to which a test requires conceptual or linguistic demands. Excessive conceptual demands (defined as conceptual knowledge required to understand test directions above age level) may pose a threat to the construct validity of the test.
Typical Age of Concept Attainment	A p value of .75 or greater, indicating that the basic concept is understood by at least 75% of preschoolers (age 3–5 years).
Degree of Cultural Content	The authors' subjective evaluation of the degree to which U.S. cultural knowledge or experience is required to perform the task. It is assumed that an examinee's level of acculturation to mainstream U.S. culture will affect his or her performance to a greater extent on subtests that are dependent upon accumulated knowledge and acquired experiences (that result from exposure to U.S. culture) than on subtests that measure basic learning processes.
High	Test performance is highly influenced by exposure to mainstream U.S. culture.
Medium	Test performance is moderately influenced by exposure to mainstream U.S. culture.
Low	Test performance is minimally influenced by exposure to mainstream U.S. culture.
Background/Environmental Influences	
Hearing difficulties	A past history of significant problems in the perception of auditory stimuli.
Vision difficulties	A past history of significant problems in the perception of visual stimuli.
Reading difficulties	A past history of significant problems with reading.
Spelling difficulties	A past history of significant problems with spelling.
Writing difficulties	A past history of significant problems with writing.

TABLE 3–2   *Continued*

Characteristic	Definition
Background/Environmental Influences (cont'd)	
Math difficulties	A past history of significant problems with mathematics.
Language stimulation	The extent to which an examinee's verbal communication skills have been influenced by frequent interaction with the environment.
Cultural opportunities and experiences	The extent to which an examinee has been exposed to a wide array of opportunities and experiences that impart knowledge of a culture.
Educational opportunities and experiences	The extent to which an examinee has been exposed to a wide array of formal and informal educational experiences.
Alertness to the environment	The extent to which an examinee is attentive to his or her surroundings.
Intellectual curiosity	The extent to which an examinee displays a tendency to seek out and explore knowledge and new learning.
Individual/Situational Influences	
Attention span	An examinee's ability to selectively focus on specific stimuli for a relatively brief period of time.
Concentration	An examinee's ability to focus on stimuli for a sustained period of time.
Distractibility	The tendency of an examinee's attention to be drawn away from stimuli that should be the focus of attention by irrelevant stimuli.
Color blindness	A congenital visual defect that results in an examinee's inability to identify and distinguish certain colors from other colors.
Visual acuity	The extent to which an examinee can accurately discriminate visual stimuli. The sharpness of the examinee's visual perception.
Hearing acuity	The extent to which an examinee can accurately discriminate auditory stimuli. The sharpness of the examinee's auditory perception.
Reflectivity vs. impulsivity	An examinee's tendency to respond either deliberately (reflective) or quickly (impulsive) when confronted with problem-solving situations.
Field dependence vs. independence	The examinee's tendency to be significantly affected (dependent) or not affected (independent) by irrelevant factors or stimuli in a perceptual field.
Verbal rehearsal	The strategy of verbally repeating (covertly or overtly) information in short-term memory to facilitate the immediate use of the information.

Continued

TABLE 3–2   *Continued*

Characteristic	Definition
Individual/Situational Influences (cont'd)	
Verbal elaboration	The strategy of verbally relating new information to already existing information to facilitate the transfer of the information to the store of acquired knowledge (i.e., long-term memory).
Visual elaboration	The strategy of visually relating new information to already existing information to facilitate the transfer of the information to the store of acquired knowledge (i.e., long-term memory).
Organization	The strategy of grouping together several different "chunks" or clusters of information to aid in the retrieval of information.
Planning	The process of developing efficient methods or solutions (i.e., plans) to a problem prior to starting the problem.
Monitoring/regulating	The process of assessing how well a selected strategy or plan is working, and then deciding whether to continue, modify, or discontinue the strategy or plan.

[1] Tests 1–14 from the WJ-R were used in the analysis. These subtests provide two relatively pure measures for each of seven *Gf-Gc* abilities.

[2] *Gf-Gc* narrow (stratum I) definitions can be found in Carroll (1993a), McGrew (1997), or Chapter 1 of this text.

Reliability

Reliability "refers to the degree to which test scores are free from errors of measurement" (APA, 1985, p. 19). The reliability of a scale affects interpretation of the test results because it guides decisions regarding the range of scores (i.e., standard error of measurement) likely to occur as the result of irrelevant chance factors. Test reliability, in its broadest sense, indicates the extent to which individual differences are attributed to true differences in the characteristics under investigation or to chance errors (Anastasi & Urbina, 1997). The degree of confidence one can place in a test score is directly related to the reliability of the instrument. Unreliable test scores can contribute to misdiagnosis and inappropriate placement and treatment. This problem can be reduced by selecting tests that have good reliability and thus little error associated with their scores. For in-depth treatment of reliability concepts, the reader is referred to Anastasi and Urbina (1997), APA (1985), Crocker and Algina (1986), Lord and Novick (1968), Salvia and Ysseldyke (1991), and Sattler (1992).

Procedure for Reporting Data
The reliabilities reported for the intelligence batteries included in the ITDR were drawn from their respective technical manuals. With the exception of speeded

tests, all reported reliabilities were estimates of how consistently examinees performed across items or subsets of items in a single test administration (i.e., *internal consistency*). For speeded tests, reported reliabilities were estimates of how consistently examinees performed on the same set of items at different times (i.e., *test-retest* or *stability* reliability). The internal consistency or test-retest reliabilities of intelligence tests published in the respective technical manuals, as reported at different age levels, were used in the ITDR.

Evaluation of Test Characteristic

Salvia and Ysseldyke (1991) presented standards for the evaluation of test reliability coefficients. For tests used to make critical educational decisions (e.g., special class placement) or diagnostic decisions, reliability coefficients of .90 or above are recommended. A value between .80 and .89 is considered appropriate for tests used to make screening decisions. Reliability coefficients below .80 are considered inadequate for making individual judgments about test performance. Since the *individual* tests (i.e., subtests) in intelligence batteries are not recommended for making critical educational or diagnostic decisions about individuals, and since the focus of interpretation in this book is on combinations of two or more tests, a .80 or above criterion was established as the minimum acceptable. It is important to note that these criteria are primarily relevant to the internal consistency reliability estimates reported for nonspeeded tests in intelligence batteries. Tests that are heavily speeded (e.g., Wechsler Coding, WJ-R Visual Matching) require the reporting of test-retest reliability coefficients, values that are considered to be lower-bound estimates of a test's reliability.

In the ITDR a reliability coefficient greater than or equal to .90 is considered *high*. Reliability coefficients that range from .80 to .89 are categorized as *medium*. Tests with medium reliability coefficients should be used for screening purposes or should be combined with other tests in a composite score. A test with a reported reliability coefficient of less than .80 is considered *low* and is therefore unreliable when used as the sole indicator upon which important judgments are made about individuals (Nunnally, 1978).

g Loadings

Intelligence tests have been interpreted often as reflecting a *general* mental ability referred to as *g* (Anastasi & Urbina, 1997; Bracken & Fagan, 1990; Carroll, 1993a; French & Hale, 1990; Horn, 1988; Jensen, 1984; Kaufman, 1979, 1994; Keith, 1997; Sattler, 1992; Thorndike & Lohman, 1990). The *g* concept was associated originally with Spearman (1904, 1927) and is considered to represent an underlying general intellectual ability (viz., the apprehension of experience and the education of relations) that is the basis for most intelligent behavior. The *g* concept has been one of the more controversial topics in psychology for decades (French & Hale, 1990; Jensen, 1992; Kamphaus, 1993; McDermott, Fantuzzo, & Glutting, 1990; McGrew, Flanagan, et al., 1997; Roid & Gyurke, 1991; Zachary, 1990). For example, a current focus of debate is whether a multiple intelligences model (Carroll, 1993a; Gardner, 1983; Horn, 1991) or a single general intelligence or *g* model explains most intelligent behavior.

Despite the inability to resolve the theoretical arguments surrounding the concept of *g*, an appreciation of each test's relationship to a general intelligence factor is considered useful in interpretation (Bracken & Fagan, 1990; Kaufman, 1979, 1990a; Roid & Gyurke, 1991). The primary value of knowing test *g* loadings is that they provide information that is necessary to anticipate which tests within an intelligence battery may vary frequently from the remainder of the test profile (Kaufman, 1979; Kamphaus, 1993). Tests that are high in their *g* factor loadings may be expected to be at a similar level of performance as most of the other tests and the global full scale score. Tests that load high on the general factor and that are markedly *discrepant* from the middle of a test profile may suggest the need for the examination of noncognitive variables (Kaufman, 1979; McGrew, 1984; Roid & Gyurke, 1991). In contrast, tests with low *g* factor loadings may vary frequently from the other tests within an intelligence battery, a finding that may not have diagnostic significance. A working knowledge of each test's loading on the general factor (*g*) within an intelligence battery can help practitioners identify unusual test variations.

Procedure for Reporting Data

As with the controversy surrounding the nature and meaning of *g*, disagreements exist about how best to calculate and report psychometric *g* estimates. All methods are based on some variant of principal component, principal factor, hierarchical factor, or confirmatory factor analysis (Jensen & Weng, 1994). Despite the different nuances between methods, in general, as long as the number of tests factored is relatively large, the tests have good reliability, a broad range of abilities is represented by the tests, and the sample is heterogeneous, the psychometric *g*'s produced by the different methods are typically very similar (Jensen & Weng, 1994). Given that the focus of this book is on intelligence batteries that are standardized on large, nationally representative samples and that most batteries include a relatively large number of reliable tests that measure a range of different abilities, differences in *g* loadings that may occur as a function of factor-analytic method are most likely trivial.

Within-Battery Procedures.   Traditionally, most reported within-battery psychometric *g* estimates for individual intelligence tests are based on each test's loading on the first unrotated factor or component in principal factor or component analysis. Published within-battery *g* estimates used in the ITDR were derived from these customary procedures. For some batteries the published estimates were not available or they were only available for very broad age categories. For these batteries, contact with the test author(s) resulted in access to unpublished within-battery test *g* loading data or the sharing of data that permitted the calculation of these estimates. Also, some published within-battery *g* estimates were calculated on the basis of a combination of cognitive and achievement tests (Kaufman & Kaufman,

1983). To ensure comparability of methods across test batteries, the ITDR reports within-battery *g* estimates that were calculated only on the basis of a test battery's *cognitive* tests. The sources of the psychometric *g* estimates reported in the ITDR are listed below.

- DAS: Unpublished analysis from test author (D. Elliott Colin, personal communication, December 7, 1994)
- K-ABC: Analysis of correlation matrices in technical manual by present authors
- KAIT: McGrew, Untiedt, and Flanagan (1996)
- SB:IV: Reynolds, Kamphaus, and Rosenthal (1988)
- WAIS-III: Analysis of correlation matrices in technical manual by present authors
- WISC-III: Analysis of correlation matrices in technical manual by present authors
- WPPSI-R: Analysis of correlation matrices in technical manual by present authors
- WJ-R: McGrew and Murphy (1995)

Cross-Battery Procedures.   Ideally, *Gf-Gc* cross-battery *g* estimates should be based on the analyses of large, nationally representative samples of subjects at different age levels who have been administered multiple intelligence batteries. Unfortunately, such an undertaking is impractical. The strategy adopted in the development of the ITDR cross-battery *g* estimates (and specificity estimates which are described later) was to use available datasets where subjects had been administered a common set of empirically validated *Gf-Gc* indicators (viz., WJ-R) together with another major intelligence battery. The datasets used were: (1) a series of validity studies reported in the WJ-R technical manual (McGrew, Werder, & Woodcock, 1991); (2) datasets used by Woodcock (1990) in a comprehensive *Gf-Gc* cross-battery analysis of the WJ-R, Wechslers, SB:IV, and K-ABC; (3) a new dataset that included tests from the WJ-R and the DAS (Laurie Ford, personal communication, October 15, 1996); and (4) a joint WJ-R/KAIT dataset used recently by Flanagan and McGrew (in press).

The critical feature of these datasets is the common use of the WJ-R, a test battery that includes empirically validated indicators of eight broad *Gf-Gc* abilities (McGrew et al., 1991; Reschly, 1990; Woodcock, 1990; Ysseldyke, 1990). As a result, each of the other intelligence batteries was analyzed together with the same set of empirically supported *Gf-Gc* test indicators (viz., the WJ-R). For each of these cross-battery analyses, test *g* loadings and communality estimates (needed for calculation of specificities, described below) were calculated separately for each battery (e.g., WISC-R alone) as well as together with the same set of strong indicators (tests) of seven *Gf-Gc* abilities (clusters) from the WJ-R battery (e.g., WJ-R and WISC-R combined). The results were then compared similarly to the way demonstrated in Table 3–1. The proportional change between the within-battery and cross-battery estimates for each test was calculated. These values were then used as scaling factors that were applied to all the standardization sample–based *g* and specificity values available for each test in each respective intelligence battery (i.e., the within-battery values reported in the ITDR). This resulted in "adjusted" norm-based cross-battery test *g* and specificity values.

The ITDR cross-battery *g* and specificity estimates are values that are likely to contain an unknown degree of error. Thus, they should be used with caution. The potential impact of this unknown error is minimized by the reporting of within- and cross-battery statistical estimates in categories (e.g., ample, adequate, inadequate). Although the exact cross-battery *g* or specificity estimates for a particular test (if computed through an ideal set of studies) would likely differ from the adjusted values reported in the ITDR, in many cases the amount of the precise difference may not result in a test's changing in its qualitative categorization (e.g., from ample to adequate).

Evaluation of Test Characteristic

In the intelligence test literature a three-category system has evolved to categorize test *g* loadings (e.g., Kaufman, 1979, 1990a). A test in an intelligence battery is classified as a *good* measure of *g* if it has a general factor or *g* loading of .70 or higher, *fair* if it has a loading of .51 to .69, and *poor* if it has a loading of .50 or lower. This *g* classification system was used for both the within- and cross-battery *g* characteristics presented in the ITDR.

Specificity

Test *specificity* refers to the portion of a test's variance that is reliable and unique to the test—"that is, not shared or held in common with other tests of the same scale" (Reynolds & Kaufman, 1990, p. 151). If a test has high specificity values (e.g., classified as "ample" or "adequate"—see evaluative criteria below), it may be interpreted as measuring an ability distinct and specific to that test. Conversely, tests with low specificity values are not recommended for individual interpretation. Test specificity assists practitioners in determining when it is appropriate to interpret individual tests as measuring distinct abilities within an intelligence battery.

Procedure for Reporting Data

Within-Battery Procedures.   Similarly to the calculation of test *g* characteristics, a number of different methods have been suggested for the calculation of test specificity (Kaufman, 1990a; Keith, 1990). The most frequently used method, which was the method used for all specificity estimates reported in the ITDR, is the one that uses squared multiple correlations (Kaufman, 1979, 1990a; Silverstein, 1976). In this procedure an estimate of each test's common or shared variance with all other tests within a specific intelligence test battery is obtained by calculating the squared multiple correlation between each test and all other tests within the battery. This value is called the test's *communality estimate*. Each test's communality estimate is then subtracted from the total reliable variance for each test (a value that is obtained by subtracting each test's reliability coefficient from unity). The difference between the total reliable variance and the communality estimate represents the amount of reliable test variance that is unique (not shared in common) for each test within the intelligence battery (i.e., specificity).

The sources of the test specificity estimates reported for the subtests of the respective intelligence batteries in the ITDR are the same as those listed for the test *g* loadings, with two exceptions: (1) The specificity estimates for the K-ABC were reported by Bracken, McCallum, and Crain (1993), and (2) the specificity estimates for the WISC-III were reported by Bracken and Howell (1989). These authors used procedures that paralleled those used for all other intelligence batteries and that were based on analyses consistent with the ITDR format (i.e., results were reported for separate age groups and the specificity estimates were not calculated together with achievement tests).

Cross-Battery Procedures.   The procedures used to develop cross-battery specificity estimates were described previously in the discussion of the cross-battery *g* estimates.

Evaluation of Test Characteristic
Individual tests are typically classified as ample, adequate, or inadequate in specificity (e.g., Cohen, 1959; Kaufman, 1979, 1990a; Sattler, 1992). Test specificity is *ample* when a test's unique reliable variance is equal to or above 25% of the total test variance and it exceeds error variance (1-reliability). When a test meets only one of these criteria, it is classified as having *adequate* specificity. If a test does not meet either of the criteria, it is classified as having *inadequate* specificity. Individual tests with ample and adequate specificity or uniqueness are considered legitimate for individual interpretation, although the latter group must be interpreted with caution (Kamphaus, 1990; Kaufman, 1979). This three-category system was used to classify both the within- and cross-battery test specificity estimates in the ITDR.

Although the terms "ample," "adequate," and "inadequate" and "good," "fair," and "poor" have been used for decades to describe test specificity and *g* loadings, respectively, these terms connote a "good–bad" continuum that can be misleading. For example, because it is recommended that tests classified as "inadequate" with regard to specificity not be interpreted as representing a unique ability, it is assumed often that these measures are not as valuable as those that are classified as "ample" in specificity. This, however, is not the case. First, tests with inadequate specificity (as well as tests that are poor indicators of *g*) may be very valuable to the interpretive process when they are included as part of a composite or cluster with other similar tests. Second, since a test's level of specificity and *g* loading are related to the breadth or diversity of tests included in the battery, these test characteristics are relative and somewhat arbitrary. Thus, specificity and *g* loading classifications are used mainly to help guide the most appropriate interpretations *within* any given battery. Although standard terminology is used in the ITDR, it may be worthwhile to classify tests as either "high," "medium," or "low" in specificity and *g* loading in the future, for the reasons just given.

Test Floors and Ceilings

Intelligence batteries with adequate floors and ceilings will yield scores that effectively discriminate among various degrees of functioning at the extremes of the cognitive ability continuum. A test with an *inadequate floor*, or an insufficient number of easy items, will not distinguish adequately between individuals functioning in the average, low average, and borderline ranges of ability. Moreover, tests with inadequate floors cannot discriminate between various degrees of mental retardation (i.e., mild, moderate, severe). Likewise, a test with an *inadequate ceiling*, or an insufficient number of difficult items, will not distinguish adequately between individuals who function in the average, high average, and superior ranges of intellectual ability. A test with an inadequate ceiling cannot discriminate between various levels of giftedness. Thus, an intelligence battery that does not have adequate floors or ceilings will provide limited information about what certain individuals can do and therefore should not be used for diagnostic, classification, or placement decisions, especially with individuals who are suspected of developmental delay or intellectual giftedness.

Procedure for Reporting Data

Information about intelligence test floors and ceilings was derived from the published norm tables of each battery included in the ITDR. A simple raw score to standard score conversion at each norm table age grouping was used to examine the adequacy of individual test floors and ceilings across the age range of all intelligence batteries in a way similar to that of Bracken (1987) and Flanagan and Alfonso (1995).

Evaluation of Test Characteristic

A test was considered to have an *inadequate* floor at any given age level if a raw score of 1 was associated with a standard score that was not *more than 2 standard deviations below* the normative mean of the test. For example, on a test with a mean of 10 and standard deviation of 3, a raw score of 1 must be associated with a standard score of 3 or less to ensure differentiation among individuals who function well below the normative mean (cf. Flanagan & Alfonso, 1995). A test was considered to have an adequate floor when a raw score of 1 was associated with a standard score greater than 2 standard deviations below the normative mean. Similarly, a test was considered to have an inadequate ceiling at any given age level when the maximum raw score for the test was associated with a standard score that was not *more than 2 standard deviations above* the normative mean of the test. For example, on a test with a mean of 100 and a standard deviation of 15, the maximum raw score must be associated with a standard score of 131 or greater to ensure differentiation among individuals who function well above the normative mean. A test was considered to have an *adequate* ceiling when the maximum raw score for the test was greater than 2 standard deviations above the normative mean.

Item Gradients

Item gradient information describes the extent to which a test effectively differentiates among various ability levels (Bracken, 1987). This characteristic is related to the density of items across a test's latent trait scale. In simple terms, a test with good item gradient characteristics has items that are approximately equally spaced in difficulty along the entire test scale and has spacing between items that is small enough to allow for reliable discrimination between individuals on the latent trait measured by the test. Item gradient information is concerned with the extent to which changes of single raw score points on a test result in excessively large changes in ability scores.

Procedure for Reporting Data

Item gradient information has received relatively little attention in the test development and evaluation literature. Bracken (1987) was one of the first researchers to highlight the importance of, and to present procedures and evaluative criteria for, item gradient characteristics. Recently, Flanagan and Alfonso (1995) reported item gradient information, using a slight modification of Bracken's procedure, for the most current intelligence batteries for preschool children. Bracken (1987) and Flanagan and Alfonso (1995) defined an *item gradient violation* as a one-unit increase in raw score points that resulted in a change of more than 1/3 standard deviation in standard score values.

Using this definition, item gradient violations reported in the ITDR were identified for each subtest in each intelligence battery by calculating the standard score change for every possible raw score change for each age-based norm table for the test. The data from the published norm tables for the respective intelligence batteries were used in these calculations. Following the procedures outlined by Flanagan and Alfonso (1995) for dealing with the different norm table age groupings (e.g., 1-month intervals on the WJ-R, 3-month intervals on the DAS, 5-month intervals on the WPPSI-R), an item gradient violation was counted once for each 1-month interval for which it occurred (see Flanagan & Alfonso, 1995, for details).

The number of item gradient violations was tallied and compared to the total number of possible item gradient violations for the test. For example, if a test had 2 item gradient violations out of a possible 50 (i.e., 50 possible raw score changes across the entire scale), the test was characterized as having 4% (2 of 50) item gradient violations. The total percent of item gradient violations for each test reported in the ITDR at every age level was calculated.

Evaluation of Test Characteristic

The procedure used to evaluate the item gradient characteristics of each test included in the ITDR differs from that reported in the literature (Bracken, 1987; Flanagan & Alfonso, 1995). Flanagan and Alfonso (1995) extended the work of Bracken (1987) by considering the significance of item gradient violations in relation to how far the violations occurred from the mean (e.g., item gradient violations that occurred closer to the mean were considered more problematic than those that occurred greater than 2 standard deviations from the mean). However, the criteria used in the ITDR do not include procedures for judging the distance that the item gradient violation occurred from the mean. In the ITDR an item gradient violation was considered undesirable regardless of where it occurred along the complete range of ability.

To establish a system of item gradient evaluation, the distribution of the percentage of item gradient violations was examined for all subtests across all age levels and across all intelligence batteries included in the ITDR. Results indicated that approximately 80% of the time, tests showed less than or equal to 5% violations; approximately 12% of the time, tests showed between 5% and 15% violations; and approximately 8% of the time, tests showed violations equal to or greater than 15%. When combined with logical considerations, these data were used to categorize tests as having *good* (≤ 5% violations), *fair* (> 5% to ≤ 15% violations), or *poor* (> 15% violations) item gradient characteristics at each age level for which the test provided norms.

Construct Validity: Gf-Gc Broad and Narrow Test Classifications

The *construct validity* of tests "focuses primarily on the test score as a measure of the psychological characteristic of interest" (APA, 1985, p. 9). In the case of intelligence tests the constructs of interest are the different cognitive abilities included in the theoretical construct of intelligence. The appropriate evaluation of the construct validity of tests requires the embedding of the constructs of interests in a conceptual framework (APA, 1985). As summarized in chapters 1 and 2, contemporary *Gf-Gc* theory provides the most comprehensive and empirically supported framework of cognitive abilities available to date. This taxonomy "provides what is essentially a 'map' of all known cognitive abilities. Such a map can be used in interpreting scores on the many tests used in individual assessment" (Carroll, 1993a, p.127).

To fulfill the objective of mapping tests to the *Gf-Gc* construct framework, the ITDR provides *Gf-Gc* broad and narrow classifications of the tests in the major intelligence batteries. These classifications not only provide evidence for the construct validity of the tests in intelligence batteries, but also provide critical information on how best to interpret performance on each test (see Figure 3–1 and the related discussion). The basis for the *Gf-Gc* classifications, as well as the ITDR classification system and terminology, is described below.

Procedure for Reporting Data

Mapping the *Gf-Gc* cognitive ability taxonomy (see Chapter 1) to the tests in intelligence batteries requires that each test be classified at both the broad (stratum II) and narrow (stratum I) levels. The broad abilities measured by tests focus on the *broad Gf-Gc* abilities, which Carroll (1993a) defined as representing "basic constitutional and longstanding characteristics of individuals that govern or influence a great variety of behaviors in a given domain" (p. 634). These broad abilities vary in differing degrees of relative emphasis on process, content, and manner of response. In contrast, *narrow* abilities "represent greater specializations of abilities, often in quite specific ways that reflect the effects of experience and learning, or the adoption of particular strategies of performance" (p. 634). As in Figure 3–1, an example of *Gf-Gc* broad and narrow ability-test-mapping is demonstrated for five Wechsler tests in Figure 3–4.

As previously described in Chapter 1, *g* subsumes the *broad* (stratum II) *Gf-Gc* abilities (of which only two are represented in Figure 3–4), which in turn subsume *narrow* (stratum I) abilities. For example, in Figure 3–4 it can be seen that the broad ability of *Gc* subsumes the specialized narrow abilities of Listening Ability, General Information, Language Development, Lexical Knowledge, and others not included in the figure (see Chapter 1). The rectangles in Figure 3–4 represent five tests from the WISC-III. In this figure the Information, Comprehension, Similarities, and Vocabulary tests are all indicators of the broad *Gc* ability. The Arithmetic test is classified as an indicator of the broad *Gq* ability.

Most of the broad *Gf-Gc* classifications for all the intelligence tests reported in the ITDR are based on Flanagan and McGrew's (1997) and McGrew's (1997) summaries of the extant *Gf-Gc* confirmatory cross-battery intelligence test research. These confirmatory cross-battery studies, which collectively will be referred to as the *CB studies* hereafter, include Woodcock's (1990) analyses of the WJ-R, Wech-

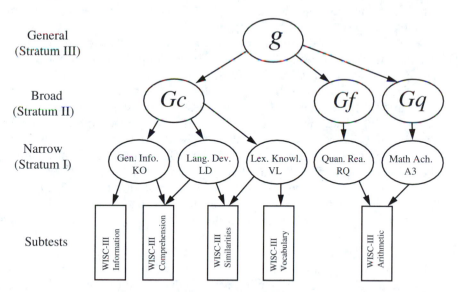

FIGURE 3–4   **The Relations Between Five WISC-III Subtests and the Three Strata (Narrow, Broad, and General) of the *Gf-Gc* Model of Intelligence. There are additional narrow abilities in the domains of *Gc, Gf,* and *Gq* that are not included in this figure.**

slers, SB:IV, and K-ABC; McGhee's (1993) analyses of the WJ-R, DAS, and Detroit Tests of Learning Aptitude-3 (DTLA-3; Hammill & Bryant, 1991); and Flanagan and McGrew's (in press) analyses of the WJ-R and KAIT.

A number of common design features across the CB studies make them important for understanding the *Gf-Gc* abilities measured by the major intelligence batteries. First, the Horn-Cattell *Gf-Gc* model of intelligence was the theoretical model used to organize each confirmatory factor analysis study. Second, all the CB data sets included tests from the WJ-R, a test battery that includes empirically validated indicators of eight broad *Gf-Gc* abilities (McGrew, 1994; McGrew et al., 1991; Reschly, 1990; Woodcock, 1990; Ysseldyke, 1990). As a result, each of the other intelligence batteries was analyzed together with a *common set of empirically supported* Gf-Gc *test indicators* from the WJ-R.

As already discussed, most of the broad *Gf-Gc* test classifications reported in the ITDR are based on empirical research studies. Thus, the resultant *Gf-Gc* classifications provide evidence of the construct validity of the tests within individual intelligence batteries. An overall summary of the broad *Gf-Gc* classifications is presented in Table 3–3.

The CB studies to date were designed to provide information about the abilities measured by tests at the broad (stratum II) *Gf-Gc* ability level. Empirically based narrow ability classification factor analysis studies would be a major undertaking and have yet to be completed. In their absence, McGrew (1997) applied a logically based expert consensus process to the narrow *Gf-Gc* ability classification of the tests in the major intelligence batteries. This involved asking a number of intelligence test experts (including most of the intelligence test authors) to match the content and task demands of each test within a battery to the narrow *Gf-Gc* ability definitions summarized in Table 1–1 (see Chapter 1). In essence, this is a form of *Gf-Gc content validity* (APA, 1985).

Figure 3–4 illustrates the result of the narrow ability classification process. In this model the five WISC-III tests are classified as measuring certain narrow abilities (e.g., Information is classified as a measure of General Information; Arithmetic is classified as a measure of Quantitative Reasoning and Math Achievement) that are subsumed by the broader *Gc*, *Gf*, and *Gq* factors. The relationship specified between the tests in intelligence batteries and the hierarchically organized narrow and broad abilities in the *Gf-Gc* model (as illustrated in figures 3–1 and 3–4) represents an important theory-application link that users and developers of intelligence tests must appreciate in order to interpret accurately the meaning of intelligence batteries.

For the ITDR every narrow test ability classification reported by McGrew (1997) was reviewed by the present authors in light of a greater understanding of the narrow ability definitions that was achieved by a re-review of earlier CB studies within the context of the more recent CB studies, a re-reading of Carroll's (1993a) text, a review of additional *Gf-Gc*–organized factor analysis studies conducted by the present authors (see Chapter 1), and communication with intelligence scholars and test authors. As a result, a handful of the narrow ability

TABLE 3–3 ***Gf-Gc* Factor Classifications of Six Major Intelligence Test Batteries**

Gf-Gc Factor	WJ-R	Wechslers
Long-Term Retrieval (*Glr*)	**Memory for Names** **Vis-Aud Learning** **Delayed Recall-MN** Delayed Recall-VAL	---------------
Short-Term Memory (*Gsm*)	**Memory for Words** Memory for Sent. (Gc*) Numbers Reversed (Gf*) Picture Recognition (Gv*)	**Digit Span** Letter-Number Sequencing[2]
Processing Speed (*Gs*)	**Visual Matching** **Cross Out**	**Coding/Digit Symbol** Symbol Search
Auditory Processing (*Ga*)	**Incomplete Words** **Sound Blending** Sound Patterns (Gf*)	---------------
Visual Processing (*Gv*)	Visual Closure Spatial Relations (Gf*)	**Block Design** **Object Assembly** Mazes Picture Comp. (Gc*) Picture Arrang. (Gc*)
Comprehension- Knowledge (*Gc*)	**Picture Vocabulary** **Oral Vocabulary** **Listening Comp.**	**Information** **Similarities** **Vocabulary** **Comprehension**
Fluid Reasoning (*Gf*)	**Analysis-Synthesis** **Concept Formation** Verbal Analogies (Gc*)	Matrix Reasoning[3]
Quantitative Ability (*Gq*)	**Calculation** **Applied Problems**	**Arithmetic**

Note: Strong measures of *Gf-Gc* factors are reported in bold-face type; measures not in bold type are moderate or mixed indicators of *Gf-Gc* abilities. Primary measures of *Gf-Gc* factors for the WJ-R are based on the empirical analyses of Woodcock (1990) and Flanagan and McGrew (in press); *Gf-Gc* factor classifications of the SB:IV, Wechslers, and K-ABC are reported in Woodcock (1990); classifications for the DAS and KAIT are reported in McGhee (1993) and Flanagan and McGrew (in press), respectively. For additional information on *Gf-Gc* factor classifications of major intelligence batteries see McGrew (1994, 1997). Copyright 1997 by Guilford Publishing Company. All rights reserved.

* Secondary factor loading.

Continued

TABLE 3–3   *Continued*

SB:IV	DAS[1]	K-ABC[1]	KAIT
----------------	**	----------------	**Rebus Learning** **Del. Rec.-RebLrn.** Del. Rec-Aud Com. (Gc*)
Memory for Digits Memory for Objects Mem. for Sent. (Gc*) Bead Memory (Gv*)	**Recall of Designs**	Number Recall Word Order Hand Move. (Gq*)	**Mem. for Blk. Des.**
----------------	**	----------------	----------------
----------------	----------------	----------------	----------------
Pattern Analysis Copying Paper Fold. (Gq*)	Pattern Construction	**Triangles** Gestalt Closure Spatial Mem Mat. Analog. (Gf*) Photo Series (Gf*)	----------------
Vocabulary **Verbal Relations** Comprehension Absurdities	**Word Definitions** **Similarities**	**Faces & Places** **Riddles** Expressive Voc.	Famous Faces Definitions (Grw*) Dbl. Meanings (Grw*) Auditory Comp. (Gsm*)
Matrices	**Matrices** Seq-Quant. Reason. (Gq*)	----------------	**Logical Steps** **Mystery Codes**
Quantitative **Number Series** **Equation Building**	**	**Arithmetic**	----------------

[1]Only a subset of DAS and K-ABC subtests were joint factor analyzed by McGhee (1993) and Woodcock (1990), respectively. Therefore, only the subtests that were included in these analyses are reported in this Table. The *Gf-Gc* factor classifications of *all* DAS and K-ABC subtests following a logical task analysis and expert consensus are reported in McGrew (1997).

** Tests measuring these abilities (i.e., *Glr, Gs, Gq*) are included on the DAS battery but have yet to be included in *Gf-Gc*–organized confirmatory cross-battery factor analyses.

[2] In the WAIS-III Letter-Number Sequencing is combined with Arithmetic and Digit Span to purportedly measure "working memory."

[3] Matrix Reasoning is found on the WAIS-III only.

classifications originally provided by McGrew (1997) were modified. Expert consensus notwithstanding, the ITDR narrow *Gf-Gc* ability classifications (like McGrew's [1997] classifications) may need modification as a result of future research and scholarly dialogue.

Evaluation of Test Characteristic

The CB studies allow the broad *Gf-Gc* test classifications to be categorized further along a number of other dimensions. The first dimension is whether the test classification is logical or empirical. *Logical* classifications are based on a task analysis of the content and demands of tests not included in CB analyses, within the context of the *Gf-Gc* taxonomy. *Empirical* classifications are those derived from a review of the results of CB studies. Typically, in these studies, tests were found to have significant or salient factor loadings on *one Gf-Gc* factor. This was considered the tests' *primary Gf-Gc* ability interpretation. However, some tests were factorially complex or mixed, displaying salient loadings on *two or more Gf-Gc* factors. In this situation the *Gf-Gc* factor upon which a test displayed its highest factor loading was considered the *primary* ability measured, and the other less salient factor loading(s) for the test was interpreted as a *secondary* ability (see Figure 3–1 and the related discussion for an illustration of this point).

A set of empirical criteria was used to categorize the tests included in the CB studies as either strong, moderate, or mixed measures of the broad *Gf-Gc* factors (McGrew, 1997; Woodcock, 1990). These operational criteria, as first specified by Woodcock (1990), were used in the ITDR and are listed here:

- *Strong*: A test had a substantial factor loading ($\geq$.50) on a primary factor and a secondary factor loading (if present) that was equal to or less than 1/2 of its loading on the primary factor.
- *Moderate*: A test had a primary factor loading of <.50 and a secondary factor loading (if present) that was less than 1/2 of the primary loading, or any primary factor loading and secondary loading between 1/2 and 7/10 of the primary loading.
- *Mixed*: A test had a factor loading on a secondary factor that was greater than 7/10 of its loading on the primary factor.

In the absence of empirical data upon which to evaluate and categorize the logically based narrow ability test classifications, McGrew's (1997) system of categorizing narrow ability classifications was adopted. That is, a *probable* designation indicates that there was a clear correspondence between the content and task demands of a test and a particular *Gf-Gc* narrow ability definition in the expert consensus process. These were also the narrow ability test classifications for which there was the most expert consensus. A *possible* categorization reflects narrow test classifications in which there was less agreement during the expert consensus process, or the correspondence between a test's content and task demands and the narrow ability definition was present, but less obvious.

Other Variables That Influence Test Performance

Based on a review of the literature that has suggested variables that may influence test performance, the following characteristics were considered most salient by the present authors and were therefore selected for inclusion in the ITDR: (1) incidence of basic concepts in intelligence test directions (applicable for instruments with norms for preschoolers); (2) degree of cultural content in cognitive ability tests, and (3) background/environmental and individual/situational variables that influence test performance.

Incidence of Basic Concepts

Practitioners who use intelligence batteries to assess the cognitive functioning of preschool children (age 3–5 years) should be aware of the basic concepts that are used during standard test administration procedures, as well as the likelihood that a young child's understanding (or conversely, misunderstanding) of these concepts may influence test performance. Many researchers have stressed the need to evaluate the difficulty of intelligence test directions by examining the incidence of basic concepts that are used during standard administration procedures, because the linguistic knowledge of preschoolers is limited (Bracken, 1986; Flanagan et al., 1995; Glutting & Kaplan, 1990; Kaufman, 1978, 1990b).

Based on the results of previous studies, it is evident that practitioners ought not to assume that preschoolers comprehend fully the standard directions of most major intelligence batteries. For instance, intelligence test directions that include "difficult" basic concepts (e.g., without, over, after), long sentences, and/or the passive voice may not be understood by preschool children (Alfonso & Flanagan, in press; Boehm, 1991; Bracken, 1986; Flanagan et al., 1995; Kaufman, 1978, 1990b). A child who does not understand test directions because of complex linguistic demands may not perform optimally, and, as a result, his or her obtained scores may underestimate ability. Moreover, intelligence batteries with directions that require conceptual or linguistic knowledge that is above age level may pose a threat to the construct validity of the instrument (Bracken, 1986). The extent to which intelligence batteries require excessive linguistic demands is especially important to consider when evaluating the performance of preschoolers and children from economically or socially disadvantaged and/or culturally diverse backgrounds (see Alfonso & Flanagan, in press; Bracken, 1986; Flanagan et al., 1995; Kaufman, 1978).

Procedure for Reporting Data

To evaluate the extent to which basic concepts have an impact on the difficulty of test directions, three characteristics of basic concepts were considered: (1) the presence (i.e., number) of basic concepts in intelligence test directions, (2) the percentage of the preschool population who understand each basic concept, and (3) the frequency with which basic concepts occur in test directions (cf. Flanagan et al., 1995). These characteristics were examined using the Bracken Basic Concept Scale

(BBCS; Bracken, 1984). The standardized test directions included in the respective administration and scoring manuals of the intelligence batteries provided the necessary information for determining the incidence of basic concepts in test directions.

The specific procedure for identifying basic concepts in intelligence test directions was as follows. First, the directions of each subtest in the intelligence batteries that are administered to preschoolers (age 2 years, 6 months through 5 years, 6 months) were reviewed for the presence of the 258 basic concepts included in the BBCS. Basic concepts were reported only if they were used in the test directions *in the same context* as that provided in the BBCS standardization procedures (see Flanagan et al. [1995] for details). Second, the proportion (p) of children in the standardization sample of the BBCS who understood each basic concept (i.e., passed the item) was recorded (p values were obtained from Bracken [1986], since BBCS standardization data were no longer available from The Psychological Corporation; Aurelio Prifitera, personal communication, March 19, 1994). Through the use of the data in Bracken (1986), it was possible to obtain p values for approximately 80% of the basic concepts found in the directions of the intelligence batteries included in the ITDR. Third, the number of times each basic concept occurred in the test directions of each intelligence battery was tabulated separately by subtest.

This review of basic concepts included only intelligence test directions that are used to guide, direct, or give feedback to the child. A restricted analysis of this kind was preferable since it eliminates the basic concepts that are inextricably bound to the ability to perform a cognitive task and includes only those directions that are essentially unrelated to the abilities or skills necessary for successful performance (cf. Flanagan et al., 1995). Thus, if the basic concepts that are revealed by this type of analysis are not understood by a preschool child, it is highly likely that the child's obtained score will underestimate his or her true ability.

Based on this criterion, subtests from certain intelligence batteries were not included in the present analysis. For example, the directions of the WPPSI-R Similarities test were not included because the child must understand the concept "alike" in order to perform the cognitive task. In addition, if an intelligence test directly assessed a child's knowledge of basic concepts, then these directions were deleted from the analysis. For example, the directions of both the Verbal Comprehension and Early Number Concepts tests of the DAS were omitted because the purpose of these tests is to assess verbal and numerical *conceptual knowledge*, respectively. Inter-rater reliability coefficients were calculated and revealed greater than 90% agreement among raters with respect to the presence and frequency of basic concepts in intelligence test directions.

Evaluation of Test Characteristic
The incidences of basic concepts data reported in the ITDR were not evaluated with respect to specific criteria. Rather, the typical age of concept attainment (i.e., 3, 4, 5, or >5 years) for those basic concepts found in test directions was reported to aid practitioners in selecting a battery that is most appropriate for working with preschool children. "Typical age of concept attainment" was defined as a p values

of .75 or greater, indicating that the basic concept is understood by at least 75% of preschoolers. For example, a review of the ITDR page for the WPPSI-R Object Assembly (OA) subtest shows that the basic concepts of "together," "through," and "fast" were found in the OA test directions. These basic concepts were listed in the column for 4-year-olds on the ITDR page. This indicates that these basic concepts are understood by at least 75% of 4-year-olds. Children younger than age 4 may have more difficulty understanding the directions of the OA test.

Degree of Cultural Content in Cognitive Ability Tests

Most major theorists include *culture* (either implicitly or explicitly) as a critical component in their conceptualizations of intelligence as for how differing experiences facilitate or inhibit intellectual behavior (e.g., Carroll, 1993a; Feuerstein, Feuerstein, Schur, 1995; Gardner, 1983; Horn, 1991; Sternberg, 1985, 1997). As such, performance on all intelligence batteries reflects, in part, the extent to which the examinee is familiar with the conventions of the mainstream culture in which the test battery was constructed and normed.

In an attempt to understand the extent to which culture may influence test performance, practitioners sometimes employ Newland's (1971) process-dominant/ product-dominant continuum when evaluating the performance of examinees from culturally or linguistically diverse backgrounds. With respect to this continuum and the intelligence batteries included in the ITDR, it is assumed that an examinee's level of acculturation, or learning of mainstream United States (U.S.) culture, will impact his or her performance to a greater extent on subtests that are dependent upon accumulated knowledge and acquired experiences (product-dominant) than on subtests that purport to measure fundamental learning processes (process-dominant) (Newland, 1971). Because all intelligence batteries include process-dominant and product-dominant tests or some combination of the two, none is *culture-free* (Humphreys, 1992). Intelligence batteries appear to measure cognitive abilities that "result from the interaction between the person's neurophysiology and the environment" (Elliott, 1990, p. 2). Therefore, the degree to which intelligence tests are *culturally loaded* probably varies. An understanding of this variability is important as it may aid practitioners in selecting more appropriate cognitive tests for use with individuals whose cultural backgrounds differ from mainstream U.S. culture (see also Chapter 14).

For example, it is assumed that an individual who is not acculturated (i.e., not familiar with the societal conventions of the U.S.) generally will perform relatively lower on product-dominant tests (i.e., tests that are generally highly influenced by U.S. culture) as compared to process-dominant tests (which are typically less influenced by exposure to mainstream U.S. culture). It is further assumed that individuals who do not have the knowledge and experiences that accumulate gradually through the process of acculturation are apt to earn product-dominant test or cluster scores that are spuriously low. Knowledge of the degree to which U.S. cultural knowledge and experience is required to perform a task may aid in making more appropriate interpretations regarding cultural demands on test performance (see Alfonso & Flanagan, in press; Armour-Thomas, 1992; Barona & Barona, 1991; Esters, Ittenbach, & Han, in press; Helms, 1997; Lopez, 1997; Rogoff & Chavajay, 1995; Vernon, Jackson, & Messick, 1988 for discussions of the importance of considering cultural influences on test performance).

Procedure for Reporting Data

Like Newland's process-dominant/product-dominant continuum, *Gf-Gc* abilities can be thought of as lying on a continuum, with abilities that depend little on direct instruction and formal learning (e.g., *Gf*) at one end and abilities that depend extensively on breadth and depth of knowledge of a culture, including the ability to communicate (especially verbally) and reason through the application of previously learned procedures (e.g., *Gc*), at the other. The remaining *Gf-Gc* abilities lie somewhere between *Gf* and *Gc* on the continuum, with their location depending on the degree to which they differ as a function of relative emphasis on process, content, and manner of response (Carroll, 1993a). Thus, classifications of all cognitive tests according to a well-researched and -validated theory (i.e., *Gf-Gc*) was considered a necessary step prior to considering how culture impacts performance on these tests (Flanagan & Alfonso, 1994; Hessler, 1993).

With this continuum in mind and with knowledge of the *Gf-Gc* classification of cognitive tests (viz., Flanagan & McGrew, 1995; Hessler, 1993; McGrew, 1997), Flanagan and Alfonso (1994) and Alfonso and Flanagan (in press) used the *Gf-Gc* theoretical framework as a basis for understanding the abilities and processes that underlie cognitive ability tests for *preschool children* (age 3–5 years). Specifically, they examined the subtests of the major intelligence batteries according to underlying process, nature of the content to be processed, and type of response to determine the relative influence of U.S. culture (i.e., high, moderate, low) on tests with norms for preschoolers (Alfonso & Flanagan, in press). The "degree of cultural content" classifications that are presented in the ITDR represent an extension of the work of Flanagan and Alfonso; that is, *all* intelligence tests were classified by the present authors, not just tests with norms for preschoolers. Also, based on the most up-to-date *Gf-Gc* classifications of cognitive ability tests (i.e., those presented in the ITDR), the present authors reviewed or re-reviewed the specific content and underlying processes and abilities of all intelligence tests in a manner consistent with Flanagan and Alfonso's approach and assigned each test either a "high," "moderate," or "low" "degree of cultural content" classification. This classification represents the degree to which U.S. cultural knowledge or experience is required to perform the task.

Evaluation of Test Characteristic

The classifications of all cognitive ability tests as either high, moderate, or low with respect to the degree to which cultural content impacts test performance are subjective. They are based predominantly on our own judgments and therefore should be used only as a guide for selecting tests that may more appropriately meet the needs of culturally diverse populations. It is important to note that the cultural content of a particular subtest or item represents only one form of potential bias in assessment. A consideration of how the cultural content of cognitive ability tests is likely to influence test performance cannot eliminate entirely the bias in test performance of culturally diverse populations. Research is necessary to provide an objective basis for understanding the U.S. cultural demands on test performance. The classifications presented in the ITDR may provide the necessary framework for conducting such research.

Background/Environmental and Individual/Situational Variables

Two additional broad categories of variables are important to consider when interpreting an individual's intelligence test performance. The background/environmental and individual/situational variables focus on placing the interpretation of an individual's test performance in an appropriate context. These sets of contextual variables can have either proximal (near or immediate) or distal (far or remote) influences on an examinee's test performance.

Background/environmental variables are influences that, although not directly operating during the testing session, have contributed to the development of the traits that are measured by a test. For example, when interpreting a very low score on a test of auditory processing (Ga), the meaning of this score would likely be different for a child with a long history of hearing difficulties due to chronic inner ear infections when compared to a similar level of performance for a child with no history of hearing difficulties. For the child with the history of hearing difficulties a possible hypothesis that a practitioner might generate is that the presence of hearing difficulties may have hindered the development of the child's Ga abilities. Background/environmental variables are distal influences—prior developmental or environmental factors that may have contributed to the development of the skill being evaluated.

Individual/situational variables include characteristics of the examinee that might exert a situational influence on test performance (in either a positive or negative direction) during the testing session. For example, if an examinee is highly distractible and inattentive during the assessment, the score(s) he or she earns may be negatively influenced. As a result, the individual's score on a particular test may not accurately portray (i.e., it may underestimate) his or her level on the trait being measured. In the context of the "big picture" (see Figure 3–1), the size of the test indicator rectangle that represents error variance may be relatively larger for this individual (resulting in a reduction of the reliable variance of the person's score).

Knowledge of the individual and situational variables that may influence performance on individual tests is necessary for appropriate test interpretation. This allows a practitioner to make informed judgments about the extent to which the proportion of reliable variance for a test (that which is the primary focus of interpretation) is a valid indicator of the abilities that are measured by the test. Failure to consider the possibility that certain environmental, situation-specific, or individual characteristics may influence test performance would be akin to blindly evaluating the running performance of a world-class sprinter based on her reported 100-meter dash time without knowledge of the unique variables that were operating during the performance (e.g., was it raining and/or windy? was the sprinter performing with a slightly pulled hamstring muscle?).

Procedure for Reporting Data

The background/environmental and individual/situational variables used in the ITDR are based on a synthesis of similar variables that have been presented in the intelligence test interpretation literature. The published interpretive material for the DAS (Elliott, 1990), K-ABC (Kaufman & Kaufman, 1983), KAIT (Kaufman & Kaufman, 1993), the Wechslers (Kaufman, 1990, 1994), and the WJ-R (McGrew, 1994), as well as a major reference book on intelligence test interpretation (Sattler, 1988), was reviewed. A table of the cross-referenced terms and statements was developed. For example, the phrases "school learning," "effect of schooling and education," and "quality of schooling" were judged to be referring to the same variable. In the ITDR this variable is referred to as "educational opportunities/ experiences."

For the ITDR the cross-referenced interpretive terms and statements were reviewed and those that were repeated frequently across sources were retained. In a sense, this was a subjective expert consensus process. Next, one of the representative terms or statements regarding a particular variable was selected or a new descriptive term or phrase was developed. In addition, certain interpretive terms that were not necessarily reported across all sources, but that were judged to be potentially important in intelligence test interpretation, were retained.

A number of interpretive terms commonly mentioned in the intelligence test literature were excluded from the ITDR. One set of interpretive terms was related to personality, attitudinal, and/or emotional factors. Examples include "perfectionistic tendencies," "motivational level," and "development of a conscience or moral sense." Although these individual characteristics may influence test performance, they were judged to refer to variables that were too general (i.e., not test-specific). Perfectionism or low motivation would most likely affect all test scores and thus would be difficult to classify as being related to specific, individual tests. Moreover, these type of factors are assessed more formally and typically in the social-emotional or personality component of the evaluation.

The second set of interpretive terms that were excluded from the ITDR were those that were judged to refer to *Gf-Gc* abilities—abilities for which tests already have been classified in the ITDR. For example, phrases such as "visual perceptual problems" (*Gv*) and "ability to listen to directions" (*Gc* and *Gsm*) were excluded. The variables represented by these phrases are not necessarily excluded from consideration in the ITDR; rather, these variables are now more accurately accounted for by the *Gf-Gc* classifications for each test.

The final set of background/environmental and individual/situational variables that were included in the ITDR are presented and defined in Table 3–2. Using the terms and definitions presented in the table, each individual test in each intelligence battery was judged according to whether one or more of these variables may potentially influence test performance. A review of the intelligence test interpretative manuals and/or books aided in this classification process.

Evaluation of the Test Characteristic

As previously described, the process of classifying each test according to background/environmental and individual/situational variables was not based on specific objective criteria. Rather, the test classifications presented in the ITDR are the authors' consensus-based judgment as to whether performance on a test may or may not be influenced by a particular variable. The process involved a simple dichotomous (yes or no) classification.

The ITDR Summary Pages

Proper interpretation of intelligence tests is an involved and important activity that often has significant implications for the individual being evaluated. It is incumbent upon those who use intelligence batteries to recognize and consider all available information about each test in the assessment and interpretation process.

Mastery and use of the wide range of quantitative and qualitative test characteristic information described in this chapter for all intelligence batteries is a daunting (but necessary) task for practitioners. To facilitate the infusion of this critical test characteristic information into the day-to-day assessment practices of practitioners, chapters 4 through 11 present two-page summaries for each subtest in each of the major individually administered intelligence batteries that were available at the time this text was being prepared. An example for the WISC-III Arithmetic subtest is presented in Figure 3–5 and Figure 3–6.

The top of the first page (Figure 3–5) reports the test battery (i.e., WISC-III) and the name of the test (i.e., Arithmetic). Next, a brief description of the test and the age range for which norms are provided is presented.

The Basic Psychometric Characteristics section follows. This section reports, in a visual-graphic format, information about each test's reliability, within- and cross-battery *g* loadings, specificity, and item gradients. The evaluation of each of these test characteristics, according to the previously described ITDR criteria (see Table 3–2), is accomplished by simply locating the appropriate age level and inspecting the color of the shading in the small square associated with that age. The meaning of the shaded box is understood by referring to the key for each test characteristic located on the ITDR pages. For example, at age 10 the Arithmetic subtest is classified as having *low* reliability, *good* within- and cross-battery *g* loadings, *ample* within-battery specificity, *inadequate* cross-battery specificity, and *poor* item gradients. In addition to these psychometric characteristics, the adequacy of test floors and ceilings is also reported. As can be seen in Figure 3–5, the Arithmetic test has *adequate* test floors and ceilings at this age. It is important to note that the classification and shading of the respective reliabilities, *g* loadings, and specificities for each test in the ITDR are based on sample statistics that were "fine-tuned" to better approximate the population parameters by reducing the effect of sampling error through the use of data-smoothing procedures that are commonly used in the development of test norms (see McGrew, 1994; McGrew & Wrightson, 1997).

TEST BATTERY: WISC-III   **TEST: Arithmetic**

Description of Test: The examinee is required to mentally solve a series of orally presented arithmetic
problems and respond orally.

Age Range: 6 to 16 years

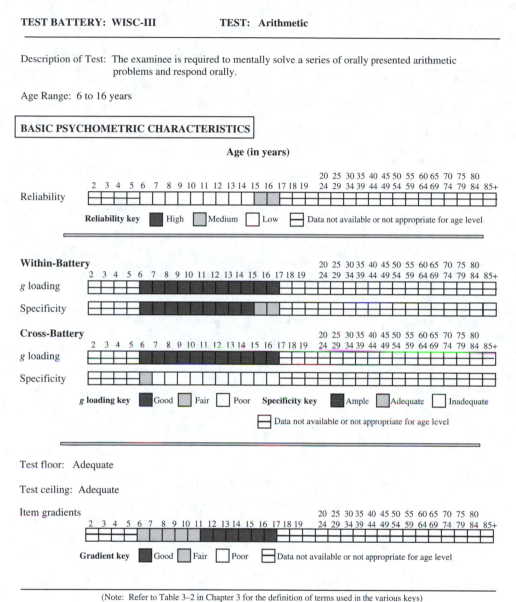

Test floor: Adequate

Test ceiling: Adequate

Item gradients

(Note: Refer to Table 3–2 in Chapter 3 for the definition of terms used in the various keys)

**FIGURE 3–5   ITDR Format Sample: First Page for WISC-III Arithmetic
Subtest.**

TEST BATTERY: WISC- III   **TEST: Arithmetic**

Gf-Gc CLASSIFICATIONS

	Primary	Secondary

Classification Key

Broad (Stratum II)   ■ Quantitative Knowledge (*Gq*)   ☐ Fluid Intelligence (*Gf*)
   ■ Empirical: strong
   ■ Empirical: moderate
   ☐ Empirical: mixed
   ☐ Logical

Narrow (Stratum I)   ■ Math Achievement (A3)   ☐ Quantitative Reasoning (RQ)
   ■ Probable
   ☐ Possible

OTHER VARIABLES THAT INFLUENCE TEST PERFORMANCE

Typical Age of Concept Attainment

Basic Concepts in Directions	3	4	5	> 5	Data not available
(Frequency of occurrence)		Not appropriate for age range covered			

Degree of Cultural Content   ☐ High   ■ Medium   ☐ Low

Additional Factors

Background/Environmental	Individual/Situational
Math difficulties	Attention span
Educational opportunities/experiences	Concentration
	Distractibility
	Visual elaboration

(Note: Refer to Table 3-2 in Chapter 3 for the definition of terms used in the various keys)

FIGURE 3–6   ITDR Format Sample: Second Page for WISC-III Arithmetic Subtest.

Inspection of the top half of the second ITDR page for the Arithmetic test (Figure 3–6) indicates that the *primary* focus of interpretation for this test should be Quantitative Knowledge (*Gq*) and Math Achievement (A3) at the broad and narrow *Gf-Gc* strata, respectively. In addition, the *secondary* narrow classification of Quantitative Reasoning (RQ), which is a narrow ability subsumed by Fluid Intelligence (*Gf*), highlights another source of variance that might explain an individual's performance on the Arithmetic subtest. The *Gq* interpretation should receive primary consideration during interpretation, however, since this is an *empirical/ strong* classification (in contrast to the logical and non–data-based *Gf* classification).

The bottom half of Figure 3–6 indicates that the potential confounding influence of a limited conceptual knowledge base on test performance, as determined through an examination of the incidence of (difficult) basic concepts in test directions, is not relevant for the Arithmetic subtest (since it does not have preschool norms—individuals who are beyond the preschool years and proficient in English are expected to have the conceptual knowledge necessary to understand test directions). As depicted in Figure 3–6, performance on the Arithmetic subtest is *moderately* influenced by cultural factors relative to all cognitive ability tests included in the ITDR. Finally, the Additional Factors section suggests that practitioners should be sensitive to the potential influence of an examinee's inability to attend, concentrate, and/or remain free from distractions during the administration of the Arithmetic subtest. Performance on this subtest may be influenced also by the use of visual elaboration strategies. Finally, during the interpretation of an Arithmetic subtest score, practitioners need to consider whether the examinee has had adequate educational opportunities and experiences and whether he or she has experienced any problems with mathematics.

In conclusion, we believe that the ITDR exemplifies Keith's (1994) admonition, "Intelligence *is* important, intelligence *is* complex" (p. 209, emphasis in the original). The ITDR was designed to facilitate a greater understanding of this important and complex construct by grounding quantitative and qualitative test characteristic information in cognitive psychology and presenting it in an easy-to-read format. In light of the numerous test features that must be considered in the selection and interpretations of intelligence batteries, it was not possible to include in the ITDR all variables that might play a role in this process. For example, variables such as ease of use and scoring, the presence of concrete manipulative test materials for preschoolers, the trade-off between psychometric sophistication and user-friendliness, the use of item response theory procedures in test development, et cetera, were not included for each test (see Harrison, Flanagan, & Genshaft [1997] for information on the technical, administration, content, and interpretive features of the major intelligence batteries). The ITDR includes those quantitative and qualitative test characteristics that were judged to be most important in the selection and interpretation of intelligence batteries. It is hoped that the information presented in the ITDR for all major intelligence batteries will promote more psychometrically and theoretically sound interpretations of cognitive ability tests within the context of relevant noncognitive factors (e.g., educational opportunities, cultural experiences, etc.).

Chapter *4*

Differential Abilities Scales (DAS)

GENERAL INFORMATION

Author: Colin D. Elliott
Publisher: The Psychological Corporation
Publication Date: 1990
Age Range[1]: Age 2-6 to 17-11
Administration Time: 45 to 60 min.
   Core subtests:
      Ages 2-6 to 3-5: 25 min.
      Ages 3-6 to 5-11: 40 min.
      Ages 6-0 to 17-11: 45 min.

   Diagnostic subtests:
      Ages 2-6 to 3-5: 10 min.
      Ages 3-6 to 5-11: 25 min.
      Ages 6-0 to 17-11: 20 min.

Note: The information in this chapter was adapted from Harrison, Flanagan, and Genshaft, 1997. Copyright 1997 Guilford Publishing Co. All rights reserved.

[1] The usual Age Range (or range corresponding to the child's chronological age) is reported for the DAS subtests in the ITDR. Several DAS subtests were normed outside this usual range. These wider or Extended Age Ranges were not reported in the ITDR.

COMPOSITE MEASURE INFORMATION

Broad Measure of Intelligence: General Conceptual Ability (GCA)

Lower-Order Composites:
Upper Preschool (Age 3-6 to 6-11)
1. Verbal Ability
2. Nonverbal Ability

School Age (5-0 to 17-11)
1. Verbal Ability
2. Nonverbal Reasoning Ability
3. Spatial Ability

SCORE INFORMATION

Peer Comparison Scores:
Percentile Rank
Standard Score

Range of Standard Scores for Total Test Composite:
Lower Preschool (Age 2-6 to 3-5): 31 to 169
Upper Preschool (Age 3-6 to 5-11): 25 to 175
School-Age (6-0 to 17-11): 25 to 164

Mean Floor of Subtests at Age 3-0[2]: −2.4

NORMING INFORMATION

Number of Subtests Normed at Each Age:
Total: 17
Age 2-6 to 2-11: 7
Age 3-0 to 3-5: 8
Age 3-6 to 3-11: 9
Age 4-0 to 4-11: 11
Age 5-0 to 6-11: 16
Age 7-0 to 7-11: 15
Age 8-0 to 8-11: 11
Age 9-0 to 17-11: 10

---

[2]Standard deviations below the mean for a raw score of 1.

Conormed with Tests of Achievement:
Yes
1. Basic Number Skills
2. Spelling
3. Word Reading

Person Variables in Norming Plan:
Gender
Race/Ethnicity (confounding race and Hispanic origin)
SES (parent education)
Educational enrollment (ages 2-6 to 5-11)

Community Variables in Norming Plan:
Location
Size

Size of Norming Sample for the Broad Measure of General Intelligence:
Preschool ages 2-6 to 4-11
N = 875
Average number per year: 350
School ages 5-0 to 17-11
N = 2600
Average number per year: 200

Age Blocks in Norm Table[3]:
3 month blocks (Age 2-6 to 7-11)
6 month blocks (Age 8-0 to 17-11)

REVIEWS

Aylward, G. P. (1992). Review of the Differential Ability Scales. In J. J. Kramer & J. C. Conoley (Eds.), *The eleventh mental measurements yearbook* (pp. 281–282). Lincoln, NE: Buros Institute.

Elliott, C. D. (1990). The nature and structure of children's abilities: Evidence from the Differential Ability Scales. *Journal of Psychoeducational Assessment, 8*(3), 376–390.

Elliott, S. N. (1990). The nature and structure of the DAS: Questioning the test's organizing model and use. *Journal of Psychoeducational Assessment, 8*, 406–411.

Flanagan, D., & Alfonso, V. (1995). A critical review of the technical characteristics of new and recently revised intelligence tests for preschool children. *Journal of Pyschoeducational Assessment, 13* (1) 66–90.

Platt, L. O., Kamphaus, R. W., Keltgen, J., & Gilliland, F. (1991). An overview and review of the Differential Ability Scales: Initial and current research findings. *Journal of School Psychology, 29* (3), 271–277.

Reinehr, R. C. (1992). Review of the Differential Ability Scales. In J. J. Kramer & J. C. Conoley (Eds.), *The eleventh mental measurements yearbook* (pp. 282–283). Lincoln, NE: Buros Institute.

[3] In most cases age blocks represent linear interpolations.

TEST BATTERY: DAS   **TEST: Block Building**

Description of Test: The examinee is required to copy two- or three-dimensional designs with wooden blocks.

Age range: 2 to 3 years

BASIC PSYCHOMETRIC CHARACTERISTICS

Age (in years)

Reliability

Reliability key ■ High   ▧ Medium   ☐ Low   ⊟ Data not available or not appropriate for age level

---

Within-Battery

g loading

Specificity

Cross-Battery

g loading

Specificity

g loading key ■ Good   ▧ Fair   ☐ Poor   **Specificity key** ■ Ample   ▧ Adequate   ☐ Inadequate

⊟ Data not available or not appropriate for age level

Test floor: *Inadequate* from ages 2:6 to 3:2

Test ceiling: Adequate

Item gradients

Gradient key ■ Good   ▧ Fair   ☐ Poor   ⊟ Data not available or not appropriate for age level

---

(Note: Refer to Table 3-2 in Chapter 3 for the definition of terms used in the various keys)

TEST BATTERY: DAS   **TEST: Block Building**

Gf-Gc **CLASSIFICATIONS**

	Primary	Secondary

Broad (Stratum II)   ☐ Visual Processing (*Gv*)
- ■ Empirical: strong
- ■ Empirical: moderate
- ☐ Empirical: mixed
- ☐ Logical

Narrow (Stratum I)   ■ Visualization (VZ)
- ■ Probable
- ☐ Possible

OTHER VARIABLES THAT INFLUENCE TEST PERFORMANCE

Typical Age of Concept Attainment

	3	4	5	> 5	Data not available
Basic Concepts in Directions (Frequency of occurrence)	big (2)	one (1) same (1)	like (12) another (12)	right (1)	

Degree of Cultural Content   ☐ High   ☐ Medium   ■ Low

Additional Factors

Background/Environmental	Individual/Situational
Environmental stimulation	Visual-motor coordination

(Note: Refer to Table 3-2 in Chapter 3 for the definition of terms used in the various keys)

TEST BATTERY: DAS   **TEST: Verbal Comprehension**

Description of Test: The examinee is required to manipulate objects or identify objects in pictures in response
to oral instructions given by the examiner.

Age range: 2 to 5 years[1]

BASIC PSYCHOMETRIC CHARACTERISTICS

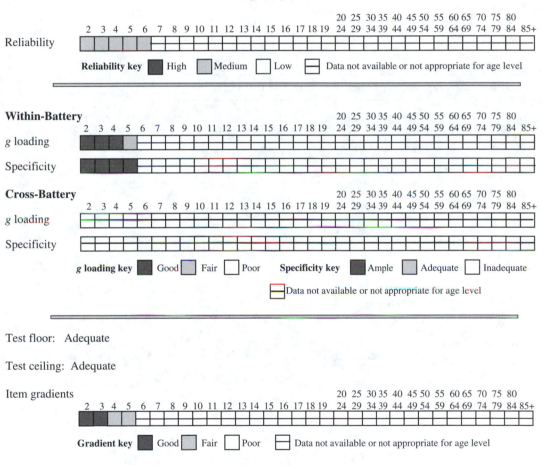

Test floor: Adequate

Test ceiling: Adequate

Item gradients

(Note: Refer to Table 3-2 in Chapter 3 for the definition of terms used in the various keys)

[1] When available, basic psychomatric characteristic information is presented for age levels which are beyond the recommended
"age ranges" reported for DAS subtests.

TEST BATTERY: DAS   TEST: Verbal Comprehension

Gf-Gc CLASSIFICATIONS

	Primary	Secondary

Broad (Stratum II)
  ■ Empirical: strong
  ■ Empirical: moderate
  □ Empirical: mixed
  □ Logical

☐ Crystallized Intelligence (*Gc*)

Narrow (Stratum I)
  ■ Probable
  □ Possible

■ Language Development (LD)
■ Listening Ability (LS)

OTHER VARIABLES THAT INFLUENCE TEST PERFORMANCE

Typical Age of Concept Attainment

	3	4	5	> 5	Data not available
Basic Concepts in Directions (Frequency of occurrence)		Conceptual knowledge is measured by this test.			

Degree of Cultural Content   ■ High   ☐ Medium   ☐ Low

Additional Factors

Background/Environmental	Individual/Situational
Language stimulation	Attention span
Environmental stimulation	Concentration
Educational opportunities/experiences	Distractibility
	Reflectivity/impulsivity

(Note: Refer to Table 3-2 in Chapter 3 for the definition of terms used in the various keys)

TEST BATTERY: DAS   **TEST: Picture Similarities**

Description of Test: The examinee is required to match a target picture to one of four stimulus pictures.

Age range: 2 to 5 years

BASIC PSYCHOMETRIC CHARACTERISTICS

Age (in years)

Reliability [1]

Reliability key: ■ High   ▧ Medium   □ Low   ⊟ Data not available or not appropriate for age level

---

Within-Battery

g loading

Specificity

Cross-Battery

g loading

Specificity

g loading key: ■ Good   ▧ Fair   □ Poor   Specificity key: ■ Ample   ▧ Adequate   □ Inadequate

⊟ Data not available or not appropriate for age level

Test floor: *Inadequate* from ages 2:6 to 2:11

Test ceiling: Adequate

Item gradients

Gradient key: ■ Good   ▧ Fair   □ Poor   ⊟ Data not available or not appropriate for age level

---

(Note: Refer to Table 3-2 in Chapter 3 for the definition of terms used in the various keys)

[1] Reliability information is also presented for ages 6 and 7, which are outside of the tests usual age range.

TEST BATTERY: DAS   **TEST: Picture Similarities**

Gf-Gc CLASSIFICATIONS

	Primary	Secondary

Broad (Stratum II)
- ■ Empirical: strong
- ■ Empirical: moderate
- ☐ Empirical: mixed
- ☐ Logical

☐ Fluid Intelligence *(Gf)*

Narrow (Stratum I)
- ■ Probable
- ☐ Possible

■ Induction (I)

OTHER VARIABLES THAT INFLUENCE TEST PERFORMANCE

Typical Age of Concept Attainment

	3	4	5	> 5	Data not available
Basic Concepts in Directions (Frequency of occurrence)	on (1)	under (2) both (4)	like (2)		four (1) row (1)

Degree of Cultural Content   ☐ High   ■ Medium   ☐ Low

Additional Factors

Background/Environmental	Individual/Situational
Language stimulation	Reflectivity/impulsivity
Environmental stimulation	Verbal elaboration
Educational opportunities/experiences	Planning
Alertness to the environment	

(Note: Refer to Table 3-2 in Chapter 3 for the definition of terms used in the various keys)

TEST BATTERY: DAS   **TEST: Naming Vocabulary**

Description of Test: The examinee is required to name objects or pictures of objects.

Age range: 2 to 5 years

| BASIC PSYCHOMETRIC CHARACTERISTICS |

Age (in years)

Reliability

Reliability key: High   Medium   Low   Data not available or not appropriate for age level

Within-Battery

g loading

Specificity

Cross-Battery

g loading

Specificity

g loading key: Good   Fair   Poor   **Specificity key** Ample   Adequate   Inadequate

Data not available or not appropriate for age level

Test floor: *Inadequate* from ages 2:6 to 2:8

Test ceiling: Adequate

Item gradients

Gradient key Good   Fair   Poor   Data not available or not appropriate for age level

(Note: Refer to Table 3-2 in Chapter 3 for the definition of terms used in the various (eys)

TEST BATTERY: DAS   **TEST: Naming Vocabulary**

Gf-Gc CLASSIFICATIONS

	Primary	Secondary

Broad (Stratum II)
- ■ Empirical: strong
- ■ Empirical: moderate
- ☐ Empirical: mixed
- ☐ Logical

☐ Crystallized Intelligence *(Gc)*

Narrow (Stratum I)
- ■ Probable
- ☐ Possible

■ Language Development (LD)
■ Lexical Knowledge (VL)

OTHER VARIABLES THAT INFLUENCE TEST PERFORMANCE

Typical Age of Concept Attainment

	3	4	5	> 5	Data not available
Basic Concepts in Directions (Frequency of occurrence) NA = data not available		Conceptual knowledge is measured by this test			

Degree of Cultural Content   ■ High   ☐ Medium   ☐ Low

Additional Factors

Background/Environmental	Individual/Situational
Language stimulation Environmental stimulation Educational opportunities/experiences Alertness to the environment Intellectual curiosity	

(Note: Refer to Table 3-2 in Chapter 3 for the definition of terms used in the various keys)

TEST BATTERY: DAS   **TEST: Recall of Objects**

Description of Test: The examinee is required to view a picture card with 20 objects and recall the names of these objects after the card is removed.

Age range: 4 to 17 years

BASIC PSYCHOMETRIC CHARACTERISTICS

Age (in years)

Reliability

Reliability key ■ High   ▢ Medium   ▢ Low   ⊟ Data not available or not appropriate for age level

Within-Battery

g loading

Specificity

Cross-Battery

g loading

Specificity

g **loading key** ■ Good   ▢ Fair   ▢ Poor   **Specificity key** ■ Ample   ▢ Adequate   ▢ Inadequate

⊟ Data not available or not appropriate for age level

Test floor: *Inadequate* from ages 4:0 to 4:2

Test ceiling: Adequate

Item gradients

Gradient key ■ Good   ▢ Fair   ▢ Poor   ⊟ Data not available or not appropriate for age level

---

(Note: Refer to Table 3-2 in Chapter 3 for the definition of terms used in the various keys)

TEST BATTERY: DAS   **TEST: Recall of Objects**

Gf-Gc CLASSIFICATIONS

	Primary	Secondary

Broad (Stratum II)
■ Empirical: strong
■ Empirical: moderate
☐ Empirical: mixed
☐ Logical

☐ Long-term Storage and Retrieval *(Glr)*
☐ Visual Processing *(Gv)*

Narrow (Stratum I)
■ Probable
☐ Possible

■ Free Recall Memory (M6)
☐ Visual Memory (MV)

OTHER VARIABLES THAT INFLUENCE TEST PERFORMANCE

	Typical Age of Concept Attainment				
	3	4	5	> 5	Data not available
Basic Concepts in Directions (Frequency of occurrence)			same (6) all (2)		some (4) more (4) as many (2) order (1) before (2)

Degree of Cultural Content   ☐ High   ■ Medium   ☐ Low

Additional Factors

Background/Environmental	**Individual/Situational**
Environmental stimulation	Attention span Concentration Distractibility Verbal rehearsal Verbal elaboration

(Note: Refer to Table 3-2 in Chapter 3 for the definition of terms used in the various keys)

TEST BATTERY: DAS   **TEST: Pattern Construction**

Description of Test: The examinee is required to use flat squares or blocks to construct a series of designs.

Age range: 3 to 17 years

BASIC PSYCHOMETRIC CHARACTERISTICS

Age (in years)

Reliability

Reliability key ■ High ▨ Medium □ Low ⊟ Data not available or not appropriate for age level

Within-Battery

g loading

Specificity

Cross-Battery

g loading

Specificity

g **loading key** ■ Good ▨ Fair □ Poor   **Specificity key** ■ Ample ▨ Adequate □ Inadequate

⊟ Data not available or not appropriate for age level

Test floor: *Inadequate* from ages 3:6 to 3:11

Test ceiling: *Inadequate* from ages 11:6 to 17:11

Item gradients

Gradient key ■ Good ▨ Fair □ Poor ⊟ Data not available or not appropriate for age level

(Note: Refer to Table 3-2 in Chapter 3 for the definition of terms used in the various keys)

TEST BATTERY: DAS   **TEST: Pattern Construction**

| *Gf-Gc* CLASSIFICATIONS |

	Primary	Secondary
Broad (Stratum II)	☐ Visual Processing (*Gv*)	
■ Empirical: strong		
■ Empirical: moderate		
☐ Empirical: mixed		
☐ Logical		
Narrow (Stratum I)	■ Spatial Relations (SR)	
■ Probable	☐ Visualization (VZ)	
☐ Possible		

| **OTHER VARIABLES THAT INFLUENCE TEST PERFORMANCE** |

	Typical Age of Concept Attainment				
	3	**4**	**5**	**> 5**	**Data not available**
Basic Concepts in Directions (Frequency of occurrence)	finished (3) in (1)	black (1 yellow (1) tops (2) together (7) both (1)	different (1) like (6) same (3) side(s) (6) pieces (6) all (3)	right (3)	straight (1)

Degree of Cultural Content   ☐ High   ☐ Medium   ■ Low

Additional Factors		
	Background/Environmental	**Individual/Situational**
	Vision difficulties Environmental stimulation	Visual-motor coordination Reflectivity/impulsivity Field dependence/independence Flexibility/inflexibility Planning Ability to perform under time pressure

(Note: Refer to Table 3-2 in Chapter 3 for the definition of terms used in the various keys)

TEST BATTERY: DAS   **TEST: Early Number Concepts**

Description of Test: The examinee is required to use colored chips or pictures to demonstrate his or her understanding of numerical concepts such as counting, number recognition, size, and basic arithmetic.

Age range: 3 to 5 years

BASIC PSYCHOMETRIC CHARACTERISTICS

Age (in years)

Reliability

Reliability key ■ High ▨ Medium □ Low ⊟ Data not available or not appropriate for age level

---

Within-Battery

g loading

Specificity

Cross-Battery

g loading

Specificity

g **loading key** ■ Good ▨ Fair □ Poor   **Specificity key** ■ Ample ▨ Adequate □ Inadequate

⊟ Data not available or not appropriate for age level

Test floor: *Inadequate* from age 3:6 to 3:11

Test ceiling: Adequate

Item gradients

Gradient key ■ Good ▨ Fair □ Poor   ⊟ Data not available or not appropriate for age level

---

(Note: Refer to Table 3-2 in Chapter 3 for the definition of terms used in the various keys)

TEST BATTERY: DAS   **TEST: Early Number Concepts**

Gf-Gc CLASSIFICATIONS

	Primary	Secondary

Broad (Stratum II)
■ Empirical: strong
■ Empirical: moderate
□ Empirical: mixed
□ Logical

☐ Quantitative Knowledge *(Gq)*

Narrow (Stratum I)
■ Probable
□ Possible

■ Math Achievement (A3)
■ Mathematical Knowledge (KM)

OTHER VARIABLES THAT INFLUENCE TEST PERFORMANCE

	Typical Age of Concept Attainment				
	3	4	5	> 5	Data not available
Basic Concepts in Directions (Frequency of occurrence)		Conceptual knowledge is measured by this test.			

Degree of Cultural Content   □ High   ■ Medium   □ Low

Additional Factors

Background/Environmental	Individual/Situational
Math difficulties	
Language stimulation	
Environmental stimulation	
Educational opportunities/experiences	

(Note: Refer to Table 3-2 in Chapter 3 for the definition of terms used in the various keys)

TEST BATTERY: DAS   **TEST: Copying**

Description of Test: The examinee is required to copy line drawings, letter shapes, or geometric figures.

Age range: 3 to 5 years

BASIC PSYCHOMETRIC CHARACTERISTICS

Age (in years)

Reliability

Reliability key ■ High   ▨ Medium   □ Low   ⊟ Data not available or not appropriate for age level

---

Within-Battery

g loading

Specificity

Cross-Battery

g loading

Specificity

g **loading key** ■ Good ▨ Fair □ Poor   **Specificity key** ■ Ample ▨ Adequate □ Inadequate

⊟ Data not available or not appropriate for age level

Test floor: *Inadequate* from ages 3:6 to 4:2

Test ceiling: Adequate

Item gradients

Gradient key ■ Good ▨ Fair □ Poor   ⊟ Data not available or not appropriate for age level

---

(Note: Refer to Table 3-2 in Chapter 3 for the definition of terms used in the various keys)

TEST BATTERY: DAS   **TEST: Copying**

Gf-Gc **CLASSIFICATIONS**

	Primary	**Secondary**

Broad (Stratum II)
- ■ Empirical: strong
- ■ Empirical: moderate
- ■ Empirical: mixed
- ☐ Logical

Secondary:
- ☐ Visual Processing (Gv)
- ☐ Psychomotor

Narrow (Stratum I)
- ■ Probable
- ☐ Possible

Secondary:
- ☐ Visualization (VZ)
- ☐ Finger Dexterity (P2)

OTHER VARIABLES THAT INFLUENCE TEST PERFORMANCE

Typical Age of Concept Attainment

Basic Concepts in Directions	3	4	5	> 5	Data not available
			same (2)		

(Frequency of occurrence)

Degree of Cultural Content   ☐ High   ☐ Medium   ■ Low

Additional Factors

Background/Environmental	Individual/Situational
Vision difficulties	Visual-motor coordination
Environmental stimulation	

(Note: Refer to Table 3-2 in Chapter 3 for the definition of terms used in the various keys)

TEST BATTERY: DAS   **TEST: Matching Letter-Like Forms**

Description of Test: The examinee is required to find an identical match of a target letter-like shape.

Age range: 4 to 5 years

BASIC PSYCHOMETRIC CHARACTERISTICS

Age (in years)

Reliability

Reliability key ■ High ▨ Medium □ Low ⊟ Data not available or not appropriate for age level

Within-Battery

g loading

Specificity

Cross-Battery

g loading

Specificity

g **loading key** ■ Good ▨ Fair □ Poor   **Specificity key** ■ Ample ▨ Adequate □ Inadequate

⊟ Data not available or not appropriate for age level

Test floor: *Inadequate* from ages 4:6 to 5:5

Test ceiling: *Inadequate* from ages 5:9 to 5:11

Item gradients

Gradient key ■ Good ▨ Fair □ Poor   ⊟ Data not available or not appropriate for age level

(Note: Refer to Table 3-2 in Chapter 3 for the definition of terms used in the various keys)

TEST BATTERY: DAS   **TEST: Matching Letter-Like Forms**

Gf-Gc **CLASSIFICATIONS**

	Primary	**Secondary**

Broad (Stratum II)   ☐ Visual Processing *(Gv)*
  ■ Empirical: strong
  ■ Empirical: moderate
  ☐ Empirical: mixed
  ☐ Logical

Narrow (Stratum I)   ■ Visualization (VZ)
  ■ Probable
  ☐ Possible

OTHER VARIABLES THAT INFLUENCE TEST PERFORMANCE

Typical Age of Concept Attainment

	3	4	5	> 5	Data not available
Basic Concepts in Directions (Frequency of occurrence)			down (4)		

Degree of Cultural Content   ☐ High   ☐ Medium   ■ Low

Additional Factors

Background/Environmental	**Individual/Situational**
Vision difficulties	Vision difficulties
Reading difficulties	Reflectivity/impulsivity
Writing difficulties	
Educational opportunities/experiences	

(Note: Refer to Table 3-2 in Chapter 3 for the definition of terms used in the various keys)

TEST BATTERY: DAS	TEST: Recall of Digits

Description of Test: The examinee is required to repeat a series of orally presented digits.

Age range: 3 to 17 years

BASIC PSYCHOMETRIC CHARACTERISTICS

Age (in years)

Reliability

Reliability key ▮ High   ▯ Medium   ☐ Low   ⊟ Data not available or not appropriate for age level

---

Within-Battery

g loading

Specificity

Cross-Battery

g loading

Specificity

***g* loading key** ▮ Good   ▯ Fair   ☐ Poor   **Specificity key** ▮ Ample   ▯ Adequate   ☐ Inadequate

⊟ Data not available or not appropriate for age level

Test floor: *Inadequate* from ages 3:0 to 3:5

Test ceiling: Adequate

Item gradients

Gradient key ▮ Good   ▯ Fair   ☐ Poor   ⊟ Data not available or not appropriate for age level

---

(Note: Refer to Table 3-2 in Chapter 3 for the definition of terms used in the various keys)

TEST BATTERY: DAS   **TEST: Recall of Digits**

Gf-Gc CLASSIFICATIONS

	Primary	**Secondary**

Broad (Stratum II)
■ Empirical: strong
■ Empirical: moderate
□ Empirical: mixed
□ Logical

☐ Short-term Memory (*Gsm*)

Narrow (Stratum I)
■ Probable
□ Possible

■ Memory Span (MS)

OTHER VARIABLES THAT INFLUENCE TEST PERFORMANCE

	Typical Age of Concept Attainment				**Data not available**
	3	**4**	**5**	**> 5**	
Basic Concepts in Directions (Frequency of occurrence)					after (>15)

Degree of Cultural Content   ☐ High   ☐ Medium   ■ Low

Additional Factors	**Background/Environmental**	**Individual/Situational**
	Hearing difficulties	Attention span
		Concentration
		Distractibility
		Verbal rehearsal
		Visual elaboration
		Organization

(Note: Refer to Table 3-2 in Chapter 3 for the definition of terms used in the various keys)

TEST BATTERY: DAS   **TEST: Recognition of Pictures**

Description of Test: The examinee is required to view pictures of objects and identify those objects in a second picture that has a larger array of objects.

Age range: 3 to 7 years

BASIC PSYCHOMETRIC CHARACTERISTICS

Age (in years)

Reliability

Reliability key   ■ High   ▨ Medium   □ Low   ▭ Data not available or not appropriate for age level

Within-Battery

g loading

Specificity

Cross-Battery

g loading

Specificity

g **loading key**   ■ Good   ▨ Fair   □ Poor   **Specificity key**   ■ Ample   ▨ Adequate   □ Inadequate

▭ Data not available or not appropriate for age level

Test floor: *Inadequate* from ages 3:0 to 3:11

Test ceiling: Adequate

Item gradients

Gradient key   ■ Good   ▨ Fair   □ Poor   ▭ Data not available or not appropriate for age level

(Note: Refer to Table 3-2 in Chapter 3 for the definition of terms used in the various keys)

TEST BATTERY: DAS   **TEST: Recognition of Pictures**

Gf-Gc **CLASSIFICATIONS**

	Primary	Secondary

Broad (Stratum II)   ☐ Visual Processing (*Gv*)
- ■ Empirical: strong
- ■ Empirical: moderate
- ☐ Empirical: mixed
- ☐ Logical

Narrow (Stratum I)   ■ Visual Memory (MV)
- ■ Probable
- ☐ Possible

OTHER VARIABLES THAT INFLUENCE TEST PERFORMANCE

Typical Age of Concept Attainment

	3	4	5	> 5	Data not available
Basic Concepts in Directions (Frequency of occurrence)	on (1)				

Degree of Cultural Content   ☐ High   ■ Medium   ☐ Low

Additional Factors

Background/Environmental	Individual/Situational
	Concentration
	Reflectivity/impulsivity
	Verbal elaboration

(Note: Refer to Table 3-2 in Chapter 3 for the definition of terms used in the various keys)

TEST BATTERY: DAS   **TEST: Recall of Designs**

Description of Test: The examinee is required to reproduce abstract line drawings from memory.

Age range: 6 to 17 years

BASIC PSYCHOMETRIC CHARACTERISTICS

Age (in years)

| | 20 25 30 35 40 45 50 55 60 65 70 75 80 |
| | 2 3 4 5 6 7 8 9 10 11 12 13 14 15 16 17 18 19 24 29 34 39 44 49 54 59 64 69 74 79 84 85+ |

Reliability

Reliability key ■ High   ▨ Medium   □ Low   ⊟ Data not available or not appropriate for age level

Within-Battery

20 25 30 35 40 45 50 55 60 65 70 75 80
2 3 4 5 6 7 8 9 10 11 12 13 14 15 16 17 18 19 24 29 34 39 44 49 54 59 64 69 74 79 84 85+

g loading

Specificity

Cross-Battery

20 25 30 35 40 45 50 55 60 65 70 75 80
2 3 4 5 6 7 8 9 10 11 12 13 14 15 16 17 18 19 24 29 34 39 44 49 54 59 64 69 74 79 84 85+

g loading

Specificity

g loading key   ■ Good   ▨ Fair   □ Poor   **Specificity key**   ■ Ample   ▨ Adequate   □ Inadequate

⊟ Data not available or not appropriate for age level

Test floor: Adequate

Test ceiling: Adequate

Item gradients

20 25 30 35 40 45 50 55 60 65 70 75 80
2 3 4 5 6 7 8 9 10 11 12 13 14 15 16 17 18 19 24 29 34 39 44 49 54 59 64 69 74 79 84 85+

Gradient key   ■ Good   ▨ Fair   □ Poor   ⊟ Data not available or not appropriate for age level

(Note: Refer to Table 3-2   in Chapter 3 for the definition of terms used in the various keys)

TEST BATTERY: DAS   **TEST: Recall of Designs**

Gf-Gc CLASSIFICATIONS

	Primary	**Secondary**

Broad (Stratum II)   ■ Visual Processing (*Gv*)
- ■ Empirical: strong
- ■ Empirical: moderate
- ☐ Empirical: mixed
- ☐ Logical

Narrow (Stratum I)   ■ Visual Memory (MV)
- ■ Probable
- ☐ Possible

OTHER VARIABLES THAT INFLUENCE TEST PERFORMANCE

	Typical Age of Concept Attainment				**Data not Available**
	3	**4**	**5**	**> 5**	
Basic Concepts in Directions *(Frequency of occurrence)*		Not appropriate for age range covered			

Degree of Cultural Content   ☐ High   ☐ Medium   ■ Low

Additional Factors

Background/Environmental	**Individual/Situational**
Vision difficulties	Concentration
	Visual-motor coordination
	Visual acuity

(Note: Refer to Table 3-2 in Chapter 3 for the definition of terms used in the various keys)

TEST BATTERY: DAS   **TEST: Word Definitions**

Description of Test: The examinee is required to define words.

Age range: 6 to 17 years

BASIC PSYCHOMETRIC CHARACTERISTICS

Age (in years)

Reliability

Reliability key: ■ High ▨ Medium □ Low ⊟ Data not available or not appropriate for age level

Within-Battery

g loading

Specificity

Cross-Battery

g loading

Specificity

g loading key: ■ Good ▨ Fair □ Poor   **Specificity key** ■ Ample ▨ Adequate □ Inadequate

⊟ Data not available or not appropriate for age level

Test floor: *Inadequate* from ages 6:0 to 6:11

Test ceiling: Adequate

Item gradients

Gradient key: ■ Good ▨ Fair □ Poor ⊟ Data not available or not appropriate for age level

(Note: Refer to Table 3-2 in Chapter 3 for the definition of terms used in the various keys)

TEST BATTERY: DAS   **TEST: Word Definitions**

| *Gf-Gc* CLASSIFICATIONS |

	Primary	**Secondary**

Broad (Stratum II)   ■ Crystallized Intelligence (*Gc*)
   ■ Empirical: strong
   ■ Empirical: moderate
   ☐ Empirical: mixed
   ☐ Logical

Narrow (Stratum I)   ■ Lexical Knowledge (VL)
   ■ Probable   ■ Language Development (LD)
   ☐ Possible

| OTHER VARIABLES THAT INFLUENCE TEST PERFORMANCE |

	Typical Age of Concept Attainment				
	3	**4**	**5**	**> 5**	**Data not available**
Basic Concepts in Directions (Frequency of occurrence)		Not appropriate for age range covered			

Degree of Cultural Content   ■ High   ☐ Medium   ☐ Low

Additional Factors

Background/Environmental	**Individual/Situational**
Language stimulation	
Environmental stimulation	
Educational opportunities/experiences	
Intellectual curiosity	

(Note: Refer to Table 3-2 in Chapter 3 for the definition of terms used in the various keys)

TEST BATTERY: DAS **TEST: Matrices**

Description of Test: The examinee is required to complete a matrix of abstract designs by choosing the correct design from among four or six designs.

Age range: 6 to 17 years

BASIC PSYCHOMETRIC CHARACTERISTICS

Age (in years)

Reliability

Reliability key ■ High ▨ Medium ☐ Low ⊟ Data not available or not appropriate for age level

---

Within-Battery

g loading

Specificity

Cross-Battery

g loading

Specificity

g loading key ■ Good ▨ Fair ☐ Poor **Specificity key** ■ Ample ▨ Adequate ☐ Inadequate

⊟ Data not available or not appropriate for age level

Test floor: Adequate

Test ceiling: Adequate

Item gradients

Gradient key ■ Good ▨ Fair ☐ Poor ⊟ Data not available or not appropriate for age level

---

(Note: Refer to Table 3-2 in Chapter 3 for the definition of terms used in the various keys)

TEST BATTERY: DAS   **TEST: Matrices**

Gf-Gc CLASSIFICATIONS

	Primary	Secondary

Broad (Stratum II)   ■ Fluid Intelligence (*Gf*)
  ■ Empirical: strong
  ■ Empirical: moderate
  □ Empirical: mixed
  □ Logical

Narrow (Stratum I)   ■ Induction (I)
  ■ Probable
  □ Possible

OTHER VARIABLES THAT INFLUENCE TEST PERFORMANCE

	Typical Age of Concept Attainment				
	3	**4**	**5**	**> 5**	**Data not available**
Basic Concepts in Directions (Frequency of occurrence)		Not appropriate for age range covered			

Degree of Cultural Content   □ High   □ Medium   ■ Low

Additional Factors

Background/Environmental	**Individual/Situational**
Vision difficulties	Reflectivity/impulsivity
	Field dependent/independent
	Flexibility/inflexibility
	Planning

(Note: Refer to Table 3-2 in Chapter 3 for the definition of terms used in the various keys)

TEST BATTERY: DAS   **TEST: Similarities**

Description of Test: The examinee is required to say how three words are similar to one another.

Age range: 6 to 17 years

BASIC PSYCHOMETRIC CHARACTERISTICS

Age (in years)

Reliability

Reliability key: ■ High   ▨ Medium   □ Low   ⊟ Data not available or not appropriate for age level

---

Within-Battery

g loading

Specificity

Cross-Battery

g loading

Specificity

g loading key: ■ Good   ▨ Fair   □ Poor   Specificity key: ■ Ample   ▨ Adequate   □ Inadequate

⊟ Data not available or not appropriate for age level

Test floor: *Inadequate* from ages 6:0 to 6:8

Test ceiling: Adequate

Item gradients

Gradient key: ■ Good   ▨ Fair   □ Poor   ⊟ Data not available or not appropriate for age level

---

(Note: Refer to Table 3-2 in Chapter 3 for the definition of terms used in the various keys)

TEST BATTERY: DAS   **TEST: Similarities**

Gf-Gc **CLASSIFICATIONS**

	Primary	**Secondary**

Broad (Stratum II)
- ■ Empirical: strong
- ■ Empirical: moderate
- □ Empirical: mixed
- □ Logical

■ Crystallized Intelligence (*Gc*)

Narrow (Stratum I)
- ■ Probable
- □ Possible

■ Language Development (LD)
□ Lexical Knowledge (VL)

OTHER VARIABLES THAT INFLUENCE TEST PERFORMANCE

	Typical Age of Concept Attainment				
	3	**4**	**5**	**> 5**	**Data not available**
Basic Concepts in Directions (Frequency of occurrence)		Not appropriate for age range covered			

Degree of Cultural Content   ■ High   □ Medium   □ Low

Additional Factors

Background/Environmental	**Individual/Situational**
Language stimulation	
Environmental stimulation	
Educational opportunities/experiences	

(Note: Refer to Table 3-2 in Chapter 3 for the definition of terms used in the various keys)

TEST BATTERY: DAS   **TEST:** Sequential and Quantitative Reasoning

Description of Test: The examinee is required to complete a series/sequence of abstract designs by identifying
the missing designs or provide the missing number to match a pattern of numbers.

Age range: 6 to 17 years

BASIC PSYCHOMETRIC CHARACTERISTICS

Age (in years)

Reliability

Reliability key   High   Medium   Low   Data not available or not appropriate for age level

Within-Battery

g loading

Specificity

Cross-Battery

g loading

Specificity

***g* loading key**   Good   Fair   Poor   **Specificity key**   Ample   Adequate   Inadequate

Data not available or not appropriate for age level

Test floor: *Inadequate* from ages 6:0 to 6:8

Test ceiling: *Inadequate* from ages 17:0 to 17:11

Item gradients

Gradient key   Good   Fair   Poor   Data not available or not appropriate for age level

(Note: Refer to Table 3-2 in Chapter 3 for the definition of terms used in the various keys)

TEST BATTERY: DAS   **TEST: Sequential and Quantitative Reasoning**

Gf-Gc CLASSIFICATIONS

	Primary	**Secondary**

Broad (Stratum II)
- ■ Empirical: strong
- ■ Empirical: moderate
- ☐ Empirical: mixed
- ☐ Logical

■ Fluid Intelligence (*Gf*)

Narrow (Stratum I)
- ■ Probable
- ☐ Possible

■ Induction (I)
■ Quantitative Reasoning (RQ)

OTHER VARIABLES THAT INFLUENCE TEST PERFORMANCE

	Typical Age of Concept Attainment				
	3	**4**	**5**	**> 5**	**Data not available**
Basic Concepts in Directions (Frequency of occurrence)		Not appropriate for age range covered			

Degree of Cultural Content   ☐ High   ☐ Medium   ■ Low

Additional Factors

Background/Environmental	**Individual/Situational**
Math difficulties	Concentration
Educational opportunities/experiences	Reflectivity/impulsivity
	Flexibility/inflexibility
	Planning

(Note: Refer to Table 3-2 in Chapter 3 for the definition of terms used in the various keys)

TEST BATTERY: DAS   **TEST: Speed of Information Processing**

Description of Test: The examinee is required to mark in each row the largest number or the circle with the most boxes as quickly as possible.

Age range: 6 to 17 years

BASIC PSYCHOMETRIC CHARACTERISTICS

Age (in years)

Reliability

Reliability key ■ High ▨ Medium □ Low ⊟ Data not available or not appropriate for age level

---

Within-Battery

g loading

Specificity

Cross-Battery

g loading

Specificity

g loading key ■ Good ▨ Fair □ Poor   **Specificity key** ■ Ample ▨ Adequate □ Inadequate

⊟ Data not available or not appropriate for age level

Test floor: *Inadequate* from ages 6:0 to 6:8

Test ceiling: Adequate

Item gradients

Gradient key ■ Good ▨ Fair □ Poor ⊟ Data not available or not appropriate for age level

---

(Note: Refer to Table 3-2 in Chapter 3 for the definition of terms used in the various keys)

TEST BATTERY: DAS   **TEST: Speed of Information Processing**

Gf-Gc **CLASSIFICATIONS**

	Primary	Secondary

Broad (Stratum II)
- ■ Empirical: strong
- ■ Empirical: moderate
- ▨ Empirical: mixed
- □ Logical

☐ Processing Speed (*Gs*)

Narrow (Stratum I)
- ■ Probable
- □ Possible

■ Mental Comparison Speed (R7)
☐ Rate-of-test-taking (R9)

OTHER VARIABLES THAT INFLUENCE TEST PERFORMANCE

Typical Age of Concept Attainment

	3	4	5	> 5	Data not available
Basic Concepts in Directions (Frequency of occurrence)		Not appropriate for age range covered			

Degree of Cultural Content   ☐ High   ☐ Medium   ■ Low

Additional Factors

Background/Environmental	Individual/Situational
Vision difficulties	Attention span
	Concentration
	Distractibility
	Visual-motor coordination
	Visual acuity
	Reflectivity/impulsivity
	Ability to perform under time pressure

(Note: Refer to Table 3-2 in Chapter 3 for the definition of terms used in the various keys

C h a p t e r 5

Kaufman Assessment Battery for Children (K-ABC)

General Information

> **Authors:** Alan S. Kaufman and Nadeen L. Kaufman
> **Publisher:** American Guidance Service
> **Publication Date:** 1983
> **Age Range:** 2-6 to 12-6
> **Administration Time:** 60 min.

Composite Measure Information

> **Broad Measure of Intelligence:**
> Mental Processing Composite (MPC)
>
> **Lower-Order Composites:**
> Sequential Processing
> Simultaneous Processing
> Verbal Intelligence (Achievement battery)[1]

Note: The above information was adapted from Harrison, Flanagan, and Genshaft (1997). Copyright 1997 Guilford Publishing Co. All rights reserved.

The descriptions of the subtests of the K-ABC were adapted from Kamphaus (1993), *Clinical Assessment of Children's Intelligence* (Needham Heights, MA: Allyn and Bacon).

[1] See Kamphaus, R. W., & Reynolds, C. R. (1987), *Clinical and research applications of the K-ABC.* (Circle Pines, MN: American Guidance Service).

Score Information

Peer Comparison Scores:
Percentile Rank
Standard Score

Range of Standard Scores for Total Test Composite: 40 to 160

Mean Floor of Subtests at Age 3-0: [2]-1.1

Norming Information

Number of Subtests Normed at Each Age:
Total: 10
Age 2-6 to 3: 5
Age 4: 7
Age 5: 7
Age 6 to 12: 8

Conormed with Tests of Achievement:
Yes
Reading
Mathematics
Knowledge (Faces & Places)

Person Variables in Norming Plan:
Gender
Race/Ethnicity (confounding race and Hispanic origin)
Family SES (parent education)

Community Variables in Norming Plan:
Location
Size

Size of Norming Sample for the Broad Measure of General Intelligence:
N = 2000
Average number per year: 222

Age Blocks in Norm Table: [3]
2-month blocks (Age 2-6 to 5-11)
3-month blocks (Age 6-0 to 12-6)

---

[2]Standard deviations below the mean for a raw score of 1.

[3]In most cases, age blocks represent linear interpolations.

Reviews

Anastasi, A. (1985). Review of Kaufman Assessment Battery for Children. In J. V. Mitchell, Jr. (Ed.), *The ninth mental measurements yearbook* (vol. 1) (pp. 769–771). Lincoln, NE: Buros Institute.

Batten Page, E. (1985). Review of Kaufman Assessment Battery for Children. In J. V. Mitchell, Jr. (Ed.), *The ninth mental measurements yearbook* (vol. 1) (pp. 773–777). Lincoln, NE: Buros Institute.

Bracken, B. A. (1985). A critical review of the Kaufman Assessment Battery for Children (K-ABC). *School Psychology Review, 14*, 21–36.

Castellanos, M., Kline, R. B., & Snyder, J. (1996). Lessons from the Kaufman Assessment Battery for Children (K-ABC): Toward a new cognitive assessment model. *Psychological Assessment, 8*(1), 7–17.

Coffman, W. E. (1985). Review of Kaufman Assessment Battery for Children. In J. V. Mitchell, Jr. (Ed.), *The ninth mental measurements yearbook* (vol. 1) (pp. 771–773). Lincoln, NE: Buros Institute.

Conoley, J. C. (1990). Review of the K-ABC: Reflecting the unobservable. *Journal of Psychoeducational Assessment, 8*(3), 369–375.

Hessler, G. (1985). Review of the Kaufman Assessment Battery for Children: Implications for assessment of the gifted. *Journal for the Education of the Gifted, 8*(2), 133–147.

Hopkins, K. D., & Hodge, S. E. (1984). Review of the Kaufman Assessment Battery for Children (K-ABC). *Journal of Counseling and Development, 63*(2), 105–107.

Kamphaus, R. W. (1990). K-ABC theory in historical and current contexts. *Journal of Psychoeducational Assessment, 8*(3), 356-368.

Kamphaus, R. W., & Reynolds, C. R. (1984). Development and structure of the Kaufman Assessment Battery for Children (K-ABC). *Journal of Special Education, 18*(3), 213–228.

Keith, T. Z. (1985). Questioning the K-ABC: What does it measure? *School Psychology Review, 14*(1), 9–20.

Mehrens, W. A. (1984). A critical analysis of the psychometric properties of the K-ABC. *Journal of Special Education, 18*(3), 297–310.

Sternberg, R. J. (1983). Should K come before A, B, and C? A review of the Kaufman Assessment Battery for Children (K-ABC). *Contemporary Education Review, 2*, 199–207.

Sternberg, R. J. (1984). The Kaufman Assessment Battery for Children: An information-processing analysis and critique. *Journal of Special Education, 18*, 269–279.

Weibe, M. J. (1986). Test review: The Kaufman Assessment Battery for Children. *Education and Training of the Mentally Retarded, 21*(1), 76–79.

TEST BATTERY: K-ABC   **TEST: Magic Window**

Description of test: The examinee is required to identify a picture that is exposed by moving it past a narrow slit or "window" (making the picture only partially visible throughout the presentation).

Age Range: 2 to 4 years

BASIC PSYCHOMETRIC CHARACTERISTICS

Age (in years)

Reliability

Reliability key ■ High ▨ Medium □ Low ⊟ Data not available or not appropriate for age level

---

Within-Battery

g loading

Specificity

Cross-Battery

g loading

Specificity

g loading key ■ Good ▨ Fair □ Poor   **Specificity key** ■ Ample ▨ Adequate □ Inadequate

⊟ Data not available or not appropriate for age level

Test floor: *Inadequate* from ages 2:6 to 3:3

Test ceiling: Adequate

Item gradients

Gradient key ■ Good ▨ Fair □ Poor ⊟ Data not available or not appropriate for age level

---

(Note: Refer to Table 3-2 in Chapter 3 for the definition of terms used in the various keys)

TEST BATTERY: K-ABC   **TEST: Magic Window**

Gf-Gc CLASSIFICATIONS

	Primary	**Secondary**

Classification Key

Broad (Stratum II)
- ■ Empirical: strong
- ■ Empirical: moderate
- ▢ Empirical: mixed
- ☐ Logical

☐ Visual Processing *(Gv)*

Narrow (Stratum I)
- ■ Probable
- ☐ Possible

■ Serial Perceptual Integration (PI)
☐ Closure Speed (CS)

OTHER VARIABLES THAT INFLUENCE TEST PERFORMANCE

Typical Age of Concept Attainment

	3	4	5	> 5	Data not available
Basic Concepts in Directions (Frequency of occurrence)		No basic concepts are included in the directions			

Degree of Cultural Content   ☐ High   ■ Medium   ☐ Low

Additional Factors

Background/Environmental	**Individual/Situational**
Environmental stimulation	Concentration
	Reflectivity/impulsivity
	Visual elaboration

(Note: Refer to Table 3-2 in Chapter 3 for the definition of terms used in the various keys)

TEST BATTERY: K-ABC   **TEST: Face Recognition**

Description of test: The examinee is required to select from a group photograph the one or two faces that were shown briefly in a preceding photograph.

Age Range: 2 to 4 years

| BASIC PSYCHOMETRIC CHARACTERISTICS |

Age (in years)

Reliability

Reliability key: ■ High ▨ Medium □ Low ⊟ Data not available or not appropriate for age level

---

Within-Battery

g loading

Specificity

Cross-Battery

g loading

Specificity

g loading key: ■ Good ▨ Fair □ Poor   Specificity key: ■ Ample ▨ Adequate □ Inadequate

⊟ Data not available or not appropriate for age level

Test floor: *Inadequate* from ages 2:6 to 4:3

Test ceiling: Adequate

Item gradients

Gradient key: ■ Good ▨ Fair □ Poor ⊟ Data not available or not appropriate for age level

---

(Note: Refer to Table 3-2 in Chapter 3 for the definition of terms used in the various keys)

TEST BATTERY: K-ABC   **TEST: Face Recognition**

Gf-Gc **CLASSIFICATIONS**

	Primary	Secondary

Classification Key

Broad (Stratum II)
  ■ Empirical: strong
  ▨ Empirical: moderate
  ▢ Empirical: mixed
  ☐ Logical

☐ Visual Processing *(Gv)*

Narrow (Stratum I)
  ■ Probable
  ☐ Possible

■ Visual Memory (MV)

OTHER VARIABLES THAT INFLUENCE TEST PERFORMANCE

	Typical Age of Concept Attainment				Data not available
	3	4	5	> 5	

Basic Concepts in Directions

(Frequency of occurrence)

No basic concepts are included in the test directions

Degree of Cultural Content   ☐ High   ▨ Medium   ☐ Low

Additional Factors

Background/Environmental	**Individual/Situational**
	Concentration
	Reflectivity/impulsivity
	Verbal elaboration

(Note: Refer to Table 3-2 in Chapter 3 for the definition of terms used in the various keys)

TEST BATTERY: K-ABC   **TEST: Hand Movements**

Description of test: The examinee is required to imitate a series of hand movements in the same sequence as performed by the examiner.

Age Range: 2 to 12 years

BASIC PSYCHOMETRIC CHARACTERISTICS

Age (in years)

Reliability

Reliability key: High   Medium   Low   Data not available or not appropriate for age level

---

Within-Battery

g loading

Specificity

Cross-Battery

g loading

Specificity

g loading key: Good Fair Poor   Specificity key: Ample Adequate Inadequate

Data not available or not appropriate for age level

Test floor: *Inadequate* from ages 2:6 to 5:3

Test ceiling: *Inadequate* from ages 9:9 to 12:5

Item gradients

Gradient key: Good Fair Poor   Data not available or not appropriate for age level

---

(Note: Refer to Table 3-2 in Chapter 3 for the definition of terms used in the various keys)

TEST BATTERY: K-ABC   **TEST: Hand Movements**

Gf-Gc CLASSIFICATIONS

	Primary	Secondary

Classification Key

Broad (Stratum II)
- ■ Empirical: strong
- ■ Empirical: moderate
- ◾ Empirical: mixed
- ☐ Logical

Secondary:
- ☐ Visual Processing *(Gv)*
- ☐ Quantitative Knowledge *(Gq)*

Narrow (Stratum I)
- ■ Probable
- ☐ Possible

Secondary:
- ■ Visual Memory (MV)
- ■ Math Achievement (A3)

OTHER VARIABLES THAT INFLUENCE TEST PERFORMANCE

Basic Concepts in Directions (Frequency of occurrence)	Typical Age of Concept Attainment				
	3	4	5	> 5	Data not available
	No basic concepts are included in the test directions				

Degree of Cultural Content   ☐ High   ☐ Medium   ◾ Low

Additional Factors

Background/Environmental	Individual/Situational
	Attention span
	Concentration
	Distractibility
	Verbal rehearsal
	Visual elaboration

(Note: Refer to Table 3-2 in Chapter 3 for the definition of terms used in the various keys)

TEST BATTERY: K-ABC   **TEST: Gestalt Closure**

Description of test: The examinee is required to name an object or scene pictured in a partially completed "inkblot" drawing.

Age Range: 2 to 12 years

BASIC PSYCHOMETRIC CHARACTERISTICS

Age (in years)

Reliability

Reliability key — High — Medium — Low — Data not available or not appropriate for age level

Within-Battery

g loading

Specificity

Cross-Battery

g loading

Specificity

g loading key — Good — Fair — Poor   Specificity key — Ample — Adequate — Inadequate

Data not available or not appropriate for age level

Test floor: *Inadequate* from ages 2:6 to 4:3

Test ceiling: *Inadequate* from ages 12:3 to 12:5

Item gradients

Gradient key — Good — Fair — Poor — Data not available or not appropriate for age level

(Note: Refer to Table 3-2 in Chapter 3 for the definition of terms used in the various keys)

TEST BATTERY: K-ABC   **TEST: Gestalt Closure**

Gf-Gc CLASSIFICATIONS

	Primary	**Secondary**

<u>Classification Key</u>

Broad (Stratum II)
- ■ Empirical: strong
- ■ Empirical: moderate
- ☐ Empirical: mixed
- ☐ Logical

■ Visual Processing *(Gv)*

Narrow (Stratum I)
- ■ Probable
- ☐ Possible

■ Closure Speed (CS)

OTHER VARIABLES THAT INFLUENCE TEST PERFORMANCE

	Typical Age of Concept Attainment				
	3	**4**	**5**	**> 5**	**Data not available**
Basic Concepts in Directions (Frequency of occurrence)		No basic concepts are included in the test directions			

Degree of Cultural Content   ☐ High   ■ Medium   ☐ Low

Additional Factors

Background/Environmental	**Individual/Situational**
Vision difficulties	Visual acuity
Environmental stimulation	Field dependence/independence

(Note: Refer to Table 3-2 in Chapter 3 for the definition of terms used in the various keys)

TEST BATTERY: K-ABC   **TEST: Number Recall**

Description of test: The examinee is required to repeat verbatim orally presented number sequences.

Age Range: 2 to 12 years

BASIC PSYCHOMETRIC CHARACTERISTICS

Age (in years)

Reliability

Reliability key ■ High   ▨ Medium   ☐ Low   ⊟ Data not available or not appropriate for age level

---

Within-Battery

g loading

Specificity

Cross-Battery

g loading

Specificity

***g* loading key** ■ Good ▨ Fair ☐ Poor   **Specificity key** ■ Ample ▨ Adequate ☐ Inadequate

⊟ Data not available or not appropriate for age level

Test floor: *Inadequate* from ages 2:6 to 4:3

Test ceiling: Adequate

Item gradients

Gradient key   ■ Good ▨ Fair ☐ Poor   ⊟ Data not available or not appropriate for age level

---

(Note: Refer to Table 3-2 in Chapter 3 for the definition of terms used in the various keys)

TEST BATTERY: K-ABC	TEST: Number Recall

Gf-Gc CLASSIFICATIONS

	Primary	**Secondary**

__Classification Key__

Broad (Stratum II)
- ■ Empirical: strong
- ■ Empirical: moderate
- ☐ Empirical: mixed
- ☐ Logical

■ Short-term Memory *(Gsm)*

Narrow (Stratum I)
- ■ Probable
- ☐ Possible

■ Memory Span (MS)

OTHER VARIABLES THAT INFLUENCE TEST PERFORMANCE

	Typical Age of Concept Attainment				
	3	**4**	**5**	**> 5**	**Data not available**
Basic Concepts in Directions (Frequency of occurrence)		some (1)			

Degree of Cultural Content   ☐ High   ☐ Medium   ■ Low

Additional Factors

Background/Environmental	**Individual/Situational**
Hearing difficulties	Attention span
	Concentration
	Distractibility
	Verbal rehearsal
	Visual elaboration
	Organization

(Note: Refer to Table 3-2 in Chapter 3 for the definition of terms used in the various keys)

TEST BATTERY: K-ABC   **TEST: Triangles**

Description of test: The examinee is required to reproduce a printed two-dimensional design using two-color triangles.

Age Range: 4 to 12 years

BASIC PSYCHOMETRIC CHARACTERISTICS

Age (in years)

Reliability

Reliability key ■ High   ▨ Medium   □ Low   ⊟ Data not available or not appropriate for age level

---

Within-Battery

g loading

Specificity

Cross-Battery

g loading

Specificity

***g* loading key** ■ Good   ▨ Fair   □ Poor   **Specificity key** ■ Ample   ▨ Adequate   □ Inadequate

⊟ Data not available or not appropriate for age level

Test floor: *Inadequate* from ages 4:0 to 7:11

Test ceiling: *Inadequate* from ages 9:0 to 12:5

Item gradients

Gradient key ■ Good   ▨ Fair   □ Poor   ⊟ Data not available or not appropriate for age level

---

(Note: Refer to Table 3-2 in Chapter 3 for the definition of terms used in the various keys)

TEST BATTERY: K-ABC   **TEST: Triangles**

Gf-Gc CLASSIFICATIONS

	Primary	Secondary

Classification Key

Broad (Stratum II)
■ Empirical: strong
■ Empirical: moderate
☐ Empirical: mixed
☐ Logical

■ Visual Processing *(Gv)*

Narrow (Stratum Level I)
■ Probable
☐ Possible

■ Visualization (VZ)
☐ Spatial Relations (SR)

OTHER VARIABLES THAT INFLUENCE TEST PERFORMANCE

Typical Age of Concept Attainment

	3	4	5	> 5	Data not available
Basic Concepts in Directions (Frequency of occurrence)		one (9) together (1)			

Degree of Cultural Content   ☐ High   ☐ Medium   ■ Low

Additional Factors

Background/Environmental	Individual/Situational
Vision difficulties Environmental stimulation	Visual-motor coordination Reflectivity/impulsivity Field dependence/independence Flexibility/inflexibility Planning

(Note: Refer to Table 3-2 in Chapter 3 for the definition of terms used in the various keys)

TEST BATTERY: K-ABC   **TEST: Word Order**

Description of test: The examinee is required to touch a series of pictures in the same sequence as they were
                     named by the examiner.

Age Range: 4 to 12 years

BASIC PSYCHOMETRIC CHARACTERISTICS

Age (in years)

Reliability

Reliability key ■ High   ▨ Medium   □ Low   ⊟ Data not available or not appropriate for age level

Within-Battery

g loading

Specificity

Cross-Battery

g loading

Specificity

g **loading key** ■ Good ▨ Fair □ Poor   **Specificity key** ■ Ample ▨ Adequate □ Inadequate

⊟ Data not available or not appropriate for age level

Test floor: *Inadequate* from ages 4:0 to 5:11

Test ceiling: *Inadequate* from ages 11:3 to 12:5

Item gradients

Gradient key ■ Good ▨ Fair □ Poor   ⊟ Data not available or not appropriate for age level

(Note: Refer to Table 3-2 in Chapter 3 for the definition of terms used in the various keys)

TEST BATTERY: K-ABC	TEST: Word Order

Gf-Gc CLASSIFICATIONS

	Primary	Secondary

Classification Key

Broad (Stratum II)
■ Empirical: strong
■ Empirical: moderate
□ Empirical: mixed
□ Logical

■ Short-term memory (*Gsm*)

Narrow (Stratum I)
■ Probable
□ Possible

■ Memory Span (MS)

OTHER VARIABLES THAT INFLUENCE TEST PERFORMANCE

Typical Age of Concept Attainment

	3	4	5	> 5	Data not available
Basic Concepts in Directions		some (1)		before (1)	
(Frequency of occurrence)					

Degree of Cultural Content   □ High   ■ Medium   □ Low

Additional Factors

Background/Environmental	Individual/Situational
Hearing difficulties	Attention
	Concentration
	Distractibility
	Verbal rehearsal
	Visual elaboration

(Note: Refer to Table 3-2 in Chapter 3 for the definition of terms used in the various keys)

TEST BATTERY: K-ABC   **TEST: Matrix Analogies**

Description of test: The examinee is required to select a picture or abstract design that completes a visual analogy.

Age Range: 5 to 12 years

BASIC PSYCHOMETRIC CHARACTERISTICS

Age (in years)

Reliability

Reliability key ▮ High   ▮ Medium   ☐ Low   ⊟ Data not available or not appropriate for age level

---

Within-Battery

g loading

Specificity

Cross-Battery

g loading

Specificity

g **loading key** ▮ Good   ▮ Fair   ☐ Poor   **Specificity key** ▮ Ample   ▮ Adequate   ☐ Inadequate

⊟ Data not available or not appropriate for age level

Test floor: *Inadequate* from ages 5:0 to 7:11

Test ceiling: *Inadequate* from ages 10:3 to 12:5

Item gradients

Gradient key ▮ Good   ▮ Fair   ☐ Poor   ⊟ Data not available or not appropriate for age level

---

(Note: Refer to Table 3-2 in Chapter 3 for the definition of terms used in the various keys)

TEST BATTERY: K-ABC   **TEST: Matrix Analogies**

Gf-Gc CLASSIFICATIONS

	Primary	Secondary

Classification Key

Broad (Stratum II)
- ■ Empirical: strong
- ■ Empirical: moderate
- □ Empirical: mixed
- □ Logical

Secondary:
- □ Fluid Intelligence (Gf)
- □ Visual Processing (Gv)

Narrow (Stratum I)
- ■ Probable
- □ Possible

Secondary:
- ■ Induction (I)
- ■ Visualization (VZ)

OTHER VARIABLES THAT INFLUENCE TEST PERFORMANCE

	Typical Age of Concept Attainment				
	3	4	5	> 5	Data not available
Basic Concepts in Directions (Frequency of occurrence)		one (>15)		right (8)	with (>15)

Degree of Cultural Content   □ High   □ Medium   ■ Low

Additional Factors

Background/Environmental	Individual/Situational
Vision difficulties	Reflectivity/impulsivity
Environmental stimulation	Field dependence/independence
	Flexibility/inflexibility
	Planning

(Note: Refer to Table 3-2 in Chapter 3 for the definition of terms used in the various keys)

TEST BATTERY: K-ABC   **TEST: Spatial Memory**

Description of test: The examinee is required to recall the placement of pictures on a page after they were
exposed for a 5-second interval.

Age Range: 5 to 12 years

BASIC PSYCHOMETRIC CHARACTERISTICS

Age (in years)

Reliability

Reliability key ☐ High   ☐ Medium   ☐ Low   ☐ Data not available or not appropriate for age level

Within-Battery

g loading

Specificity

Cross-Battery

g loading

Specificity

g loading key ☐ Good ☐ Fair ☐ Poor   **Specificity key** ☐ Ample ☐ Adequate ☐ Inadequate

☐ Data not available or not appropriate for age level

Test floor: *Inadequate* from ages 5:0 to 6:2

Test ceiling: *Inadequate* from ages 9:9 to 12:5

Item gradients

Gradient key ☐ Good ☐ Fair ☐ Poor   ☐ Data not available or not appropriate for age level

(Note: Refer to Table 3-2 in Chapter 3 for the definition of terms used in the various keys)

TEST BATTERY: K-ABC   **TEST: Spatial Memory**

Gf-Gc CLASSIFICATIONS

	Primary	**Secondary**

Broad (Stratum II)
- ■ Empirical: strong
- ■ Empirical: moderate
- ☐ Empirical: mixed
- ☐ Logical

Secondary:
- ☐ Visual Processing *(Gv)*
- ☐ Short-term Memory *(Gsm)*

Narrow (Stratum I)
- ■ Probable
- ☐ Possible

Secondary:
- ■ Visual Memory (MV)
- ■ Spatial Relations (SR)
- ☐ Memory Span (MS)

OTHER VARIABLES THAT INFLUENCE TEST PERFORMANCE

Typical Age of Concept Attainment

	3	4	5	> 5	Data not available
Basic Concepts in Directions (Frequency of occurrence)		No basic concepts are included in the test directions			

Degree of Cultural Content   ☐ High   ■ Medium   ☐ Low

Additional Factors

Background/Environmental	**Individual/Situational**
Environmental stimulation	Concentration
	Verbal rehearsal

(Note: Refer to Table 3-2 in Chapter 3 for the definition of terms used in the various keys)

TEST BATTERY: K-ABC   **TEST: Photo Series**

Description of test: The examinee is required to place photographs of an event in chronological order.

Age Range: 6 to 12 years

BASIC PSYCHOMETRIC CHARACTERISTICS

Age (in years)

Reliability

Reliability key   ■ High   ▨ Medium   □ Low   ⊟ Data not available or not appropriate for age level

Within-Battery

g loading

Specificity

Cross-Battery

g loading

Specificity

g **loading key**   ■ Good   ▨ Fair   □ Poor   **Specificity key**   ■ Ample   ▨ Adequate   □ Inadequate

⊟ Data not available or not appropriate for age level

Test floor: *Inadequate* from ages 6:0 to 7:8

Test ceiling: *Inadequate* from ages 9:6 to 12:5

Item gradients

Gradient key   ■ Good   ▨ Fair   □ Poor   ⊟ Data not available or not appropriate for age level

(Note: Refer to Table 3-2 in Chapter 3 for the definition of terms used in the various keys)

TEST BATTERY: K-ABC　　　　　　**TEST: Photo Series**

Gf-Gc CLASSIFICATIONS

	Primary	**Secondary**

Classification Key

Broad (Stratum II)
- ■ Empirical: strong
- ■ Empirical: moderate
- ▨ Empirical: mixed
- ☐ Logical

Secondary:
- ☐ Visual Processing (Gv)
- ☐ Fluid Intelligence (Gf)

Narrow (Stratum I)
- ■ Probable
- ☐ Possible

Secondary:
- ■ Visualization (VZ)
- ■ Induction (I)

OTHER VARIABLES THAT INFLUENCE TEST PERFORMANCE

	Typical Age of Concept Attainment				
	3	**4**	**5**	**> 5**	**Data not available**
Basic Concepts in Directions (Frequency of occurrence)		Not appropriate for age range covered			

Degree of Cultural Content　　☐ High　　■ Medium　　☐ Low

Additional Factors

Background/Environmental	**Individual/Situational**
Environmental stimulation	Visual-motor coordination
Alertness to the environment	Reflectivity/impulsivity
	Flexibility/inflexibility
	Planning

(Note: Refer to Table 3-2 in Chapter 3 for the definition of terms used in the various keys)

Kaufman Adolescent and Adult Intelligence Test (KAIT)

General Information

Authors: Alan S. Kaufman and Nadeen L. Kaufman

Publisher: American Guidance Service

Publication Date: 1993

Age Range: Age 11- 0 to 85+

Administration Time:
Core Battery: 65 min.
Extended Battery: 90 min.

Composite Measure Information

Broad Measure of Intelligence: Composite IQ

Lower-Order Composites:
Fluid Scale
Crystallized Scale
Long-Term Retrieval

Score Information

Peer Comparison Scores:
Percentile Rank
Standard Score

Range of Standard Scores for Total Test Composite: 40 to 160

Mean Floor of Subtests at Age 3-0:[1] N/A

Norming Information

Number of Subtests Normed at Each Age:
Total: 10
Age 11-0 to 85+: 10

Conormed with Tests of Achievement: No

Person Variables in Norming Plan:
Gender
Race/Ethnicity (confounding race and Hispanic origin)
SES (educational level)

Community Variables in Norming Plan:
Location
Size

Size of Norming Sample for the Broad Measure of General Intelligence:
School ages 11–19 (5 age groups)
N = 650
Average number per age group: 130

Adult ages 20–85+ (8 age groups)
N = 1350
Average number per age group: 169

Note: The above information was adapted from Harrison, Flanagan, and Genshaft (1997). Copyright 1997 Guilford Publishing Co. All rights reserved.

The description of the subtests of the KAIT were adapted from *Kaufman Adolescent and Adult Test (KAIT)* by Alan S. Kaufman and Nadeen L. Kaufman © (1993) American Guidance Service, Inc., 4201 Woodland Road, Circle Pine, Minnesota 55014–1796. Used with permission of the publisher. All rights reserved.

[1]Standard deviations below the mean for a raw score of 1.

Age Blocks in Norm Table:[2]
4-month blocks (Age 11-0 to 16-11)
6-month blocks (Age 17-0 to 18-11)
1-year blocks (Age 19-0 to 20-11)
2-year blocks (Age 21 to 24)
5-year blocks (Age 25 to 84)

Reviews

Brown, D. T. (1994). Review of the Kaufman Adolescent and Adult Intelligence Test (KAIT). *Journal of School Psychology, 32,* 85–99.

Dumont, R., & Hagberg, C. (1994). Test reviews: Kaufman Adolescent and Adult Intelligence Test. *Journal of Psychoeducational Assessment, 12*(2), 190–196.

Flanagan, D. P. (1995). Review of the Kaufman Adolescent and Adult Intelligence Test. In J. C. Conoley & J. C. Impara (Eds.), *The twelfth mental measurements yearbook* (pp. 527–530). Lincoln, NE: Buros Institute.

Flanagan, D. P., Alfonso, V. C., & Flanagan, R. (1994). A review of the Kaufman Adolescent and Adult Intelligence Test: An advancement in cognitive assessment? *School Psychology Review, 23,* 512–525.

Flanagan, D. P., Genshaft, J. L., & Boyce, D. M. (in press). A review of the Kaufman Adolescent and Adult Intelligence Test (KAIT). *Journal of Psychoeducational Assessment.*

Keith, T. Z. (1995). Review of the Kaufman Adolescent and Adult Intelligence Test. In J. C. Conoley & J. C. Impara (Eds.), *The twelfth mental measurements yearbook* (pp. 530–532). Lincoln, NE: Buros Institute.

---

[2] In most cases, age blocks represent linear interpolations.

TEST BATTERY: KAIT   **TEST: Definitions**

Description of test: The examinee is required to figure out a word by studying the word shown with some of its letters missing and hearing or reading a clue about its meaning.

Age range: 11 to 85+ years

BASIC PSYCHOMETRIC CHARACTERISTICS

Age (in years)

Reliability

Reliability key ■ High   ▨ Medium   □ Low   ▭ Data not available or not appropriate for age level

Within-Battery

g loading

Specificity

Cross-Battery

g loading

Specificity

g loading key ■ Good   ▨ Fair   □ Poor   **Specificity key** ■ Ample   ▨ Adequate   □ Inadequate

▭ Data not available or not appropriate for age level

Test floor: *Inadequate* from ages 11:0 to 11:7 and 60 to 85+

Test ceiling: Adequate

Item gradients

Gradient key ■ Good   ▨ Fair   □ Poor   ▭ Data not available or not appropriate for age level

(Note: Refer to Table 3-2 in Chapter 3 for the definition of terms used in the various keys)

TEST BATTERY: KAIT   TEST: Definitions

Gf-Gc CLASSIFICATIONS

	Primary	Secondary

Classification Key

Broad (Stratum II)
- ■ Empirical: strong
- ■ Empirical: moderate
- ☐ Empirical: mixed
- ☐ Logical

- ☐ Crystallized Intelligence *(Gc)*
- ☐ Reading/writing *(Grw)*

Narrow (Stratum I)
- ■ Probable
- ☐ Possible

- ■ Language Development (LD)
- ■ Lexical Knowledge (VL)
- ■ Spelling Ability (SG)
- ☐ Reading Decoding (RD)

OTHER VARIABLES THAT INFLUENCE TEST PERFORMANCE

	Typical Age of Concept Attainment				
	3	4	5	> 5	Data not available
Basic Concepts in Directions (Frequency of occurrence)			Not appropriate for age range covered		

Degree of Cultural Content   ■ High   ☐ Medium   ☐ Low

Additional Factors

Background/Environmental	Individual/Situational
Reading difficulties Spelling difficulties Language stimulation Environmental stimulation Educational opportunities/experiences	

(Note: Refer to Table 3-2 in Chapter 3 for the definition of terms used in the various keys)

BATTERY: KAIT   **TEST: Rebus Learning**

Description of test: The examinee is required to learn the word or concept associated with a particular rebus (drawing) and then "read" phrases and sentences composed of these rebuses.

Age range: 11 to 85+ years

BASIC PSYCHOMETRIC CHARACTERISTICS

Age (in years)

Reliability

Reliability key ▉ High   ▩ Medium   ☐ Low   ⊟ Data not available or not appropriate for age level

Within-Battery

g loading

Specificity

Cross-Battery

g loading

Specificity

g loading key ▉ Good   ▩ Fair   ☐ Poor   **Specificity key** ▉ Ample   ▩ Adequate   ☐ Inadequate

⊟ Data not available or not appropriate for age level

Test floor: *Inadequate* from ages 60 to 85+

Test ceiling: Adequate

Item gradients

Gradient key ▉ Good   ▩ Fair   ☐ Poor   ⊟ Data not available or not appropriate for age level

(Note: Refer to Table 3-2 in Chapter 3 for the definition of terms used in the various keys)

TEST BATTERY: KAIT   **TEST: Rebus Learning**

Gf-Gc CLASSIFICATIONS

	Primary	**Secondary**

<u>Classification Key</u>

Broad (Stratum II)
- ■ Empirical: strong
- ■ Empirical: moderate
- □ Empirical: mixed
- □ Logical

■ Long-term Storage and
Retrieval *(Glr)*

Narrow (Stratum I)
- ■ Probable
- □ Possible

■ Associative Memory (MA)
□ Meaningful Memory (MM)

OTHER VARIABLES THAT INFLUENCE TEST PERFORMANCE

Typical Age of Concept Attainment

Basic Concepts in Directions	3	4	5	> 5	Data not available
(Frequency of occurrence)		Not appropriate for age range covered			

Degree of Cultural Content   □ High   ■ Medium   □ Low

Additional Factors

Background/Environmental	**Individual/Situational**
Reading difficulties	Concentration
Educational opportunities/experiences	Verbal elaboration
	Visual elaboration
	Ability to use feedback to modify performance

(Note: Refer to Table 3-2 in Chapter 3 for the definition of terms used in the various keys)

BATTERY: KAIT   **TEST: Logical Steps**

Description of test: The examinee is required to attend to logical premises presented both visually and aurally, and then respond to a question by making use of the logical premise.

Age range: 11 to 85+ years

BASIC PSYCHOMETRIC CHARACTERISTICS

Age (in years)

Reliability

Reliability key ■ High ▨ Medium ☐ Low ⊟ Data not available or not appropriate for age level

Within-Battery

g loading

Specificity

Cross-Battery

g loading

Specificity

g loading key ■ Good ▨ Fair ☐ Poor   **Specificity key** ■ Ample ▨ Adequate ☐ Inadequate

⊟ Data not available or not appropriate for age level

Test floor: *Inadequate* from ages 11:0 to 15:3 and 35 to 85+

Test ceiling: Adequate

Item gradients

Gradient key ■ Good ▨ Fair ☐ Poor ⊟ Data not available or not appropriate for age level

(Note: Refer to Table 3-2 in Chapter 3 for the definition of terms used in the various keys)

TEST BATTERY: KAIT   **TEST: Logical Steps**

Gf-Gc CLASSIFICATIONS

	Primary	**Secondary**

__Classification Key__

Broad (Stratum II)
- ■ Empirical: strong
- ■ Empirical: moderate
- ▢ Empirical: mixed
- ☐ Logical

■ Fluid Intelligence *(Gf)*

Narrow (Stratum I)
- ■ Probable
- ☐ Possible

■ General Sequential Reasoning (RG)
☐ Induction (I)

OTHER VARIABLES THAT INFLUENCE TEST PERFORMANCE

Typical Age of Concept Attainment

Basic Concepts in Directions (Frequency of occurrence)	3	4	5	> 5	Data not available
	Not appropriate for age range covered				

Degree of Cultural Content   ☐ High   ■ Medium   ☐ Low

Additional Factors

Background/Environmental	**Individual/Situational**
Math difficulties Educational opportunities/experiences	Concentration Reflectivity/impulsivity Flexibility/inflexibility Planning

(Note: Refer to Table 3-2 in Chapter 3 for the definition of terms used in the various keys)

BATTERY: KAIT　　　　　　**TEST: Auditory Comprehension**

Description of test: The examinee is required to listen to a recording of a news story and then answer literal and inferential questions about the story.

Age range: 11 to 85+ years

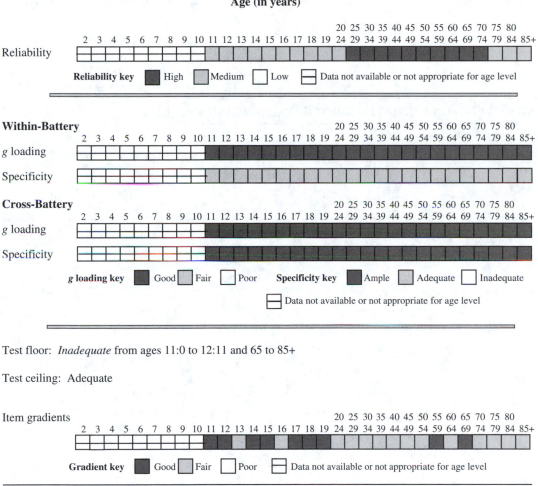

| BASIC PSYCHOMETRIC CHARACTERISTICS |

Age (in years)

Reliability

Reliability key ■ High ▨ Medium □ Low ⊟ Data not available or not appropriate for age level

Within-Battery

g loading

Specificity

Cross-Battery

g loading

Specificity

g loading key ■ Good ▨ Fair □ Poor　**Specificity key** ■ Ample ▨ Adequate □ Inadequate

⊟ Data not available or not appropriate for age level

Test floor: *Inadequate* from ages 11:0 to 12:11 and 65 to 85+

Test ceiling: Adequate

Item gradients

Gradient key ■ Good ▨ Fair □ Poor　⊟ Data not available or not appropriate for age level

(Note: Refer to Table 3-2 in Chapter 3 for the definition of terms used in the various keys)

TEST BATTERY: KAIT   **TEST: Auditory Comprehension**

Gf-Gc CLASSIFICATIONS

	Primary	Secondary

Classification Key

Broad (Stratum II)
- ■ Empirical: strong
- ■ Empirical: moderate
- ▢ Empirical: mixed
- ☐ Logical

- ☐ Crystallized Intelligence *(Gc)*
- ☐ Short-term Memory *(Gsm)*
- ☐ Long-term Storage & Retrieval *(Glr)*

Narrow (Stratum I)
- ■ Probable
- ☐ Possible

- ■ Language Development (LD)
- ■ Listening Ability (LS)
- ■ Memory Span (MS)
- ☐ Meaningful Memory (MM)

OTHER VARIABLES THAT INFLUENCE TEST PERFORMANCE

Typical Age of Concept Attainment

	3	4	5	> 5	Data not available
Basic Concepts in Directions *(Frequency of occurrence)*		Not appropriate for age range covered			

Degree of Cultural Content   ■ High   ☐ Medium   ☐ Low

Additional Factors

Background/Environmental	Individual/Situational
Hearing difficulties	Attention span
Language stimulation	Concentration
Environmental stimulation	Distractibility
Educational opportunities/experiences	

(Note: Refer to Table 3-2 in Chapter 3 for the definition of terms used in the various keys)

BATTERY: KAIT   **TEST: Mystery Codes**

Description of test: The examinee is required to study the identifying codes associated with a set of pictorial stimuli and then figure out the code for a novel pictorial stimulus.

Age range: 11 to 85+ years

BASIC PSYCHOMETRIC CHARACTERISTICS

Age (in years)

Reliability

Reliability key High   Medium   Low   Data not available or not appropriate for age level

Within-Battery

g loading

Specificity

Cross-Battery

g loading

Specificity

***g* loading key** Good   Fair   Poor   **Specificity key** Ample   Adequate   Inadequate

Data not available or not appropriate for age level

Test floor: *Inadequate* from ages 75 to 85+

Test ceiling: Adequate

Item gradients

Gradient key Good   Fair   Poor   Data not available or not appropriate for age level

(Note: Refer to Table 3-2 in Chapter 3 for the definition of terms used in the various keys)

TEST BATTERY: KAIT   **TEST: Mystery Codes**

Gf-Gc **CLASSIFICATIONS**

	Primary	**Secondary**
<u>**Classification Key**</u>		
Broad (Stratum II)	■ Fluid Intelligence *(Gf)*	
■ Empirical: strong		
■ Empirical: moderate		
☐ Empirical: mixed		
☐ Logical		
Narrow (Stratum I)	■ Induction (I)	
■ Probable		
☐ Possible		

OTHER VARIABLES THAT INFLUENCE TEST PERFORMANCE

Typical Age of Concept Attainment

	3	4	5	> 5	Data not available
Basic Concepts in Directions *(Frequency of occurrence)*		Not appropriate for age range covered			

Degree of Cultural Content   ☐ High   ■ Medium   ☐ Low

Additional Factors

Background/Environmental	**Individual/Situational**
	Concentration
	Reflectivity/impulsivity
	Flexibility/inflexibility
	Planning
	Ability to use feedback to modify performance

(Note: Refer to Table 3-3 in Chapter 3 for the definition of terms used in the various keys)

BATTERY: KAIT   **TEST: Double Meanings**

Description of test: The examinee is required to study two sets of word clues and then think of a word with two meanings that relates closely to both sets of clues.

Age range: 11 to 85+ years

BASIC PSYCHOMETRIC CHARACTERISTICS

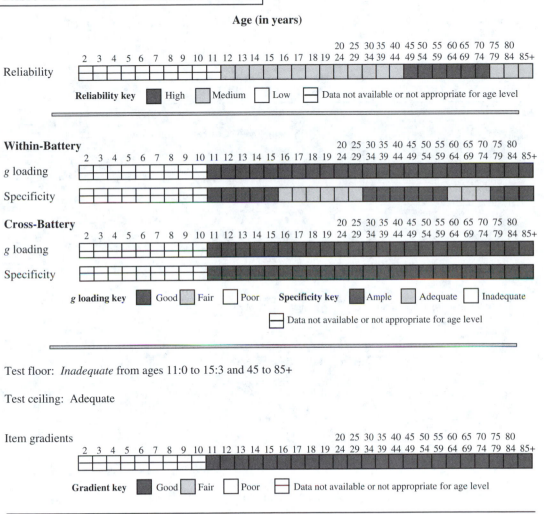

Test floor: *Inadequate* from ages 11:0 to 15:3 and 45 to 85+

Test ceiling: Adequate

(Note: Refer to Table 3-2 in Chapter 3 for the definition of terms used in the various keys)

Gf-Gc CLASSIFICATIONS

	Primary	**Secondary**

Classification Key

Broad (Stratum II)
- ■ Empirical: strong
- ■ Empirical: moderate
- ☐ Empirical: mixed
- ☐ Logical

☐ Crystallized Intelligence *(Gc)*
☐ Reading/writing *(Grw)*

Narrow (Stratum I)
- ■ Probable
- ☐ Possible

■ Lexical Knowledge (VL)
■ Verbal Language Comprehension (V)

OTHER VARIABLES THAT INFLUENCE TEST PERFORMANCE

Typical Age of Concept Attainment

	3	4	5	> 5	Data not available
Basic Concepts in Directions (Frequency of occurrence)		Not appropriate for age range covered			

Degree of Cultural Content   ■ High   ☐ Medium   ☐ Low

Additional Factors

Background/Environmental	**Individual/Situational**
Reading difficulties	
Language stimulation	
Environmental stimulation	
Educational opportunities/experiences	

(Note: Refer to Table 3-2 in Chapter 3 for the definition of terms used in the various keys)

BATTERY: KAIT   **TEST: Memory for Block Designs**

Description of test: The examinee is required to study a printed abstract design that is exposed briefly, and then copy the design from memory using six yellow and black wooden blocks and a tray.

Age range: 11 to 85+ years

BASIC PSYCHOMETRIC CHARACTERISTICS

Age (in years)

Reliability

Reliability key ■ High   ■ Medium   □ Low   ⊟ Data not available or not appropriate for age level

Within-Battery

g loading

Specificity

Cross-Battery

g loading

Specificity

g loading key ■ Good ■ Fair □ Poor   **Specificity key** ■ Ample ■ Adequate □ Inadequate

⊟ Data not available or not appropriate for age level

Test floor: *Inadequate* from ages 60 to 85+

Test ceiling: Adequate

Item gradients

Gradient key ■ Good ■ Fair □ Poor   ⊟ Data not available or not appropriate for age level

(Note: Refer to Table 3-2 in Chapter 3 for the definition of terms used in the various keys)

TEST BATTERY: KAIT   **TEST: Memory for Block Designs**

Gf-Gc CLASSIFICATIONS

	Primary	**Secondary**

<u>Classification Key</u>

Broad (Stratum II)   ■ Visual Processing *(Gv)*
 ■ Empirical: strong
 ■ Empirical: moderate
 □ Empirical: mixed
 □ Logical

Narrow (Stratum I)   ■ Visual Memory (MV)
 ■ Probable
 □ Possible

OTHER VARIABLES THAT INFLUENCE TEST PERFORMANCE

Typical Age of Concept Attainment

	3	4	5	> 5	Data not available
Basic Concepts in Directions (Frequency of occurrence)		Not appropriate for age range covered			

Degree of Cultural Content   □ High   □ Medium   ■ Low

Additional Factors

Background/Environmental	**Individual/Situational**
Vision difficulties	Concentration
Environmental stimulation	Reflectivity/impulsivity
	Field dependence/independence
	Flexibility/inflexibility
	Planning

(Note: Refer to Table 3-2 in Chapter 3 for the definition of terms used in the various keys)

TEST BATTERY: KAIT   **TEST: Famous Faces**

Description of test: The examinee is required to name people of current or historical fame, based on their photographs and a verbal clue about them.

Age range: 11 to 85+ years

BASIC PSYCHOMETRIC CHARACTERISTICS

Age (in years)

Reliability

Reliability key ■ High ■ Medium □ Low ⊟ Data not available or not appropriate for age level

Within-Battery

g loading

Specificity

Cross-Battery

g loading

Specificity

g loading key ■ Good ■ Fair □ Poor   **Specificity key** ■ Ample ■ Adequate □ Inadequate

⊟ Data not available or not appropriate for age level

Test floor: *Inadequate* from ages 11:0 to 14:11 and 75 to 85+

Test ceiling: Adequate

Item gradients

Gradient key ■ Good ■ Fair □ Poor ⊟ Data not available or not appropriate for age level

---

(Note: Refer to Table 3-2 in Chapter 3 for the definition of terms used in the various keys)

TEST BATTERY: KAIT   TEST: Famous Faces

Gf-Gc CLASSIFICATIONS

	Primary	Secondary

Broad (Stratum II)
- ■ Empirical: strong
- ■ Empirical: moderate
- ☐ Empirical: mixed
- ☐ Logical

■ Crystallized Intelligence *(Gc)*

Narrow (Stratum I)
- ■ Probable
- ☐ Possible

■ Information about Culture (K2)
☐ General Information (KO)

OTHER VARIABLES THAT INFLUENCE TEST PERFORMANCE

Typical Age of Concept Attainment				
3	4	5	> 5	Data not available
Basic Concepts in Directions *(Frequency of occurrence)*		Not appropriate for age range covered		

Degree of Cultural Content   ■ High   ☐ Medium   ☐ Low

Additional Factors

Background/Environmental	Individual/Situational
Language stimulation	
Environmental stimulation	
Educational opportunities/experiences	
Alertness to the environment	
Intellectual curiosity	

(Note: Refer to Table 3-2 in Chapter 3 for the definition of terms used in the various keys)

TEST BATTERY: KAIT   **TEST: Rebus Delayed Recall**

Description of test: The examinee is required to "read" phrases and sentences composed of rebuses they
learned about 45 minutes earlier during the Rebus Learning test.

Age range: 11 to 85+ years

BASIC PSYCHOMETRIC CHARACTERISTICS

Age (in years)

Reliability

Reliability key ▪ High ▪ Medium ▫ Low ▭ Data not available or not appropriate for age level

Within-Battery

g loading

Specificity

Cross-Battery

g loading

Specificity

g loading key ▪ Good ▪ Fair ▫ Poor **Specificity key** ▪ Ample ▪ Adequate ▫ Inadequate

▭ Data not available or not appropriate for age level

Test floor: *Inadequate* from ages 11:0 to 16:11 and 25 to 85+

Test ceiling: Adequate

Item gradients

Gradient key ▪ Good ▪ Fair ▫ Poor ▭ Data not available or not appropriate for age level

(Note: Refer to Table 3-2 in Chapter 3 for the definition of terms used in the various keys)

TEST BATTERY: KAIT   **TEST: Rebus Delayed Recall**

Gf-Gc CLASSIFICATIONS

	Primary	Secondary

Classification Key

Broad (Stratum II)
- ■ Empirical: strong
- ■ Empirical: moderate
- ▨ Empirical: mixed
- ☐ Logical

■ Long-term Storage and Retrieval *(Glr)*

Narrow (Stratum I)
- ■ Probable
- ☐ Possible

■ Associative Memory (MA)
☐ Meaningful Memory (MM)

OTHER VARIABLES THAT INFLUENCE TEST PERFORMANCE

Typical Age of Concept Attainment

	3	4	5	> 5	Data not available
Basic Concepts in Directions (Frequency of occurrence)		Not appropriate for age range covered			

Degree of Cultural Content   ☐ High   ■ Medium   ☐ Low

Additional Factors

Background/Environmental	**Individual/Situational**
Reading difficulties	Concentration
Educational opportunities/experiences	Verbal elaboration
	Visual elaboration

(Note: Refer to Table 3-2 in Chapter 3 for the definition of terms used in the various keys)

TEST BATTERY: KAIT   **TEST: Auditory Delayed Recall**

Description of test: The examinee is required to answer literal and inferential questions about news stories they heard approximately 25 minutes earlier during the Auditory Comprehension test.

Age range: 11 to 85+ years

BASIC PSYCHOMETRIC CHARACTERISTICS

Age (in years)

Reliability

Reliability key ■ High ▨ Medium ☐ Low ⊟ Data not available or not appropriate for age level

Within-Battery

g loading

Specificity

Cross-Battery

g loading

Specificity

g **loading key** ■ Good ▨ Fair ☐ Poor   **Specificity key** ■ Ample ▨ Adequate ☐ Inadequate

⊟ Data not available or not appropriate for age level

Test floor: *Inadequate* from ages 11:0 to 85+

Test ceiling: Adequate

Item gradients

Gradient key ■ Good ▨ Fair ☐ Poor ⊟ Data not available or not appropriate for age level

---

(Note: Refer to Table 3-2 in Chapter 3 for the definition of terms used in the various keys)

TEST BATTERY: KAIT   **TEST: Auditory Delayed Recall**

Gf-Gc CLASSIFICATIONS

<u>Classification Key</u>

	Primary	Secondary

Broad (Stratum II)
- ■ Empirical: strong
- ■ Empirical: moderate
- ▨ Empirical: mixed
- ☐ Logical

Narrow (Stratum I)
- ▨ Probable
- ☐ Possible

Secondary:
- ☐ Long-term Storage and Retrieval *(Glr)*
- ▨ Crystallized Intelligence *(Gc)*
- ■ Meaningful Memory (MM)
- ☐ Language Development (LD)

OTHER VARIABLES THAT INFLUENCE TEST PERFORMANCE

Typical Age of Concept Attainment

	3	4	5	> 5	Data not available
Basic Concepts in Directions *(Frequency of occurrence)*		Not appropriate for age range covered			

Degree of Cultural Content   ■ High   ☐ Medium   ☐ Low

Additional Factors

Background/Environmental	Individual/Situational
Hearing difficulties	Attention span
Language stimulation	Concentration
Environmental stimulation	
Educational opportunities/experiences	

(Note: Refer to Table 3-2 in Chapter 3 for the definition of terms used in the various keys)

Stanford-Binet Intelligence Scale: Fourth Edition (SB:IV)

General Information

Authors: Robert L. Thorndike, Elizabeth P. Hagen, and Jerome M. Sattler

Publisher: The Riverside Publishing Company

Publication Date: 1916–1986

Age Range: Age 2-0 to 24

Administration Time: 60 to 90 min.

Composite Measure Information

Broad Measure of Intelligence: Test Composite

Lower-Order Composites:
Verbal Reasoning
Abstract/Visual Reasoning
Quantitative Reasoning
Short-Term Memory

Score Information

Peer Comparison Scores:
Percentile Rank
Standard Age Score

Range of Standard Scores for Total Test Composite: 36 to 164

Mean Floor of Subtests at Age 3-0:[1] –1.4

Norming Information

Number of Subtests Normed at Each Age:
Total: 15
Age 2-0 to 6: 8
Age 7 to 11: 12
Age 12 to 13: 15
Age 14: 14
Age 15 to 24: 13

Conormed with Tests of Achievement: No

Person Variables in Norming Plan:
Gender
Race/Ethnicity (confounding race and Hispanic origin)
Family SES (parent occupation and education)

Community Variables in Norming Plan:
Location
Size

Size of Norming Sample for the Broad Measure of General Intelligence:
Preschool ages 2-0 to 4-11
N = 901

Note: The above information was adapted from Harrison, Flanagan, and Genshaft (1997). Copyright 1997 Guilford Publishing Co. All rights reserved.

The descriptions of the subtests of the SB:IV were adapted from Kamphaus, *Clinical Assessment of Children's Intelligence.* Copyright © 1993 by Allyn and Bacon. Adapted by permission.

[1]Standard deviations below the mean for a raw score of 1.

Average number per year: 300
School ages 5-0 to 17-11
    N = 3918
Average number per year: 490
Adult ages 18-0 to 24-11
    N = 194

Age Blocks in Norm Table:[2]
4-month blocks (Age 2-0 to 5-11)
6-month blocks (Age 6-0 to 10-11)
1-year blocks (Age 11 to 17)
6-year blocks (Age 18 to 24)

Reviews

Anastasi, A. (1989). Review of the Stanford-Binet Intelligence Scale, Fourth Edition. In J. C. Conoley & J. J. Kramer (Eds.), *The tenth mental measurements yearbook* (pp. 771–773). Lincoln, NE: Buros Institute.

Cronbach, L. J. (1989). Review of the Stanford-Binet Intelligence Scale, Fourth Edition. In J. C. Conoley & J. J. Kramer (Eds.), *The tenth mental measurements yearbook* (pp. 773–775). Lincoln, NE: Buros Institute.

Flanagan, D., & Alfonso, V. (1995). A critical review of the technical characteristics of new and recently revised intelligence tests for preschool children. *Journal of Psychoeducational Assessment, 13*(1), 66–90.

Glutting, J. J. (1989). Introduction to the structure and application of the Stanford-Binet Intelligence Scale: Fourth Edition. *Journal of School Psychology, 27,* 69–80.

Laurent, J., Swerdlik, M., & Ryburn, M. (1992). Review of validity research on the Stanford-Binet Intelligence Scale: Fourth Edition. *Psychological Assessment, 4,* 102–112.

McCallum, R. S. (1990). Determining the factor structure of the Stanford-Binet—Fourth Edition: The right choice. *Journal of Psychoeducational Assessment, 8*(3), 436–442.

Thorndike, R. M. (1990). Would the real factors of the Stanford-Binet—Fourth Edition please come forward? *Journal of Psychoeducational Assessment, 8*(3), 412–435.

[2] In most cases, age blocks represent linear interpolations.

TEST BATTERY: SB:IV **TEST: Vocabulary**

Description of test: The examinee either is required to point to pictures named by the examiner or (later) orally define words.

Age range: 2 to 24 years

| BASIC PSYCHOMETRIC CHARACTERISTICS |

Age (in years)

Reliability

Reliability key ■ High ▨ Medium □ Low ⊟ Data not available or not appropriate for age level

Within-Battery

g loading

Specificity

Cross-Battery

g loading

Specificity

g **loading key** ■ Good ▨ Fair □ Poor   **Specificity key** ■ Ample ▨ Adequate □ Inadequate

⊟ Data not available or not appropriate for age level

Test floor: *Inadequate* from ages 2:0 to 3:3

Test ceiling: Adequate

Item gradients

Gradient key ■ Good ▨ Fair □ Poor ⊟ Data not available or not appropriate for age level

(Note: Refer to Table 3-2 in Chapter 3 for the definition of terms used in the various keys)

TEST BATTERY: SB:IV   **TEST: Vocabulary**

Gf-Gc CLASSIFICATIONS

	Primary	**Secondary**

Classification Key

Broad (Stratum II)
- ■ Empirical: strong
- ■ Empirical: moderate
- ☐ Empirical: mixed
- ☐ Logical

■ Crystallized Intelligence *(Gc)*

Narrow (Stratum I)
- ■ Probable
- ☐ Possible

■ Language Development (LD)
■ Lexical Knowledge (VL)

OTHER VARIABLES THAT INFLUENCE TEST PERFORMANCE

Typical Age of Concept Attainment

Basic Concepts in Directions (Frequency of occurrence)	**3**	**4**	**5**	**> 5**	**Data not available**
	on (4) in (2)	top (2) some (1)	different (1)	another (13)	in front (2) dollar (2)

Degree of Cultural Content   ■ High   ☐ Medium   ☐ Low

Additional Factors

Background/Environmental	**Individual/Situational**
Language stimulation	
Environmental stimulation	
Educational opportunities/experiences	
Intellectual curiosity	

(Note: Refer to Table 3-2 in Chapter 3 for the definition of terms used in the various keys)

TEST BATTERY: SB:IV   **TEST: Bead Memory**

Description of test: For the first 10 items, the examinee is required to recall which of one or two beads was exposed. For items 11 through 42 the examinee is required to place beads on a stick in the same sequence as shown in a picture (following a 5-second exposure)

Age range: 2 to 24 years

BASIC PSYCHOMETRIC CHARACTERISTICS

Age (in years)

Reliability

Reliability key ■ High   ▨ Medium   ☐ Low   ⊟ Data not available or not appropriate for age level

---

Within-Battery

g loading

Specificity

Cross-Battery

g loading

Specificity

***g* loading key** ■ Good ▨ Fair ☐ Poor   **Specificity key** ■ Ample ▨ Adequate ☐ Inadequate

⊟ Data not available or not appropriate for age level

Test floor: *Inadequate* from ages 2:0 to 4:3

Test ceiling: Adequate

Item gradients

Gradient key ■ Good ▨ Fair ☐ Poor   ⊟ Data not available or not appropriate for age level

---

(Note: Refer to Table 3-2 in Chapter 3 for the definition of terms used in the various keys)

TEST BATTERY: SB:IV   **TEST: Bead Memory**

Gf-Gc CLASSIFICATIONS

	Primary	Secondary

<u>Classification Key</u>

Broad (Stratum II)
  ■ Empirical: strong
  ■ Empirical: moderate
  □ Empirical: mixed
  □ Logical

■ Visual Processing *(Gv)*

Narrow (Stratum I)
  ■ Probable
  □ Possible

■ Visual Memory (MV)

OTHER VARIABLES THAT INFLUENCE TEST PERFORMANCE

Typical Age of Concept Attainment

Basic Concepts in Directions (Frequency of occurrence)	3	4	5	> 5	Data not available
	on (2) in (5)	one (1) two (1) some (1)	like (>15) away (3)	over [direction] (1)	

Degree of Cultural Content   □ High   □ Medium   ■ Low

Additional Factors

Background/Environmental	Individual/Situational
Vision difficulties	Concentration
Environmental stimulation	Reflectivity/impulsivity
	Field dependence/independence
	Flexibility/inflexibility
	Verbal rehearsal

(Note: Refer to Table 3-2 in Chapter 3 for the definition of terms used in the various keys)

TEST BATTERY: SB:IV   **TEST: Quantitative**

Description of test: The examinee is required to solve applied mathematics problems and show knowledge of mathematics concepts.

Age range: 2 to 24 years

BASIC PSYCHOMETRIC CHARACTERISTICS

Age (in years)

Reliability

Reliability key   ■ High   ▨ Medium   ☐ Low   ⊞ Data not available or not appropriate for age level

Within-Battery

g loading

Specificity

Cross-Battery

g loading

Specificity

***g* loading key**   ■ Good   ▨ Fair   ☐ Poor   **Specificity key**   ■ Ample   ▨ Adequate   ☐ Inadequate

⊞ Data not available or not appropriate for age level

Test floor: *Inadequate* from ages 2:0 to 4:11

Test ceiling: *Inadequate* from ages 17:11 to 24:11

Item gradients

Gradient key   ■ Good   ▨ Fair   ☐ Poor   ⊞ Data not available or not appropriate for age level

(Note: Refer to Table 3-2 in Chapter 3 for the definition of terms used in the various keys)

TEST BATTERY: SB:IV   TEST: Quantitative

Gf-Gc CLASSIFICATIONS

	Primary	Secondary
Classification Key		
Broad (Stratum II) ■ Empirical: strong ▨ Empirical: moderate ▢ Empirical: mixed ☐ Logical	■ Quantitative Knowledge *(Gq)*	☐ Fluid Intelligence *(Gf)*
Narrow (Stratum I) ▨ Probable ☐ Possible	■ Math Achievement (A3)	☐ Quantitative Reasoning (RQ)

OTHER VARIABLES THAT INFLUENCE TEST PERFORMANCE

	Typical Age of Concept Attainment				
	3	**4**	**5**	**> 5**	**Data not available**
Basic Concepts in Directions (Frequency of occurrence)	on (5) up (2) in (2)	one (1) two (2) top (8) some (3) together (4)	different (2) like (7) side (1) all (3) next (1) order (2)	another (1)	next to (1) beside (1) with (5)

Degree of Cultural Content   ☐ High   ▨ Medium   ☐ Low

Additional Factors

Background/Environmental	**Individual/Situational**
Math difficulties	Concentration
Environmental stimulation	Reflectivity/impulsivity
Educational opportunities/experiences	Flexibility/inflexibility

(Note: Refer to Table 3-2 in Chapter 3 for the definition of terms used in the various keys)

TEST BATTERY: SB:IV   **TEST: Memory for Sentences**

Description of test: The examinee is required to repeat sentences exactly as presented by the examiner.

Age range: 2 to 24 years

BASIC PSYCHOMETRIC CHARACTERISTICS

Age (in years)

Reliability

Reliability key ■ High   ▨ Medium   □ Low   ⊞ Data not available or not appropriate for age level

---

Within-Battery

g loading

Specificity

Cross-Battery

g loading

Specificity

g loading key ■ Good ▨ Fair □ Poor   Specificity key ■ Ample ▨ Adequate □ Inadequate

⊞ Data not available or not appropriate for age level

Test floor: *Inadequate* from ages 2:0 to 3:11

Test ceiling: Adequate

Item gradients

Gradient key ■ Good ▨ Fair □ Poor   ⊞ Data not available or not appropriate for age level

(Note: Refer to Table 3-2 in Chapter 3 for the definition of terms used in the various keys)

TEST BATTERY: SB:IV   **TEST: Memory for Sentences**

Gf-Gc CLASSIFICATIONS

	Primary	Secondary

Classification Key

Broad (Stratum II)
- ■ Empirical: strong
- ■ Empirical: moderate
- ☐ Empirical: mixed
- ☐ Logical

Secondary:
- ☐ Short-term Memory *(Gsm)*
- ☐ Crystallized Intelligence *(Gc)*

Narrow (Stratum I)
- ■ Probable
- ☐ Possible

Secondary:
- ■ Memory Span (MS)
- ■ Language Development (LD)

OTHER VARIABLES THAT INFLUENCE TEST PERFORMANCE

Typical Age of Concept Attainment

Basic Concepts in Directions	3	4	5	> 5	Data not available
(Frequency of occurrence)		No basic concepts are included in the test directions			

Degree of Cultural Content   ☐ High   ■ Medium   ☐ Low

Additional Factors

Background/Environmental	Individual/Situational
Hearing difficulties	Attention span
Language stimulation	Concentration
	Distractibility
	Verbal rehearsal
	Visual elaboration

(Note: Refer to Table 3-2 in Chapter 3 for the definition of terms used in the various keys)

TEST BATTERY: SB:IV   **TEST: Pattern Analysis**

Description of test: For the first six items the examinee is required to place puzzle pieces into a form board.
In subsequent items the examinee reproduces patterns with blocks. This is a timed test.

Age range: 2 to 24 years

BASIC PSYCHOMETRIC CHARACTERISTICS

Age (in years)

Reliability

Reliability key   ■ High   ▨ Medium   □ Low   ⊟ Data not available or not appropriate for age level

---

Within-Battery

g loading

Specificity

Cross-Battery

g loading

Specificity

g loading key   ■ Good   ▨ Fair   □ Poor   **Specificity key**   ■ Ample   ▨ Adequate   □ Inadequate

⊟ Data not available or not appropriate for age level

Test floor: *Inadequate* from ages 2:0 to 3:3

Test ceiling: *Inadequate* from ages 9:11 to 24:11

Item gradients

Gradient key   ■ Good   ▨ Fair   □ Poor   ⊟ Data not available or not appropriate for age level

---

(Note: Refer to Table 3-2 in Chapter 3 for the definition of terms used in the various keys)

TEST BATTERY: SB:IV   **TEST: Pattern Analysis**

Gf-Gc CLASSIFICATIONS

	Primary	**Secondary**
<u>Classification Key</u>		

Broad (Stratum II)   ■ Visual Processing *(Gv)*
   ■ Empirical: strong
   ■ Empirical: moderate
   ☐ Empirical: mixed
   ☐ Logical

Narrow (Stratum I)   ■ Visualization (VZ)
   ■ Probable   ☐ Spatial Relations (SR)
   ☐ Possible

OTHER VARIABLES THAT INFLUENCE TEST PERFORMANCE

Typical Age of Concept Attainment

	3	4	5	> 5	Data not available
Basic Concepts in Directions (Frequency of occurrence)	finished (1) in (1)	top (14) together (4) into (6)	different (1) like (15) all (6)	another (2)	

Degree of Cultural Content   ☐ High   ☐ Medium   ■ Low

Additional Factors

Background/Environmental	**Individual/Situational**
Vision difficulties	Visual-motor coordination
Environmental stimulation	Reflectivity/impulsivity
	Field dependence/independence
	Flexibility/inflexibility

(Note: Refer to Table 3-2 in Chapter 3 for the definition of terms used in the various keys)

TEST BATTERY: SB:IV   **TEST: Comprehension**

Description of test: For items 1 through 6, the examinee is required to identify body parts on a card with a picture of a child. For items 7 through 42, the examinee is required to respond to questions about everyday problem situations ranging from survival behavior to civic duties.

Age range: 2 to 24 years

BASIC PSYCHOMETRIC CHARACTERISTICS

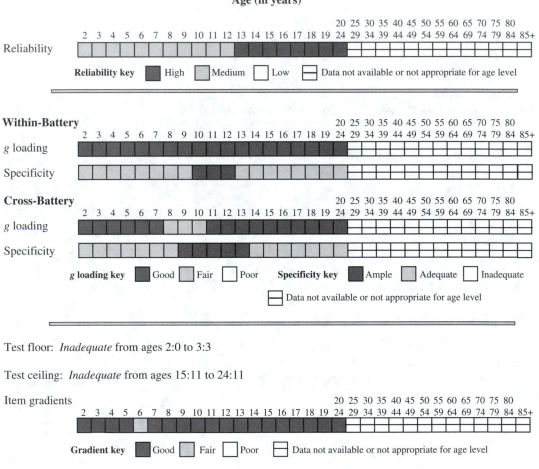

Age (in years)

Reliability

Reliability key   High   Medium   Low   Data not available or not appropriate for age level

Within-Battery

g loading

Specificity

Cross-Battery

g loading

Specificity

g loading key   Good   Fair   Poor   **Specificity key**   Ample   Adequate   Inadequate

Data not available or not appropriate for age level

Test floor: *Inadequate* from ages 2:0 to 3:3

Test ceiling: *Inadequate* from ages 15:11 to 24:11

Item gradients

Gradient key   Good   Fair   Poor   Data not available or not appropriate for age level

(Note: Refer to Table 3-2 in Chapter 3 for the definition of terms used in the various keys)

TEST BATTERY: SB:IV   **TEST: Comprehension**

Gf-Gc CLASSIFICATIONS

	Primary	Secondary

Classification Key

Broad (Stratum II)
- ■ Empirical: strong
- ■ Empirical: moderate
- ☐ Empirical: mixed
- ☐ Logical

■ Crystallized Intelligence *(Gc)*

Narrow (Stratum I)
- ■ Probable
- ☐ Possible

■ Language Development (LD)
■ General Information (KO)

OTHER VARIABLES THAT INFLUENCE TEST PERFORMANCE

Typical Age of Concept Attainment

	3	4	5	> 5	Data not available
Basic Concepts in Directions *(Frequency of occurrence)*		some (1)			

Degree of Cultural Content   ■ High   ☐ Medium   ☐ Low

Additional Factors

Background/Environmental	Individual/Situational
Language stimulation	
Environmental stimulation	
Educational opportunities/experiences	
Alertness to the environment	

(Note: Refer to Table 3-2 in Chapter 3 for the definition of terms used in the various keys)

TEST BATTERY: SB:IV   **TEST: Absurdities**

Description of test: The examinee is required to point to or describe the absurdity in a presented situation
that is contrary to common sense.

Age range: 2 to 14 years

BASIC PSYCHOMETRIC CHARACTERISTICS

Age (in years)

Reliability

Reliability key: High   Medium   Low   Data not available or not appropriate for age level

Within-Battery

g loading

Specificity

Cross-Battery

g loading

Specificity

g loading key: Good   Fair   Poor   Specificity key: Ample   Adequate   Inadequate

Data not available or not appropriate for age level

Test floor: *Inadequate* from ages 2:0 to 4:3

Test ceiling: *Inadequate* from ages 11:11 to 14:11

Item gradients

Gradient key: Good   Fair   Poor   Data not available or not appropriate for age level

(Note: Refer to Table 3-2 in Chapter 3 for the definition of terms used in the various keys.)

TEST BATTERY: SB:IV   **TEST: Absurdities**

Gf-Gc CLASSIFICATIONS

	Primary	Secondary

Classification Key

Broad (Stratum II)
- ■ Empirical: strong
- ■ Empirical: moderate
- ▨ Empirical: mixed
- □ Logical

■ Crystallized Intelligence *(Gc)*

Narrow (Stratum I)
- ■ Probable
- □ Possible

■ Language Development (LD)
□ General Information (KO)

OTHER VARIABLES THAT INFLUENCE TEST PERFORMANCE

Typical Age of Concept Attainment

	3	4	5	> 5	Data not available
Basic Concepts in Directions (Frequency of occurrence)		some (1)			

Degree of Cultural Content   ■ High   □ Medium   □ Low

Additional Factors

Background/Environmental	Individual/Situational
Language stimulation	
Environmental stimulation	
Educational opportunities/experiences	
Alertness to the environment	

(Note: Refer to Table 3-2 in Chapter 3 for the definition of terms used in the various keys)

TEST BATTERY: SB:IV   **TEST: Memory for Digits**

Description of test: The examinee is required to repeat digits exactly as they were stated by the examiner and, for some items, in reverse order.

Age range: 7 to 24 years

BASIC PSYCHOMETRIC CHARACTERISTICS

Age (in years)

Reliability

Reliability key ■ High ▨ Medium □ Low ⊟ Data not available or not appropriate for age level

---

Within-Battery

g loading

Specificity

Cross-Battery

g loading

Specificity

***g* loading key** ■ Good ▨ Fair □ Poor   **Specificity key** ■ Ample ▨ Adequate □ Inadequate

⊟ Data not available or not appropriate for age level

Test floor: *Inadequate* from ages 6:11 to 9:5

Test ceiling: Adequate

Item gradients

Gradient key ■ Good ▨ Fair □ Poor ⊟ Data not available or not appropriate for age level

---

(Note: Refer to Table 3-2 in Chapter 3 for the definition of terms used in the various keys)

TEST BATTERY: SB:IV   **TEST: Memory for Digits**

Gf-Gc CLASSIFICATIONS

	Primary	Secondary

Classification Key

Broad (Stratum II)   ■ Short-term Memory *(Gsm)*
   ■ Empirical: strong
   ■ Empirical: moderate
   ☐ Empirical: mixed
   ☐ Logical

Narrow (Stratum I)   ■ Memory Span (MS)
   ■ Probable
   ☐ Possible

OTHER VARIABLES THAT INFLUENCE TEST PERFORMANCE

	Typical Age of Concept Attainment				
	3	4	5	> 5	Data not available
Basic Concepts in Directions (Frequency of occurrence)			Not appropriate for age range covered		

Degree of Cultural Content	☐ High	☐ Medium	■ Low

Additional Factors

Background/Environmental	Individual/Situational
Hearing difficulties	Attention span
	Concentration
	Distractibility
	Verbal rehearsal
	Visual elaboration
	Organization

(Note: Refer to Table 3-2 in Chapter 3 for the definition of terms used in the various keys)

TEST BATTERY: SB:IV   **TEST: Copying**

Description of test: The examinee is required to produce models with single-color blocks or use pencil
and paper to draw a variety of designs to match a model.

Age range: 2 to 13 years

BASIC PSYCHOMETRIC CHARACTERISTICS

Age (in years)

Reliability

Reliability key ■ High   ▨ Medium   □ Low   ⊟ Data not available or not appropriate for age level

Within-Battery

g loading

Specificity

Cross-Battery

g loading

Specificity

g loading key ■ Good ▨ Fair □ Poor   **Specificity key** ■ Ample ▨ Adequate □ Inadequate

⊟ Data not available or not appropriate for age level

Test floor: *Inadequate* from ages 2:0 to 3:11

Test ceiling: *Inadequate* from ages 9:5 to 13:11

Item gradients

Gradient key ■ Good ▨ Fair □ Poor   ⊟ Data not available or not appropriate for age level

(Note: Refer to Table 3-2 in Chapter 3 for the definition of terms used in the various keys)

TEST BATTERY: SB:IV   **TEST: Copying**

Gf-Gc CLASSIFICATIONS

	Primary	Secondary

Classification Key

Broad (Stratum II)
- ■ Empirical: strong
- ■ Empirical: moderate
- ◻ Empirical: mixed
- ☐ Logical

☐ Visual Processing *(Gv)*
☐ Psychomotor

Narrow (Stratum I)
- ■ Probable
- ☐ Possible

☐ Visualization (VZ)
☐ Finger Dexterity (P2)

OTHER VARIABLES THAT INFLUENCE TEST PERFORMANCE

Typical Age of Concept Attainment

	3	4	5	> 5	Data not available
Basic Concepts in Directions (Frequency of occurrence)		some (1)	like (>15)		with (1)

Degree of Cultural Content   ☐ High   ☐ Medium   ■ Low

Additional Factors

Background/Environmental	Individual/Situational
Vision difficulties	Visual-motor coordination
Environmental stimulation	

(Note: Refer to Table 3-2 in Chapter 3 for the definition of terms used in the various keys)

TEST BATTERY: SB:IV   **TEST: Memory for Objects**

Description of test: The examinee is required to identify objects in the correct order from a larger array of presented objects.

Age range: 7 to 24 years

BASIC PSYCHOMETRIC CHARACTERISTICS

Age (in years)

Reliability

Reliability key   High   Medium   Low   Data not available or not appropriate for age level

Within-Battery

g loading

Specificity

Cross-Battery

g loading

Specificity

g loading key   Good   Fair   Poor   Specificity key   Ample   Adequate   Inadequate

Data not available or not appropriate for age level

Test floor: *Inadequate* from ages 6:11 to 9:11

Test ceiling: Adequate

Item gradients

Gradient key   Good   Fair   Poor   Data not available or not appropriate for age level

---

(Note: Refer to Table 3-2 in Chapter 3 for the definition of terms used in the various keys)

TEST BATTERY: SB:IV   **TEST: Memory for Objects**

Gf-Gc CLASSIFICATIONS

	Primary	Secondary
Classification Key		

Broad (Stratum II)
- ■ Empirical: strong
- ◨ Empirical: moderate
- ▨ Empirical: mixed
- ☐ Logical

Secondary: ◨ Visual Processing *(Gv)*

Narrow (Stratum I)
- ■ Probable
- ☐ Possible

Secondary: ■ Visual Memory (MV)

OTHER VARIABLES THAT INFLUENCE TEST PERFORMANCE

Typical Age of Concept Attainment

	3	4	5	> 5	Data not available
Basic Concepts in Directions (Frequency of occurrence)		Not appropriate for age range covered			

Degree of Cultural Content   ☐ High   ■ Medium   ☐ Low

Additional Factors

Background/Environmental	Individual/Situational
Environmental stimulation	Attention span
	Reflectivity/impulsivity
	Verbal rehearsal
	Verbal elaboration

(Note: Refer to Table 3-2 in Chapter 3 for the definition of terms used in the various keys)

TEST BATTERY: SB:IV   **TEST: Matrices**

Description of test: When presented with figural matrices in which one portion of the matrix is missing, the examinee is required to identify the missing element from multiple-choice alternatives.

Age range: 7 to 24 years

BASIC PSYCHOMETRIC CHARACTERISTICS

Age (in years)

Reliability

Reliability key ■ High ▨ Medium □ Low ⊟ Data not available or not appropriate for age level

Within-Battery

g loading

Specificity

Cross-Battery

g loading

Specificity

g loading key ■ Good ▨ Fair □ Poor   **Specificity key** ■ Ample ▨ Adequate □ Inadequate

⊟ Data not available or not appropriate for age level

Test floor: *Inadequate* from ages 6:11 to 10:5

Test ceiling: *Inadequate* from ages 17:11 to 24:11

Item gradients

Gradient key ■ Good ▨ Fair □ Poor ⊟ Data not available or not appropriate for age level

---

(Note: Refer to Table 3-2 in Chapter 3 for the definition of terms used in the various keys)

TEST BATTERY: SB:IV   TEST: Matrices

Gf-Gc CLASSIFICATIONS

	Primary	Secondary

Classification Key

Broad (Stratum II)
  ■ Empirical: strong
  ■ Empirical: moderate
  ▫ Empirical: mixed
  ☐ Logical

■ Fluid Intelligence *(Gf)*

Narrow (Stratum I)
  ■ Probable
  ☐ Possible

■ Induction (I)

OTHER VARIABLES THAT INFLUENCE TEST PERFORMANCE

Typical Age of Concept Attainment

	3	4	5	> 5	Data not available
Basic Concepts in Directions (Frequency of occurrence)		Not appropriate for age range covered			

Degree of Cultural Content   ☐ High   ☐ Medium   ■ Low

Additional Factors

Background/Environmental	Individual/Situational
Vision difficulties	Reflectivity/impulsivity
	Field dependence/independence
	Flexibility/inflexibility
	Planning

(Note: Refer to Table 3-2 in Chapter 3 for the definition of terms used in the various keys)

TEST BATTERY: SB:IV   **TEST: Number Series**

Description of test: After reviewing a series of four or more numbers, the examinee is required to generate the next two numbers in the series in a manner consistent with the principle underlying the number series.

Age range: 7 to 24 years

BASIC PSYCHOMETRIC CHARACTERISTICS

Age (in years)

Reliability

Reliability key   High   Medium   Low   Data not available or not appropriate for age level

Within-Battery

g loading

Specificity

Cross-Battery

g loading

Specificity

***g* loading key**   Good   Fair   Poor   **Specificity key**   Ample   Adequate   Inadequate

Data not available or not appropriate for age level

Test floor: *Inadequate* from ages 6:11 to 11:11

Test ceiling: *Inadequate* from ages 13:11 to 24:11

Item gradients

Gradient key   Good   Fair   Poor   Data not available or not appropriate for age level

---

(Note: Refer to Table 3-2 in Chapter 3 for the definition of terms used in the various keys.)

TEST BATTERY: SB:IV   **TEST: Number Series**

Gf-Gc CLASSIFICATIONS

	Primary	Secondary

Broad (Stratum II)
- ■ Empirical: strong
- ■ Empirical: moderate
- ▢ Empirical: mixed
- ☐ Logical

☐ Fluid Intelligence *(Gf)*

Narrow (Stratum I)
- ■ Probable
- ☐ Possible

■ Quantitative Reasoning (RQ)

OTHER VARIABLES THAT INFLUENCE TEST PERFORMANCE

Typical Age of Concept Attainment

	3	4	5	> 5	Data not available
Basic Concepts in Directions (Frequency of occurrence)		Not appropriate for age range covered			

Degree of Cultural Content   ☐ High   ☐ Medium   ■ Low

Additional Factors

Background/Environmental	Individual/Situational
Math difficulties	Reflectivity/impulsivity
Educational opportunities/experiences	Flexibility/inflexibility
	Planning

(Note: Refer to Table 3-2 in Chapter 3 for the definition of terms used in the various keys)

TEST BATTERY: SB:IV   **TEST: Paper Folding and Cutting**

Description of test: The examinee is required to choose the correct picture from a multiple-choice format
that shows how a piece of folded and cut paper might look if it were unfolded.

Age range: 12 years to 24 years

BASIC PSYCHOMETRIC CHARACTERISTICS

Age (in years)

Reliability

Reliability key   ■ High   ▨ Medium   □ Low   ⊟ Data not available or not appropriate for age level

Within-Battery

g loading

Specificity

Cross-Battery

g loading

Specificity

***g* loading key**   ■ Good   ▨ Fair   □ Poor   **Specificity key**   ■ Ample   ▨ Adequate   □ Inadequate

⊟ Data not available or not appropriate for age level

Test floor: *Inadequate* from ages 11:11 to 24:11

Test ceiling: *Inadequate* from ages 14:11 to 24:11

Item gradients

Gradient key   ■ Good   ▨ Fair   □ Poor   ⊟ Data not available or not appropriate for age level

(Note: Refer to Table 3-2 in Chapter 3 for the definition of terms used in the various keys)

TEST BATTERY: SB:IV   **TEST: Paper Folding and Cutting**

Gf-Gc CLASSIFICATIONS

	Primary	Secondary

<u>Classification Key</u>

Broad (Stratum II)
- ■ Empirical: strong
- ■ Empirical: moderate
- ☐ Empirical: mixed
- ☐ Logical

Narrow (Stratum I)
- ■ Probable
- ☐ Possible

Secondary:
- ☐ Visual Processing *(Gv)*
- ☐ Quantitative Knowledge *(Gq)*

- ■ Visualization (VZ)
- ■ Math Achievement (A3)

OTHER VARIABLES THAT INFLUENCE TEST PERFORMANCE

Typical Age of Concept Attainment

	3	4	5	> 5	Data not available
Basic Concepts in Directions (Frequency of occurrence)		Not appropriate for age range covered			

Degree of Cultural Content   ☐ High   ☐ Medium   ■ Low

Additional Factors

Background/Environmental	Individual/Situational
	Field dependence/independence

(Note: Refer to Table 3-2 in Chapter 3 for the definition of terms used in the various keys)

TEST BATTERY: SB:IV   **TEST: Verbal Relations**

Description of test: When given four words, the examinee is required to state how three words out of the four-word set are similar.

Age range: 12 to 24 years

BASIC PSYCHOMETRIC CHARACTERISTICS

Age (in years)

Reliability

Reliability key ■ High ▨ Medium ☐ Low ⊟ Data not available or not appropriate for age level

Within-Battery

g loading

Specificity

Cross-Battery

g loading

Specificity

g loading key ■ Good ▨ Fair ☐ Poor   **Specificity key** ■ Ample ▨ Adequate ☐ Inadequate

⊟ Data not available or not appropriate for age level

Test floor: *Inadequate* from ages 11:11 to 24:11

Test ceiling: *Inadequate* from ages 15:11 to 24:11

Item gradients

Gradient key ■ Good ▨ Fair ☐ Poor ⊟ Data not available or not appropriate for age level

(Note: Refer to Table 3-2 in Chapter 3 for the definition of terms used in the various keys)

TEST BATTERY: SB:IV   **TEST: Verbal Relations**

Gf-Gc CLASSIFICATIONS

	Primary	**Secondary**

Classification Key

Broad (Stratum II)
- ■ Empirical: strong
- ▨ Empirical: moderate
- ▢ Empirical: mixed
- ☐ Logical

■ Crystallized Intelligence (*Gc*)

Narrow (Stratum I)
- ▨ Probable
- ☐ Possible

▨ Language Development (LD)
☐ Lexical Knowledge (VL)

OTHER VARIABLES THAT INFLUENCE TEST PERFORMANCE

Typical Age of Concept Attainment

	3	4	5	> 5	Data not available
Basic Concepts in Directions (Frequency of occurrence)		Not appropriate for age range covered			

Degree of Cultural Content   ■ High   ☐ Medium   ☐ Low

Additional Factors

Background/Environmental	**Individual/Situational**
Environmental stimulation	Reflectivity/impulsivity
Educational opportunities/experiences	Flexibility/inflexibility
Alertness to the environment	Visual elaboration
	Planning

(Note: Refer to Table 3-2 in Chapter 3 for the definition of terms used in the various keys.)

TEST BATTERY: SB:IV   **TEST: Equation Building**

Description of test: The examinee is required to take numerals and mathematical signs and resequence them in order to produce a correct solution (i.e., equation).

Age range: 12 to 24 years

BASIC PSYCHOMETRIC CHARACTERISTICS

Age (in years)

```
                                    20 25 30 35 40 45 50 55 60 65 70 75 80
        2  3  4  5  6  7  8  9 10 11 12 13 14 15 16 17 18 19 24 29 34 39 44 49 54 59 64 69 74 79 84 85+
```

Reliability

Reliability key ▮ High ▢ Medium ☐ Low ⊟ Data not available or not appropriate for age level

Within-Battery

g loading

Specificity

Cross-Battery

g loading

Specificity

g **loading key** ▮ Good ▮ Fair ☐ Poor   **Specificity key** ▮ Ample ▮ Adequate ☐ Inadequate

⊟ Data not available or not appropriate for age level

Test floor: *Inadequate* from ages 11:11 to 24:11

Test ceiling: Adequate

Item gradients

Gradient key ▮ Good ▮ Fair ☐ Poor ⊟ Data not available or not appropriate for age level

(Note: Refer to Table 3-2 in Chapter 3 for the definition of terms used in the various keys)

TEST BATTERY: SB: IV   **TEST: Equation Building**

Gf-Gc CLASSIFICATIONS

	Primary	**Secondary**
Classification Key		

Broad (Stratum II)
- ■ Empirical: strong
- ■ Empirical: moderate
- ▢ Empirical: mixed
- ☐ Logical

Narrow (Stratum I)
- ■ Probable
- ☐ Possible

Primary
- ■ Fluid Intelligence *(Gf)*
- ■ Quantitative Reasoning (RQ)

Secondary
- ☐ Quantitative Knowledge *(Gq)*
- ☐ Mathematical Knowledge (KM)

OTHER VARIABLES THAT INFLUENCE TEST PERFORMANCE

Typical Age of Concept Attainment

	3	4	5	> 5	Data not available
Basic Concepts in Directions *(Frequency of occurrence)*		Not appropriate for age range covered			

Degree of Cultural Content   ☐ High   ■ Medium   ☐ Low

Additional Factors

Background/Environmental	**Individual/Situational**
Math difficulties Educational opportunities/experiences	Planning

(Note: Refer to Table 3-2 in Chapter 3 for the definition of terms used in the various keys)

Chapter 8

Wechsler Adult Intelligence Scale—Third Edition (WAIS-III)

General Information

Author: David Wechsler

Publisher: The Psychological Corporation

Publication Date: 1939–1997

Age Range: Age 16 to 89

Administration Time: 60 to 90 min.

Composite Measure Information

Broad Measure of Intelligence: Full Scale IQ (FSIQ)

Lower-Order Composites:
Verbal Scale
Performance Scale
Verbal Comprehension Index
Perceptual Organization Index
Working Memory Index
Processing Speed Index

Score Information

Peer Comparison Scores:
Percentile Rank
IQ/Index

Range of Standard Scores for Total Test Composite: 45 to 155

Mean Floor of Subtests at Age 3-0:[1] N/A

Norming Information

Number of Subtests Normed at Each Age:
Total: 14 across age range

Conormed with Tests of Achievement:
No (Linked scores with WIAT for ages 16–19)
Reading
Mathematics
Language
Writing

Person Variables in Norming Plan:
Gender
Race/Ethnicity (confounding race and Hispanic origin)
Education level (parent education used for ages 16–19)

Community Variables in Norming Plan:
Location
Size

Note: In the following WAIS-III ITDR pages the *Gf-Gc* subtest classifications are noted to be "empirical." Although the WAIS-III has not yet been subjected to appropriately designed cross-battery factor analysis studies, the robust Wechsler (viz., WAIS, WAIS-R) factor analysis literature would suggest that the WAIS-III subtests that were in the prior versions of the battery would load on the same *Gf-Gc* broad factors found in existing WAIS-R cross-battery studies. The three exceptions are the new Symbol Search, Matrix Reasoning, and Letter-Number Sequencing subtests, for which the *Gf-Gc* classifications are designated as "logical."

Note: The descriptions of the subtests of the WAIS-III were adapted with permission from Wechsler (1981), *WAIS-R Manual* and Wechsler (1997), *WAIS-III Administration and Scoring Manual* (San Antonio, TX: The Psychological Corporation).

[1] Standard deviations below the mean for a raw score of 1.

Size of Norming Sample for the Broad Measure of General Intelligence:
N = 2450
Average number per age group: 200

Age Blocks in Norm Table:[2]
2-year blocks (Age 16 to 19)
5-year blocks (Age 20 to 34; 65 to 89)
10-year blocks (Age 35 to 64)

Reviews

(No reviews were available for the WAIS-III at the time this book manuscript was completed.)

---

[2] In most cases, age blocks represent linear interpolations.

TEST BATTERY: WAIS-III   **TEST: Picture Completion**

Description of test: The examinee is required to identify an important part that is missing from a set of pictures of common objects and scenes.

Age Range: 16 to 89 years

BASIC PSYCHOMETRIC CHARACTERISTICS

Age (in years)

Reliability

Reliability key ▮ High ▯ Medium ▯ Low ⊟ Data not available or not appropriate for age level

Within-Battery

g loading

Specificity

Cross-Battery

g loading

Specificity

g loading key ▮ Good ▯ Fair ▯ Poor   Specificity key ▮ Ample ▯ Adequate ▯ Inadequate

⊟ Data not available or not appropriate for age level

Test floor: Adequate

Test ceiling: Adequate

Item gradients

Gradient key ▮ Good ▯ Fair ▯ Poor   ⊟ Data not available or not appropriate for age level

---

(Note: Refer to Table 3-2 in Chapter 3 for the definition of terms used in the various keys.)

TEST BATTERY: WAIS-III   **TEST: Picture Completion**

Gf-Gc CLASSIFICATIONS

	Primary	Secondary

Classification Key

Broad (Stratum II)
- ■ Empirical: strong
- ■ Empirical: moderate
- ☐ Empirical: mixed
- ☐ Logical

Secondary:
- ☐ Visual Processing (*Gv*)
- ☐ Crystallized Intelligence (*Gc*)

Narrow (Stratum I)
- ■ Probable
- ☐ Possible

Secondary:
- ☐ Flexibility of Closure (CF)
- ☐ General Information (KO)

OTHER VARIABLES THAT INFLUENCE TEST PERFORMANCE

Typical Age of Concept Attainment

Basic Concepts in Directions	3	4	5	> 5	Data not available
(Frequency of occurrence)		Not appropriate for age range covered			

Degree of Cultural Content   ☐ High   ■ Medium   ☐ Low

Additional Factors

Background/Environmental	Individual/Situational
Vision difficulties	Visual acuity
Alertness to the environment	Field dependence/independence

(Note: Refer to Table 3-2 in Chapter 3 for the definition of terms used in the various keys.)

TEST BATTERY: WAIS-III **TEST: Vocabulary**

Description of test: The examinee is required to orally define a series of orally presented words.

Age Range: 16 to 89 years

BASIC PSYCHOMETRIC CHARACTERISTICS

Age (in years)

Reliability

Reliability key: ■ High ▨ Medium ☐ Low ⊟ Data not available or not appropriate for age level

Within-Battery

g loading

Specificity

Cross-Battery

g loading

Specificity

g loading key: ■ Good ▨ Fair ☐ Poor **Specificity key:** ■ Ample ▨ Adequate ☐ Inadequate

⊟ Data not available or not appropriate for age level

Test floor: Adequate

Test ceiling: Adequate

Item gradients

Gradient key: ■ Good ▨ Fair ☐ Poor ⊟ Data not available or not appropriate for age level

(Note: Refer to Table 3-2 in Chapter 3 for the definition of terms used in the various keys.)

TEST BATTERY: WAIS-III   **TEST: Vocabulary**

Gf-Gc CLASSIFICATIONS	**Primary**	**Secondary**

Classification Key

Broad (Stratum II)   ■ Crystallized Intelligence (*Gc*)
  ■ Empirical: strong
  ■ Empirical: moderate
  ☐ Empirical: mixed
  ☐ Logical

Narrow (Stratum I)   ■ Language Development (LD)
  ■ Probable   ■ Lexical Knowledge (VL)
  ☐ Possible

OTHER VARIABLES THAT INFLUENCE TEST PERFORMANCE

Typical Age of Concept Attainment

	3	4	5	> 5	Data not available
Basic Concepts in Directions					
(Frequency of occurrence)		Not appropriate for age range covered			

Degree of Cultural Content   ■ High   ☐ Medium   ☐ Low

Additional Factors

Background/Environmental	**Individual/Situational**
Language stimulation	
Environmental stimulation	
Educational opportunities/experiences	
Alertness to the environment	
Intellectual curiosity	

(Note: Refer to Table 3-2 in Chapter 3 for the definition of terms used in the various keys.)

TEST BATTERY: WAIS-III   **TEST: Digit Symbol-Coding**

Description of test: The examinee is required to draw symbols that are paired with a series of numbers
according to a key. The examinee is required to perform this task as quickly as possible.
This is a timed test.

Age Range: 16 to 89 years

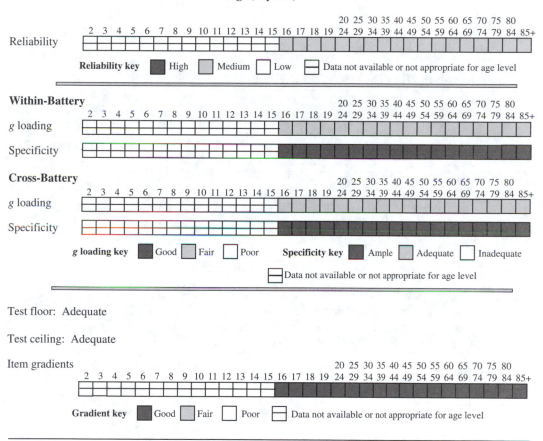

Test floor: Adequate

Test ceiling: Adequate

(Note: Refer to Table 3-2 in Chapter 3 for the definition of terms used in the various keys.)

TEST BATTERY: WAIS-III   **TEST: Digit Symbol-Coding**

Gf-Gc CLASSIFICATIONS

	Primary	Secondary

Classification Key

Broad (Stratum II)
- ■ Empirical: strong
- ■ Empirical: moderate
- ☐ Empirical: mixed
- ☐ Logical

■ Processing Speed (*Gs*)

Narrow (Stratum I)
- ■ Probable
- ☐ Possible

■ Rate-of-test-taking (R9)

OTHER VARIABLES THAT INFLUENCE TEST PERFORMANCE

Typical Age of Concept Attainment

	3	4	5	> 5	Data not available
Basic Concepts in Directions (Frequency of occurrence)		Not appropriate for age range covered			

Degree of Cultural Content   ☐ High   ☐ Medium   ■ Low

Additional Factors

Background/Environmental	Individual/Situational
Vision difficulties	Attention span
	Concentration
	Distractibility
	Visual Acuity
	Reflectivity/impulsivity
	Verbal elaboration
	Visual elaboration
	Planning
	Ability to perform under time pressure

(Note: Refer to Table 3-2 in Chapter 3 for the definition of terms used in the various keys.)

TEST BATTERY: WAIS-III   **TEST: Similarities**

Description of test: The examinee is presented pairs of words orally and is required to explain the similarity of the common objects or concepts they represent.

Age Range: 16 to 89 years

BASIC PSYCHOMETRIC CHARACTERISTICS

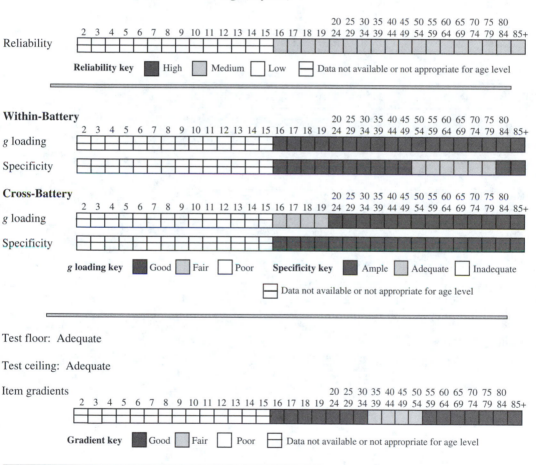

Test floor: Adequate

Test ceiling: Adequate

Item gradients

(Note: Refer to Table 3-2 in Chapter 3 for the definition of terms used in the various keys.)

TEST BATTERY: WAIS-III   **TEST: Similarities**

| *Gf-Gc* CLASSIFICATIONS |

Classification Key   **Primary**   **Secondary**

Broad (Stratum II)   ■ Crystallized Intelligence (*Gc*)
    ■ Empirical: strong
    ■ Empirical: moderate
    ☐ Empirical: mixed
    ☐ Logical

Narrow (Stratum I)   ■ Language Development (LD)
    ■ Probable   ☐ Lexical Knowledge (VL)
    ☐ Possible

| **OTHER VARIABLES THAT INFLUENCE TEST PERFORMANCE** |

Typical Age of Concept Attainment

	3	4	5	> 5	Data not available
Basic Concepts in Directions (Frequency of occurrence)		Not appropriate for age range covered			

Degree of Cultural Content   ■ High   ☐ Medium   ☐ Low

Additional Factors

Background/Environmental	**Individual/Situational**
Language stimulation	
Environmental stimulation	
Educational opportunities/experiences	

(Note: Refer to Table 3-2 in Chapter 3 for the definition of terms used in the various keys.)

TEST BATTERY: WAIS-III   **TEST: Block Design**

Description of test: The examinee is required to replicate a set of modeled or printed two-dimensional geometric patterns using two-color cubes. This is a timed test.

Age Range: 16 to 89 years

| BASIC PSYCHOMETRIC CHARACTERISTICS |

Age (in years)

Reliability

Reliability key ■ High   ▨ Medium   ☐ Low   ⊟ Data not available or not appropriate for age level

Within-Battery

g loading

Specificity

Cross-Battery

g loading

Specificity

g loading key ■ Good   ▨ Fair   ☐ Poor   Specificity key ■ Ample   ▨ Adequate   ☐ Inadequate

⊟ Data not available or not appropriate for age level

Test floor: Adequate

Test ceiling: Adequate

Item gradients

Gradient key ■ Good   ▨ Fair   ☐ Poor   ⊟ Data not available or not appropriate for age level

(Note: Refer to Table 3-2 in Chapter 3 for the definition of terms used in the various keys.)

TEST BATTERY: WAIS-III   **TEST: Block Design**

Gf-Gc CLASSIFICATIONS	Primary	Secondary

<u>Classsification Key</u>

Broad (Stratum II)   ■ Visual Processing (*Gv*)
   ■ Empirical: strong
   ■ Empirical: moderate
   ☐ Empirical: mixed
   ☐ Logical

Narrow (Stratum I)   ■ Spatial Relations (SR)
   ■ Probable   ☐ Visualization (VZ)
   ☐ Possible

OTHER VARIABLES THAT INFLUENCE TEST PERFORMANCE

Typical Age of Concept Attainment

Basic Concepts in Directions	3	4	5	> 5	Data not available
(Frequency of occurrence)			Not appropriate for age range covered		

Degree of Cultural Content   ☐ High   ☐ Medium   ■ Low

Additional Factors

Background/Environmental	Individual/Situational
	Color blindness
	Reflectivity/impulsivity
	Field dependence/independence
	Flexibility/inflexibility
	Planning
	Ability to perform under time pressure

(Note: Refer to Table 3-2 in Chapter 3 for the definition of terms used in the various keys.)

TEST BATTERY: WAIS-III   **TEST: Arithmetic**

Description of test: The examinee is required to mentally solve a series of orally presented arithmetic problems and respond orally.

Age Range: 16 to 89 years

BASIC PSYCHOMETRIC CHARACTERISTICS

Age (in years)

Reliability

Reliability key ■ High ▨ Medium □ Low ⊟ Data not available or not appropriate for age level

---

Within-Battery

g loading

Specificity

Cross-Battery

g loading

Specificity

g loading key ■ Good ▨ Fair □ Poor   Specificity key ■ Ample ▨ Adequate □ Inadequate

⊟ Data not available or not appropriate for age level

Test floor: Adequate

Test ceiling: Adequate

Item gradients

Gradient key ■ Good ▨ Fair □ Poor ⊟ Data not available or not appropriate for age level

---

(Note: Refer to Table 3-2 in Chapter 3 for the definition of terms used in the various keys.)

TEST BATTERY: WAIS-III   **TEST: Arithmetic**

Gf-Gc CLASSIFICATIONS

	Primary	Secondary

<u>Classification Key</u>

Broad (Stratum II)
- ■ Empirical: strong
- ■ Empirical: moderate
- ☐ Empirical: mixed
- ☐ Logical

■ Quantitative Knowledge (*Gq*)   ☐ Fluid Intelligence (*Gf*)

Narrow (Stratum I)
- ■ Probable
- ☐ Possible

■ Math Achievement (A3)   ☐ Quantitative Reasoning (RQ)

OTHER VARIABLES THAT INFLUENCE TEST PERFORMANCE

Typical Age of Concept Attainment

	3	4	5	> 5	Data not available

Basic Concepts in Directions

(Frequency of occurrence)

Not appropriate for age range covered

Degree of Cultural Content   ☐ High   ■ Medium   ☐ Low

Additional Factors

Background/Environmental	**Individual/Situational**
Math difficulties	Attention span
Educational opportunities/experiences	Concentration
	Distractibility
	Visual elaboration

(Note: Refer to Table 3-2 in Chapter 3 for the definition of terms used in the various keys.)

TEST BATTERY: WAIS-III   **TEST: Matrix Reasoning**

Description of test: The examinee is presented a series of geometric shapes in an incomplete grid and must identify the correct answer that completes the grid from five different options.

Age Range: 16 to 89 years

| BASIC PSYCHOMETRIC CHARACTERISTICS |

Age (in years)

Reliability

Reliability key ■ High ▨ Medium □ Low ⊟ Data not available or not appropriate for age level

Within-Battery

g loading

Specificity

Cross-Battery

g loading

Specificity

g **loading key** ■ Good ▨ Fair □ Poor   **Specificity key** ■ Ample ▨ Adequate □ Inadequate

⊟ Data not available or not appropriate for age level

Test floor: Adequate

Test ceiling: Adequate

Item gradients

Gradient key ■ Good ▨ Fair □ Poor ⊟ Data not available or not appropriate for age level

(Note: Refer to Table 3-2 in Chapter 3 for the definition of terms used in the various keys.)

TEST BATTERY: WAIS-III   **TEST: Matrix Reasoning**

Gf-Gc CLASSIFICATIONS

	Primary	**Secondary**

<u>Classification Key</u>

Broad (Stratum II)
- ■ Empirical: strong
- ▨ Empirical: moderate
- ▢ Empirical: mixed
- ☐ Logical

☐ Fluid Intelligence (*Gf*)

Narrow (Stratum I)
- ■ Probable
- ☐ Possible

■ Induction (I)

OTHER VARIABLES THAT INFLUENCE TEST PERFORMANCE

Typical Age of Concept Attainment

Basic Concepts in Directions	3	4	5	> 5	Data not available
(Frequency of occurrence)		Not appropriate for age range covered			

Degree of Cultural Content   ☐ High   ☐ Medium   ■ Low

Additional Factors

Background/Environmental	**Individual/Situational**
Vision difficulties	Reflectivity/impulsivity
	Field dependence/independence
	Flexibility/inflexibility
	Planning

(Note: Refer to Table 3-2 in Chapter 3 for the definition of terms used in the various keys.)

TEST BATTERY: WAIS-III   **TEST: Digit Span**

Description of test: The examinee is required to repeat verbatim or in a reversed order a series of orally presented number sequences.

Age Range: 16 to 89 years

BASIC PSYCHOMETRIC CHARACTERISTICS

Age (in years)

Reliability

Reliability key ■ High   ■ Medium   □ Low   ⊟ Data not available or not appropriate for age level

---

Within-Battery

g loading

Specificity

Cross-Battery

g loading

Specificity

***g* loading key** ■ Good   ■ Fair   □ Poor   **Specificity key** ■ Ample   ■ Adequate   □ Inadequate

⊟ Data not available or not appropriate for age level

Test floor: Adequate

Test ceiling: Adequate

Item gradients

Gradient key ■ Good   ■ Fair   □ Poor   ⊟ Data not available or not appropriate for age level

---

(Note: Refer to Table 3-2 in Chapter 3 for the definition of terms used in the various keys.)

TEST BATTERY: WAIS-III   **TEST: Digit Span**

Gf-Gc CLASSIFICATIONS		
	Primary	**Secondary**

Classification Key

Broad (Stratum II)
- ■ Empirical: strong
- ▨ Empirical: moderate
- ☐ Empirical: mixed
- ☐ Logical

■ Short-term Memory (*Gsm*)

Narrow (Stratum I)
- ▨ Probable
- ☐ Possible

▨ Memory Span (MS)

OTHER VARIABLES THAT INFLUENCE TEST PERFORMANCE

Typical Age of Concept Attainment

	3	4	5	> 5	Data not available
Basic Concepts in Directions (Frequency of occurrence)		Not appropriate for age range covered			

Degree of Cultural Content   ☐ High   ☐ Medium   ■ Low

Additional Factors

Background/Environmental	**Individual/Situational**
	Attention span
	Concentration
	Distractibility
	Verbal rehearsal
	Visual elaboration
	Organization

(Note: Refer to Table 3-2 in Chapter 3 for the definition of terms used in the various keys.)

TEST BATTERY: WAIS-III   **TEST: Information**

Description of test: The examinee is required to respond to a series of orally presented questions that tap
ones knowledge about common events, objects, places, and people.

Age Range: 16 to 89 years

BASIC PSYCHOMETRIC CHARACTERISTICS

Age (in years)

Reliability

Reliability key ■ High   ■ Medium   □ Low   ⊟ Data not available or not appropriate for age level

Within-Battery

g loading

Specificity

Cross-Battery

g loading

Specificity

g loading key ■ Good   ■ Fair   □ Poor   **Specificity key** ■ Ample   ■ Adequate   □ Inadequate

⊟ Data not available or not appropriate for age level

Test floor: Adequate

Test ceiling: Adequate

Item gradients

Gradient key ■ Good   ■ Fair   □ Poor   ⊟ Data not available or not appropriate for age level

---

(Note: Refer to Table 3-2 in Chapter 3 for the definition of terms used in the various keys.)

TEST BATTERY: WAIS-III   **TEST: Information**

Gf-Gc CLASSIFICATIONS

	Primary	**Secondary**
<u>Classification Key</u>		

Broad (Stratum II)
- ■ Empirical: strong
- ▪ Empirical: moderate
- ☐ Empirical: mixed
- ☐ Logical

■ Crystallized Intelligence (*Gc*)

Narrow (Stratum I)
- ▪ Probable
- ☐ Possible

▪ General Information (K0)

OTHER VARIABLES THAT INFLUENCE TEST PERFORMANCE

Typical Age of Concept Attainment

Basic Concepts in Directions	3	4	5	> 5	Data not available
(Frequency of occurrence)		Not appropriate for age range covered			

Degree of Cultural Content   ■ High   ☐ Medium   ☐ Low

Additional Factors

Background/Environmental	**Individual/Situational**
Environmental stimulation	
Educational opportunities/experiences	
Alertness to the environment	
Intellectual curiosity	

(Note: Refer to Table 3-2 in Chapter 3 for the definition of terms used in the various keys.)

TEST BATTERY: WAIS-III **TEST: Picture Arrangement**

Description of test: The examinee is required to arrange a set of pictures, presented in a mixed-up order, into a logical story sequence. This is a timed test.

Age Range: 16 to 89 years

BASIC PSYCHOMETRIC CHARACTERISTICS

Age (in years)

Reliability

Reliability key ■ High ▨ Medium ☐ Low ⊟ Data not available or not appropriate for age level

Within-Battery

g loading

Specificity

Cross-Battery

g loading

Specificity

g loading key ■ Good ▨ Fair ☐ Poor **Specificity key** ■ Ample ▨ Adequate ☐ Inadequate

⊟ Data not available or not appropriate for age level

Test floor: *Inadequate* from ages 65 to 89

Test ceiling: Adequate

Item gradients

Gradient key ■ Good ▨ Fair ☐ Poor ⊟ Data not available or not appropriate for age level

(Note: Refer to Table 3-2 in Chapter 3 for the definition of terms used in the various keys.)

TEST BATTERY: WAIS-III   **TEST: Picture Arrangement**

Gf-Gc CLASSIFICATIONS

	Primary	**Secondary**

Classification Key

Broad (Stratum II)
- ■ Empirical: strong
- ▨ Empirical: moderate
- ▢ Empirical: mixed
- ☐ Logical

Secondary:
- ▨ Visual Processing (*Gv*)
- ▨ Crystallized Intelligence (*Gc*)

Narrow (Stratum I)
- ▨ Probable
- ☐ Possible

Secondary:
- ☐ Visualization (VZ)
- ☐ General Information (K0)

OTHER VARIABLES THAT INFLUENCE TEST PERFORMANCE

Typical Age of Concept Attainment

	3	4	5	> 5	Data not available
Basic Concepts in Directions (Frequency of occurrence)		Not appropriate for age range covered			

Degree of Cultural Content   ☐ High   ▨ Medium   ☐ Low

Additional Factors

Background/Environmental	**Individual/Situational**
Alertness to the environment	Reflectivity/impulsivity
Educational opportunities/experiences	Flexibility/inflexibility
	Planning
	Ability to perform under time pressure

(Note: Refer to Table 3-2 in Chapter 3 for the definition of terms used in the various keys.)

TEST BATTERY: WAIS-III   **TEST: Comprehension**

Description of test: The examinee is required to respond orally to orally presented questions that focus on everyday problems or understanding of social rules and concepts.

Age Range: 16 to 89 years

BASIC PSYCHOMETRIC CHARACTERISTICS

Age (in years)

Reliability

Reliability key: ■ High ▨ Medium ☐ Low ⊟ Data not available or not appropriate for age level

Within-Battery

g loading

Specificity

Cross-Battery

g loading

Specificity

g loading key: ■ Good ▨ Fair ☐ Poor   Specificity key: ■ Ample ▨ Adequate ☐ Inadequate

⊟ Data not available or not appropriate for age level

Test floor: Adequate

Test ceiling: Adequate

Item gradients

Gradient key: ■ Good ▨ Fair ☐ Poor ⊟ Data not available or not appropriate for age level

(Note: Refer to Table 3-2 in Chapter 3 for the definition of terms used in the various keys.)

TEST BATTERY: WAIS-III   **TEST: Comprehension**

Gf-Gc CLASSIFICATIONS

	Primary	Secondary

Classification Key

Broad (Stratum II)
- ■ Empirical: strong
- ■ Empirical: moderate
- ☐ Empirical: mixed
- ☐ Logical

■ Crystallized Intelligence (*Gc*)

Narrow (Stratum I)
- ■ Probable
- ☐ Possible

■ Language Development (LD)
■ General Information (KO)

OTHER VARIABLES THAT INFLUENCE TEST PERFORMANCE

Typical Age of Concept Attainment

	3	4	5	> 5	Data not available

Basic Concepts in Directions

(Frequency of occurrence)

Not appropriate for age range covered

Degree of Cultural Content   ■ High   ☐ Medium   ☐ Low

Additional Factors

Background/Environmental	Individual/Situational

Language stimulation
Environmental stimulation
Educational opportunities/experiences
Alertness to the environment

(Note: Refer to Table 3-2 in Chapter 3 for the definition of terms used in the various keys.)

TEST BATTERY: WAIS-III   **TEST: Symbol Search**

Description of test: The examinee is required to scan a series of paired groups of symbols, each pair consisting of a target group and a search group, and indicate whether or not a target symbol appears in the search group. The examinee is required to perform this task as quickly as possible. This is a timed test.

Age Range: 16 to 89 years

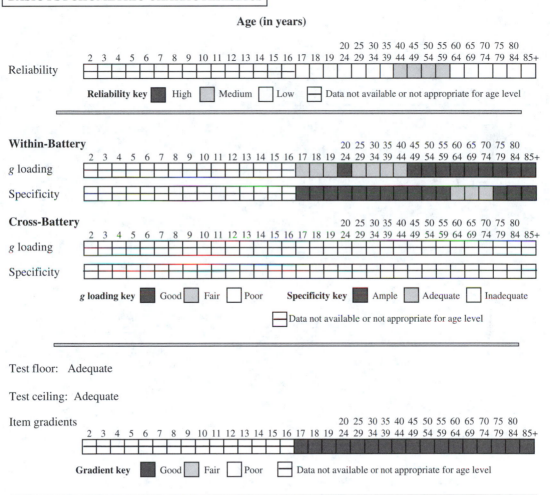

BASIC PSYCHOMETRIC CHARACTERISTICS

Test floor: Adequate

Test ceiling: Adequate

Item gradients

(Note: Refer to Table 3-2 in Chapter 3 for the definition of terms used in the various keys.)

TEST BATTERY: WAIS-III   **TEST: Symbol Search**

Gf-Gc CLASSIFICATIONS

	Primary	**Secondary**

Classification Key

Broad (Stratum II)   ☐ Processing Speed (*Gs*)
- ■ Empirical: strong
- ■ Empirical: moderate
- ☐ Empirical: mixed
- ☐ Logical

Narrow (Stratum I)   ■ Perceptual Speed (P)
- ■ Probable   ■ Rate-of-test-taking (R9)
- ☐ Possible

OTHER VARIABLES THAT INFLUENCE TEST PERFORMANCE

Typical Age of Concept Attainment

Basic Concepts in Directions (Frequency of occurrence)	3	4	5	> 5	Data not available
		Not appropriate for age range covered			

Degree of Cultural Content   ☐ High   ☐ Medium   ■ Low

Additional Factors

Background/Environmental	**Individual/Situational**
Vision difficulties	Attention span
	Concentration
	Distractibility
	Visual acuity
	Reflectivity/impulsivity
	Verbal elaboration
	Visual elaboration
	Planning
	Ability to perform under time pressure

(Note: Refer to Table 3-2 in Chapter 3 for the definition of terms used in the various keys.)

TEST BATTERY: WAIS-III   **TEST: Letter-Number Sequencing**

Description of test: The examinee is presented orally a series of letters and numbers in a mixed-up order and then is required to reorder and say the complete list with the numbers first in ascending order and then the letters in alphabetical order.

Age Range: 16 to 89 years

BASIC PSYCHOMETRIC CHARACTERISTICS

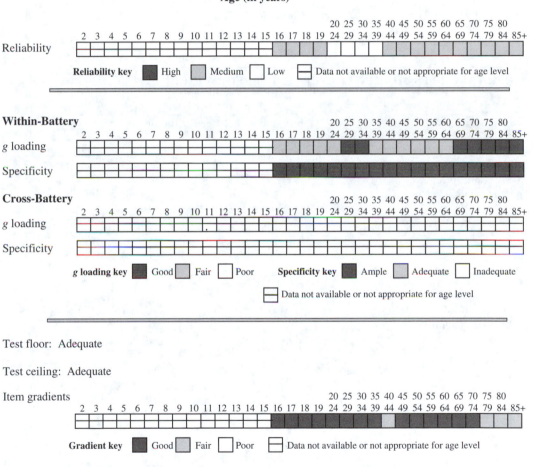

Test floor: Adequate

Test ceiling: Adequate

Item gradients

(Note: Refer to Table 3-2 in Chapter 3 for the definition of terms used in the various keys.)

TEST BATTERY: WAIS-III   **TEST: Letter-Number Sequencing**

Gf-Gc CLASSIFICATIONS

<u>Classification Key</u>

	Primary	Secondary

Broad (Stratum II)
- ■ Empirical: strong
- ■ Empirical: moderate
- ☐ Empirical: mixed
- ☐ Logical

☐ Short-term Memory (*Gsm*)

Narrow (Stratum I)
- ■ Probable
- ☐ Possible

■ Memory Span (MS)

OTHER VARIABLES THAT INFLUENCE TEST PERFORMANCE

Typical Age of Concept Attainment

Basic Concepts in Directions	3	4	5	> 5	Data not available
(Frequency of occurrence)		Not appropriate for age range covered			

Degree of Cultural Content   ■ High   ☐ Medium   ☐ Low

Additional Factors

Background/Environmental	Individual/Situational
	Attention span
	Concentration
	Distractibility
	Verbal rehearsal
	Visual elaboration

(Note: Refer to Table 3-2 in Chapter 3 for the definition of terms used in the various keys.)

TEST BATTERY: WAIS-III   **TEST: Object Assembly**

Description of test: The examinee is required to assemble a set of puzzles of common objects into
meaningful wholes. This is a timed test.

Age Range: 16 to 89 years

BASIC PSYCHOMETRIC CHARACTERISTICS

Age (in years)

Reliability

Reliability key   ■ High   ▨ Medium   □ Low   ⊟ Data not available or not appropriate for age level

---

Within-Battery

g loading

Specificity

Cross-Battery

g loading

Specificity

***g* loading key**   ■ Good   ▨ Fair   □ Poor   **Specificity key**   ■ Ample   ▨ Adequate   □ Inadequate

⊟ Data not available or not appropriate for age level

Test floor: Adequate

Test ceiling: Adequate

Item gradients

Gradient key   ■ Good   ▨ Fair   □ Poor   ⊟ Data not available or not appropriate for age level

---

(Note: Refer to Table 3-2 in Chapter 3 for the definition of terms used in the various keys.)

TEST BATTERY: WAIS-III   **TEST: Object Assembly**

Gf-Gc CLASSIFICATIONS

	Primary	Secondary

Broad (Stratum II)
- ■ Empirical: strong
- ■ Empirical: moderate
- ☐ Empirical: mixed
- ☐ Logical

■ Visual Processing (*Gv*)

Narrow (Stratum I)
- ■ Probable
- ☐ Possible

■ Closure Speed (CS)
☐ Spatial Relations (SR)

OTHER VARIABLES THAT INFLUENCE TEST PERFORMANCE

Typical Age of Concept Attainment

	3	4	5	> 5	Data not available
Basic Concepts in Directions *(Frequency of occurrence)*			Not appropriate for age range covered		

Degree of Cultural Content   ☐ High   ■ Medium   ☐ Low

Additional Factors

Background/Environmental	Individual/Situational
Alertness to the environment	Reflectivity/impulsivity
	Field dependence/independence
	Planning
	Ability to perform under time pressure

(Note: Refer to Table 3-2 in Chapter 3 for the definition of terms used in the various keys.)

Wechsler Intelligence Scale for Children—Third Edition (WISC-III)

General Information

Author: David Wechsler

Publisher: The Psychological Corporation

Publication Date: 1949–1991

Age Range: Age 6-0 to 16-11

Administration Time:
50 to 70 min.
Supplementary subtests: 10 to 15 min.

Composite Measure Information

Broad Measure of Intelligence: Full Scale IQ (FSIQ)

Lower-Order Composites:
Verbal Comprehension
Perceptual Organization

Freedom from Distractibility
Processing Speed

Score Information

Peer Comparison Scores:
Percentile Rank
IQ/Index

Range of Standard Scores for Total Test Composite: 40 to 160

Mean Floor of Subtests at Age 3-0:[1] N/A

Norming Information

Number of Subtests Normed at Each Age:
Total: 13 across age range

Conormed with Tests of Achievement:
No (Equated scores for WIAT)
Reading
Mathematics
Language
Writing

Person Variables in Norming Plan:
Gender
Race/Ethnicity (confounding race and Hispanic origin)
Family SES (occupation and education)

Note: The above information was adapted from Harrison, Flanagan, and Genshaft (1997). Copyright 1997 Guilford Publishing Co. All rights reserved.

Descriptions of the WISC-III subtests are adapted from *Wechsler Intelligence Scale for Children: Third Edition.* Copyright © 1990 by The Psychological Corporation. Reproduced by permission. All rights reserved. "Wechsler Intelligence Scale for Children" and "WISC-III" are registered trademarks of The Psychological Corporation.

In the following WISC-IIII ITDR pages the *Gf-Gc* subtest classifications are noted to be "empirical." Although the WISC-III has not yet been subjected to appropriately designed cross-battery factor analysis studies, the robust Wechsler (viz., WISC; WISC-R) factor analysis literature would suggest that the WISC-III subtests would load on the same *Gf-Gc* broad factors found in existing WISC-R cross-battery studies. The one exception is the new Symbol Search subtest, for which the *Gf-Gc* classifications are designated as "logical."

[1] Standard deviations below the mean for a raw score of 1.

Community Variables in Norming Plan:
Location
Size

Size of Norming Sample for the Broad Measure of General Intelligence:
N = 2200
Average number per year: 200

Age Blocks in Norm Table:[2]
4-month blocks

Reviews

Braden, J. P. (1995). Review of the Wechsler Intelligence Scale for Children, Third Edition. In J. C. Conoley & J. C. Impara (Eds.), *The twelfth mental measurements yearbook* (pp. 1098–1103). Lincoln, NE: Buros Institute.

Carroll, J. B. (1993). What abilities are measured by the WISC-III? *Journal of Psychoeducational Assessment, WISC-III Monograph*, 134–143.

Edelman, S. (1996). A review of the Wechsler Intelligence Scale for Children—Third Edition (WISC-III). *Measurement and Evaluation in Counseling and Development, 28*, 219–224.

Kaufman, A. S. (1993). King WISC the Third assumes the throne. *Journal of School Psychology, 31*, 345–354.

Little, S. G. (1992). The WISC-III: Everything old is new again. *School Psychology Quarterly, 7* (2), 148–154.

Post, K. R., & Mitchell, H. R. (1993). The WISC-III: A reality check. *Journal of School Psychology, 31*, 541–545.

Sandoval, J. (1995). Review of the Wechsler Intelligence Scale for Children, Third Edition. In J. C. Conoley & J. C. Impara (Eds.), *The twelfth mental measurements yearbook* (pp. 1103–1104). Lincoln, NE: Buros Institute.

Shaw, S. R., Swerdlik, M. E., & Laurent, J. (1993). Review of the WISC-III. *Journal of Psychoeducational Assessment, WISC-III Monograph*, 151–160.

Sternberg, R. J. (1993). Rocky's back again: A review of the WISC-III. *Journal of Psychoeducational Assessment, WISC-III Monograph*, 161–164.

---

[2] In most cases, age blocks represent linear interpolations.

TEST BATTERY: WISC-III   **TEST: Picture Completion**

Description of test : The examinee is required to identify an important part that is missing from a set of pictures of common objects and scenes.

Age Range: 6 to 16 years

BASIC PSYCHOMETRIC CHARACTERISTICS

Age (in years)

Reliability

Reliability key ▮ High ▧ Medium ☐ Low ⊟ Data not available or not appropriate for age level

---

Within-Battery

g loading

Specificity

Cross-Battery

g loading

Specificity

g loading key ▮ Good ▧ Fair ☐ Poor   **Specificity key** ▮ Ample ▧ Adequate ☐ Inadequate

⊟ Data not available or not appropriate for age level

Test floor: Adequate

Test ceiling: Adequate

Item gradients

Gradient key ▮ Good ▧ Fair ☐ Poor   ⊟ Data not available or not appropriate for age level

---

(Note: Refer to Table 3-2 in Chapter 3 for the definition of terms used in the various keys.)

TEST BATTERY: WISC- III   **TEST: Picture Completion**

Gf-Gc CLASSIFICATIONS

Classification Key

	Primary	Secondary

Broad (Stratum II)
- ■ Empirical: strong
- ■ Empirical: moderate
- ☐ Empirical: mixed
- ☐ Logical

Secondary:
- ☐ Visual Processing *(Gv)*
- ☐ Crystallized Intelligence *(Gc)*

Narrow (Stratum I)
- ■ Probable
- ☐ Possible

Secondary:
- ☐ Flexibility of Closure (CF)
- ☐ General Information (KO)

OTHER VARIABLES THAT INFLUENCE TEST PERFORMANCE

Typical Age of Concept Attainment

Basic Concepts in Directions	3	4	5	> 5	Data not available
(Frequency of occurrence)		Not appropriate for age range covered			

Degree of Cultural Content   ☐ High   ■ Medium   ☐ Low

Additional Factors

Background/Environmental	Individual/Situational
Vision difficulties	Visual acuity
Alertness to the environment	Field dependence/independence

(Note: Refer to Table 3-2 in Chapter 3 for the definition of terms used in the various keys)

TEST BATTERY: WISC-III   **TEST: Information**

Description of test: The examinee is required to respond to a series of orally presented questions that tap knowledge about common events, objects, places, and people.

Age Range: 6 to 16 years

BASIC PSYCHOMETRIC CHARACTERISTICS

Age (in years)

Reliability

Reliability key: ■ High   ▨ Medium   □ Low   ⊟ Data not available or not appropriate for age level

---

Within-Battery

g loading

Specificity

Cross-Battery

g loading

Specificity

g loading key: ■ Good   ▨ Fair   □ Poor   Specificity key: ■ Ample   ▨ Adequate   □ Inadequate

⊟ Data not available or not appropriate for age level

Test floor: *Inadequate* from ages 6:0 to 6:3

Test ceiling: Adequate

Item gradients

Gradient key: ■ Good   ▨ Fair   □ Poor   ⊟ Data not available or not appropriate for age level

---

(Note: Refer to Table 3-2 in Chapter 3 for the definition of terms used in the various keys)

TEST BATTERY: WISC- III   **TEST: Information**

Gf-Gc CLASSIFICATIONS

	Primary	**Secondary**

Classification Key

Broad (Stratum II)
■ Empirical: strong
■ Empirical: moderate
☐ Empirical: mixed
☐ Logical

■ Crystallized Intelligence *(Gc)*

Narrow (Stratum I)
■ Probable
☐ Possible

■ General Information (KO)

OTHER VARIABLES THAT INFLUENCE TEST PERFORMANCE

Typical Age of Concept Attainment

	3	4	5	> 5	Data not available

Basic Concepts in Directions

(Frequency of occurrence)

Not appropriate for age range covered

Degree of Cultural Content   ■ High   ☐ Medium   ☐ Low

Additional Factors

Background/Environmental	**Individual/Situational**

Environmental stimulation
Educational opportunities/experiences
Alertness to the environment
Intellectual curiosity

(Note: Refer to Table 3-2 in Chapter 3 for the definition of terms used in the various keys)

TEST BATTERY: WISC-III   **TEST: Coding**

Description of test: The examinee is required to draw symbols that are paired with a series of simple shapes (Coding A) or numbers (Coding B) according to a key. The examinee is required to perform the task as quickly as possible. The test is timed.

Age Range: 6 to 16 years

BASIC PSYCHOMETRIC CHARACTERISTICS

Age (in years)

Reliability

Reliability key: ■ High   ▨ Medium   □ Low   ⊟ Data not available or not appropriate for age level

---

Within-Battery

g loading

Specificity

Cross-Battery

g loading

Specificity

g loading key: ■ Good   ▨ Fair   □ Poor   Specificity key: ■ Ample   ▨ Adequate   □ Inadequate

⊟ Data not available or not appropriate for age level

Test floor: Adequate

Test ceiling: Adequate

Item gradients

Gradient key: ■ Good   ▨ Fair   □ Poor   ⊟ Data not available or not appropriate for age level

(Note: Refer to Table 3-2 in Chapter 3 for the definition of terms used in the various keys)

TEST BATTERY: WISC- III   **TEST: Coding**

Gf-Gc CLASSIFICATIONS

	Primary	**Secondary**

Classification Key

Broad (Stratum II)
- ■ Empirical: strong
- ◼ Empirical: moderate
- ◻ Empirical: mixed
- ☐ Logical

■ Processing Speed *(Gs)*

Narrow (Stratum I)
- ◼ Probable
- ☐ Possible

◼ Rate-of-test-taking (R9)

OTHER VARIABLES THAT INFLUENCE TEST PERFORMANCE

Typical Age of Concept Attainment

Basic Concepts in Directions (Frequency of occurrence)	3	4	5	> 5	Data not available
		Not appropriate for age range covered			

Degree of Cultural Content   ☐ High   ☐ Medium   ◼ Low

Additional Factors

Background/Environmental	**Individual/Situational**
Vision difficulties	Attention span
	Concentration
	Distractibility
	Visual Acuity
	Reflectivity/impulsivity
	Verbal elaboration
	Visual elaboration
	Planning
	Ability to perform under time pressure

(Note: Refer to Table 3-2 in Chapter 3 for the definition of terms used in the various keys)

TEST BATTERY: WISC-III   **TEST: Similarities**

Description of test: The examinee is presented pairs of words orally and is required to explain the
similarity of the common objects or concepts they represent.

Age Range: 6 to 16 years

BASIC PSYCHOMETRIC CHARACTERISTICS

Age (in years)

Reliability

Reliability key ■ High   ▨ Medium   ☐ Low   ⊟ Data not available or not appropriate for age level

---

Within-Battery

g loading

Specificity

Cross-Battery

g loading

Specificity

***g* loading key** ■ Good   ▨ Fair   ☐ Poor   **Specificity key** ■ Ample   ▨ Adequate   ☐ Inadequate

⊟ Data not available or not appropriate for age level

Test floor: *Inadequate* from ages 6:0 to 6:3

Test ceiling: Adequate

Item gradients

Gradient key ■ Good   ▨ Fair   ☐ Poor   ⊟ Data not available or not appropriate for age level

---

(Note: Refer to Table 3-2 in Chapter 3 for the definition of terms used in the various keys)

TEST BATTERY: WISC- III   **TEST: Similarities**

Gf-Gc CLASSIFICATIONS

	Primary	**Secondary**

Classification Key

Broad (Stratum II)
- ■ Empirical: strong
- ■ Empirical: moderate
- ☐ Empirical: mixed
- ☐ Logical

■ Crystallized Intelligence *(Gc)*

Narrow (Stratum I)
- ■ Probable
- ☐ Possible

■ Language Development (LD)
☐ Lexical Knowledge (VL)

OTHER VARIABLES THAT INFLUENCE TEST PERFORMANCE

Typical Age of Concept Attainment

	3	4	5	> 5	Data not available
Basic Concepts in Directions (Frequency of occurrence)		Not appropriate for age range covered			

Degree of Cultural Content   ■ High   ☐ Medium   ☐ Low

Additional Factors

Background/Environmental	**Individual/Situational**
Language stimulation Environmental stimulation Educational opportunities/experiences	

(Note: Refer to Table 3-2 in Chapter 3 for the definition of terms used in the various keys)

TEST BATTERY: WISC-III   **TEST: Picture Arrangement**

Description of test: The examinee is required to arrange a set of pictures, presented in a mixed-up order, into a logical story sequence. This is a timed test.

Age Range: 6 to 16 years

BASIC PSYCHOMETRIC CHARACTERISTICS

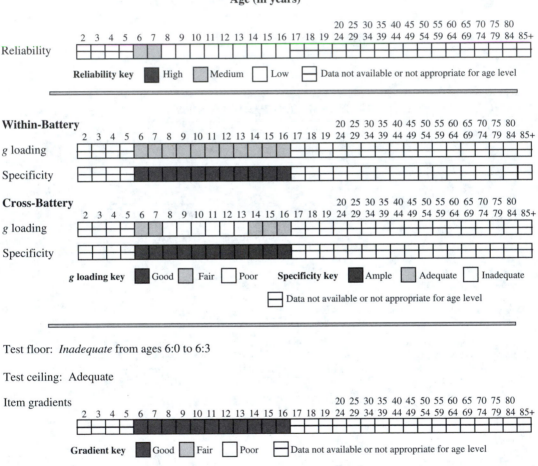

Test floor: *Inadequate* from ages 6:0 to 6:3

Test ceiling: Adequate

Item gradients

(Note: Refer to Table 3-2 in Chapter 3 for the definition of terms used in the various keys)

TEST BATTERY: WISC- III   **TEST: Picture Arrangement**

Gf-Gc CLASSIFICATIONS

	Primary	**Secondary**

Classification Key

Broad (Stratum II)
- ■ Empirical: strong
- ■ Empirical: moderate
- ☐ Empirical: mixed
- ☐ Logical

Secondary:
- ☐ Visual Processing *(Gv)*
- ☐ Crystallized Intelligence *(Gc)*

Narrow (Stratum I)
- ■ Probable
- ☐ Possible

Secondary:
- ☐ Visualization (VZ)
- ☐ General Information (KO)

OTHER VARIABLES THAT INFLUENCE TEST PERFORMANCE

Typical Age of Concept Attainment

	3	4	5	> 5	Data not available
Basic Concepts in Directions (Frequency of occurrence)		Not appropriate for age range covered			

Degree of Cultural Content   ☐ High   ■ Medium   ☐ Low

Additional Factors

Background/Environmental	**Individual/Situational**
Alertness to the environment	Reflectivity/impulsivity
Educational opportunities/experiences	Flexibility/inflexibility
	Planning
	Ability to perform under time pressure

(Note: Refer to Table 3-2 in Chapter 3 for the definition of terms used in the various keys)

TEST BATTERY: WISC-III   **TEST: Arithmetic**

Description of test: The examinee is required to mentally solve a series of orally presented arithmetic
problems and respond orally.

Age Range: 6 to 16 years

| BASIC PSYCHOMETRIC CHARACTERISTICS |

Age (in years)

Reliability

Reliability key ■ High   ▨ Medium   □ Low   ▭ Data not available or not appropriate for age level

Within-Battery

g loading

Specificity

Cross-Battery

g loading

Specificity

g loading key ■ Good   ▨ Fair   □ Poor   **Specificity key** ■ Ample   ▨ Adequate   □ Inadequate

▭ Data not available or not appropriate for age level

Test floor: Adequate

Test ceiling: Adequate

Item gradients

Gradient key ■ Good   ▨ Fair   □ Poor   ▭ Data not available or not appropriate for age level

---

(Note: Refer to Table 3-2 in Chapter 3 for the definition of terms used in the various keys)

TEST BATTERY: WISC- III   **TEST: Arithmetic**

Gf-Gc CLASSIFICATIONS

<u>Classification Key</u>

	Primary	Secondary

Broad (Stratum II)
- ■ Empirical: strong
- ■ Empirical: moderate
- ☐ Empirical: mixed
- ☐ Logical

■ Quantitative Knowledge *(Gq)*   ☐ Fluid Intelligence *(Gf)*

Narrow (Stratum I)
- ■ Probable
- ☐ Possible

■ Math Achievement (A3)   ☐ Quantitative Reasoning (RQ)

OTHER VARIABLES THAT INFLUENCE TEST PERFORMANCE

Typical Age of Concept Attainment

	3	4	5	> 5	Data not available

Basic Concepts in Directions

(Frequency of occurrence)

Not appropriate for age range covered

Degree of Cultural Content   ☐ High   ■ Medium   ☐ Low

Additional Factors

Background/Environmental	Individual/Situational
Math difficulties	Attention span
Educational opportunities/experiences	Concentration
	Distractibility
	Visual elaboration

(Note: Refer to Table 3-2 in Chapter 3 for the definition of terms used in the various keys)

TEST BATTERY: WISC-III   **TEST: Block Design**

Description of test: The examinee is required to replicate a set of modeled or printed two-dimensional geometric patterns using two-color cubes. This is a timed test.

Age Range: 6 to 16 years

BASIC PSYCHOMETRIC CHARACTERISTICS

Age (in years)

Reliability

Reliability key ■ High   ▨ Medium   □ Low   ⊟ Data not available or not appropriate for age level

---

Within-Battery

g loading

Specificity

Cross-Battery

g loading

Specificity

g **loading key** ■ Good   ▨ Fair   □ Poor   **Specificity key** ■ Ample   ▨ Adequate   □ Inadequate

⊟ Data not available or not appropriate for age level

Test floor: *Inadequate* from ages 6:0 to 6:3

Test ceiling: Adequate

Item gradients

Gradient key ■ Good   ▨ Fair   □ Poor   ⊟ Data not available or not appropriate for age level

---

(Note: Refer to Table 3-2 in Chapter 3 for the definition of terms used in the various keys)

TEST BATTERY: WISC-III   **TEST: Block Design**

Gf-Gc CLASSIFICATIONS

	Primary	**Secondary**

Classification Key

Broad (Stratum II)
- ■ Empirical: strong
- ■ Empirical: moderate
- ☐ Empirical: mixed
- ☐ Logical

■ Visual Processing *(Gv)*

Narrow (Stratum I)
- ■ Probable
- ☐ Possible

■ Spatial Relations (SR)
☐ Visualization (VZ)

OTHER VARIABLES THAT INFLUENCE TEST PERFORMANCE

Typical Age of Concept Attainment

	3	4	5	> 5	Data not available
Basic Concepts in Directions (Frequency of occurrence)		Not appropriate for age range covered			

Degree of Cultural Content   ☐ High   ☐ Medium   ■ Low

Additional Factors

Background/Environmental	**Individual/Situational**
	Color blindness
	Reflectivity/impulsivity
	Field dependence/independence
	Flexibility/inflexibility
	Planning
	Ability to perform under time pressure

(Note: Refer to Table 3-2 in Chapter 3 for the definition of terms used in the various keys)

TEST BATTERY: WISC-III   **TEST: Vocabulary**

Description of test: The examinee is required to define orally a series of orally presented words.

Age Range: 6 to 16 years

BASIC PSYCHOMETRIC CHARACTERISTICS

Age (in years)

Reliability

Reliability key   ■ High   ▣ Medium   ☐ Low   ⊟ Data not available or not appropriate for age level

---

Within-Battery

g loading

Specificity

Cross-Battery

g loading

Specificity

g loading key   ■ Good   ▣ Fair   ☐ Poor   **Specificity key**   ■ Ample   ▣ Adequate   ☐ Inadequate

⊟ Data not available or not appropriate for age level

Test floor: Adequate

Test ceiling: Adequate

Item gradients

Gradient key   ■ Good   ▣ Fair   ☐ Poor   ⊟ Data not available or not appropriate for age level

(Note: Refer to Table 3-2 in Chapter 3 for the definition of terms used in the various keys)

TEST BATTERY: WISC-III   **TEST: Vocabulary**

Gf-Gc CLASSIFICATIONS

	Primary	Secondary

Classification Key

Broad (Stratum II)
- ■ Empirical: strong
- ■ Empirical: moderate
- ◻ Empirical: mixed
- ☐ Logical

■ Crystallized Intelligence *(Gc)*

Narrow (Stratum I)
- ■ Probable
- ☐ Possible

■ Language Development (LD)
■ Lexical Knowledge (VL)

OTHER VARIABLES THAT INFLUENCE TEST PERFORMANCE

Typical Age of Concept Attainment

	3	4	5	> 5	Data not available
Basic Concepts in Directions (Frequency of occurrence)		Not appropriate for age range covered			

Degree of Cultural Content   ■ High   ☐ Medium   ☐ Low

Additional Factors

Background/Environmental	Individual/Situational
Language stimulation	
Environmental stimulation	
Educational opportunities/experiences	
Alertness to the environment	
Intellectual curiosity	

(Note: Refer to Table 3-2 in Chapter 3 for the definition of terms used in the various keys)

TEST BATTERY: WISC-III   **TEST: Object Assembly**

Description of test: The examinee is required to assemble a set of puzzles of common objects into meaningful wholes. This is a timed test.

Age Range: 6 to 16 years

BASIC PSYCHOMETRIC CHARACTERISTICS

Age (in years)

Reliability

Reliability key   High   Medium   Low   Data not available or not appropriate for age level

Within-Battery

g loading

Specificity

Cross-Battery

g loading

Specificity

g loading key   Good   Fair   Poor   **Specificity key**   Ample   Adequate   Inadequate

Data not available or not appropriate for age level

Test floor: Adequate

Test ceiling: Adequate

Item gradients

Gradient key   Good   Fair   Poor   Data not available or not appropriate for age level

(Note: Refer to Table 3-2 in Chapter 3 for the definition of terms used in the various keys)

TEST BATTERY: WISC-III   **TEST: Object Assembly**

Gf-Gc CLASSIFICATIONS

	Primary	Secondary

Classification Key

Broad (Stratum II)
- ■ Empirical: strong
- ■ Empirical: moderate
- ☐ Empirical: mixed
- ☐ Logical

■ Visual Processing *(Gv)*

Narrow (Stratum I)
- ■ Probable
- ☐ Possible

■ Closure Speed (CS)
☐ Spatial Relations (SR)

OTHER VARIABLES THAT INFLUENCE TEST PERFORMANCE

Typical Age of Concept Attainment

	3	4	5	> 5	Data not available
Basic Concepts in Directions (Frequency of occurrence)		Not appropriate for age range covered			

Degree of Cultural Content   ☐ High   ■ Medium   ☐ Low

Additional Factors

Background/Environmental	**Individual/Situational**
Alertness to the environment	Reflectivity/impulsivity
	Field dependence/independence
	Planning
	Ability to perform under time pressure

(Note: Refer to Table 3-2 in Chapter 3 for the definition of terms used in the various keys)

TEST BATTERY: WISC-III   **TEST: Comprehension**

Description of test: The examinee is required to respond orally to orally presented questions that focus on everyday problems or understanding of social rules and concepts.

Age Range: 6 to 16 years

BASIC PSYCHOMETRIC CHARACTERISTICS

Age (in years)

Reliability

Reliability key: High | Medium | Low | Data not available or not appropriate for age level

Within-Battery

g loading

Specificity

Cross-Battery

g loading

Specificity

g loading key: Good | Fair | Poor   Specificity key: Ample | Adequate | Inadequate

Data not available or not appropriate for age level

Test floor: Adequate

Test ceiling: Adequate

Item gradients

Gradient key: Good | Fair | Poor   Data not available or not appropriate for age level

(Note: Refer to Table 3-2 in Chapter 3 for the definition of terms used in the various keys)

TEST BATTERY: WISC-III   **TEST: Comprehension**

Gf-Gc CLASSIFICATIONS

	Primary	Secondary

Classification Key

Broad (Stratum II)
- ▪ Empirical: strong
- ▪ Empirical: moderate
- ☐ Empirical: mixed
- ☐ Logical

▪ Crystallized Intelligence *(Gc)*

Narrow (Stratum I)
- ▪ Probable
- ☐ Possible

▪ Language Development (LD)
▪ General Information (KO)

OTHER VARIABLES THAT INFLUENCE TEST PERFORMANCE

Typical Age of Concept Attainment

	3	4	5	> 5	Data not available
Basic Concepts in Directions (Frequency of occurrence)			Not appropriate for age range covered		

Degree of Cultural Content   ▪ High   ☐ Medium   ☐ Low

Additional Factors

Background/Environmental	Individual/Situational
Language stimulation	
Environmental stimulation	
Educational opportunities/experiences	
Alertness to the environment	

(Note: Refer to Table 3-2 in Chapter 3 for the definition of terms used in the various keys)

TEST BATTERY: WISC-III   **TEST: Symbol Search**

Description of test: The examinee is required to scan a series of paired groups of symbols, each pair consisting of a target group and a search group, and indicate whether or not a target symbol appears in the search group. The examinee is required to perform this task as quickly as possible. This is a timed test.

Age Range: 6 to 16 years

BASIC PSYCHOMETRIC CHARACTERISTICS

Age (in years)

Reliability

Reliability key   ■ High   ▨ Medium   □ Low   ⊟ Data not available or not appropriate for age level

Within-Battery

g loading

Specificity

Cross-Battery

g loading

Specificity

g loading key   ■ Good   ▨ Fair   □ Poor   **Specificity key**   ■ Ample   ▨ Adequate   □ Inadequate

⊟ Data not available or not appropriate for age level

Test floor: Adequate

Test ceiling: Adequate

Item gradients

Gradient key   ■ Good   ▨ Fair   □ Poor   ⊟ Data not available or not appropriate for age level

(Note: Refer to Table 3-2 in Chapter 3 for the definition of terms used in the various keys)

TEST BATTERY: WISC-III   **TEST: Symbol Search**

Gf-Gc CLASSIFICATIONS

	Primary	Secondary

Classification Key

Broad (Stratum II)
- ■ Empirical: strong
- ■ Empirical: moderate
- ☐ Empirical: mixed
- ☐ Logical

☐ Processing Speed *(Gs)*

Narrow (Stratum I)
- ■ Probable
- ☐ Possible

■ Perceptual Speed (P)
■ Rate-of-test-taking (R9)

OTHER VARIABLES THAT INFLUENCE TEST PERFORMANCE

Typical Age of Concept Attainment

	3	4	5	> 5	Data not available
Basic Concepts in Directions (Frequency of occurrence)		Not appropriate for age range covered			

Degree of Cultural Content   ☐ High   ☐ Medium   ■ Low

Additional Factors

Background/Environmental	Individual/Situational
Vision difficulties	Attention span
	Concentration
	Distractibility
	Visual Acuity
	Reflectivity/impulsivity
	Verbal elaboration
	Visual elaboration
	Planning
	Ability to perform under time pressure

(Note: Refer to Table 3-2 in Chapter 3 for the definition of terms used in the various keys)

TEST BATTERY: WISC-III   **TEST: Digit Span**

Description of test: The examinee is required to repeat verbatim or in a reversed order a series of orally
presented number sequences.

Age Range: 6 to 16 years

BASIC PSYCHOMETRIC CHARACTERISTICS

Age (in years)

Reliability

Reliability key: High / Medium / Low / Data not available or not appropriate for age level

---

Within-Battery

g loading

Specificity

Cross-Battery

g loading

Specificity

g loading key: Good / Fair / Poor   Specificity key: Ample / Adequate / Inadequate

Data not available or not appropriate for age level

Test floor: Adequate

Test ceiling: Adequate

Item gradients

Gradient key: Good / Fair / Poor   Data not available or not appropriate for age level

---

(Note: Refer to Table 3-2 in Chapter 3 for the definition of terms used in the various keys)

TEST BATTERY: WISC-III   **TEST: Digit Span**

Gf-Gc CLASSIFICATIONS

	Primary	Secondary

Classification Key

Broad (Stratum II)   ■ Short-term Memory *(Gsm)*
  ■ Empirical: strong
  ■ Empirical: moderate
  □ Empirical: mixed
  □ Logical

Narrow (Stratum I)   ■ Memory Span (MS)
  ■ Probable
  □ Possible

OTHER VARIABLES THAT INFLUENCE TEST PERFORMANCE

Typical Age of Concept Attainment

	3	4	5	> 5	Data not available
Basic Concepts in Directions (Frequency of occurrence)		Not appropriate for age range covered			

Degree of Cultural Content   □ High   □ Medium   ■ Low

Additional Factors

Background/Environmental	Individual/Situational
	Attention span
	Concentration
	Distractibility
	Verbal rehearsal
	Visual elaboration
	Organization

(Note: Refer to Table 3-2 in Chapter 3 for the definition of terms used in the various keys)

TEST BATTERY: WISC-III   **TEST: Mazes**

Description of test: The examinee is required to solve, with a pencil, a series of increasingly difficult mazes.

Age Range: 6 to 16 years

BASIC PSYCHOMETRIC CHARACTERISTICS

Age (in years)

Reliability

Reliability key ■ High ▨ Medium □ Low ⊟ Data not available or not appropriate for age level

Within-Battery

g loading

Specificity

Cross-Battery

g loading

Specificity

g loading key ■ Good ▨ Fair □ Poor   Specificity key ■ Ample ▨ Adequate □ Inadequate

⊟ Data not available or not appropriate for age level

Test floor: Adequate

Test ceiling: Adequate

Item gradients

Gradient key ■ Good ▨ Fair □ Poor   ⊟ Data not available or not appropriate for age level

---

(Note: Refer to Table 3-2 in Chapter 3 for the definition of terms used in the various keys)

TEST BATTERY: WISC-III   **TEST: Mazes**

Gf-Gc **CLASSIFICATIONS**	**Primary**	**Secondary**

Classification Key

Broad (Stratum II)
- ■ Empirical: strong
- ◾ Empirical: moderate
- ☐ Empirical: mixed
- ☐ Logical

■ Visual Processing *(Gv)*

Narrow (Stratum I)
- ◾ Probable
- ☐ Possible

■ Spatial Scanning (SS)

OTHER VARIABLES THAT INFLUENCE TEST PERFORMANCE

	Typical Age of Concept Attainment				
	3	**4**	**5**	**> 5**	**Data not available**
Basic Concepts in Directions (Frequency of occurrence)		Not appropriate for age range covered			

Degree of Cultural Content   ☐ High   ☐ Medium   ■ Low

Additional Factors

Background/Environmental	**Individual/Situational**
Vision difficulties	Visual-motor coordination
	Reflectivity/impulsivity
	Field dependence/independence
	Planning
	Ability to perform under time pressure

(Note: Refer to Table 3-2 in Chapter 3 for the definition of terms used in the various keys)

Chapter *10*

Wechsler Preschool and Primary Scale of Intelligence—Revised (WPPSI-R)

General Information

Author: David Wechsler

Publisher: The Psychological Corporation

Publication Date: 1949–1989

Age Range: Age 2-11 to 7-3

Administration Time:
50 to 70 min.
Optional subtests: 10 to 15 min.

Composite Measure Information

Broad Measure of Intelligence: Full Scale IQ (FSIQ)

Lower-Order Composites:
Verbal Scale
Performance Scale

Score Information

Peer Comparison Scores:
Percentile Rank
IQ/Index

Range of Standard Scores for Total Test Composite: 41 to 160

Mean Floor of Subtests at Age 3-0:[1] –1.6

Norming Information

Number of Subtests Normed at Each Age:
Total: 12 across age range

Conormed with Tests of Achievement:
No (Equated scores for WIAT)
Reading
Mathematics
Language
Writing

Person Variables in Norming Plan:
Gender
Race/Ethnicity (confounding race and Hispanic origin)
Family SES (occupation and education)

Community Variables in Norming Plan:
Location
Size

Note: The above information was adapted from Harrison, Flanagan, and Genshaft (1997). Copyright 1997 Guilford Publishing Co. All rights reserved.

Descriptions of the WPPSI-R subtests are adapted from *Wechsler Preschool and Primary Scale of Intelligence; Revised.* Copyright © 1989 by The Psychological Corporation. Reproduced by permission. All rights reserved. "Wechsler Preschool and Primary Scale of Intelligence—Revised" and "WPPSI-R" are registered trademarks of The Psychological Corporation.

[1]Standard deviations below the mean for a raw score of 1.

Size of Norming Sample for the Broad Measure of General Intelligence:
N = 1700
Average number per year: 183

Age Blocks in Norm Table:[2]
3-month blocks

Reviews

Bracken, B. A. (1992). Review of the Wechsler Preschool and Primary Scale of Intelligence—
Revised. In J. J. Kramer & J. C. Conoley (Eds.),
The eleventh mental measurements yearbook (pp.
1027–1029). Lincoln, NE: Buros Institute.

Braden, J. P. (1992). Review of the Wechsler Preschool and Primary Scale of Intelligence—
Revised. In J. J. Kramer & J. C. Conoley (Eds.),
The eleventh mental measurements yearbook (pp.
1029–1031). Lincoln, NE: Buros Institute.

Flanagan, D., & Alfonso, V. (1995). A critical
review of the technical characteristics of new
and recently revised intelligence tests for preschool children. *Journal of Psychoeducational
Assessment, 13*(1), 66–90.

Kaufman, A. S. (1990). The WPPSI-R: You can't
judge a test by its colors. *Journal of School Psychology, 29*(4), 387–394.

---

[2] In most cases, age blocks represent linear interpolations.

TEST BATTERY: WPPSI-R   **TEST: Object Assembly**

Description of test: The examinee is required to assemble a set of puzzles of common objects into meaningful wholes. This is a timed test.

Age Range: 3 to 7 years

BASIC PSYCHOMETRIC CHARACTERISTICS

Age (in years)

Reliability

Reliability key ■ High   ■ Medium   □ Low   ⊟ Data not available or not appropriate for age level

Within-Battery

g loading

Specificity

Cross-Battery

g loading

Specificity

g loading key ■ Good ■ Fair □ Poor   **Specificity key** ■ Ample ■ Adequate □ Inadequate

⊟ Data not available or not appropriate for age level

Test floor: Adequate

Test ceiling: *Inadequate* from ages 6:5 to 7:3

Item gradients

Gradient key ■ Good ■ Fair □ Poor   ⊟ Data not available or not appropriate for age level

(Note: Refer to Table 3-2 in Chapter 3 for the definition of terms used in the various keys)

TEST BATTERY: WPPSI-R   **TEST: Object Assembly**

Gf-Gc CLASSIFICATIONS

	Primary	Secondary

Classification Key

Broad (Stratum II)   ■ Visual Processing *(Gv)*
- ■ Empirical: strong
- ■ Empirical: moderate
- ☐ Empirical: mixed
- ☐ Logical

Narrow (Stratum I)   ■ Closure Speed (CS)
- ■ Probable   ☐ Spatial Relations (SR)
- ☐ Possible

OTHER VARIABLES THAT INFLUENCE TEST PERFORMANCE

	Typical Age of Concept Attainment				
	3	**4**	**5**	**> 5**	**Data not available**
Basic Concepts in Directions	in (5)	together (6)	like (1)	some (1)	
	big (2)	through (2)	pieces (12)		
(Frequency of occurrence)		fast (5)	all (2)		

Degree of Cultural Content   ☐ High   ■ Medium   ☐ Low

Additional Factors

Background/Environmental	**Individual/Situational**
Alertness to the environment	Reflectivity/impulsivity
	Field dependence/independence
	Planning
	Ability to perform under time pressure

(Note: Refer to Table 3-2 in Chapter 3 for the definition of terms used in the various keys)

TEST BATTERY: WPPSI-R   **TEST: Information**

Description of test: The examinee is required to respond to a series of orally presented questions that measure ones knowledge about common events, objects, places, and people.

Age Range: 3 to 7 years

BASIC PSYCHOMETRIC CHARACTERISTICS

Age (in years)

Reliability

Reliability key   ■ High   ▨ Medium   □ Low   ⊟ Data not available or not appropriate for age level

---

Within-Battery

g loading

Specificity

Cross-Battery

g loading

Specificity

***g* loading key**   ■ Good   ▨ Fair   □ Poor   **Specificity key**   ■ Ample   ▨ Adequate   □ Inadequate

⊟ Data not available or not appropriate for age level

Test floor: *Inadequate* from ages 2:11 to 3:11

Test ceiling: Adequate

Item gradients

Gradient key   ■ Good   ▨ Fair   □ Poor   ⊟ Data not available or not appropriate for age level

---

(Note: Refer to Table 3-2 in Chapter 3 for the definition of terms used in the various keys)

TEST BATTERY: WPPSI-R   **TEST: Information**

Gf-Gc CLASSIFICATIONS

<u>Classification Key</u>

Broad (Stratum II)
- ■ Empirical: strong
- ◼ Empirical: moderate
- ◻ Empirical: mixed
- ☐ Logical

Narrow (Stratum I)
- ■ Probable
- ☐ Possible

	Primary	Secondary
	■ Crystallized Intelligence (*Gc*)	
	◼ General Information (K0)	

OTHER VARIABLES THAT INFLUENCE TEST PERFORMANCE

	Typical Age of Concept Attainment				
	3	**4**	**5**	**> 5**	**Data not available**
Basic Concepts in Directions	on (5)	two (3)	pieces (1)	another (1)	four (1)
	in (2)	together (1)		before (1)	night (1)
(Frequency of occurrence)					after (1)
					wood (1)

Degree of Cultural Content   ◼ High   ☐ Medium   ☐ Low

Additional Factors

Background/Environmental	**Individual/Situational**
Environmental stimulation	
Educational opportunities/experiences	
Alertness to the environment	
Intellectual curiosity	

(Note: Refer to Table 3-2 in Chapter 3 for the definition of terms used in the various keys.)

TEST BATTERY: WPPSI-R   **TEST: Geometric Designs**

Description of test: The examinee is required to examine a simple design, and, with the stimulus in
view, point to a design that is exactly like it from an array of four designs. The examinee
is then required to draw geometric designs from a printed model.

Age Range: 3 to 7 years

BASIC PSYCHOMETRIC CHARACTERISTICS

Age (in years)

Reliability

Reliability key ■ High   ▨ Medium   ☐ Low   ⊟ Data not available or not appropriate for age level

Within-Battery

g loading

Specificity

Cross-Battery

g loading

Specificity

g loading key ■ Good   ▨ Fair   ☐ Poor   **Specificity key** ■ Ample   ▨ Adequate   ☐ Inadequate

⊟ Data not available or not appropriate for age level

Test floor: *Inadequate* from ages 2:11 to 3:11

Test ceiling: *Inadequate* from ages 6:5 to 7:3

Item gradients

Gradient key ■ Good   ▨ Fair   ☐ Poor   ⊟ Data not available or not appropriate for age level

(Note: Refer to Table 3-2 in Chapter 3 for the definition of terms used in the various keys)

TEST BATTERY: WPPSI-R   **TEST: Geometric Designs**

Gf-Gc **CLASSIFICATIONS**	**Primary**	**Secondary**

Classification Key

Broad (Stratum II)
- ■ Empirical: strong
- ■ Empirical: moderate
- □ Empirical: mixed
- □ Logical

Secondary:
- □ Visual Processing *(Gv)*
- □ Psychomotor

Narrow (Stratum I))
- ■ Probable
- □ Possible

Secondary:
- ■ Visualization (VZ)
- ■ Finger Dexterity (P2)

OTHER VARIABLES THAT INFLUENCE TEST PERFORMANCE

Typical Age of Concept Attainment

Basic Concepts in Directions	3	4	5	> 5	Data not available
(Frequency of occurrence)	up (1) finished (1)	two (2) both (1)	like/alike (>15)		

Degree of Cultural Content   □ High   □ Medium   ■ Low

Additional Factors

Background/Environmental	**Individual/Situational**
Vision difficulties Environmental stimulation	Visual-motor coordination

(Note: Refer to Table 3-2 in Chapter 3 for the definition of terms used in the various keys)

TEST BATTERY: WPPSI-R   **TEST: Comprehension**

Description of test: The examinee is required to respond orally to orally presented questions that focus on everyday problems or understanding of social rules and concepts.

Age Range: 3 to 7 years

BASIC PSYCHOMETRIC CHARACTERISTICS

Age (in years)

Reliability

Reliability key: ■ High ▨ Medium □ Low ⊟ Data not available or not appropriate for age level

---

Within-Battery

g loading

Specificity

Cross-Battery

g loading

Specificity

g loading key: ■ Good ▨ Fair □ Poor   Specificity key: ■ Ample ▨ Adequate □ Inadequate

⊟ Data not available or not appropriate for age level

Test floor: *Inadequate* from ages 2:11 to 4:8

Test ceiling: Adequate

Item gradients

Gradient key: ■ Good ▨ Fair □ Poor   ⊟ Data not available or not appropriate for age level

---

(Note: Refer to Table 3-2 in Chapter 3 for the definition of terms used in the various keys)

TEST BATTERY: WPPSI-R   **TEST: Comprehension**

Gf-Gc CLASSIFICATIONS

	Primary	**Secondary**

<u>Classification Key</u>

Broad (Stratum II)   ■ Crystallized Intelligence (*Gc*)
  ■ Empirical: strong
  ■ Empirical: moderate
  ☐ Empirical: mixed
  ☐ Logical

Narrow (Stratum I)   ■ Language Development (LD)
  ■ Probable   ■ General Information (K0)
  ☐ Possible

OTHER VARIABLES THAT INFLUENCE TEST PERFORMANCE

	Typical Age of Concept Attainment				**Data not available**
	3	**4**	**5**	**> 5**	
Basic Concepts in Directions	in (1)	one (1)		another (1)	sick (1) before (1) hot (2) cold (1)
(Frequency of occurrence)					

Degree of Cultural Content   ■ High   ☐ Medium   ☐ Low

Additional Factors

Background/Environmental	**Individual/Situational**
Language stimulation	
Environmental stimulation	
Educational opportunities/experiences	
Alertness to the environment	

(Note: Refer to Table 3-2 in Chapter 3 for the definition of terms used in the various keys.)

TEST BATTERY: WPPSI-R   **TEST: Block Design**

Description of test: The examinee is required to replicate a set of modeled or printed two-dimensional geometric patterns using two-color cubes. This is a timed test.

Age Range: 3 to 7 years

BASIC PSYCHOMETRIC CHARACTERISTICS

Age (in years)

Reliability

Reliability key ■ High ▨ Medium □ Low ⊟ Data not available or not appropriate for age level

---

Within-Battery

g loading

Specificity

Cross-Battery

g loading

Specificity

g **loading key** ■ Good ▨ Fair □ Poor   **Specificity key** ■ Ample ▨ Adequate □ Inadequate

⊟ Data not available or not appropriate for age level

Test floor: *Inadequate* from ages 2:11 to 4:5

Test ceiling: Adequate

Item gradients

Gradient key ■ Good ▨ Fair □ Poor ⊟ Data not available or not appropriate for age level

---

(Note: Refer to Table 3-2 in Chapter 3 for the definition of terms used in the various keys)

TEST BATTERY: WPPSI-R   **TEST: Block Design**

Gf-Gc CLASSIFICATIONS

<u>Classification Key</u>

	Primary	Secondary

Broad (Stratum II)
- ■ Empirical: strong
- ■ Empirical: moderate
- ▢ Empirical: mixed
- ☐ Logical

■ Visual Processing *(Gv)*

Narrow (Stratum I)
- ■ Probable
- ☐ Possible

■ Spatial Relations (SR)
☐ Visualization (VZ)

OTHER VARIABLES THAT INFLUENCE TEST PERFORMANCE

	Typical Age of Concept Attainment				
	3	**4**	**5**	**> 5**	**Data not available**
Basic Concepts in Directions (Frequency of occurrence)	red (1) up (1) on (1)	one (1) white (3) together (1) through (1)	side (1) like (>15) same (2)	some (1) another (1)	next to (1)

Degree of Cultural Content   ☐ High   ☐ Medium   ■ Low

Additional Factors

Background/Environmental	Individual/Situational
	Color blindness
	Reflectivity/impulsivity
	Field dependence/independence
	Flexibility/inflexibility
	Planning
	Ability to work under time pressure

(Note: Refer to Table 3-2 in Chapter 3 for the definition of terms used in the various keys)

TEST BATTERY: WPPSI-R   **TEST: Arithmetic**

Description of test: The examinee is required to mentally solve and respond orally to a series of orally
presented arithmetic problems.

Age Range: 3 to 7 years

BASIC PSYCHOMETRIC CHARACTERISTICS

Age (in years)

Reliability

Reliability key ■ High   ▨ Medium   □ Low   ⊟ Data not available or not appropriate for age level

Within-Battery

g loading

Specificity

Cross-Battery

g loading

Specificity

g **loading key** ■ Good   ▨ Fair   □ Poor   **Specificity key** ■ Ample   ▨ Adequate   □ Inadequate

⊟ Data not available or not appropriate for age level

Test floor: *Inadequate* from ages 2:11 to 3:8

Test ceiling: *Inadequate* from ages 6:8 to 7:3

Item gradients

Gradient key ■ Good   ▨ Fair   □ Poor   ⊟ Data not available or not appropriate for age level

(Note: Refer to Table 3-2 in Chapter 3 for the definition of terms used in the various keys)

TEST BATTERY: WPPSI-R   **TEST: Arithmetic**

Gf-Gc CLASSIFICATIONS

	Primary	Secondary

Classification Key

Broad (Stratum II)
- ■ Empirical: strong
- ■ Empirical: moderate
- ☐ Empirical: mixed
- ☐ Logical

■ Quantitative Knowledge *(Gq)*   ☐ Fluid Intelligence *(Gf)*

Narrow (Stratum I)
- ■ Probable
- ☐ Possible

■ Math Achievement (A3)   ☐ Quantitative Reasoning (RQ)

OTHER VARIABLES THAT INFLUENCE TEST PERFORMANCE

	Typical Age of Concept Attainment				
	3	**4**	**5**	**> 5**	**Data not available**
Basic Concepts in Directions	on (4) in (2)				some (7)
(Frequency of occurrence)					

Degree of Cultural Content   ☐ High   ■ Medium   ☐ Low

Additional Factors

Background/Environmental	Individual/Situational
Math difficulties	Attention span
Educational opportunities/experiences	Concentration
	Distractibility
	Visual elaboration

(Note: Refer to Table 3-2 in Chapter 3 for the definition of terms used in the various keys)

TEST BATTERY: WPPSI-R   **TEST: Mazes**

Description of test: The examinee is required to solve, with a pencil, a series of increasingly difficult mazes.

Age Range: 3 to 7 years

BASIC PSYCHOMETRIC CHARACTERISTICS

Age (in years)

Reliability

Reliability key   High   Medium   Low   Data not available or not appropriate for age level

Within-Battery

g loading

Specificity

Cross-Battery

g loading

Specificity

g loading key   Good   Fair   Poor   **Specificity key**   Ample   Adequate   Inadequate

Data not available or not appropriate for age level

Test floor: *Inadequate* from ages 2:11 to 3:8

Test ceiling: Adequate

Item gradients

Gradient key   Good   Fair   Poor   Data not available or not appropriate for age level

(Note: Refer to Table 3-2 in Chapter 3 for the definition of terms used in the various keys)

TEST BATTERY: WPPSI-R   **TEST: Mazes**

Gf-Gc CLASSIFICATIONS

	Primary	**Secondary**

Classification Key

Broad (Stratum II)
- ■ Empirical: strong
- ▩ Empirical: moderate
- ▨ Empirical: mixed
- ☐ Logical

Secondary: ■ Visual Processing *(Gv)*

Narrow (Stratum I)
- ▩ Probable
- ☐ Possible

Secondary: ■ Spatial Scanning (SS)

OTHER VARIABLES THAT INFLUENCE TEST PERFORMANCE

	Typical Age of Concept Attainment				
	3	**4**	**5**	**> 5**	**Data not available**
Basic Concepts in Directions *(Frequency of occurrence)*	on (6) in (2) up (1) out of (1) boy (2) little (2) finished (1)	inside (4) into (7) middle (1)	like (2) wrong (1) all (5)	without (4) another (1) over [direction] (3)	over [time] (2)

Degree of Cultural Content   ☐ High   ☐ Medium   ■ Low

Additional Factors

Background/Environmental	**Individual/Situational**
Vision difficulties	Visual-motor coordination Reflectivity/impulsivity Field dependence/independence Planning Ability to perform under time pressure

(Note: Refer to Table 3-2 in Chapter 3 for the definition of terms used in the various keys)

TEST BATTERY: WPPSI-R   **TEST: Vocabulary**

Description of test: The examinee is required to orally define a series of orally presented words.

Age Range: 3 to 7 years

BASIC PSYCHOMETRIC CHARACTERISTICS

Age (in years)

Reliability

Reliability key   ■ High   ▨ Medium   □ Low   ⊟ Data not available or not appropriate for age level

Within-Battery

g loading

Specificity

Cross-Battery

g loading

Specificity

***g* loading key**   ■ Good   ▨ Fair   □ Poor   **Specificity key**   ■ Ample   ▨ Adequate   □ Inadequate

⊟ Data not available or not appropriate for age level

Test floor: *Inadequate* from ages 2:11 to 3:2

Test ceiling: Adequate

Item gradients

Gradient key   ■ Good   ▨ Fair   □ Poor   ⊟ Data not available or not appropriate for age level

(Note: Refer to Table 3-2 in Chapter 3 for the definition of terms used in the various keys)

TEST BATTERY: WPPSI-R   **TEST: Vocabulary**

Gf-Gc CLASSIFICATIONS

	Primary	Secondary

Classification Key

Broad (Stratum II)
- ■ Empirical: strong
- ■ Empirical: moderate
- ☐ Empirical: mixed
- ☐ Logical

■ Crystallized Intelligence (*Gc*)

Narrow (Stratum I)
- ■ Probable
- ☐ Possible

■ Language Development (LD)
■ Lexical Knowledge (VL)

OTHER VARIABLES THAT INFLUENCE TEST PERFORMANCE

Typical Age of Concept Attainment

	3	4	5	> 5	Data not available
Basic Concepts in Directions *(Frequency of occurrence)*				some (2)	

Degree of Cultural Content   ■ High   ☐ Medium   ☐ Low

Additional Factors

Background/Environmental	**Individual/Situational**
Language stimulation	
Environmental stimulation	
Educational opportunities/experiences	
Alertness to the environment	
Intellectual curiosity	

(Note: Refer to Table 3-2 in Chapter 3 for the definition of terms used in the various keys.)

TEST BATTERY: WPPSI-R   **TEST: Picture Completion**

Description of test: The examinee is required to identify an important part that is missing from a set of pictures of common objects and scenes. This is a timed test.

Age Range: 3 to 7 years

BASIC PSYCHOMETRIC CHARACTERISTICS

Age (in years)

Reliability

Reliability key ■ High ▨ Medium □ Low ⊟ Data not available or not appropriate for age level

Within-Battery

g loading

Specificity

Cross-Battery

g loading

Specificity

***g* loading key** ■ Good ▨ Fair □ Poor   **Specificity key** ■ Ample ▨ Adequate □ Inadequate

⊟ Data not available or not appropriate for age level

Test floor: *Inadequate* from ages 2:11 to 3:11

Test ceiling: Adequate

Item gradients

Gradient key ■ Good ▨ Fair □ Poor ⊟ Data not available or not appropriate for age level

(Note: Refer to Table 3-2 in Chapter 3 for the definition of terms used in the various keys)

TEST BATTERY: WPPSI-R   **TEST: Picture Completion**

Gf-Gc CLASSIFICATIONS

	Primary	Secondary

Classification Key

Broad (Stratum II)
- ■ Empirical: strong
- ■ Empirical: moderate
- ◻ Empirical: mixed
- ☐ Logical

☐ Visual Processing *(Gv)*
☐ Crystallized Intelligence *(Gc)*

Narrow (Stratum I)
- ■ Probable
- ☐ Possible

☐ Flexibility of Closure (CF)
☐ General Information (KO)

OTHER VARIABLES THAT INFLUENCE TEST PERFORMANCE

Typical Age of Concept Attainment

	3	4	5	> 5	Data not available
Basic Concepts in Directions (Frequency of occurrence)	in (>15)	missing (>15)			

Degree of Cultural Content   ☐ High   ■ Medium   ☐ Low

Additional Factors

Background/Environmental	Individual/Situational
Vision difficulties	Visual acuity
Alertness to the environment	Field dependence/independence

(Note: Refer to Table 3-2 in Chapter 3 for the definition of terms used in the various keys)

TEST BATTERY: WPPSI-R   **TEST: Similarities**

Description of test: The examinee is presented pairs of words orally and is required to explain the
similarity of the common objects or concepts they represent.

Age Range: 3 to 7 years

BASIC PSYCHOMETRIC CHARACTERISTICS

Age (in years)

Reliability

Reliability key   ■ High   ▨ Medium   ☐ Low   ⊟ Data not available or not appropriate for age level

---

Within-Battery

g loading

Specificity

Cross-Battery

g loading

Specificity

***g* loading key** ■ Good ▨ Fair ☐ Poor   **Specificity key** ■ Ample ▨ Adequate ☐ Inadequate

⊟ Data not available or not appropriate for age level

Test floor: *Inadequate* from ages 2:11 to 4:2

Test ceiling: Adequate

Item gradients

Gradient key ■ Good ▨ Fair ☐ Poor   ⊟ Data not available or not appropriate for age level

(Note: Refer to Table 3-2 in Chapter 3 for the definition of terms used in the various keys)

TEST BATTERY: WPPSI-R   **TEST: Similarities**

Gf-Gc CLASSIFICATIONS		

	Primary	Secondary

Classification Key

Broad (Stratum II)
■ Empirical: strong
■ Empirical: moderate
□ Empirical: mixed
□ Logical

■ Crystallized Intelligence (*Gc*)

Narrow (Stratum I)
■ Probable
□ Possible

■ Language Development (LD)
□ Lexical Knowledge (VL)

OTHER VARIABLES THAT INFLUENCE TEST PERFORMANCE

	Typical Age of Concept Attainment				
	3	4	5	> 5	Data not available
Basic Concepts in Directions	in (2)	together (1)	like/alike (4)	another (5)	nickle (1)
	up (1)	both (1)	all (4)		penny (1)
(Frequency of occurrence)					

Degree of Cultural Content   ■ High   □ Medium   □ Low

Additional Factors

Background/Environmental	Individual/Situational
Language stimluation	
Environmental stimulation	
Educational opportunities/experiences	

(Note: Refer to Table 3-2 in Chapter 3 for the definition of terms used in the various keys.)

TEST BATTERY: WPPSI-R   **TEST: Animal Pegs**

Description of test: The examinee is required to place colored pegs in holes on a board according to a key at the top of the board. This is a timed test.

Age Range: 3 to 7 years

BASIC PSYCHOMETRIC CHARACTERISTICS

Age (in years)

Reliability

Reliability key High   Medium   Low   Data not available or not appropriate for age level

Within-Battery

g loading

Specificity

Cross-Battery

g loading

Specificity

***g* loading key** Good Fair Poor   **Specificity key** Ample Adequate Inadequate

Data not available or not appropriate for age level

Test floor: *Inadequate* from ages 2:11 to 4:2

Test ceiling: Adequate

Item gradients

Gradient key Good Fair Poor   Data not available or not appropriate for age level

(Note: Refer to Table 3-2 in Chapter 3 for the definition of terms used in the various keys.)

TEST BATTERY: WPPSI-R   **TEST: Animal Pegs**

Gf-Gc CLASSIFICATIONS

	Primary	**Secondary**

Broad (Stratum II)   ☐ Processing Speed *(Gs)*
   ■ Empirical: strong
   ■ Empirical: moderate
   ☐ Empirical: mixed
   ☐ Logical

Narrow (Stratum I)   ■ Rate-of-test-taking (R9)
   ■ Probable
   ☐ Possible

OTHER VARIABLES THAT INFLUENCE TEST PERFORMANCE

	Typical Age of Concept Attainment				
	3	**4**	**5**	**> 5**	**Data not available**
Basic Concepts in Directions	up (1)	white (3)	piece (1)	right (2)	black (1)
	in (2)	under (2)	different (1)	after (1)	blue (3)
(Frequency of occurrence)		top (1)	next (1)		yellow (1)
		fast (1)			row (2)
					with (7)

Degree of Cultural Content   ☐ High   ■ Medium   ☐ Low

Additional Factors

Background/Environmental	**Individual/Situational**
Vision difficulties	Attention span
	Concentration
	Distractibility
	Visual acuity
	Reflectivity/impulsivity
	Verbal elaboration
	Visual elaboration
	Planning
	Visual-motor coordination
	Ability to perform under time pressure

(Note: Refer to Table 3-2 in Chapter 3 for the definition of terms used in the various keys)

TEST BATTERY: WPPSI-R   **TEST: Sentences**

Description of test: The examinee is required to repeat verbatim sentences that are presented orally.

Age Range: 3 to 7 years

BASIC PSYCHOMETRIC CHARACTERISTICS

Age (in years)

Reliability

Reliability key ■ High ▨ Medium □ Low ⊟ Data not available or not appropriate for age level

Within-Battery

g loading

Specificity

Cross-Battery

g loading

Specificity

***g* loading key** ■ Good ▨ Fair □ Poor   **Specificity key** ■ Ample ▨ Adequate □ Inadequate

⊟ Data not available or not appropriate for age level

Test floor: *Inadequate* from ages 2:11 to 3:8

Test ceiling: Adequate

Item gradients

Gradient key ■ Good ▨ Fair □ Poor ⊟ Data not available or not appropriate for age level

(Note: Refer to Table 3-2 in Chapter 3 for the definition of terms used in the various keys)

TEST BATTERY: WPPSI-R   **TEST: Sentences**

Gf-Gc CLASSIFICATIONS

	Primary	Secondary

Classification Key

Broad (Stratum II)
- ■ Empirical: strong
- ■ Empirical: moderate
- ☐ Empirical: mixed
- ☐ Logical

Secondary:
- ☐ Short-term Memory *(Gsm)*
- ☐ Crystallized Intelligence *(Gc)*

Narrow (Stratum I)
- ■ Probable
- ☐ Possible

Secondary:
- ■ Memory Span (MS)
- ■ Language Development (LD)

OTHER VARIABLES THAT INFLUENCE TEST PERFORMANCE

	Typical Age of Concept Attainment				
	3	4	5	> 5	Data not available
Basic Concepts in Directions (Frequency of occurrence)			same (1)	after (1)	

Degreee of Cultural Content   ☐ High   ■ Medium   ☐ Low

Additional Factors

Background/Environmental	Individual/Situational
Hearing difficulties Language stimulation	Attention span Concentration Distractibility Verbal rehearsal Visual elaboration

(Note: Refer to Table 3-2 in Chapter 3 for the definition of terms used in the various keys)

Chapter *11*

Woodcock-Johnson Psychoeducational Battery— Revised (WJ-R)

General Information

Author: Richard W. Woodcock

Publisher: The Riverside Publishing Company

Publication Date: 1977–1991

Age Range: Age 2-0 to 90+

Administration Time:
BCA—Early Development: 30 to 40 min.
BCA—Standard Scale: 40 to 50 min.
BCA—Extended Scale: 90 to 100 min.

Composite Measure Information

Broad Measure of Intelligence: Broad Cognitive Ability (BCA)

Lower-Order Composites:
Long-Term Retrieval
Short-Term Memory

Processing Speed
Auditory Processing
Visual Processing
Comprehension-Knowledge
Fluid Reasoning
Quantitative Ability (in WJ-R ACH)

Score Information

Peer Comparison Scores:
Percentile Rank
Standard Score

Range of Standard Scores for Total Test Composite: 0 to 200

Mean Floor of Subtests at Age 3-0[1]: –3.5

Norming Information

Number of Subtests Normed at Each Age:
Total: 21
Age 2-0 to 90+: 5
Age 4 to 90+: 21

Conormed with Tests of Achievement:
Yes
Reading
Mathematics
Written Language
Knowledge

Person Variables in Norming Plan:
Gender
Race
Hispanic origin
SES (occupation and education) (for adult sample only)

Note: The above information was adapted from Harrison, Flanagan, and Genshaft (1997), Guilford Publishing Co. All rights reserved.

Descriptions of WJ-R subtests Copyright © 1991 by The Riverside Publishing Company. Adapted from *Woodcock-Johnson—Revised Technical Manual* by Kevin S. McGrew, Judy K. Werder, and Richard W. Woodcock with permission of the publisher. All rights reserved.

[1]Standard deviations below the mean for a raw score of 1.

Community Variables in Norming Plan:
Location
Size
13 community socioeconomic categories[2]

Size of Norming Sample for the Broad Measure of General Intelligence:
BCA—Early Development Scale:
Preschool ages 2–5 years
N = 806
Average number per year: 201
BCA—Standard Scale
School ages 6–19 years
N = 2701
Average number per year: 193
Adult ages 20–80+ years
N = 918
Average number for 7 age groups: 131

Age Blocks in Norm Table[3]:
1-month blocks (Age 2-0 to 18-11)
1-year blocks (Age 19 to 90+)

REVIEWS

Cummings, J. A. (1995). Review of the Woodcock-Johnson Psycho-Educational Battery—Revised. In J. C. Conoley & J. C. Impara (Eds.), *The twelfth mental measurements yearbook* (pp. 1113–1116). Lincoln, NE: Buros Institute.

Flanagan, D., & Alfonso, V. (1995). A critical review of technical characteristics of new and recently revised intelligence tests for preschool children. *Journal of Psychoeducational Assessment, 13*(1), 66–90.

Hicks, P., & Bolen, L. M. (1996). Review of the Woodcock-Johnson Psycho-Educational Battery—Revised. *Journal of School Psychology, 34*(1), 93–102.

Lee, S. W., & Stefany, E. F. (1995). Review of the Woodcock-Johnson Psycho-Educational Battery—Revised. In. J. C. Conoley & J. C. Impara (Eds.), *The twelfth mental measurements yearbook* (pp. 1116–1117). Lincoln, NE: Buros Institute.

Woodcock, R. W. (1990). Theoretical foundations of the WJ-R measures of cognitive ability. *Journal of Psychoeducational Assessment, 8*(3), 231–258.

Ysseldyke, J. E. (1990). Goodness of fit of the Woodcock-Johnson Psycho-Educational Battery—Revised to the Horn-Cattell *Gf-Gc* theory. *Journal of Psychoeducational Assessment, 8*(3), 268–275.

[2] Distribution of values controlled in the set of communities: three levels of adult education, three classes of occupational status, and three classes of occupation. For colleges and universities: two types of institution and two sources of funding.

[3] In most cases, age blocks represent linear interpolations.

TEST BATTERY: WJ-R   **TEST: Memory for Names**

Description of test: The examinee is required to learn associations between unfamiliar auditory and visual stimuli (an auditory-visual association task).

Age range: 2 to 85+ years

BASIC PSYCHOMETRIC CHARACTERISTICS

Age (in years)

Reliability

Reliability key   ■ High   ▦ Medium   □ Low   ⊟ Data not available or not appropriate for age level

---

Within-Battery

g loading

Specificity

Cross-Battery

g loading

Specificity

g loading key ■ Good ▦ Fair □ Poor   **Specificity key** ■ Ample ▦ Adequate □ Inadequate

⊟ Data not available or not appropriate for age level

Test floor: *Inadequate* from ages 2:0 to 2:5

Test ceiling: Adequate

Item gradients

Gradient key   ■ Good   ▦ Fair   □ Poor   ⊟ Data not available or not appropriate for age level

---

(Note: Refer to Table 3-2 in Chapter 3 for the definition of terms used in the various keys)

TEST BATTERY: WJ-R   **TEST: Memory for Names**

Gf-Gc CLASSIFICATIONS   **Primary**   **Secondary**

Classification Key

Broad (Stratum II)   ■ Long-term storage and
  ■ Empirical: strong   Retrieval *(Glr)*
  ■ Empirical: moderate
  □ Empirical: mixed
  □ Logical

Narrow (Stratum I)   ■ Associative Memory (MA)
  ■ Probable
  □ Possible

OTHER VARIABLES THAT INFLUENCE TEST PERFORMANCE

Typical Age of Concept Attainment

	3	4	5	> 5	Data not available
Basic Concepts in Directions (Frequency of occurrence)				more (1)	

Degree of Cultural Content   □ High   □ Medium   ■ Low

Additional Factors

Background/Environmental	**Individual/Situational**
Environmental stimulation	Concentration
	Reflectivity/impulsivity
	Verbal elaboration
	Visual elaboration
	Ability to use feedback to modify performance

(Note: Refer to Table 3-2 in Chapter 3 for the definition of terms used in the various keys)

TEST BATTERY: WJ-R   **TEST: Memory for Sentences**

Description of test: The examinee is required to remember and repeat phrases and sentences presented auditorily by use of a tape player or, in special cases, by an examiner.

Age range: 2 to 85+ years

BASIC PSYCHOMETRIC CHARACTERISTICS

Age (in years)

Reliability

Reliability key ☐ High ☐ Medium ☐ Low ☐ Data not available or not appropriate for age level

---

Within-Battery

g loading

Specificity

Cross-Battery

g loading

Specificity

***g* loading key** ☐ Good ☐ Fair ☐ Poor   **Specificity key** ☐ Ample ☐ Adequate ☐ Inadequate

☐ Data not available or not appropriate for age level

Test floor: Adequate

Test ceiling: Adequate

Item gradients

Gradient key ☐ Good ☐ Fair ☐ Poor ☐ Data not available or not appropriate for age level

---

(Note: Refer to Table 3-2 in Chapter 3 for the definition of terms used in the various keys.)

TEST BATTERY: WJ-R   **TEST: Memory for Sentences**

Gf-Gc **CLASSIFICATIONS**		
	Primary	**Secondary**

Classification Key

Broad (Stratum II)
- ■ Empirical: strong
- ■ Empirical: moderate
- ▨ Empirical: mixed
- ☐ Logical

Secondary
- ☐ Short-Term Memory *(Gsm)*
- ☐ Crystallized Intellignece *(Gc)*

Narrow (Stratum I)
- ■ Probable
- ☐ Possible

- ■ Memory Span (MS)
- ■ Language Development (LD)

OTHER VARIABLES THAT INFLUENCE TEST PERFORMANCE

Typical Age of Concept Attainment

Basic Concepts in Directions	3	4	5	> 5	Data not available
(Frequency of occurrence)	on (1)	two (1)	same (1)	some (1) after (1)	

Degree of Cultural Content   ☐ High   ■ Medium   ☐ Low

Additional Factors

Background/Environmental	**Individual/Situational**
Hearing difficulties	Attention span
Language stimulation	Concentration
	Distractibility
	Verbal rehearsal
	Visual elaboration

(Note: Refer to Table 3-2 in Chapter 3 for the definition of terms used in the various keys)

TEST BATTERY: WJ-R   **TEST: Visual Matching**

Description of test: The examinee is required to locate and circle the two identical numbers in a row of six
                     numbers. The task proceeds in difficulty from single-digit numbers to triple-digit numbers
                     and has a 3-minute time limit.

Age range: 4 to 85+ years

BASIC PSYCHOMETRIC CHARACTERISTICS

Age (in years)

Reliability

Reliability key ■ High   ▨ Medium   □ Low   ⊟ Data not available or not appropriate for age level

---

Within-Battery

g loading

Specificity

Cross-Battery

g loading

Specificity

g loading key ■ Good ▨ Fair □ Poor   Specificity key ■ Ample ▨ Adequate □ Inadequate

⊟ Data not available or not appropriate for age level

Test floor: *Inadequate* from ages 4:0 to 4:11

Test ceiling: Adequate

Item gradients

Gradient key ■ Good ▨ Fair □ Poor   ⊟ Data not available or not appropriate for age level

---

(Note: Refer to Table 3-2 in Chapter 3 for the definition of terms used in the various keys.)

TEST BATTERY: WJ-R   **TEST: Visual Matching**

Gf-Gc CLASSIFICATIONS

	Primary	**Secondary**

<u>Classification Key</u>

Broad (Stratum II)   ■ Processing Speed *(Gs)*
   ■ Empirical: strong
   ■ Empirical: moderate
   □ Empirical: mixed
   □ Logical

Narrow (Stratum I)   ■ Perceptual Speed (P)
   ■ Probable   ■ Rate-of-test-taking (R9)
   □ Possible

OTHER VARIABLES THAT INFLUENCE TEST PERFORMANCE

Typical Age of Concept Attainment

	3	4	5	> 5	Data not available

Basic Concepts in Directions

Test not recommended for preschoolers

(Frequency of occurrence)

Degree of Cultural Content   □ High   □ Medium   ■ Low

Additional Factors

Background/Environmental	**Individual/Situational**
Vision difficulties	Attention span
	Concentration
	Distractibility
	Visual-motor coordination
	Visual acuity
	Reflectivity/impulsivity
	Ability to perform under time pressure

(Note: Refer to Table 3-2 in Chapter 3 for the definition of terms used in the various keys)

TEST BATTERY: WJ-R   **TEST: Incomplete Words**

Description of test: After hearing a recorded word that has one or more phonemes missing, the examinee is required to identify the complete word.

Age range: 2 to 85+ years

BASIC PSYCHOMETRIC CHARACTERISTICS

Age (in years)

Reliability

Reliability key: High | Medium | Low | Data not available or not appropriate for age level

Within-Battery

g loading

Specificity

Cross-Battery

g loading

Specificity

g loading key: Good | Fair | Poor   Specificity key: Ample | Adequate | Inadequate

Data not available or not appropriate for age level

Test floor: *Inadequate* from ages 2:0 to 4:3 and 90+

Test ceiling: Adequate

Item gradients

Gradient key: Good | Fair | Poor   Data not available or not appropriate for age level

---

(Note: Refer to Table 3-2 in Chapter 3 for the definition of terms used in the various keys)

TEST BATTERY: WJ-R   **TEST: Incomplete Words**

Gf-Gc CLASSIFICATIONS

	Primary	**Secondary**

Classification Key

Broad (Stratum II)
- ■ Empirical: strong
- ■ Empirical: moderate
- ☐ Empirical: mixed
- ☐ Logical

■ Auditory Processing (*Ga*)

Narrow (Stratum I)
- ■ Probable
- ☐ Possible

■ Phonetic Coding (PC)
☐ Resistance to Auditory
Stimulus Distortion (UR)

OTHER VARIABLES THAT INFLUENCE TEST PERFORMANCE

Typical Age of Concept Attainment

	3	**4**	**5**	**> 5**	**Data not available**
Basic Concepts in Directions	on (1)	two (1) whole (>15)	next (2)	some (1) after (1)	woman (1)
(Frequency of occurrence)					

Degree of Cultural Content   ☐ High   ■ Medium   ☐ Low

Additional Factors

Background/Environmental	**Individual/Situational**
Hearing difficulties	Attention span
Reading difficulties	Concentration
Environmental stimulation	Distractibility
Educational opportunities/experiences	Hearing acuity
	Verbal rehearsal

(Note: Refer to Table 3-2 in Chapter 3 for the definition of terms used in the various keys.)

TEST BATTERY: WJ-R   **TEST: Visual Closure**

Description of test: The examinee is required to identify a drawing or picture that is altered in one of several ways. The picture may be distorted, have missing lines or areas, or have a superimposed pattern.

Age range: 2 to 85+ years

BASIC PSYCHOMETRIC CHARACTERISTICS

Age (in years)

Reliability

Reliability key   ■ High   ▨ Medium   □ Low   ⊟ Data not available or not appropriate for age level

---

Within-Battery

g loading

Specificity

Cross-Battery

g loading

Specificity

***g* loading key**   ■ Good   ▨ Fair   □ Poor   **Specificity key**   ■ Ample   ▨ Adequate   □ Inadequate

⊟ Data not available or not appropriate for age level

Test floor: Adequate

Test ceiling: Adequate

Item gradients

Gradient key   ■ Good   ▨ Fair   □ Poor   ⊟ Data not available or not appropriate for age level

---

(Note: Refer to Table 3-2 in Chapter 3 for the definition of terms used in the various keys)

TEST BATTERY: WJ-R   **TEST: Visual Closure**

Gf-Gc **CLASSIFICATIONS**

	Primary	Secondary

Classification Key

Broad (Stratum II)
- ■ Empirical: strong
- ■ Empirical: moderate
- ▨ Empirical: mixed
- ☐ Logical

■ Visual Processing *(Gv)*

Narrow (Stratum I)
- ■ Probable
- ☐ Possible

■ Closure Speed (CS)

OTHER VARIABLES THAT INFLUENCE TEST PERFORMANCE

Typical Age of Concept Attainment

Basic Concepts in Directions	3	4	5	> 5	Data not available
(Frequency of occurrence)	behind (1) in (2)			another (>15)	

Degree of Cultural Content   ☐ High   ▨ Medium   ☐ Low

Additional Factors

Background/Environmental	Individual/Situational
Vision difficulties	Visual acuity
Environmental stimulation	Field dependence/independence

(Note: Refer to Table 3-2 in Chapter 3 for the definition of terms used in the various keys)

TEST BATTERY: WJ-R   **TEST: Picture Vocabulary**

Description of test: The examinee is required to name familiar and unfamiliar pictured objects.

Age range: 2 to 85+ years

BASIC PSYCHOMETRIC CHARACTERISTICS

Age (in years)

Reliability

Reliability key ■ High   ▨ Medium   □ Low   ⊟ Data not available or not appropriate for age level

---

Within-Battery

g loading

Specificity

Cross-Battery

g loading

Specificity

g loading key ■ Good   ▨ Fair   □ Poor   **Specificity key** ■ Ample   ▨ Adequate   □ Inadequate

⊟ Data not available or not appropriate for age level

Test floor: *Inadequate* from ages 2:0 to 2:1

Test ceiling: Adequate

Item gradients

Gradient key ■ Good   ▨ Fair   □ Poor   ⊟ Data not available or not appropriate for age level

---

(Note: Refer to Table 3-2 in Chapter 3 for the definition of terms used in the various keys)

TEST BATTERY: WJ-R   **TEST: Picture Vocabulary**

Gf-Gc CLASSIFICATIONS

	Primary	Secondary

<u>Classification Key</u>

Broad (Stratum II)
- ■ Empirical: strong
- ■ Empirical: moderate
- ☐ Empirical: mixed
- ☐ Logical

■ Crystallized Intelligence *(Gc)*

Narrow (Stratum I)
- ■ Probable
- ☐ Possible

■ Lexical Knowledge (VL)
■ General Information (KO)
☐ Language Development (LD)

OTHER VARIABLES THAT INFLUENCE TEST PERFORMANCE

Typical Age of Concept Attainment

Basic Concepts in Directions	3	4	5	> 5	Data not available
(Frequency of occurrence)	on (12)			another (9)	

Degree of Cultural Content   ■ High   ☐ Medium   ☐ Low

Additional Factors

Background/Environmental	Individual/Situational
Language stimulation	
Environmental stimulation	
Educational opportunities/experiences	
Alertness to the environment	
Intellectual curiosity	

(Note: Refer to Table 3-2 in Chapter 3 for the definition of terms used in the various keys)

TEST BATTERY: WJ-R   **TEST: Analysis Synthesis**

Description of test: The examinee is required to analyze the presented components of an incomplete logic
puzzle and to identify the missing components. This is a controlled-learning task in
which the examinee is given instructions on how to perform an increasingly complex
procedure. The examinee is given feedback regarding the correctness of his or
her response.

Age range: 4 to 85+ years

BASIC PSYCHOMETRIC CHARACTERISTICS

Age (in years)

Reliability

Reliability key ■ High ▨ Medium □ Low ⊞ Data not available or not appropriate for age level

---

Within-Battery

g loading

Specificity

Cross-Battery

g loading

Specificity

***g* loading key** ■ Good ▨ Fair □ Poor   **Specificity key** ■ Ample ▨ Adequate □ Inadequate

⊟ Data not available or not appropriate for age level

Test floor: *Inadequate* from ages 4:0 to 6:4 and 64 to 90+

Test ceiling: Adequate

Item gradients

Gradient key ■ Good ▨ Fair □ Poor ⊟ Data not available or not appropriate for age level

---

(Note: Refer to Table 3-2 in Chapter 3 for the definition of terms used in the various keys)

TEST BATTERY: WJ-R   **TEST: Analysis Synthesis**

Gf-Gc CLASSIFICATIONS

	Primary	Secondary

Broad (Stratum II)
- ■ Empirical: strong
- ■ Empirical: moderate
- ☐ Empirical: mixed
- ☐ Logical

■ Fluid Intelligence *(Gf)*

Narrow (Stratum I)
- ■ Probable
- ☐ Possible

■ General Sequential Reasoning (RG)
☐ Quantitative Reasoning (RQ)

OTHER VARIABLES THAT INFLUENCE TEST PERFORMANCE

Typical Age of Concept Attainment

	3	4	5	> 5	Data not available
Basic Concepts in Directions (Frequency of occurrence)		Test not recommended for preschoolers			

Degree of Cultural Content   ☐ High   ☐ Medium   ■ Low

Additional Factors

Background/Environmental	Individual/Situational
	Concentration
	Color blindness
	Reflectivity/impulsivity
	Flexibility/inflexibility
	Planning
	Ability to use feedback to modify performance

(Note: Refer to Table 3-2 in Chapter 3 for the definition of terms used in the various keys)

TEST BATTERY: WJ-R   **TEST: Visual-Auditory Learning**

Description of test: The examinee is required to associate novel visual symbols (rebuses) with familiar words
in oral languageand to translate a series of symbols into verbal sentences (a visual-
auditory association task). This test is a controlled-learning test in which the examinee's
errors are corrected. This task simulates a learning-to-read test.

Age range: 4 to 85+ years

BASIC PSYCHOMETRIC CHARACTERISTICS

Age (in years)

Reliability

Reliability key   ■ High   ▨ Medium   □ Low   ⊟ Data not available or not appropriate for age level

---

Within-Battery

g loading

Specificity

Cross-Battery

g loading

Specificity

g **loading key**   ■ Good   ▨ Fair   □ Poor   **Specificity key**   ■ Ample   ▨ Adequate   □ Inadequate

⊟ Data not available or not appropriate for age level

Test floor: *Inadequate* from ages 73 to 90+

Test ceiling: Adequate

Item gradients

Gradient key   ■ Good   ▨ Fair   □ Poor   ⊟ Data not available or not appropriate for age level

---

(Note: Refer to Table 3-2 in Chapter 3 for the definition of terms used in the various keys)

TEST BATTERY: WJ-R   **TEST: Visual-Auditory Learning**

Gf-Gc CLASSIFICATIONS

	Primary	Secondary

Classification Key

Broad (Stratum II)
- ■ Empirical: strong
- ■ Empirical: moderate
- ☐ Empirical: mixed
- ☐ Logical

■ Long-term Storage and Retrieval *(Glr)*

Narrow (Stratum I)
- ■ Probable
- ☐ Possible

■ Associative Memory (MA)
☐ Meaningful Memory (MM)

OTHER VARIABLES THAT INFLUENCE TEST PERFORMANCE

Typical Age of Concept Attainment

	3	4	5	> 5	Data not available
Basic Concepts in Directions (Frequency of occurrence)		Test not recommended for preschoolers			

Degree of Cultural Content   ☐ High   ■ Medium   ☐ Low

Additional Factors

Background/Environmental	**Individual/Situational**
Reading difficulties	Concentration
Educational opportunities/experiences	Reflectivity/impulsivity
	Verbal elaboration
	Visual elaboration
	Ability to use feedback to modify performance

(Note: Refer to Table 3-2 in Chapter 3 for the definition of terms used in the various keys)

TEST BATTERY: WJ-R   **TEST: Memory for Words**

Description of test: The examinee is required to repeat lists of unrelated words in the correct sequence after they are presented auditorily by use of a tape player, or, in special cases, by an examiner.

Age range: 4 to 85+ years

BASIC PSYCHOMETRIC CHARACTERISTICS

Age (in years)

Reliability

Reliability key ■ High ▨ Medium □ Low ⊟ Data not available or not appropriate for age level

---

Within-Battery

g loading

Specificity

Cross-Battery

g loading

Specificity

g loading key ■ Good ▨ Fair □ Poor   **Specificity key** ■ Ample ▨ Adequate □ Inadequate

⊟ Data not available or not appropriate for age level

Test floor: *Inadequate* from ages 90+

Test ceiling: Adequate

Item gradients

Gradient key ■ Good ▨ Fair □ Poor ⊟ Data not available or not appropriate for age level

---

(Note: Refer to Table 3-2 in Chapter 3 for the definition of terms used in the various keys.)

TEST BATTERY: WJ-R   **TEST: Memory for Words**

Gf-Gc CLASSIFICATIONS

<u>Classification Key</u>

	Primary	**Secondary**

Broad (Stratum II)
- ■ Empirical: strong
- ■ Empirical: moderate
- ☐ Empirical: mixed
- ☐ Logical

■ Short-term Memory (*Gsm*)

Narrow (Stratum I)
- ■ Probable
- ☐ Possible

■ Memory Span (MS)

OTHER VARIABLES THAT INFLUENCE TEST PERFORMANCE

Typical Age of Concept Attainment

	3	4	5	> 5	Data not available
Basic Concepts in Directions (Frequency of occurrence)		Test not recommended for preschoolers			

Degree of Cultural Content   ☐ High   ■ Medium   ☐ Low

Additional Factors

Background/Environmental	**Individual/Situational**
Hearing difficulties	Attention span
	Concentration
	Distractibility
	Verbal rehearsal
	Visual elaboration

(Note: Refer to Table 3-2 in Chapter 3 for the definition of terms used in the various keys)

TEST BATTERY: WJ-R	TEST: Cross Out

Description of test: The examinee is required to scan and compare visual information quickly. The examinee must mark the five drawings in a row of 20 drawings that are identical to the first drawing in the row. The examinee is given a 3-minute time limit to complete as many rows of items as possible.

Age range: 4 to 85+ years

BASIC PSYCHOMETRIC CHARACTERISTICS

Age (in years)

Reliability

Reliability key ■ High ▨ Medium □ Low ⊟ Data not available or not appropriate for age level

---

Within-Battery

g loading

Specificity

Cross-Battery

g loading

Specificity

g loading key ■ Good ▨ Fair □ Poor   Specificity key ■ Ample ▨ Adequate □ Inadequate

⊟ Data not available or not appropriate for age level

Test floor: *Inadequate* from ages 4:0 to 5:0 and 82 to 90+

Test ceiling: Adequate

Item gradients

Gradient key ■ Good ▨ Fair □ Poor ⊟ Data not available or not appropriate for age level

---

(Note: Refer to Table 3-2 in Chapter 3 for the definition of terms used in the various keys)

TEST BATTERY: WJ-R   **TEST: Cross Out**

| *Gf-Gc* CLASSIFICATIONS | Primary | Secondary |

<u>Classification Key</u>

Broad (Stratum II)
- ■ Empirical: strong
- ■ Empirical: moderate
- ☐ Empirical: mixed
- ☐ Logical

Primary

■ Processing Speed *(Gs)*

Narrow (Stratum I)
- ■ Probable
- ☐ Possible

■ Perceptual Speed (P)
☐ Rate-of-test-taking (R9)

OTHER VARIABLES THAT INFLUENCE TEST PERFORMANCE

Typical Age of Concept Attainment

	3	4	5	> 5	Data not available
Basic Concepts in Directions (Frequency of occurrence)		Test not recommended for preschoolers			

Degree of Cultural Content   ☐ High   ☐ Medium   ■ Low

Additional Factors

Background/Environmental	**Individual/Situational**
Vision difficulties	Attention span
	Concentration
	Distractibility
	Visual-motor coordination
	Visual acuity
	Reflectivity/impulsivity
	Field dependence/independence
	Ability to use feedback to modify performance

(Note: Refer to Table 3-2 in Chapter 3 for the definition of terms used in the various keys)

TEST BATTERY: WJ-R   **TEST: Sound Blending**

Description of test: The examinee is required to integrate and then say whole words after hearing part
(syllables and/or phonemes) of the words presented via an audio tape player.

Age range: 4 to 85+ years

BASIC PSYCHOMETRIC CHARACTERISTICS

Age (in years)

Reliability

Reliability key   ■ High   ▨ Medium   □ Low   ⊟ Data not available or not appropriate for age level

---

Within-Battery

g loading

Specificity

Cross-Battery

g loading

Specificity

g loading key   ■ Good   ▨ Fair   □ Poor   **Specificity key**   ■ Ample   ▨ Adequate   □ Inadequate

⊟ Data not available or not appropriate for age level

Test floor: *Inadequate* from ages 4:0 to 4:9 and 63 to 90+

Test ceiling: Adequate

Item gradients

Gradient key   ■ Good   ▨ Fair   □ Poor   ⊟ Data not available or not appropriate for age level

---

(Note: Refer to Table 3-2 in Chapter 3 for the definition of terms used in the various keys)

TEST BATTERY: WJ-R   **TEST: Sound Blending**

Gf-Gc CLASSIFICATIONS

	Primary	Secondary

Classification Key

Broad (Stratum II)
- ■ Empirical: strong
- ■ Empirical: moderate
- ☐ Empirical: mixed
- ☐ Logical

■ Auditory Processing (*Ga*)

Narrow (Stratum I)
- ■ Probable
- ☐ Possible

■ Phonetic Coding (PC)

OTHER VARIABLES THAT INFLUENCE TEST PERFORMANCE

Typical Age of Concept Attainment

	3	4	5	> 5	Data not available
Basic Concepts in Directions (Frequency of occurrence)		Test not recommended for prescholers			

Degree of Cultural Content   ☐ High   ■ Medium   ☐ Low

Additional Factors

Background/Environmental	Individual/Situational
Hearing difficulties	Attention span
Reading difficulties	Concentration
Environmental stimulation	Distractibility
Educational opportunities/experiences	Hearing acuity
	Verbal rehearsal

(Note: Refer to Table 3-2 in Chapter 3 for the definition of terms used in the various keys.)

TEST BATTERY: WJ-R   **TEST: Picture Recognition**

Description of test: The examinee is required to recognize a subset of previously presented pictures within a field of distracting pictures.

Age range: 4 to 85+ years

BASIC PSYCHOMETRIC CHARACTERISTICS

Age (in years)

Reliability

Reliability key: ■ High   ▨ Medium   ☐ Low   ⊟ Data not available or not appropriate for age level

---

Within-Battery

g loading

Specificity

Cross-Battery

g loading

Specificity

g loading key: ■ Good   ▨ Fair   ☐ Poor

Specificity key: ■ Ample   ▨ Adequate   ☐ Inadequate

⊟ Data not available or not appropriate for age level

Test floor: *Inadequate* from ages 4:0 to 4:5

Test ceiling: Adequate

Item gradients

Gradient key: ■ Good   ▨ Fair   ☐ Poor   ⊟ Data not available or not appropriate for age level

(Note: Refer to Table 3-2 in Chapter 3 for the definition of terms used in the various keys)

TEST BATTERY: WJ-R   **TEST: Picture Recognition**

Gf-Gc CLASSIFICATIONS

	Primary　　　　　　　　**Secondary**

Classification Key

Broad (Stratum II)
- ■ Empirical: strong
- ■ Empirical: moderate
- ☐ Empirical: mixed
- ☐ Logical

■ Visual Processing *(Gv)*

Narrow (Stratum I)
- ■ Probable
- ☐ Possible

■ Visual Memory (MV)

OTHER VARIABLES THAT INFLUENCE TEST PERFORMANCE

	Typical Age of Concept Attainment				
	3	**4**	**5**	**> 5**	**Data not available**
Basic Concepts in Directions (Frequency of occurrence)		Not appropriate for age range covered			

Degree of Cultural Content   ☐ High   ■ Medium   ☐ Low

Additional Factors

Background/Environmental	**Individual/Situational**
	Concentration
	Reflectivity/impulsivity
	Verbal elaboration

(Note: Refer to Table 3-2 in Chapter 3 for the definition of terms used in the various keys)

TEST BATTERY: WJ-R   **TEST: Oral Vocabulary**

Description of test: In part A (Synonyms), the examinee is required to state a word similar in meaning to the word presented. In part B (Antonyms), the examinee must state a word that is opposite in meaning to the word presented.

Age range: 4 to 85+ years

BASIC PSYCHOMETRIC CHARACTERISTICS

Age (in years)

Reliability

Reliability key ■ High ▨ Medium ☐ Low ⊟ Data not available or not appropriate for age level

---

Within-Battery

g loading

Specificity

Cross-Battery

g loading

Specificity

g loading key ■ Good ▨ Fair ☐ Poor   Specificity key ■ Ample ▨ Adequate ☐ Inadequate

⊟ Data not available or not appropriate for age level

Test floor: *Inadequate* from ages 4:0 to 6:2 and 81 to 90+

Test ceiling: Adequate

Item gradients

Gradient key ■ Good ▨ Fair ☐ Poor ⊟ Data not available or not appropriate for age level

---

(Note: Refer to Table 3-2 in Chapter 3 for the definition of terms used in the various keys)

TEST BATTERY: WJ-R   **TEST: Oral Vocabulary**

Gf-Gc CLASSIFICATIONS

	Primary	**Secondary**

Broad (Stratum II)
- ■ Empirical: strong
- ■ Empirical: moderate
- ☐ Empirical: mixed
- ☐ Logical

■ Crystallized Intelligence *(Gc)*

Narrow (Stratum I)
- ■ Probable
- ☐ Possible

■ Language Development (LD)
■ Lexical Knowledge (VL)

OTHER VARIABLES THAT INFLUENCE TEST PERFORMANCE

	Typical Age of Concept Attainment				
	3	**4**	**5**	**> 5**	**Data not available**
Basic Concepts in Directions (Frequency of occurrence)		Not appropriate for age range covered			

Degree of Cultural Content   ■ High   ☐ Medium   ☐ Low

Additional Factors

Background/Environmental	**Individual/Situational**
Language stimulation	
Environmental stimulation	
Educational opportunities/experiences	
Intellectual curiosity	

(Note: Refer to Table 3-2 in Chapter 3 for the definition of terms used in the various keys)

TEST BATTERY: WJ-R   **TEST: Concept Formation**

Description of test: The examinee is required to identify the rules for concepts when shown illustrations of instances of the concept and non-instances of the concepts. This is a controlled-learning task that involves categorical reasoning based on principles of formal logic. The examinee is given feedback regarding the correctness of each response.

Age range: 4 to 85+ years

BASIC PSYCHOMETRIC CHARACTERISTICS

Age (in years)

Reliability

Reliability key ■ High ▨ Medium □ Low ⊟ Data not available or not appropriate for age level

Within-Battery

g loading

Specificity

Cross-Battery

g loading

Specificity

***g* loading key** ■ Good ▨ Fair □ Poor   **Specificity key** ■ Ample ▨ Adequate □ Inadequate

⊟ Data not available or not appropriate for age level

Test floor: *Inadequate* from ages 4:0 to 8:4 and 59 to 90+

Test ceiling: Adequate

Item gradients

Gradient key ■ Good ▨ Fair □ Poor ⊟ Data not available or not appropriate for age level

(Note: Refer to Table 3-2 in Chapter 3 for the definition of terms used in the various keys)

TEST BATTERY: WJ-R   **TEST: Concept Formation**

Gf-Gc CLASSIFICATIONS		

	Primary	**Secondary**

Classification Key

Broad (Stratum II)
- ■ Empirical: strong
- ▦ Empirical: moderate
- ☐ Empirical: mixed
- ☐ Logical

■ Fluid Intelligence *(Gf)*

Narrow (Stratum I)
- ▦ Probable
- ☐ Possible

▦ Induction (I)
☐ Quantitative Reasoning (RQ)

OTHER VARIABLES THAT INFLUENCE TEST PERFORMANCE

Typical Age of Concept Attainment

	3	4	5	> 5	Data not available
Basic Concepts in Directions (Frequency of occurrence)		Test not recommended for preschoolers			

Degree of Cultural Content   ☐ High   ☐ Medium   ■ Low

Additional Factors

Background/Environmental	**Individual/Situational**
	Concentration
	Reflectivity/impulsivity
	Flexibility/inflexibility
	Planning
	Ability to use feedback to modify performance

(Note: Refer to Table 3-2 in Chapter 3 for the definition of terms used in the various keys)

TEST BATTERY: WJ-R   **TEST: Delayed Recall: Memory for Names**

Description of test: The examinee is required to recall (after 1 to 8 days) the space creatures presented in the Memory for Names test. The examinee is not told that subsequent testing will occur.

Age range: 4 to 85+ years

BASIC PSYCHOMETRIC CHARACTERISTICS

Age (in years)

Reliability

Reliability key ■ High ▨ Medium □ Low ⊟ Data not available or not appropriate for age level

---

Within-Battery

g loading

Specificity

Cross-Battery

g loading

Specificity

***g* loading key** ■ Good ▨ Fair □ Poor   **Specificity key** ■ Ample ▨ Adequate □ Inadequate

⊟ Data not available or not appropriate for age level

Test floor: *Inadequate* from ages 80 to 90+ (1 day); 78 to 90+ (2-3 days); 75 to 90+ (4-6 days); and 74 to 90+ (7-8 days)

Test ceiling: *Inadequate* from ages 27 to 36 (1-2 days)

Item gradients

Gradient key ■ Good ▨ Fair □ Poor ⊟ Data not available or not appropriate for age level

---

(Note: Refer to Table 3-2 in Chapter 3 for the definition of terms used in the various keys)

TEST BATTERY: WJ-R   **TEST: Delayed Recall: Memory for Names**

Gf-Gc CLASSIFICATIONS		
	Primary	**Secondary**

Classification Key

Broad (Stratum II)
- ■ Empirical: strong
- ■ Empirical: moderate
- ☐ Empirical: mixed
- ☐ Logical

Narrow (Stratum I)
- ■ Probable
- ☐ Possible

■ Long-term Storage and Retrieval *(Glr)*

■ Associative Memory (MA)

OTHER VARIABLES THAT INFLUENCE TEST PERFORMANCE

Typical Age of Concept Attainment

	3	4	5	> 5	Data not available
Basic Concepts in Directions (Frequency of occurrence)		Test not recommended for preschoolers			

Degree of Cultural Content   ☐ High   ☐ Medium   ■ Low

Additional Factors

Background/Environmental	**Individual/Situational**
	Concentration
	Verbal elaboration
	Visual elaboration

(Note: Refer to Table 3-2 in Chapter 3 for the definition of terms used in the various keys)

TEST BATTERY: WJ-R　　　　**TEST: Delayed Recall: Visual-Auditory Learning**

Description of test: The examinee is required to recall (after 1 to 8 days) the symbols (rebuses) presented in the Visual-Auditory Learning test. The examinee is not told that subsequent testing will occur.

• Age range: 4 to 85+ years

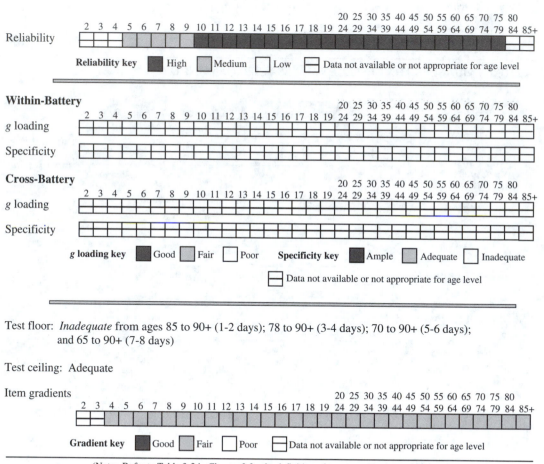

BASIC PSYCHOMETRIC CHARACTERISTICS

Test floor: *Inadequate* from ages 85 to 90+ (1-2 days); 78 to 90+ (3-4 days); 70 to 90+ (5-6 days); and 65 to 90+ (7-8 days)

Test ceiling: Adequate

(Note: Refer to Table 3-2 in Chapter 3 for the definition of terms used in the various keys)

TEST BATTERY: WJ-R   **TEST: Delayed Recall: Visual-Auditory Learning**

Gf-Gc CLASSIFICATIONS

	Primary	Secondary

<u>Classification Key</u>

Broad (Stratum II)
- ■ Empirical: strong
- ■ Empirical: moderate
- ☐ Empirical: mixed
- ☐ Logical

■ Long-term Storage and Retrieval *(Glr)*

Narrow (Stratum I)
- ■ Probable
- ☐ Possible

■ Associative Memory (MA)
☐ Meaningful Memory (MM)

OTHER VARIABLES THAT INFLUENCE TEST PERFORMANCE

Typical Age of Concept Attainment

	3	4	5	> 5	Data not available
Basic Concepts in Directions (Frequency of occurrence)		Test not recommended for preschoolers			

Degree of Cultural Content   ☐ High   ■ Medium   ☐ Low

Additional Factors

Background/Environmental	**Individual/Situational**
Reading difficulties	Concentration
Educational opportunities/experiences	Verbal elaboration
	Visual elaboration

(Note: Refer to Table 3-2 in Chapter 3 for the definition of terms used in the various keys)

TEST BATTERY: WJ-R   **TEST: Numbers Reversed**

Description of test: The examinee is required to say a series of random numbers backwards.

Age range: 4 to 85+ years

BASIC PSYCHOMETRIC CHARACTERISTICS

Age (in years)

Reliability

Reliability key ■ High   ▨ Medium   □ Low   ⊟ Data not available or not appropriate for age level

---

Within-Battery

g loading

Specificity

Cross-Battery

g loading

Specificity

g **loading key** ■ Good   ▨ Fair   □ Poor   **Specificity key** ■ Ample   ▨ Adequate   □ Inadequate

⊟ Data not available or not appropriate for age level

Test floor: *Inadequate* from ages 4:0 to 6:5

Test ceiling: Adequate

Item gradients

Gradient key ■ Good   ▨ Fair   □ Poor   ⊟ Data not available or not appropriate for age level

---

(Note: Refer to Table 3-2 in Chapter 3 for the definition of terms used in the various keys)

TEST BATTERY: WJ-R   **TEST: Numbers Reversed**

Gf-Gc CLASSIFICATIONS

	Primary	**Secondary**

Classification Key

Broad (Stratum II)
- ■ Empirical: strong
- ■ Empirical: moderate
- ▨ Empirical: mixed
- ☐ Logical

Secondary:
- ☐ Short-term Memory *(Gsm)*
- ☐ Fluid Intelligence *(Gf)*

Narrow (Stratum I)
- ■ Probable
- ☐ Possible

Secondary:
- ■ Memory Span (MS)
- ■ General Sequential Reasoning (RG)

OTHER VARIABLES THAT INFLUENCE TEST PERFORMANCE

Typical Age of Concept Attainment

Basic Concepts in Directions	3	4	5	> 5	Data not available
(Frequency of occurrence)		Test not recommended for preschoolers			

Degree of Cultural Content   ☐ High   ☐ Medium   ■ Low

Additional Factors

Background/Environmental	**Individual/Situational**
Hearing difficulties	Attention span
	Concentration
	Distractibility
	Verbal rehearsal
	Visual elaboration
	Organization

(Note: Refer to Table 3-2 in Chapter 3 for the definition of terms used in the various keys)

TEST BATTERY: WJ-R   **TEST: Sound Patterns**

Description of test: The examinee is required to indicate whether pairs of complex sound patterns presented via an audio tape player are the same or different. The patterns may differ in pitch, rhythm, or content.

Age range: 4 to 85+ years

BASIC PSYCHOMETRIC CHARACTERISTICS

Age (in years)

Reliability

Reliability key: ■ High ▦ Medium □ Low ⊟ Data not available or not appropriate for age level

Within-Battery

g loading

Specificity

Cross-Battery

g loading

Specificity

g loading key: ■ Good ▦ Fair □ Poor   **Specificity key:** ■ Ample ▦ Adequate □ Inadequate

⊟ Data not available or not appropriate for age level

Test floor: *Inadequate* from ages 4:0 to 4:1

Test ceiling: Adequate

Item gradients

Gradient key: ■ Good ▦ Fair □ Poor ⊟ Data not available or not appropriate for age level

(Note: Refer to Table 3-2 in Chapter 3 for the definition of terms used in the various keys.)

TEST BATTERY: WJ-R   **TEST: Sound Patterns**

***Gf-Gc* CLASSIFICATIONS**		

<u>**Classification Key**</u>

	Primary	**Secondary**

Broad (Stratum II)
- ■ Empirical: strong
- ▨ Empirical: moderate
- ▢ Empirical: mixed
- ☐ Logical

Secondary (Broad):
- ▨ Auditory Processing *(Ga)*
- ☐ Fluid Intelligence *(Gf)*

Narrow (Stratum I)
- ▨ Probable
- ☐ Possible

Secondary (Narrow):
- ■ Speech Sound Discrimination (US)
- ☐ Memory for Sound Patterns (UM)
- ☐ General Sequential Reasoning (RG)

OTHER VARIABLES THAT INFLUENCE TEST PERFORMANCE

Typical Age of Concept Attainment

	3	4	5	> 5	Data not available
Basic Concepts in Directions *(Frequency of occurrence)*		Not appropriate for age range covered			

Degree of Cultural Content   ☐ High   ☐ Medium   ■ Low

Additional Factors

Background/Environmental	**Individual/Situational**
Hearing difficulties	Attention span
	Concentration
	Distractibility
	Hearing acuity
	Verbal rehearsal

(Note: Refer to Table 3-2 in Chapter 3 for the definition of terms used in the various keys)

TEST BATTERY: WJ-R   **TEST: Spatial Relations**

Description of test: The examinee is required to match shapes visually. The examinee must select, from a series of shapes, the component parts needed to make a given whole shape.

Age range: 4 to 85+ years

BASIC PSYCHOMETRIC CHARACTERISTICS

Age (in years)

Reliability

Reliability key: ■ High ▨ Medium □ Low ⊟ Data not available or not appropriate for age level

---

Within-Battery

g loading

Specificity

Cross-Battery

g loading

Specificity

g loading key: ■ Good ▨ Fair □ Poor   Specificity key: ■ Ample ▨ Adequate □ Inadequate

⊟ Data not available or not appropriate for age level

Test floor: Adequate

Test ceiling: Adequate

Item gradients

Gradient key: ■ Good ▨ Fair □ Poor ⊟ Data not available or not appropriate for age level

---

(Note: Refer to Table 3-2 in Chapter 3 for the definition of terms used in the various keys)

TEST BATTERY: WJ-R   **TEST: Spatial Relations**

Gf-Gc CLASSIFICATIONS

	Primary	Secondary

Classification Key

Broad (Stratum II)
- ■ Empirical: strong
- ■ Empirical: moderate
- ◻ Empirical: mixed
- ☐ Logical

Narrow (Stratum I)
- ■ Probable
- ☐ Possible

Secondary
- ◻ Visual Processing *(Gv)*
- ◻ Fluid Intelligence *(Gf)*

- ■ Spatial Relations (SR)
- ■ Visualization (VZ)
- ■ General Sequential Reasoning (RG)

OTHER VARIABLES THAT INFLUENCE TEST PERFORMANCE

Typical Age of Concept Attainment

	3	4	5	> 5	Data not available

Basic Concepts in Directions

(Frequency of occurrence)

Test not recommended for preschoolers

Degree of Cultural Content   ☐ High   ☐ Medium   ■ Low

Additional Factors

Background/Environmental	Individual/Situational
Vision difficulties	Reflectivity/impulsivity
Environmental stimulation	Field dependence/independence
	Flexibility/inflexibility
	Planning

(Note: Refer to Table 3-2 in Chapter 3 for the definition of terms used in the various keys)

TEST BATTERY: WJ-R   **TEST: Listening Comprehension**

Description of test: The examinee is required to listen to a short tape-recorded passage and supply the single word missing at the end of the passage.

Age range: 4 to 85+ years

BASIC PSYCHOMETRIC CHARACTERISTICS

Age (in years)

Reliability

Reliability key ■ High   ▨ Medium   □ Low   ⊟ Data not available or not appropriate for age level

---

Within-Battery

g loading

Specificity

Cross-Battery

g loading

Specificity

g loading key ■ Good   ▨ Fair   □ Poor   **Specificity key** ■ Ample   ▨ Adequate   □ Inadequate

⊟ Data not available or not appropriate for age level

Test floor: Adequate

Test ceiling: Adequate

Item gradients

Gradient key ■ Good   ▨ Fair   □ Poor   ⊟ Data not available or not appropriate for age level

(Note: Refer to Table 3-2 in Chapter 3 for the definition of terms used in the various keys)

TEST BATTERY: WJ-R   **TEST: Listening Comprehension**

Gf-Gc CLASSIFICATIONS

	Primary	Secondary

<u>Classification Key</u>

Broad (Stratum II)   ■ Crystallized Intelligence *(Gc)*
  ■ Empirical: strong
  ■ Empirical: moderate
  □ Empirical: mixed
  □ Logical

Narrow (Stratum I)   ■ Listening Ability (LS)
  ■ Probable   ■ Language Development (LD)
  □ Possible

OTHER VARIABLES THAT INFLUENCE TEST PERFORMANCE

Typical Age of Concept Attainment

	3	4	5	> 5	Data not available
Basic Concepts in Directions (Frequency of occurrence)		Test not recommended for preschoolers			

Degree of Cultural Content   ■ High   □ Medium   □ Low

Additional Factors

Background/Environmental	**Individual/Situational**
Hearing difficulties	Attention span
Language stimulation	Concentration
Environmental stimulation	Distractibility
Educational opportunities/experiences	

(Note: Refer to Table 3-2 in Chapter 3 for the definition of terms used in the various keys)

TEST BATTERY: WJ-R   **TEST: Verbal Analogies**

Description of test: The examinee is required to complete phrases with words that indicate appropriate analogies.

Age range: 4 to 85+ years

BASIC PSYCHOMETRIC CHARACTERISTICS

Age (in years)

Reliability

Reliability key ■ High ▨ Medium □ Low ⊟ Data not available or not appropriate for age level

---

Within-Battery

g loading

Specificity

Cross-Battery

g loading

Specificity

g loading key ■ Good ▨ Fair □ Poor   **Specificity key** ■ Ample ▨ Adequate □ Inadequate

⊟ Data not available or not appropriate for age level

Test floor: *Inadequate* from ages 4:0 to 7:10 and 60 to 90+

Test ceiling: Adequate

Item gradients

Gradient key ■ Good ▨ Fair □ Poor ⊟ Data not available or not appropriate for age level

---

(Note: Refer to Table 3-2 in Chapter 3 for the definition of terms used in the various keys)

TEST BATTERY: WJ-R   **TEST: Verbal Analogies**

Gf-Gc CLASSIFICATIONS

	Primary	Secondary

Classification Key

Broad (Stratum II)
- ■ Empirical: strong
- ■ Empirical: moderate
- ☐ Empirical: mixed
- ☐ Logical

Secondary:
- ☐ Crystallized Intelligence *(Gc)*
- ☐ Fluid Intelligence *(Gf)*

Narrow (Stratum I)
- ■ Probable
- ☐ Possible

Secondary:
- ■ Language Development (LD)
- ■ Lexical Knowledge (VL)
- ■ Induction (I)

OTHER VARIABLES THAT INFLUENCE TEST PERFORMANCE

Typical Age of Concept Attainment

	3	4	5	> 5	Data not available
Basic Concepts in Directions (Frequency of occurrence)		Test not recommended for preschoolers			

Degree of Cultural Content   ■ High   ☐ Medium   ☐ Low

Additional Factors

Background/Environmental	Individual/Situational
Language stimulation	
Environmental stimulation	
Educational opportunities/experiences	

(Note: Refer to Table 3-2 in Chapter 3 for the definition of terms used in the various keys)

Chapter 12

Commonly Used and New "Special Purpose" Tests of Gf-Gc Abilities

Special Purpose Tests: A Supplement to Standard Intelligence Batteries

Practitioners routinely administer "special purpose" tests to provide additional information about cognitive functioning over and above that provided by a standard intelligence battery. Additional information is sought for a variety of reasons including the following: (1) to test hypotheses about cognitive strengths or weaknesses identified initially by a standard intelligence battery; (2) to gain information about abilities not measured or not measured adequately by a standard intelligence battery (e.g., fluid reasoning, long-term memory); (3) to seek a more culturally or linguistically "fair" measure of cognitive potential in individuals from diverse cultural or linguistic backgrounds; (4) to determine the cognitive capabilities of individuals with speech/communication disorders or hearing impairments; (5) to determine the cognitive capabilities of individuals with motor impairments; (6) to assess cognitive processes in individuals with neurological impairments or traumatic brain injury; and (7) to assess selective, sustained, and divided attention in individuals suspected of attention deficit hyperactivity disorder (ADHD).

Because standard intelligence batteries often have extensive language demands, individuals with limited hearing abilities, receptive and expressive language disabilities, or learners of English as a second language (or dual-language learners) are often at an unfair disadvantage when assessed by these conventional tests. Likewise, because individually administered, standardized tests of intelligence are defined and created from a unique cultural perspective, individuals with diverse cultural backgrounds or with sociolinguistic patterns that differ substantially from those of the test's developers may be at an unfair disadvantage when assessed with such instruments. Also, some special purpose tests provide norm-referenced information on abilities and processes (e.g., attention) that is not available through conventional intelligence measures. Thus, many special purpose tests (1) offer practitioners an alternative means to assessing a variety of populations whose performance is likely to be underestimated by traditional intelligence batteries, and (2) yield information about abilities and/or processes not adequately or directly measured by conventional batteries.

However, while this is often the case, it is important to understand that special purpose tests are characterized by the same types of problems as tests of intelligence. The problem lies not so much in linguistic differences or cultural bias (which are important factors), but, rather, in the fundamental principles upon which such tests are based—test norms. While such factors as gender, socioeconomic status, geographic location, and ethnicity are well controlled in major intelligence batteries, culture is *not* one of the stratified variables. In addition, in most cases of cultural difference there is a concomitant language difference. Since every school-age child in the United States is taught to speak and use English, the U.S. population is, in fact, bi- or even multilingual (from very limited English proficient through fully balanced and everything in between). There are no tests with appropriate norms for such children because multilingualism is not a controlled variable in norming samples. Therefore, because of the importance of language and culture in cognitive test performance, it cannot possibly be known how the performance of a bilingual child (to whatever degree) compares with other bilingual children of the same level of proficiency, acculturation, et cetera—the only appropriate comparison group—since that information is not available (Samuel Ortiz, July 1997, personal communication).

Purpose

In the preceding chapters the tests of eight major intelligence batteries were classified according to the broad (stratum II) and narrow (stratum I) *Gf-Gc* abilities they measure. Most of the classifications at the broad level were empirical. That is, they were based on the results of a series of cross-battery factor analyses. All of the classifications at the narrow level were logical (i.e., based on expert consensus) (see Chapter 3 for details). The *Gf-Gc* classifications were reported to aid practitioners in making cognitive test interpretations that are grounded in contemporary theory and research. In addition, these classifications provided the necessary foundation for organizing cross-battery assessments (described in Part III of this text). That is, classifying all tests according to *Gf-Gc* theory enables practitioners to select appropriate supplemental tests to measure important abilities that are not measured or not measured adequately by a given intelligence battery. The purpose of this chapter is to describe commonly used and new special purpose tests in terms of the abilities they measure according to contemporary *Gf-Gc* theory so that they can be used in cross-battery and selective-cross battery assessments (see chapters 13 and 14, respectively).

Table 12–1 includes 17 special purpose tests, consisting of 113 cognitive tests (and/or subtests) in all. The definition and age range of each subtest are provided along with the classifications of the broad and narrow *Gf-Gc* abilities that are believed to be measured by these tests. The *Gf-Gc* classifications were made in the following way. Each of the subtests presented in Table 12–1 was compared to the 109 subtests included in chapters 4 through 11 to determine similarity in content and task demands. When the special purpose tests were found to be similar (or identical) in content and task demand to the subtests of the major intelligence batteries, the broad and narrow ability classifications for the intelligence battery subtests were adopted for the special purpose tests and reported in Table 12–1. In instances when a special purpose subtest appeared to measure an ability not directly measured by any of the subtests of the major intelligence batteries, then it was classified by the present authors. The present authors' classifications were made based on an understanding of Carroll's (1993a) text, the results of their own and recent *Gf-Gc*–organized factor analysis studies (see Chapter 3), and communication with intelligence scholars and test authors. Because of the subjective nature of this classification process, the narrow (and perhaps some broad) *Gf-Gc* ability classifications presented in Table 12–1 may need modification as a result of future research and scholarly dialogue.

It is important to note that the list of tests presented in Table 12–1 is not exhaustive. There are literally hundreds of special purpose tests available. Those selected for inclusion in the table are frequently used tests as well as new tests that are likely to gain widespread use. As can be seen in Table 12–1, special purpose tests measure a wide range of *Gf-Gc* abilities, including Fluid Intelligence (*Gf*), Visual Processing (*Gv*), Short-Term Memory (*Gsm*), and Long-Term Storage and Retrieval (*Glr*). It is noteworthy that, with the exception of *Gv*, these broad abilities are largely underrepresented or not measured adequately by commonly used intelligence tests (e.g., Wechslers) (see Chapter 13 for a discussion). Since these broad abilities are differentially related to various achievement and/or occupational outcomes across the lifespan (see Chapter 2), they represent necessary supplements to standard intelligence batteries, depending on the purpose of assessment.

It is also noteworthy that the *depth* of coverage within certain broad *Gf-Gc* areas represented in some special purpose tests exceeds that of most major intelligence batteries. For example, Table 12–1 shows that the Test of Memory and Learning (TOMAL; Reynolds & Bigler, 1994) includes six measures of *Glr*, representing three *different narrow abilities* within that domain (i.e., Associative Memory—MA, Meaningful Memory—MM, and Free Recall Memory—M6). According to one of the principles underlying the cross-battery approach (discussed in Chapter 13), two or more *qualitatively different* narrow abilities must be measured within a broad *Gf-Gc* area before making generalizations about ability in that domain. None of the major intelligence batteries meets this criterion for the broad ability of *Glr*. Therefore, when an individual is suspected of having significant long-term memory difficulties, it is necessary to supplement most major intelligence batteries to adequately assess functioning in this area.

TABLE 12–1 Descriptions and *Gf-Gc* Classifications for Special Purpose Tests

Test and Subtests	Author(s) (Publication date)	Age Range in Years	Description	Stratum II	Stratum I
				Gf-Gc Classification	
Cognitive Assessment System (CAS)	J. A. Naglieri & J. P. Das (1997)				
Planned Codes		5–17	The examinee is required to use a strategy to match symbols to letters as quickly as possible.	Gs	R9
Matching Numbers		5–17	The examinee is required to develop a plan to find two identical numbers on several rows.	Gs	P, R9
Planned Connections		5–17	The examinee is required to complete a pattern of letters and numbers.	Gs / Gv	R9 / SS
Number Detection		5–17	The examinee is required to find specific numbers to match a sample while resisting response to distracting numbers.	Gs	R7, R9
Receptive Attention		5–17	The examinee is required to identify pairs of pictures or letters while resisting distractions.	Gs	P, R4
Expressive Attention		5–17	The examinee is required to identify the name of a color used to print a word when both are different (e.g., the word "red" is printed in green ink).	Glr / Gs	NA / R9
Verbal Spatial Relations		5–17	The examinee is required to choose one of six pictures that respond to a verbal question about spatial relationships.	Gc / Gv	LD, LS / VZ
Nonverbal Matrices		5–17	The examinee is required to select one of six options to complete a nonverbal progressive matrix.	Gf	I
Figure Memory		5–17	The examinee is required to identify a geometric figure that is within a more complex design.	Gv	CF, MV
Word Series		5–17	The examinee is required to repeat a series of words in the same order in which they were presented by the examiner.	Gsm	MS
Sentence Repetition		5–17	The examinee is required to repeat sentences that are syntactically correct but essentially meaningless.	Gsm / Gc	MS / LD
Sentence Questions		8–17	The examinee is required to answer questions about syntax-based statements.	Gc / Gsm	LD / MS

Continued

TABLE 12–1 *Continued*

Test and Subtests	Author(s) (Publication date)	Age Range in Years	Description	*Gf-Gc* Classification Stratum II	Stratum I
Speech Rate		5–7	The examinee is required to quickly and accurately repeat a series of words 10 times.	P. Motor	PT[1]
Comprehensive Test of Nonverbal Intelligence (CTONI)	D. D. Hammill, N. A. Pearson, & J. L. Wiederholt (1996)				
Pictorial Analogies		6–18	The examinee is required to complete a 2 × 2 matrix using pictures of common objects.	Gf Gc	RG KO
Geometric Analogies		6–18	The examinee is required to complete a 2 × 2 matrix of geometric shapes.	Gf Gv	I, RG VZ
Pictorial Categories		6–18	The examinee is required to deduce the relationship between two stimulus pictures and to select an object from a group of items that shares this same relationship.	Gf Gc	I, RG KO
Geometric Categories		6–18	The examinee is required to deduce the relationship between two stimulus geometric shapes and to select a shape that shares this same relationship.	Gf Gv	I, RG VZ
Pictorial Sequences		6–18	The examinee is presented with a series of stimulus pictures that have a sequential relationship. The examinee is required to complete the last box in this series by choosing the correct item from an array of items.	Gf Gc	I, RG KO
Geometric Sequences		6–18	The examinee is presented with a series of stimulus geometric shapes that have a sequential relationship. The examinee is required to complete the last box in this series by choosing the correct item from an array of items.	Gf Gv	I, RG VZ
Detroit Tests of Learning Aptitude—3 (DTLA-3) Word Opposites	D. D. Hammill & B. R. Bryant (1991)	6–17	After the examiner presents a word, the examinee is required to present a word that is opposite in meaning.	Gc*	LD, VL

Subtest	Author (date)	Age	Description	Broad	Narrow
Design Sequences		6–17	The examinee is presented with a series of pictured designs for 5 seconds and is required to replicate the designs with a group of cubes.	Gv*	MV
Sentence Imitation		6–17	The examinee is presented with a sentence and is required to imitate the sentence.	Gsm* Gc	MS LD
Reversed Letters		6–17	The examinee is presented with a series of letters and is required to write the series of letters in reverse order in a small box, without touching or surpassing the boundaries of the box.	Gv* Gsm Gf	MV MS RG
Story Construction		6–17	The examinee is required to make up stories about a series of pictures.	Gc*	LD, OP
Design Reproduction		6–17	The examinee is presented with a geometric figure for a specified time and is required to draw the figure from memory.	Gv*	MV
Basic Information		6–17	The examinee is required to verbally answer a series of common knowledge questions.	Gc*	KO
Symbolic Relations		6–17	The examinee is presented with a series of geometric or line drawings in which one design is absent. The examinee is then presented with six possible designs and is required to choose the missing design.	Gf*	I
Word Sequences		6–17	The examinee is required to repeat a series of unrelated words that were previously read by the examiner.	Gsm*	MS
Story Sequences		6–17	The examinee is required to put a series of cartoon-like pictures in a particular order that will portray a meaningful and funny story by placing numbered chips under the pictures.	Gv* Gc	VZ LD
Picture Fragments		6–17	The examinee is presented with a series of pictures in which different elements are missing from otherwise common objects and is required to verbally identify the names of these objects in the pictures.	Gv*	CS
Expressive Vocabulary Test (EVT)	K. T. Williams (1997)	2–85+	The examinee is presented with pictures and is required to verbally provide the name of the pictures or a synonym for the picture.	Gc	VL, LD
Kaufman Brief Intelligence Test (K-BIT)	A. S. Kaufman & N. L. Kaufman (1990)				
Expressive Vocabulary		4–90	The examinee is presented with pictures of 45 items and is required to provide a name for each item.	Gc	VL, KO, LD

Continued

TABLE 12–1 *Continued*

Test and Subtests	Author(s) (Publication date)	Age Range in Years	Description	Gf-Gc Classification Stratum II	Stratum I
Definitions		8–90	The examinee is presented with a description and a partial spelling of a word. With these two clues the examinee is required to provide the best fitting word.	Gc Grw	LD, VL SG, RD
Matrices		4–90	The examinee is presented with several abstract visual stimuli and is required to solve either a 2 × 2 matrix, a 3 × 3 matrix, or to complete a pattern of dots.	Gf	I
Kaufman Short Neuropsychological Assessment Procedure (K-SNAP)	A. S. Kaufman & N. L. Kaufman (1994)				
Number Recall		11–85	The examinee is required to repeat a series of numbers in the same order as the examiner presents them.	Gsm	MS
Gestalt Closure		11–85	The examinee is presented with a partially completed "inkblot" drawing and is required to name an object or scene in the drawing.	Gv	CS
Four-Letter Words		11–85	The examinee is presented with clues involving a series of four-letter words and is required to discover "secret" words by studying these clues. On one item the examinee is required to rapidly form four-letter words by rearranging jumbled sets of four letters.	Gf	I
Learning and Memory Battery (LAMB)	J. P. Schmidt & T. Tombaugh (1995)				
Paragraph		20–60	The examinee is required to recall a paragraph using free recall, cued recall, and retention recall trials.	Glr Gc	MM, M6 LS
Wordlist		20–60	The examinee is required to recall a 15-word list using free recall, cued recall, and retention recall trials.	Glr	M6, MA
Word Pairs		20–60	The examinee is required to recall the second word of 14 word pairs using free recall and retention recall trials.	Glr	MA, FI
Digit Span		20–60	The examinee is required to recall a series of digits both forward and backward.	Gsm	MS

Subtest	Author	Age	Description		
Supraspan Digit		20–60	The examinee is required to learn a number that is two digits longer than the longest number that was successfully recalled on Digit Span forward, and to recall the number using free recall and retention recall trials.	Gsm	MS
Simple Figure		20–60	The examinee is presented with four simple geometric designs for 15 seconds and is required to draw them first from memory and later while viewing the designs.	Gv	MV
Complex Figure		20–60	The examinee is presented with one complex figure for 30 seconds and is required to draw it first from memory, and later while viewing the figure.	Gv	MV
Leiter International Performance Scale—Revised (LEITER-R)	G. H. Roid & L. J. Miller (1997)				
Design Analogies		5–18+	The examinee is presented with 2 × 2 and 4 × 2 matrices and is required to complete these matrices using geometric shapes.	Gf	I
Repeated Patterns		2–18+	The examinee is presented with patterns of pictorial or figural objects. These patterns are presented again and the examinee is required to supply the "missing" portion of the pattern by moving response cards into alignment with the easel.	Gf	I
Sequential Order		2–18+	The examinee is presented with a progressive series of pictorial or figural objects and is required to select appropriate items that fit the progression.	Gf	I
Classification		2–6	The examinee is required to categorize objects or geometric designs.	Gf	I
Matching		2–10	The examinee is presented with a series of visual stimuli and is required to select response cards to match these stimuli.	Gv	VZ
Figure Ground		2–18+	The examinee is required to identify embedded figures or designs within a complex stimulus.	Gv	CF
Picture Context		2–10	The examinee is required to recognize an object that has been removed from a larger display using visual context clues.	Gf	RG
Form Completion		2–18+	The examinee is required to recognize a "whole object" from a randomly displayed array of its parts.	Gv	VZ, SR

Continued

TABLE 12–1 *Continued*

Test and Subtests	Author(s) (Publication date)	Age Range in Years	Description	*Gf-Gc* Classification Stratum II	Stratum I
Paper Folding		11–18+	The examinee is required to mentally "fold" an unfolded object displayed in two dimensions and match it to a target.	Gv	VZ
Figure Rotation		11–18+	The examinee is required to mentally rotate a two- or three-dimensional object or geometric figure.	Gv	VZ, SR
Immediate Recognition		4–10	A stimulus array of pictured objects is shown for 5 seconds. After its removal the examinee is required to discriminate between objects that are present and objects that are absent.	Gv	MV
Delayed Recognition		4–10	After a 20-minute delay the examinee is required to recognize the objects presented in the Immediate Recognition subtest.	Glr	MA
Associated Pairs		2–18+	Pairs of pictured objects are displayed for 5 to 10 seconds. After their removal the examinee is required to make meaningful and nonmeaningful associations.	Glr	MA, MM
Delayed Pairs		6–18+	After a 20-minute delay the examinee is required to recognize the objects associated in the Associated Pairs subtest.	Glr	MA, MM
Forward Memory		2–18+	After the examiner points to a series of pictures in a given sequence, the examinee is required to repeat the pointing sequence.	Gv Gsm	MV MS
Reverse Memory		6–18+	After the examiner points to a series of pictures in a given sequence, the examinee is required to repeat the pointing sequence in the reverse order.	Gv Gf	MV RG
Spatial Memory		6–18+	The examinee is presented with an increasingly complex display of pictured objects in a matrix format for 10 seconds. After their removal the examinee is required to place the cards in order on a blank matrix display.	Gv Gsm	MV, SR MS
Visual Coding		6–18+	The examinee is required to code symbols associated with pictorial objects, geometric objects, and numbers.	Gf	RG

Test	Author (Year)	Ages	Description		
Attention Sustained		2–18+	The examinee is required to identify specific stimuli among an array of different stimuli.	Gs	P, R9
Attention Divided		6–18+	The examinee is required to sort numbered playing cards while a moving display is presented on a sheath.	Attention Gv	AC^2 SS
Matrix Analogies Test (MAT)	J. A. Naglieri (1985)	5–17	The examinee is required to solve matrices that are organized into four groups: Pattern Completion, Reasoning by Analogy, Serial Reasoning, and Spatial Visualization.	Gf	I, RG
Peabody Picture Vocabulary Test—Third Edition (PPVT-3)	L. M. Dunn, L. M. Dunn, & K. T. Williams (1997)	2–85	The examiner presents a series of pictures and says a corresponding stimulus word. The examinee is required to point to the picture that matches the word presented by the examiner.	Gc	VL, KO LD
Raven's Progressive Matrices	J. C. Raven (1938)	5–18+	The examinee is required to solve problems presented in abstract figures and designs that involve the ability to deduce relationships.	Gf	I
Test of Memory and Learning (TOMAL)	C. R. Reynolds & E. D. Bigler (1994)				
Memory for Stories		5–19	The examinee is required to recall a verbally presented short story.	Glr Gc	MM LS MV
Facial Memory		5–19	The examinee is required to identify particular faces from a set of diversions.	Gv	MV
Word Selective Reminding		5–19	The examinee is required to learn and recall a word list within eight trials.	Glr	M6
Visual Selective Reminding		5–19	After the examiner points to specific dots on a card, the examinee is required to point to the same sequence of dots, being allowed eight trials to master each sequence.	Gsm Gv	MS MV
Object Recall		5–19	The examinee is presented with a series of pictures that are named by the examiner. The examinee is required to recall the names of the pictures within four trials.	Gsm Gv	MS MV
Abstract Visual Memory		5–19	The examinee is presented with a standard stimulus and is required to identify the standard among six deviations.	Gv	MV
Digits Forward		5–19	The examinee is required to recall a sequence of numbers.	Gsm	MS

Continued

TABLE 12–1 *Continued*

Test and Subtests	Author(s) (Publication date)	Age Range in Years	Description	*Gf-Gc* Classification Stratum II	*Gf-Gc* Classification Stratum I
Visual Sequential Memory		5–19	Geometric designs are presented in a specific order. The order is rearranged and the examinee is required to recall the original order.	Gv Gsm	MV MS
Paired Recall		5–19	The examinee is presented with a list of word pairs and is required to recall the word pairs after the first word of each pair is presented by the examiner.	Glr	MA
Memory for Location		5–19	The examinee is presented with a group of big dots dispersed on a page and is required to recall the position of the dots in any particular order.	Gv Gsm	MV, SR MS
Manual Imitation		5–19	The examinee is required to imitate a set of ordered hand movements in the same order in which the examiner performed them.	Gv Gsm	MV MS
Letters Forward		5–19	The examinee is required to recall a sequence of letters.	Gsm	MS
Digits Backward		5–19	The examinee is required to recall a sequence of numbers in reverse order.	Gsm Gf	MS RG
Letters Backward		5–19	The examinee is required to recall a sequence of letters in reverse order.	Gsm Gf	MS RG
Delayed Recall of Memory for Stories		5–19	The examinee is required to perform a delayed recall of Memory for Stories 30 minutes after completion.	Glr Gc	MM LD
Delayed Recall of Facial Memory		5–19	The examinee is required to perform a delayed recall trial of the Facial Memory subtest 30 minutes after completion.	Glr Gv	M6 MV
Delayed Recall of Word Selective Reminding		5–19	The examinee is required to perform a delayed recall of the Word Selective Reminding subtest 30 minutes after completion.	Glr	M6
Delayed Recall of Visual Selective Reminding		5–19	The examinee is required to perform a delayed recall of the Visual Selective Reminding subtest 30 minutes after the last trial in Visual Selective Reminding is completed.	Gv	MV

Test	Author	Age	Description		
Test of Nonverbal Intelligence—Third Edition (TONI-3)	L. Brown, R. J. Sherbenou, & S. K. Johnsen (1997)	5–85	The examinee is required to identify a problem-solving rule that defines the relationship among various stimulus figures and to select a correct response from an array of figures.	Gf	I
Test of Phonological Awareness (TOPA)	J. K. Torgesen & B. R. Bryant (1994)	5–8	The examinee is required to isolate individual phonemes in spoken words.	Ga	PC
Universal Nonverbal Intelligence Test (UNIT)	R. S. McCallum & B. A. Bracken (in press)				
Symbolic Memory		5–17	The examinee is required to recall and recreate sequences of visually presented universal symbols (e.g., green boy, black woman).	Gv*	MV
Spatial Memory		5–17	The examinee is required to remember and recreate the placement of black and/or green chips on a 3 × 3 or 4 × 4 cell grid.	Gv*	MV, SR
Object Memory		5–17	The examinee is shown a visual array of common objects (e.g., shoe, telephone, tree) for 5 seconds, after which the examinee identifies the pictured objects from a larger array of pictured objects.	Gv*	MV
Cube Design		5–17	The examinee completes a three-dimensional block design task using between one and nine green and white blocks.	Gf*	RG
Analogic Reasoning		5–17	The examinee completes a matrix analogies task using common objects (e.g., hand/glove, foot/___?) and novel geometric figures.	Gf*	I
Mazes		5–17	The examinee completes a maze task by tracing a path through each maze from the center starting point to an exit.	Gv*	SS
Wechsler Memory Scale—Revised (WMS-R)	D. Wechsler (1987)				
Figural Memory		16–74	The examinee is shown a set of abstract designs, after which the examinee is required to identify the designs from a larger array of designs.	Gv	MV
Logical Memory I		16–74	The examinee is required to listen to two brief stories and then immediately recall each story.	Glr / Gc	MM / LS
Visual Paired Associates I		16–74	The examinee is required to learn associations between colors and six abstract line drawings.	Glr	MA

Continued

TABLE 12–1 *Continued*

Test and Subtests	Author(s) (Publication date)	Age Range in Years	Description	*Gf-Gc* Classification	
				Stratum II	Stratum I
Verbal Paired Associates I		16–74	The examinee is required to learn eight word pairs.	Glr	MA
Visual Reproduction I		16–74	The examinee is required to draw simple geometric designs from memory after the designs are each exposed for 10 seconds.	Gv	MV
Digit Span		16–74	The examinee is required to repeat a series of digits both forward and backward.	Gsm Gf	MS RG
Visual Memory Span		16–74	The examinee is required to touch a series of colored squares first in the same order and then in the reverse order that they were presented by the examiner.	Gv Gsm	MV MS
Logical Memory II		16 -74	The examinee is required to perform a delayed recall trial of Logical Memory I subtest 30 minutes after completion.	Glr	MM
Visual Paired Associates II		16–74	The examinee is required to perform a delayed recall trial of the Visual Paired Associates I subtest 30 minutes after completion.	Glr	MA
Verbal Paired Associates II		16–74	The examinee is required to perform a delayed recall trial of the Verbal Paired Associates I subtest 30 minutes after completion.	Glr	MA
Visual Reproduction II		16–74	The examinee is required to perform a delayed recall trial of the Visual Reproduction I subtest 30 minutes after completion.	Gv Glr	MV M6
Wide Range Assessment of Memory and Learning (WRAML)	D. Sheslow & W. Adams (1990)				
Picture Memory		5–17	The examinee is presented with a complicated scene followed by a second, similar scene. The examinee is required to identify components that have been changed in the second scene.	Gv	MV
Design Memory		5–17	The examinee is presented with four designs and is asked to draw the designs after a 10-second delay.	Gv	MV

Verbal Learning	5–17	The examinee is required to recall a list of words immediately after they are read aloud. A delayed recall trial is given after the Story Memory subtest is presented.	Glr	M6
Story Memory	5–17	The examinee is required to recall components of two short stories.	Glr / Gc	MM / LS
Finger Windows	5–17	The examinee is required to reproduce a series of visually presented spatial sequences.	Gv / Gsm	MV / MS
Sound Symbol	5–17	The examinee is required to recall sounds correlated with diverse abstract figures. A delayed recall trial is given.	Glr	MA
Sentence Memory	5–17	The examinee is required to repeat a series of sentences.	Gsm / Gc	MS / LD
Visual Learning	5–17	The examinee is required to recall the spatial locations of visual designs presented on a board. A delayed recall trial is presented.	Gv / Gsm	MV, SR / MS
Number/Letter Memory	5–17	The examinee is required to repeat an indiscriminate combination of verbally presented letters and numbers beginning with 2 units and increasing to a maximum of 10 units.	Gsm	MS

Note: The *Gf-Gc* classification codes and definitions are presented in Chapter 2 of this text. Classifications are not presented for any test for which standard scores are not available.

*Indicates empirical classifications that are based on cross-battery factor analysis studies. DTLA-3 classifications were based on McGhee (1995). UNIT classifications were based on reanalysis of Reed and McCallum (1995) data by the current authors.

[1] PT is the code for "speech anticulation speed" (Carroll, 1993).

[2] AC is the code for "attention/concentration" (Carroll, 1993).

Another important broad *Gf-Gc* ability that is amply represented among the special purpose tests (with two or more qualitatively different indicators) is *Gf*. With the exception of the DAS (Elliott, 1990a), KAIT (Kaufman & Kaufman, 1993), and WJ-R (Woodcock & Johnson, 1989), all major intelligence batteries either do not measure or do not measure adequately fluid reasoning. Finally, it is important to note that some special purpose batteries such as the Comprehensive Test of Nonverbal Intelligence (CTONI; Hammill, Pearson, & Wiederholt, 1996), the Leiter International Performance Scale—-Revised (Leiter-R; Roid & Miller, 1997), and the Universal Nonverbal Intelligence Test (UNIT; McCallum & Bracken, in press) are capable of assessing between one and four broad *Gf-Gc* abilities while requiring only a low level of linguistic proficiency in comprehension or response. These tests can be administered entirely in pantomime (i.e., nonverbally). Because the CTONI, Leiter-R, and UNIT were normed using a nonverbal communication format, test scores can be compared to an appropriate norm group (see McCallum & Bracken, 1997, for a discussion). Other special purpose tests, such as the Raven's Progressive Matrices test, also have significantly reduced language requirements (e.g., minimal receptive language requirements and no expressive language requirements), which makes them useful for a variety of populations (e.g., dual-language learners) (see Chapter 14 for categorizations of tests according to level of language demands).

Conclusion

It is clear from the information presented in the ITDR section of this book that none of the eight major intelligence batteries currently available measures the breadth and depth of cognitive abilities that define the structure of intelligence according to contemporary *Gf-Gc* theory and research. Therefore, *depending on the purpose of assessment*, each intelligence battery may need to be supplemented with other tests to assess adequately the abilities not measured by the instrument or to obtain a more valid and complete evaluation of intellectual functioning. The special purpose batteries and tests presented in Table 12–1 serve as valuable supplements to the major intelligence batteries. In addition, many incorporate unique features that make them useful in the assessment of culturally and linguistically diverse populations. The next section of this text demonstrates how special purpose tests figure prominently in cross-battery and selective cross-battery assessments.

Chapter 13

The Gf-Gc *Cross-Battery Approach*

Definition and Application

After you've done a thing the same way for two years, look it over carefully. After five years, look at it with suspicion. And after ten years, throw it away and start all over.
—ALFRED EDWARD PERLMAN,
The New York Times, *July 3, 1958*

Since the late 1900s the Wechsler batteries have dominated the field of intelligence testing. Despite the significant contributions that the Wechslers have made to research and practice in psychology as well as in special education, they have been criticized in recent years. The major criticisms of the Wechsler batteries are that they are based on a relatively narrow concept of intelligence, were not developed from a well-researched theoretical model of intelligence, and do not reflect recent advances in cognitive psychology (see Carroll, 1993a, 1993b, 1997; Das, Naglieri, & Kirby, 1994; Flanagan, Genshaft, & Harrison, 1997; Flanagan & McGrew, 1995, 1997; Gardner, 1983; Lezak, 1995; Mackintosh, 1986; McGrew, 1993, 1994, 1997; Naglieri, 1997; Shaw, Swerdlik, & Laurent, 1993; Sternberg, 1986, 1992, 1993, 1997). As discussed in Chapter 1, it is clear that dominant testing practices (i.e., the Wechsler batteries) lag considerably behind current cognitive theories. The way traditional intelligence batteries are typically used impedes the advancement of applied intelligence testing.

Despite the publication of new and revised intelligence batteries (e.g., DAS, WJ-R), most practitioners and researchers continue to rely on the Wechsler scales to assess cognitive functioning (see Flanagan & Genshaft, 1997; Harrison, et al., 1988; Stinnett, Havey, & Oehler-Stinnett, 1994; Wilson & Reschly, 1996). Therefore, it seems that many professionals continue to implicitly or explicitly define intelligence as general ability (i.e., a full-scale IQ) that subsumes either dichotomous abilities (i.e., verbal and performance) or four different indices of functioning (e.g., verbal comprehension, perceptual organization, freedom from distractibility, and processing speed). However, as presented in Chapter 1, at the forefront of intelligence theory and research are reviews of the extant factor analysis research (e.g., Carroll, 1983, 1989, 1993a, 1997; Gustafsson, 1984, 1988; Horn, 1988, 1991, 1994; Lohman, 1989; Snow, 1986; Woodcock, 1990) that have clarified our understanding of the general, broad, and narrow cognitive abilities that underlie the construct of intelligence and the batteries used to measure the construct. These reviews show that the scientific evidence does not support either a single general intelligence (*g*) model, any of several dichotomous models (e.g., verbal/nonverbal, fluid/crystallized, simultaneous/sequential), or incomplete multiple intelligences models. Rather, many researchers in the psychometric tradition have converged on the contemporary *Gf-Gc* multiple intelligences theory (see Chapter 1 for a summary).

As discussed in Chapter 1, Horn and Cattell's *Gf-Gc* theory (Horn, 1985, 1988, 1991, 1994; Horn & Noll, 1997) and Carroll's (1993a, 1997) hierarchical three-stratum theory of human cognitive abilities are the most prominent of the psychometric theories of multiple intelligences to date. The structure of intelligence that has emerged from this body of research is significantly different from the conceptualization of intelligence that underlies the Wechsler scales. Given the extensive body of supporting evidence (see Chapter 2) for the Horn and Carroll *Gf-Gc* models, it is clear that these contemporary *Gf-Gc* models provide the most appropriate basis for understanding and interpreting the cognitive constructs that underlie intelligence tests (Carroll, 1997; Flanagan, Genshaft, & Harrison, 1997; Flanagan & McGrew, 1995, 1997; McGrew, 1997; Woodcock, 1990; Ysseldyke, 1990). Therefore, the purpose of this chapter is to demonstrate how the *Gf-Gc* theoretical framework can be used as a foundation for understanding the breadth and depth of abilities that are measured by all major intelligence batteries. Furthermore, for cases in which the measurement of important cognitive abilities cannot be achieved through the administration of a particular intelligence battery, procedures are recommended for augmenting the battery with other tests to ensure that such abilities are measured.

Just as a neuropsychological test battery "must be able to measure the full range of behavioral functions subserved by the brain" (Reitan & Wolfsen, 1985, p. 1), an intelligence battery ought to be able to measure the full range of broad cognitive abilities that define the structure of intelligence. Although this goal is virtually impossible to achieve, steps can be taken to approximate the goal of more complete assessments of cognitive abilities than can be achieved by any single battery. To this end, this chapter presents a *Gf-Gc* "cross-battery" approach to assessing cognitive abilities that arose, primarily, out of the finding that *none* of the major intelligence batteries adequately measures the full range of important *broad Gf-Gc* abilities according to contemporary theory and research (see Chapter 3). A set of guiding principles is offered for augmenting any given intelligence battery with the most psychometrically sound and theoretically pure tests (according to ITDR criteria—see Chapter 3) so that a broader, more complete range of *Gf-Gc* abilities can be assessed. A step-by-step approach to *Gf-Gc* cross-battery assessment is offered for improving the validity of intellectual assessment, thereby narrowing the intelligence testing theory–practice gap described in Chapter 1.

The cross-battery approach presented in this chapter should not be misinterpreted to mean that cross-battery assessments *always* need to measure the full range of broad cognitive abilities specified in *Gf-Gc* theory. The "best practices" principles of (1) conducting assessments only after other preassessment activities have been tried (e.g., prevention, prereferral intervention), (2) pursuing intellectual assessments only when the results have direct relevance to well-defined referral questions, (3) embedding assessments in a multifactored approach, and (4) tailoring the assessment to the unique needs of the individual case hold true for *Gf-Gc*–designed cross-battery assessments. For cases in which a comprehensive *Gf-Gc* assessment is not considered necessary, a selective cross-battery approach may be implemented. This approach is described in Chapter 14.

Unless an effort is made to devise new ways of measuring cognitive abilities, "we shall remain limited by obsolescent testing methods that do not reflect modern theories of cognition" (Hunt, 1990, p. 238). The "crossing" of batteries is not a new method of intellectual assessment per se, as it is commonplace in neuropsychological assessment (e.g., Lezak, 1976). However, the method of crossing intelligence batteries has never been formally operationalized. The cross-battery approach presented here provides a systematic means for practitioners to make valid, *up-to-date* interpretations of all intelligence tests and to augment them in a way that is consistent with the empirically supported *Gf-Gc* theoretical model. Moving beyond the boundaries of a single intelligence battery by adopting the psychometrically and theoretically defensible cross-battery principles outlined here is a *first step* toward a new and improved method of measuring cognitive abilities.

A Definition of the **Gf-Gc** *Cross-Battery Approach*

According to Carroll (1997), the *Gf-Gc* taxonomy of human cognitive abilities "appears to prescribe that individuals should be assessed with regard to the *total range* of abilities the theory specifies" (p. 129). He admitted, however, that "any such prescription would of course create enormous problems" and that "[r]esearch is needed to spell out how the assessor can select what abilities need to be tested in particular cases" (p. 129). The *Gf-Gc* cross-battery approach is an attempt to "spell out" how practitioners can conduct assessments that approximate the total range of broad cognitive abilities more adequately than does any single intelligence battery.

Specifically, *the Gf-Gc cross-battery approach is a time-efficient method of intellectual assessment that allows practitioners to measure validly a wider range (or a more in-depth but selective range) of cognitive abilities than that represented by any one intelligence battery in a way consistent with contemporary psychometric theory and research on the structure of intelligence.* The cross-battery approach is based on three foundational sources or pillars of information (Flanagan & McGrew, 1997).

Cross-Battery Pillar #1

The first pillar of the cross-battery approach is the *synthesized Horn-Cattell/Carroll Gf-Gc model* of human cognitive abilities (McGrew, 1997). Because this model was described at length in Chapter 1, it will not be explained again here. The *Gf-Gc* model is the one around which cross-battery assessments are designed because it has a more comprehensive network of validity evidence than do other multidimensional conceptualizations of intelligence (Horn, 1994; Horn & Noll, 1997; Messick, 1992) (see also Chapter 2).

Cross-Battery Pillar #2

The second pillar of the cross-battery approach is the *Gf-Gc broad (stratum II) classifications* of cognitive ability tests reported in the ITDR (Part II). A total of 222 broad ability classifications were made, the number of tests and subtests of 8 major intelligence batteries and 17 "special purpose" batteries and tests. The way these classifications were made was described in Chapter 3. Classification of all tests at the broad ability level was necessary to improve upon the validity of intellectual assessment and interpretation. Specifically, these broad ability classifications were necessary to ensure that the *Gf-Gc* constructs that underlie cross-battery assessments are minimally affected by construct-irrelevant variance (Messick, 1995).

According to Messick (1995), *construct-irrelevant variance* is present when an "assessment is too broad, containing excess reliable variance associated with other distinct constructs...that affects responses in a manner irrelevant to the interpreted constructs" (p. 742). For example, Figure 13–1 shows that the Wechsler Verbal IQ (VIQ) contains construct irrelevant variance because, in addition to its four strong indicators of *Gc* (i.e., Information, Similarities, Vocabulary, Comprehension), it contains one strong indicator of *Gq* (i.e., Arithmetic). Therefore, the VIQ is a *mixed* measure of two distinct, broad *Gf-Gc* abilities (*Gc* and *Gq*). It contains reliable variance (associated with *Gq*) that is irrelevant to the interpreted construct of *Gc*. Thus, as depicted in Figure 13–1, the *purest* (or cleanest) *Gc* composite on the WISC-III is the Verbal Comprehension Index, since it contains only construct-*relevant* variance. A composite score will provide a valid estimate of a broad *Gf-Gc* ability when it contains at least two reliable measures of two different narrow (stratum I) abilities subsumed by that broad ability only.[1] Composite scores that contain excess reliable variance (i.e., measures of narrow abilities subsumed by two or more broad abilities) will confound interpretation. Thus, the assumption

---

[1] In factor analysis a minimum of *three* variables are necessary to form a factor (Zwick & Velicer, 1986). The tests that are recommended for use in cross-battery assessments had either strong or moderate (but not mixed) loadings on their respective factors in studies in which three or more indicators typically formed a factor (see Chapter 3 for a summary). However, in the cross-battery approach a minimum of *two* narrow ability measures is recommended for constructing *Gf-Gc* broad ability composites for practical reasons (viz., time-efficient assessment).

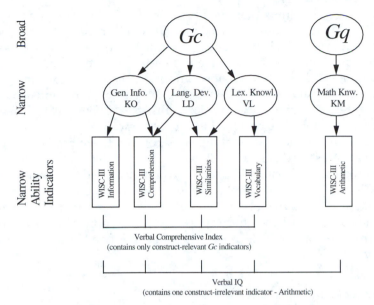

**FIGURE 13–1   Examples of WISC-III Construct-Relevant
and Construct-Irrelevant *Gc* Composites**

behind the *Gf-Gc* cross-battery approach is that "*a single scale ought to measure a single construct*" (Briggs & Cheek, 1986, italics in the original).

The results of within-battery factor analyses (described in Chapter 3) are often misleading because they do not contain a sufficient number of reasonably pure (or clean) measures for each of the factors present so that the factor structure of the instrument can be identified clearly and interpreted appropriately (see also Woodcock, 1990). When two or more broad abilities are each represented by only one narrow ability indicator, they may not emerge as separate factors because there is an insufficient number of indicators to represent the broad abilities. In this situation, narrow indicators of different broad abilities may form a factor of their own. For example, on the WISC-III the Digit Span subtest (a narrow ability indicator of *Gsm*) and the Arithmetic subtest (a narrow ability indicator of *Gq*) formed the "Freedom From Distractibility" (FFD) factor (Wechsler, 1991). Since these subtests measure narrow abilities subsumed by different broad *Gf-Gc* abilities, the resultant factor is complex (i.e., mixed). According to Carroll (1993a), the FFD factor is "an artifact of the factor analysis of a severely limited battery of tests, and is not to be considered as a basic primary factor in mental organization" (p. 258). Thus, factorial complexity masks the "true" factor structure of an instrument and complicates or misinforms interpretation. In the cross-battery approach, test classifications are used to organize relatively pure *Gf-Gc* clusters, thereby circumventing this problem in assessment.

Construct-irrelevant variance may also be present at the subtest level. Some subtests, such as the WJ-R Verbal Analogies test, are mixed measures of two or more narrow abilities that are subsumed by two or more broad *Gf-Gc* abilities. The Verbal Analogies test is a mixed measure of *Gf* and *Gc*. As can be seen in Table 13–1 (column 4), which provides a description of the abilities measured by all the major intelligence batteries, many subtests are mixed measures of two or more *Gf-Gc* abilities. "[A]ny test that measures more than one common factor to a substantial degree yields scores that are psychologically ambiguous and very difficult to interpret" (Guilford, 1954, p. 356; cf. Briggs & Cheek, 1986). Therefore, cross-battery assessments are designed using only empirically strong or moderate (but not mixed) measures of *Gf-Gc* abilities.[2] If constructs are broad and multifaceted, like those represented at stratum II in the *Gf-Gc* model, then each component (i.e., *Gf-Gc* broad ability) "should be specified and measured as *cleanly* as possible" (Briggs & Cheek, 1986, p. 130, emphasis added). By combining only empirically strong (or moderate) measures of *Gf-Gc* abilities into appropriate (i.e., construct-relevant) composites, the cross-battery approach offers a more valid means of measuring the narrow and broad *Gf-Gc* constructs than that offered by any single intelligence battery.

Cross-Battery Pillar #3

The third pillar of the cross-battery approach is the *Gf-Gc narrow (stratum I) classifications* of cognitive ability tests reported in the ITDR. The 222 tests mentioned above were also classified at the *Gf-Gc* narrow ability level (see Chapter 3 for narrow ability test classification procedures). Classifications at this level were necessary to *further* improve upon the validity of intellectual assessment and interpretation. Specifically, these narrow ability classifications were necessary to ensure that the *Gf-Gc* constructs that underlie cross-battery assessments are well represented (Messick, 1995).

According to Messick (1995), *construct underrepresentation* is present when an "assessment is too narrow and fails to include important dimensions or facets of the construct" (p. 742). Two examples of construct underrepresentation inherent in cognitive assessment follow.

First, construct underrepresentation is present when an *individual test* (i.e., subtest) is interpreted as measuring a *broad (stratum II) Gf-Gc* ability. For example, interpreting the SB:IV Vocabulary subtest as a measure of *Gc* is inappropriate. *Gc* is a broad ability that subsumes several narrow abilities, including Language Development (LD), Lexical Knowledge (VL), Listening Ability (LS), General Information (KO), and Information about Culture (K2), to name a few (see Table 1–1). Although the SB:IV Vocabulary subtest measures VL, an important component of *Gc*, it represents only one narrow aspect of this broad ability. In order for a construct to be well represented, *two or more qualitatively different indicators* (i.e., measures of two or more narrow abilities subsumed by the broad ability) are needed (see Comrey, 1988). Thus, the aggregate of SB:IV Vocabulary (VL), Comprehension (LD), Absurdities (LD), and Verbal Relations (LD) (i.e., the Verbal Reasoning SAS;

---

[2] Definitions of "strong," "moderate," and "mixed" are provided in Chapter 3.

TABLE 13–1 Description of the Abilities Measured by Intelligence Batteries

Battery Subtest	Age Range in Years	Ability Measured According to Test Author(s)	Broad and (Narrow) Abilities Measured According to Recent Gf-Gc Analyses[1]	Under-represented Gf-Gc Constructs	Gf-Gc Constructs Not Measured by the Battery
Differential Ability Scales (DAS)	2–17			Gq, Gsm, Glr, Gs	Ga
Verbal Comprehension	2–5	Verbal Ability	Crystallized Intelligence (Gc) (*Language Development—LD, Listening Ability—LS*)		
Naming Vocabulary	2–5	Verbal Ability	Crystallized Intelligence (Gc) (*Language Development—LD, Lexical Knowledge—VL*)		
Word Definitions	6–17	Verbal Ability	**CRYSTALLIZED INTELLIGENCE (Gc)** (*Lexical Knowledge—VL, Language Development—LD*)		
Similarities	6–17	Verbal Ability	**CRYSTALLIZED INTELLIGENCE (Gc)** (*Language Development—LD, Lexical Knowledge—VL*)		
Picture Similarities	2–5	Nonverbal Ability	Fluid Intelligence (Gf) (*Induction—I*)		
Pattern Construction[2]	3–17	Nonverbal Ability Spatial Ability	Visual Processing (Gv) (*Spatial Relations—SR, Visualization—VZ*)		
Copying	3–5	Nonverbal Ability	Visual Processing (Gv) (*Visualization—VZ, Finger Dexterity—P2*)		
Matrices	6–17	Nonverbal Reasoning Ability	**FLUID INTELLIGENCE (Gf)** (*Induction—I*)		
Sequential & Quantitative Reasoning	6–17	Nonverbal Reasoning Ability	**FLUID INTELLIGENCE (Gf)** (*Induction—I, Quantitative Reasoning—RQ*)		
Recall of Designs	6–17	Spatial Ability	**VISUAL PROCESSING (Gv)** (*Visual Memory—MV*)		
Early Number Concepts	3–5	General Conceptual Ability	Quantitative Knowledge (Gq) (*Math Achievement—A3, Mathematical Knowledge—KM*)		

Continued

TABLE 13–1 *Continued*

Battery Subtest	Age Range in Years	Ability Measured According to Test Author(s)	Broad and (Narrow) Abilities Measured According to Recent Gf-Gc Analyses[1]	Under-represented Gf-Gc Constructs	Gf-Gc Constructs Not Measured by the Battery
Block Building	2–3	Perceptual-Motor Ability	Visual Processing (Gv) (Visualization—VZ)		
Matching Letter-Like Forms	4–5	Visual-Perceptual Matching	Visual Processing (Gv) (Visualization—VZ)		
Recall of Digits	3–17	Short-Term Auditory Memory	Short-Term Memory (Gsm) (Memory Span—MS)		
Recall of Objects	4–17	Short- and Intermediate-Term Verbal Memory	Long-Term Storage & Retrieval (Glr) (Free Recall Memory—M6) Visual Processing (Gv) (Visual Memory—MV)		
Recognition of Pictures	3–7	Short-Term Visual Memory	Visual Processing (Gv) (Visual Memory—MV)		
Speed of Information Processing	6–17	Speed of Information Processing	Processing Speed (Gs) (Mental Comparison Speed—R7, Rate-of-Test-Taking—R9)		
Kaufman Assessment Battery for Children (K-ABC)	2–12			Gf, Gsm	Gc³, Ga, Glr, Gs, Gq
Magic Window	2–4	Simultaneous Processing	Visual Processing (Gv) (Serial Perceptual Integration—PI, Closure Speed—CS)		
Face Recognition	2–4	Simultaneous Processing	Visual Processing (Gv) (Visual Memory—MV)		
Gestalt Closure	2–12	Simultaneous Processing	Visual Processing (Gv) (Closure Speed—CS)		
Triangles	4–12	Simultaneous Processing	VISUAL PROCESSING (Gv) (Visualization—VZ, Spatial Relations—SR)		
Matrix Analogies	5–12	Simultaneous Processing	[Fluid Intelligence (Gf)] (Induction—I) [Visual Processing (Gv)] (Visualization—VZ)		

Subtest	Age	Scale	CHC Broad (Narrow) Abilities	
				Ga, Gq, Gs
				Gv, Gsm
Spatial Memory	5–12	Simultaneous Processing	[Visual Processing (*Gv*)] (*Visual Memory—MV, Spatial Relations—SR*) [Short-Term Memory (*Gsm*)] (*Memory Span—MS*)	
Photo Series	6–12	Simultaneous Processing	[Visual Processing (*Gv*)] (*Visualization—VZ*) [Fluid Intelligence (*Gf*)] (*Induction—I*)	
Hand Movements	2–12	Sequential Processing	[Visual Processing (*Gv*)] (*Visual Memory—MV*) [Quantitative Knowledge (*Gq*)] (*Math Achievement—A3*)	
Number Recall	2–12	Sequential Processing	**SHORT-TERM MEMORY (*Gsm*)** (*Memory Span—MS*)	
Word Order	4–12	Sequential Processing	**SHORT-TERM MEMORY (*Gsm*)** (*Memory Span—MS*)	
Kaufman Adolescent and Adult Intelligence Test (KAIT)				
Definitions	11–85+	Crystallized Intelligence (*Gc*)	[Crystallized Intelligence (*Gc*)] (*Language Development—LD, Lexical Knowledge—VL*) [Reading/writing (*Grw*)] (*Spelling Ability—SG, Reading Decoding—RD*)	
Double Meanings	11–85+	Crystallized Intelligence (*Gc*)	[Crystallized Intelligence (*Gc*)] (*Lexical Knowledge—VL*) [Reading/writing (*Grw*)] (*Verbal Language Comprehension—V*)	
Auditory Comprehension	11–85+	Crystallized Intelligence (*Gc*)	[Crystallized Intelligence (*Gc*)] (*Language Development—LD, Listening Ability—LS*) [Short-Term Memory (*Gsm*)] (*Memory Span—MS*)	
Famous Faces	11–85+	Crystallized Intelligence (*Gc*)	**CRYSTALLIZED INTELLIGENCE (*Gc*)** (*Information about Culture—K2, General Information—KO*)	

Continued

TABLE 13–1 *Continued*

Battery Subtest	Age Range in Years	Ability Measured According to Test Author(s)	Broad and (Narrow) Abilities Measured According to Recent Gf-Gc Analyses[1]	Under-represented Gf-Gc Constructs	Gf-Gc Constructs Not Measured by the Battery
Logical Steps	11–85+	Fluid Intelligence (*Gf*)	**FLUID INTELLIGENCE (*Gf*)** (*General Sequential Reasoning—RG, Induction—I*)		
Mystery Codes	11–85+	Fluid Intelligence (*Gf*)	**FLUID INTELLIGENCE (*Gf*)** (*Induction—I*)		
Rebus Learning	11–85+	Fluid Intelligence (*Gf*)	**LONG-TERM STORAGE & RETRIEVAL (*Glr*)** (*Associative Memory—MA, Meaningful Memory—MM*)		
Memory for Block Designs	11–85+	Fluid Intelligence (*Gf*)	**VISUAL PROCESSING (*Gv*)** (*Visual Memory—MV*)		
Rebus Delayed Recall	11–85+	Delayed Memory	**LONG-TERM STORAGE & RETRIEVAL (*Glr*)** (*Associative Memory—MA, Meaningful Memory—MM*)		
Auditory Delayed Recall	11–85+	Delayed Memory	[Long-Term Storage & Retrieval (*Glr*) (*Meaningful Memory—MM*)] [Crystallized Intelligence (*Gc*) (*Language Development—LD*)]	*Gq, Gsm*	*Ga, Glr, Gs*
Stanford-Binet Intelligence Scale: Fourth Edition (SB:IV)	2–24				
Vocabulary	2–24	Crystallized Intelligence (*Gc*) Verbal Reasoning	**CRYSTALLIZED INTELLIGENCE (*Gc*)** (*Language Development—LD, Lexical Knowledge—VL*)		
Comprehension	2–24	Crystallized Intelligence (*Gc*) Verbal Reasoning	Crystallized Intelligence (*Gc*) (*Language Development—LD, General Information—KO*)		
Absurdities	2–14	Crystallized Intelligence (*Gc*) Verbal Reasoning	Crystallized Intelligence (*Gc*) (*Language Development—LD, General Information—KO*)		
Verbal Relations	12–24	Crystallized Intelligence (*Gc*) Verbal Reasoning	**CRYSTALLIZED INTELLIGENCE (*Gc*)** (*Language Development—LD, Lexical Knowledge—VL*)		

Pattern Analysis	2–24	Fluid Intelligence (Gf) Abstract/Visual Reasoning	**VISUAL PROCESSING (Gv)** *(Visualization—VZ, Spatial Relations—SR)*	
Copying	2–13	Fluid Intelligence (Gf) Abstract/Visual Reasoning	[Visual Processing (Gv) *(Visualization—VZ, Finger Dexterity—P2)*]	
Matrices	7–24	Fluid Intelligence (Gf) Abstract/Visual Reasoning	**FLUID INTELLIGENCE (Gf)** *(Induction—I)*	
Paper Folding and Cutting	12–24	Fluid Intelligence (Gf) Abstract/Visual Reasoning	[Visual Processing (Gv) *(Visualization—VZ)* [Quantitative Knowledge (Gq)] *(Math Achievement—A3)*	
Quantitative	2–24	Crystallized Intelligence (Gc) Quantitative Reasoning	**QUANTITATIVE KNOWLEDGE (Gq)** *(Math Achievement—A3)* Fluid Intelligence (Gf) *(Quantitative Reasoning—RQ)*	
Number Series	7–24	Crystallized Intelligence (Gc) Quantitative Reasoning	Fluid Intelligence (Gf) *(Quantitative Reasoning—RQ)*	
Equation Building	12–24	Crystallized Intelligence (Gc) Quantitative Reasoning	**FLUID INTELLIGENCE (Gf)** *(Quantitative Reasoning—RQ)* Quantitative Knowledge (Gq) *(Mathematical Knowledge—KM)*	
Bead Memory	2–24	Short-Term Memory (Gsm)	Visual Processing (Gv) *(Visual Memory—MV)*	
Memory for Sentences	2–24	Short-Term Memory (Gsm)	[Short-Term Memory (Gsm)] *(Memory Span—MS)* [Crystallized Intelligence (Gc)] *(Language Development—LD)*	
Memory for Digits	7–24	Short-Term Memory (Gsm)	**SHORT-TERM MEMORY (Gsm)** *(Memory Span—MS)*	
Memory for Objects	7–24	Short-Term Memory (Gsm)	Visual Processing (Gv) *(Visual Memory—MV)*	
Wechsler Batteries (WPPSI-R, WISC-III, & WAIS-III)	3–89[4]			*Gsm, Gq, Gs[5]* *Ga, Glr, Gf*
Information	3–89	Verbal Comprehension	**CRYSTALLIZED INTELLIGENCE (Gc)** *(General Information—KO)*	
Vocabulary	3–89	Verbal Comprehension	**CRYSTALLIZED INTELLIGENCE (Gc)** *(Language Development—LD, Lexical Knowledge—VL)*	

TABLE 13–1 *Continued*

Battery Subtest	Age Range in Years	Ability Measured According to Test Author(s)	Broad and (Narrow) Abilities Measured According to Recent Gf-Gc Analyses[1]	Under-represented Gf-Gc Constructs	Gf-Gc Constructs Not Measured by the Battery
Arithmetic[6]	3–89	Verbal Comprehension	**QUANTITATIVE KNOWLEDGE (Gq)** *(Math Achievement—A3)* Fluid Intelligence (Gf) *(Quantitative Reasoning—RQ)*		
Comprehension[7]	3–89	Verbal Comprehension	**CRYSTALLIZED INTELLIGENCE (Gc)** *(Language Development—LD, General Information—KO)*		
Similarities	3–89	Verbal Comprehension	**CRYSTALLIZED INTELLIGENCE (Gc)** *(Language Development—LD, Lexical Knowledge—VL)*		
Picture Completion	3–89	Perceptual Organization	[Visual Processing (Gv)] *(Flexibility of Closure—CF)* [Crystallized Intelligence (Gc) *(General Information—KO)*		
Block Design	3–89	Perceptual Organization	**VISUAL PROCESSING (Gv)** *(Spatial Relations—SR, Visualization—VZ)*		
Object Assembly[8]	3–89	Perceptual Organization	**VISUAL PROCESSING (Gv)** *(Closure Speed—CS, Spatial Relations—SR)*		
Digit Span[9] (WISC-III, WAIS-III only)	6–89	Verbal Comprehension	**SHORT-TERM MEMORY (Gsm)** *(Memory Span—MS)*		
Picture Arrangement[10] (WISC-III, WAIS-III only)	6–89	Perceptual Organization	[Visual Processing (Gv)] *(Visualization—VZ)* [Crystallized Intelligence (Gc) *(General Information—KO)*		
Coding[11] (WISC-III, WAIS-III only)	6–89	Processing Speed	**PROCESSING SPEED (Gs)** *(Rate-of-Test-Taking—R9)*		
Symbol Search (WISC-III, WAIS-III only)	6–89	Processing Speed	Processing Speed (Gs) *(Perceptual Speed—P, Rate-of-Test-Taking—R9)*		

Continued

Subtest	Age	Broad Ability	Narrow Ability
Matrix Reasoning (WAIS-III only)	16–89	Perceptual Organization	Fluid Intelligence (Gf) (Induction—I)
Letter-Number Sequencing (WAIS-III only)	16–89	Working Memory	Short-Term Memory (Gsm) (Memory Span—MS)
Mazes[12] (WPPSI-R, WISC-III only)	3–16	Perceptual Organization	Visual Processing (Gv)[12] (Spatial Scanning—SS)
Geometric Design (WPPSI-R Only)	3–7	Perceptual Organization	Visual Processing (Gv) (Visualization—VZ, Finger Dexterity—P2)
Animal Pegs (WPPSI-R only)	3–7	Perceptual Organization	Processing Speed (Gs) (Rate-of-Test-Taking—R9)
Sentences (WPPSI-R only)	3–7	Verbal Comprehension	Short-Term Memory (Gsm) (Memory Span—MS) Crystallized Intelligence (Gc) (Language Development—LD)
Woodcock-Johnson Psychoeducational Battery—Revised (WJ-R)	2–85+		Glr, Gsm, Gs, Ga, Gc
Memory for Names	2–85+	Long-Term Storage & Retrieval (Glr)	LONG-TERM STORAGE & RETRIEVAL (Glr) (Associative Memory—MA)
Visual-Auditory Learning	4–85+	Long-Term Storage & Retrieval (Glr)	LONG-TERM STORAGE & RETRIEVAL (Glr) (Associative Memory—MA, Meaningful Memory—MM)
Memory for Sentences	2–85+	Short-Term Memory (Gsm)	[Short-Term Memory (Gsm)] [Crystallized Intelligence (Gc)] (Language Development-LD)
Memory for Words	4–85+	Short-Term Memory (Gsm)	SHORT-TERM MEMORY (Gsm) (Memory Span—MS)
Visual Matching	4–85+	Processing Speed (Gs)	PROCESSING SPEED (Gs) (Perceptual Speed—P, Rate-of-Test-Taking—R9)
Cross Out	4–85+	Processing Speed (Gs)	PROCESSING SPEED (Gs) (Perceptual Speed—P, Rate-of-Test-Taking—R9)

TABLE 13–1 *Continued*

Battery Subtest	Age Range in Years	Ability Measured According to Test Author(s)	Broad and (Narrow) Abilities Measured According to Recent Gf-Gc Analyses[1]	Under-represented Gf-Gc Constructs	Gf-Gc Constructs Not Measured by the Battery
Incomplete Words	2–85+	Auditory Processing (*Ga*)	**AUDITORY PROCESSING (*Ga*)** (*Phonetic Coding—PC, Resistance to Auditory Stimulus Distortion—UR*)		
Sound Blending	4–85+	Auditory Processing (*Ga*)	**AUDITORY PROCESSING (*Ga*)** (*Phonetic Coding—PC*)		
Visual Closure	2–85+	Visual Processing (*Gv*)	**Visual Processing (*Gv*)** (*Closure Speed—CS*)		
Picture Recognition	4–85+	Visual Processing (*Gv*)	**Visual Processing (*Gv*)** (*Visual Memory—MV*)		
Picture Vocabulary	2–85+	Crystallized Intelligence (*Gc*)	**CRYSTALLIZED INTELLIGENCE (*Gc*)** (*Lexical Knowledge—VL, General Information—KO, Language Development—LD*)		
Oral Vocabulary	4–85+	Crystallized Intelligence (*Gc*)	**CRYSTALLIZED INTELLIGENCE (*Gc*)** (*Lexical Knowledge—VL, Language Development—LD*)		
Analysis Synthesis	4–85+	Fluid Intelligence (*Gf*)	**FLUID INTELLIGENCE (*Gf*)** (*General Sequential Reasoning—RG, Quantitative Reasoning—RQ*)		
Concept Formation	4–85+	Fluid Intelligence (*Gf*)	**FLUID INTELLIGENCE (*Gf*)** (*Induction—I, Quantitative Reasoning—RQ*)		
Delayed Recall—Memory for Names	4–85+	Long-Term Storage & Retrieval (*Glr*)	**LONG-TERM STORAGE & RETRIEVAL (*Glr*)** (*Associative Memory—MA*)		
Delayed Recall—Visual Auditory Learning	4–85+	Long-Term Storage & Retrieval (*Glr*)	**Long-Term Storage & Retrieval (*Glr*)** (*Associative Memory—MA, Meaningful Memory—MM*)		
Numbers Reversed	4–85+	Short-Term Memory (*Gsm*)	[**Short-Term Memory (*Gsm*)**] (*Memory Span—MS*) [Fluid Intelligence (*Gf*)] (*General Sequential Reasoning—RG*)		

Sound Patterns	4–85+	Auditory Processing (*Ga*) Fluid Intelligence (*Gf*)	[Auditory Processing (*Ga*)] (**Speech Sound Discrimination—US,** Memory *for Sound Patterns—UM*) [Fluid Intelligence (*Gf*)] (*General Sequential Reasoning—RG*)
Spatial Relations	4–85+	Visual Processing (*Gv*) Fluid Intelligence (*Gf*)	[Visual Processing (*Gv*)] (***Spatial Relations—SR,*** ***Visualization—VZ***) [Fluid Intelligence (*Gf*)] (***General Sequential Reasoning—RG***)
Listening Comprehension	4–85+	Crystallized Intelligence (*Gc*)	**CRYSTALLIZED INTELLIGENCE (*Gc*)** (*Listening Ability—LS,* *Language Development—LD*)
Verbal Analogies	4–85+	Crystallized Intelligence (*Gc*) Fluid Intelligence (*Gf*)	[Crystallized Intelligence (*Gc*)] (*Language Development—LD,* *Lexical Knowledge—VL*) [Fluid Intelligence (*Gf*)] (***Induction—I***)

[1] *Gf–Gc* classifications are taken from the ITDR of this text and are therefore based on the method and criteria used therein. Broad ability classifications in bold/uppercase letters are "empirical: strong" measures; broad abilities in bold/lowercase letters are "empirical: moderate" measures; broad abilities in brackets ([ ]) are "empirical: mixed" measures; broad abilities in regular type/lowercase are logically based measures. All narrow abilities in italics are "empirical: moderate" measures. Narrow abilities in bold/italics are "probable" measures; narrow abilities in regular type/italics are "possible" measures.

[2] Pattern Construction purportedly measures Nonverbal Ability at the younger ages (3–6 to 5–11) and Spatial Ability at the older ages (6–0 to 17–11) (Elliott, 1990).

[3] The K-ABC Achievement Test provides qualitatively different indicators of *Gc*.

[4] The three Wechsler batteries cover the age range from 2 to 89 years. The age ranges for the separate batteries are: WPPSI-R: 2–7 years; WISC-III: 6–16 years; and WAIS-III: 16–89 years.

[5] *Gs* is *not* underrepresented in the WISC-III.

[6] In the WISC-III the Arithmetic subtest purportedly measures Freedom from Distractibility.

[7] In the WAIS-III Comprehension is not included in the calculation of index scores.

[8] In the WAIS-III Object Assembly is not included in the calculation of index scores.

[9] In the WAIS-III the Digit Span subtest purportedly measures Freedom from Distractibility.

[10] In the WAIS-III Picture Arrangement is not included in the calculation of index scores.

[11] In the WAIS-III this subtest is named Digit Symbol-Coding.

[12] The Mazes subtest on the WPPSI-R is an "empirical: moderate" measure of Visual Processing (*Gv*).

Thorndike et al., 1986) provides a good index of the broad *Gc* ability because these subtests measure qualitatively different narrow abilities subsumed by *Gc* (see Table 13–1). Likewise, Figure 13–1 shows that the aggregate of WISC-III Information (KO), Comprehension (LD), Similarities (LD), and Vocabulary (VL) (i.e., the Verbal Comprehension Index) is a good estimate of *Gc*. (It is noteworthy that there are very few composites among the eight intelligence batteries that are both pure [i.e., contain only construct-relevant tests] and well represented [i.e., contain qualitatively different measures of the broad ability represented by the composite].)

A review of Table 13–1 (column 5) shows that two or more constructs are underrepresented on *all* the major intelligence batteries. For example, the important constructs *Gsm* and *Gq* are underrepresented on the WISC-III. The WISC-III Digit Span subtest measures a narrow ability subsumed by *Gsm* (i.e., Memory Span—MS) and the WISC-III Arithmetic subtest measures a narrow ability subsumed by *Gq* (i.e., Math Achievement—A3). Interpreting these tests as measures of the broad abilities of *Gsm* and *Gq*, respectively, is inappropriate because there are not enough qualitatively different indicators of these broad abilities included on the WISC-III to represent them adequately. Therefore, before one makes interpretations or generalizations about an individual's ability in the broad domains of *Gsm* and *Gq*, the WISC-III must be supplemented with at least one additional, qualitatively different, narrow indicator of *Gsm* and *Gq*.

Second, construct underrepresentation is present when the aggregate of two or more measures of the same narrow (stratum I) ability is interpreted as measuring a broad (stratum II) *Gf-Gc* ability. Examples of this type of construct underrepresentation can be seen by examining the cognitive tests of the WJ-R in Table 13–1. According to the information presented in this table, the two tests that make up the WJ-R *Glr* cluster (Memory for Names and Visual-Auditory Learning) are primarily measures of Associative Memory (MA), a narrow ability subsumed by *Glr*. Thus, the more appropriate description of the ability underlying the WJ-R *Glr* cluster is not *broad Glr* as purported, but, rather, the narrow ability of MA that is subsumed by *Glr*.

With regard to factor analysis, the results of within-battery analyses (described in Chapter 3) may be misleading if they do not contain qualitatively different indicators for each of the factors present (e.g., Comrey, 1988; Woodcock, 1990). Subtests that measure the same narrow abilities will, of course, load on the same factor. However, that factor may be misinterpreted as representing a broad (stratum II) rather than narrow (stratum I) ability construct. For example, a factor composed of two or more subtests that measure Induction (I), a narrow ability subsumed by *Gf*, is most appropriately labeled "I," not "*Gf*." The factor is simply not sufficiently broad to warrant a broad (stratum II) label. If the factor contained at least one qualitatively different indicator of *Gf* in addition to I, such as General Sequential Reasoning (RG), then it would be more appropriately labeled "*Gf*."

Having two or more measures of the same narrow ability on the same battery seems redundant and unnecessary and is analogous to having reworded versions of the same item or alternate forms of the same test on a scale (Comrey, 1988). When one is included, the others contribute little, if any, incremental information

(Clark & Watson, 1995). That is, "the items (or tests) together will yield little more construct-relevant information than any one item (or test) individually. Accordingly, a scale [or broad *Gf-Gc* ability cluster] will yield far more information—and, hence, be a more valid measure of a construct—if it contains more differentiated items [or tests]" (Clark & Watson, 1995). In the case of the WJ-R, the *Gv* and *Gf* broad ability clusters contain more differentiated measures than the remaining five clusters (see Table 13–1) and therefore are probably more valid measures of these broad (stratum II) abilities than the other clusters are of their respective *Gf-Gc* (stratum II) abilities. In fact, the second-order *Gf-Gc* factors of *Gc*, *Glr*, *Gsm*, *Ga*, and *Gs* on the WJ-R are described more appropriately by the predominant narrow (stratum I) ability underlying the measures (i.e., Lexical Knowledge—VL, Associative Memory—MA, Memory Span—MS, Phonetic Coding—PC, and Perceptual Speed—P, respectively). This is because these *Gf-Gc* constructs are so narrowly focused that they cannot adequately represent broad second-order (stratum II) constructs (see Comrey, 1988).

With regard to scale differentiation, as the average inter-item or inter-test (i.e., tests within the same *Gf-Gc* broad ability cluster) correlation increases, indices that reflect scale homogeneity (e.g., internal consistency reliability for items, magnitude of factor loadings for tests) will also increase. However, maximization of the absolute magnitude of indices of scale homogeneity may occur at the expense of construct validity. This situation is referred to as the "attenuation paradox" in the reliability literature (e.g., Boyle, 1991; Clark & Watson, 1995; Loevinger, 1954). Therefore, it is recommended that inter-item and inter-test correlations be moderate (not high) in magnitude (e.g., Clark & Watson, 1995). This is achieved through developing items (or tests) that measure related but different (rather than redundant) aspects of a construct. Thus, the cross-battery approach suggests circumventing misinterpretations that may result when constructs are underrepresented by using two or more qualitatively different indicators to represent each broad *Gf-Gc* ability. Construct validity is thus maximized rather than compromised.

In sum, the latter two cross-battery pillars guard against two ubiquitous sources of invalidity in assessment—construct-irrelevant variance and construct underrepresentation. Taken together, the three pillars provide the necessary foundation from which to build more theoretically driven, comprehensive, and valid measures of human cognitive abilities.

Rationale for the Gf-Gc *Cross-Battery Approach*

The *Gf-Gc* cross-battery approach was developed to improve on the validity of assessment and interpretation of intelligence tests. The notion of "crossing" intelligence batteries to measure all broad abilities included in contemporary *Gf-Gc* theory was first advanced by Woodcock (1990), following his compilation of a series of cross-battery factor analyses of several intelligence batteries. The conclusions drawn from Woodcock's set of analyses, as well as from other similar cross-battery analyses (see Chapter 3), sparked the development of the cross-battery approach to assessment presented here. The more specific and fundamental reasons for developing the cross-battery method are discussed briefly here in terms of practice, research, and test development.

First, the cross-battery approach was developed to provide "a much needed and updated bridge between current intellectual theory and research and practice" (Flanagan & McGrew, 1997, p. 322). The results of the recent cross-battery factor analyses summarized in Chapter 3 demonstrate that none of our current intelligence batteries adequately measures the full range of broad *Gf-Gc* abilities that define the structure of intelligence in contemporary theory. As can be seen in Table 13–1, of the eight major intelligence batteries currently available, six fail to measure three or more broad *Gf-Gc* abilities (viz., *Ga, Glr, Gf, Gs*) that are important in understanding and predicting school achievement (McGrew, 1993; McGrew, Flanagan, et al., 1997; McGrew & Hessler, 1995; McGrew & Knopik, 1993) (see Chapter 2 for a summary). In fact, *Gf*, often considered to be the *essence* of intelligence, is either not measured or not measured adequately (i.e., underrepresented) by half of the intelligence batteries (i.e., WAIS-III, WISC-III, WPPSI-R, WAIS-R, and K-ABC).

The absence of any strong indicators (or measures) of *Gf* on the Wechsler batteries (i.e., WAIS-R, WISC-III, and WPPSI-R) is particularly noteworthy, since the Wechsler Performance tests are often misinterpreted as measures of fluid reasoning (see McGrew & Flanagan, 1996, for a discussion). Also noteworthy is the omission of measures of auditory (or phonological) processing (*Ga*) on all intelligence batteries except the WJ-R. Since phonological processes appear to be the core cognitive deficits associated with reading difficulties (one of the most common reasons for referral among elementary school children) (Felton & Pepper, 1995; McBride-Chang, 1995; Stahl & Murray, 1994; Torgesen et al., 1994; Wagner et al., 1994), it seems pertinent to assess these processing skills in all children who are experiencing reading problems. The body of recent factor-analytic research with the major intelligence batteries demonstrates that appropriately designed and conducted *cross-battery assessments* will result in a more thorough evaluation of an individual's broad *Gf-Gc* abilities, since any battery by itself is limited (i.e., *incomplete*). The procedure of augmenting intelligence batteries through cross-battery assessment brings theory and practice closer together (see Figure 1–1 in Chapter 1).

Second, most disciplines have a common set of terms and definitions (i.e., a standard nomenclature) that facilitates communication among professionals and guards against misinterpretations. In chemistry this standard nomenclature is reflected in the Table of Periodic Elements. Carroll (1993a) has provided an analogous table for intelligence, and the cross-battery approach is an attempt to operationalize this "Table of Human Cognitive Elements," advancing a standard nomenclature that can be used to enhance communication among practitioners, researchers, and scholars in the field of intelligence testing. The cross-battery approach was developed to improve communication between and among practitioners, researchers, and scholars.

For example, one aspect of intelligence testing that leads to confusion in understanding and interpreting cognitive performance is the inconsistency of terminology used to describe abilities measured by subtests and composites that exists across batteries. For example, as can be seen in Table 13–1, considerable variability exists across batteries in the labels used by test authors to describe a standard block design test. The SB:IV Pattern Analysis test is purported to measure Abstract-Visual Reasoning (which is subsumed by fluid ability according to the theoretical model underlying the instrument), whereas WISC-III Block Design, K-ABC Triangles, and DAS Pattern Construction are purported to measure Perceptual Organization, Simultaneous Processing, and Spatial Ability, respectively. Notwithstanding this variability in terms, a standard block design task is often interpreted as a measure of inductive and deductive reasoning (i.e., *Gf*) in the intelligence test literature (e.g., Kaufman, 1994). Considering that the demands of the Pattern Analysis, Block Design, Triangles, and Pattern Construction tests are essentially identical, which label is correct? With the possible exception of the description offered by the authors of the SB:IV, all labels appear to depict, at least in part, the ability measured by a standard block design task (viz., visual-spatial). However, within the context of contemporary *Gf-Gc* theory and research, *none* is correct. Since these labels are not consistent with the language of current theory and research, they may be misleading (and test interpretations may convey inaccurate information). For instance, interpreting any of these block design tests as *strong measures* of fluid intelligence would be inaccurate.

According to the *Gf-Gc* framework, Carroll's (1993a) classification of block design tests, and the results of recent cross-battery factor analyses (see Chapter 3), the standard block design–type tests measure aspects of the broad ability of Visual Processing (*Gv*). Specifically, block design tests measure two narrow abilities subsumed by *Gv*—namely Visualization (VZ) and Spatial Relations (SR) (see Table 1–1 for definitions of *Gf-Gc* narrow abilities). These labels should therefore be used to describe block design–type tests and interpretations of the abilities that underlie performance on these tests. Regardless of a practitioner's or researcher's preferred intelligence battery, the conceptualization and implementation of cross-battery assessments within a common *Gf-Gc* theoretical framework will appropriately reflect similarities across instruments as well as the *Gf-Gc* abilities that underlie all cognitive tests (see Table 13–1). As a result, communication between and among practitioners, researchers, and scholars will be enhanced and misinterpretations of cognitive test performance that result from armchair speculation will be minimized.

Third, the cross-battery approach was developed to facilitate a greater understanding of the relationship between cognitive abilities and important outcome criteria. Because cross-battery assessments are based on the empirically supported *Gf-Gc* theory of intelligence, their use results in a valid measure of cognitive constructs. It is noteworthy that when second-order constructs are composed of (moderately) correlated but qualitatively distinct measures, they will likely correlate more highly with complex criteria (e.g., academic achievement) than will lower-order constructs because they are broader in what they measure (Comrey, 1988). Predictive statements about different achievements (i.e., criterion-related inferences) that are made from cross-battery assessments, therefore, are based on a more solid foundation because the predictor constructs represent relatively pure measures of broad *Gf-Gc* abilities. Thus, improving the validity of measures of *Gf-Gc* abilities may elucidate further the empirically established relations between specific *Gf-Gc* abilities and different achievement and vocational/occupational outcomes (see Chapter 2 and McGrew, Flanagan, et al., 1997, for a discussion).

Fourth, the cross-battery approach was developed as a means of potentially improving aptitude-treatment-interaction (ATI) research. The use of properly designed cross-battery assessments in research may increase the likelihood of isolating important ATIs. Because a well-validated theory of the structure of intelligence underlies the cross-battery approach, its use may facilitate more methodologically sound ATI research. That is, we may now begin to explore whether instrumentation that more adequately operationalizes current intelligence theory (i.e., *Gf-Gc* cross-battery assessment) provides information that has direct relevance to treatment (Ysseldyke, 1990). The cross-battery approach may lead to better ATI research because it encourages the use of better measures of *Gf-Gc* constructs than those that are used typically in such research (Flanagan, Andrews, & Genshaft, 1997; Flanagan & McGrew, 1997).

Finally, the three pillars of the cross-battery approach represent a guide or "blueprint" for developing tests with stronger evidence of content validity (see Kamphaus, Petoskey, & Morgan, 1997). As already stated, none of the current intelligence batteries measures the full range of *Gf-Gc* abilities, and many fail to measure some important abilities adequately. The cross-battery approach highlights the breadth and depth of coverage of broad cognitive constructs that would be necessary to include in new or revised intelligence batteries to measure intelligence more completely, advance the field, and narrow the gap between practice and advances in cognitive psychology.

In summary, the cross-battery approach was developed to provide practitioners with a means of conducting more valid and comprehensive intellectual assessments. Also, the cross-battery approach provides researchers with an arsenal of theory-driven and empirically supported classifications of intelligence tests that can be used to design and improve research studies on human cognitive abilities. Until test developers construct new instruments or revise existing batteries that reflect advances in cognitive psychology and that allow for the *selective measurement* of the broad range of *Gf-Gc* abilities, a cross-battery assessment approach is needed to advance and inform the use and interpretation of intelligence tests.

Application of the Gf-Gc Cross-Battery Approach

Guiding Principles

First, when constructing broad (stratum II) ability composites or clusters, one should include only relatively pure *Gf-Gc* indicators. *Relatively pure indicators* are those tests that had either *strong* or *moderate* (but not mixed) loadings on their respective *Gf-Gc* factors in cross-battery factor analyses (see Chapter 3 for a discussion). This factor loading information is available in the ITDR (chapters 4 through 11) and is included on the *Gf-Gc* cross-battery worksheets presented in the next section of this chapter (as well as in Appendix A).

There is one exception to this principle. A test that was *logically* classified at the broad (stratum II) level may be used in cross-battery assessments if there is a clear, established relation between it and the format of a test that was *empirically* classified. For example, although the DAS Recall of Digits test has not yet been included in adequately designed cross-battery factor analyses (following the criteria specified in Chapter 3), it can be assumed to be a relatively pure measure of a narrow ability (i.e., Memory Span—MS) subsumed by the broad ability of *Gsm*. This is because it is very similar in testing format (e.g., administration procedure, task demand, nature of stimuli) to the Wechsler Digit Span test, a test that consistently was found to have a strong loading on a broad *Gsm* factor in adequately designed cross-battery factor analyses (e.g., Woodcock, 1990; see also Chapter 3). Thus, Recall of Digits and Digit Span measure MS, a narrow ability subsumed by *Gsm*. A good rule of thumb is to select empirically classified tests over logically classified tests whenever possible. This will ensure that only *construct-relevant* tests are included in cross-battery assessment.

Second, when constructing broad (stratum II) ability composites, *include two or more qualitatively different* narrow (stratum I) ability indicators. Following this principle will ensure appropriate *construct representation*. It is important to note that in some instances it may be necessary to use logically classified tests together with empirically classified tests to adequately represent constructs (this situation will be elaborated on below). If there are insufficient empirically and/or logically classified tests available to adequately represent constructs, then inferences about an individual's broad (stratum II) ability cannot be made. For example, when a composite is derived from two measures of Induction (I), it is inappropriate to generalize about an individual's *broad Gf* ability because the *Gf* construct is underrepresented. In this case the composite is interpreted best as a measure of Induction (a narrow stratum I ability) rather than *Gf* (a broad stratum II ability). Alternatively, inferences can be made about an individual's broad *Gf* ability based on a composite that is derived from one measure of Induction and one measure of General Sequential Reasoning (i.e., two qualitatively different indicators of *Gf*). Of course, the more broadly an ability is represented through the derivation of composites based on *multiple* qualitatively different narrow ability indicators, the more confidence one has in drawing inferences about that broad ability based on the composite score. A minimum of two qualitatively different indicators per *Gf-Gc* composite is recommended in the cross-battery approach for practical reasons (viz., time-efficient assessment).

Third, when conducting cross-battery assessments, select tests from the *smallest number* of batteries to minimize the effect of norming differences. This principle is directed at minimizing the effect of spurious differences between test scores that may be due to differences in the characteristics of independent norm samples (McGrew, 1994). For example, the "Flynn effect" (Kamphaus, 1993) indicates that, on average, a difference of 3 standard score points would be expected between test scores based on tests that were standardized 10 years apart. Using the WJ-R to augment the WISC-III or vice versa following the steps outlined below will ensure a valid and comprehensive assessment of most *Gf-Gc* broad abilities. Because the WISC-III and WJ-R were normed within 2 years of one another and both were found to have very adequate standardization sample characteristics (Kamphaus, 1993; Kaufman, 1990; Salvia & Ysseldyke, 1991), this combination of batteries would be appropriate for cross-battery assessments.

There are times, however, when crossing more than two batteries is necessary to gain enough information to test hypotheses about cognitive strengths or weaknesses, to answer specific referral questions, and so forth. For example, in order to conduct an in-depth assessment of an individual's functioning in the area of *Glr*, multiple narrow indicators of this ability would need to be administered. Since *Glr* is either underrepresented on or not measured by many intelligence batteries (see Table 13–1), it may be necessary to cross more than two intelligence batteries or to use a special purpose test of *Glr* (see Chapter 12) to acquire the information necessary to fully understand functioning in this cognitive domain. Typically, it is necessary to cross more than two intelligence batteries when conducting *selective cross-battery assessments* (see Chapter 14).

Bridging the Gap Between Gf-Gc *Theory and Practice*

The aforementioned cross-battery pillars and guiding principles provide the necessary foundation from which to conduct a comprehensive assessment of the broad *Gf-Gc* abilities that define the structure of intelligence in current psychometric research within cognitive psychology. The essence of the cross-battery approach can be understood by reviewing Figure 13–2. This figure graphically summarizes how the three pillars of the cross-battery approach are translated into practice. The first pillar (the empirically supported *Gf-Gc* theory of the structure of intelligence) is represented by the rectangles in the top portion of the figure labeled "Broad (*str. II*) *Gf-Gc* Abilities." This portion of the figure includes the 10 broad *Gf-Gc* abilities that are included in the integrated Horn-Cattell/Carroll *Gf-Gc* model discussed in Chapter 1 (i.e., *Gf, Gc, Gq, Grw,* etc.). One of the broad abilities (i.e., *Gv*) is enlarged in Figure 13–2 to demonstrate how the second and third cross-battery pillars are translated into practice.

The center of Figure 13–2, labeled "Test Indicators," lists all the tests of the eight intelligence batteries as well as the special purpose tests and batteries included in the ITDR according to their *Gv* classification. The empirically classified *Gv* tests represent the second pillar of the cross-battery approach and should be used instead of the logically classified tests whenever possible. The empirically classified tests are those that practitioners must consider in order to (1) ensure that the measures selected to assess *Gv* are *construct-relevant* and (2) adhere to the first guiding principle of the cross-battery approach (i.e., include only relatively pure measures of ability in cross-battery assessment).

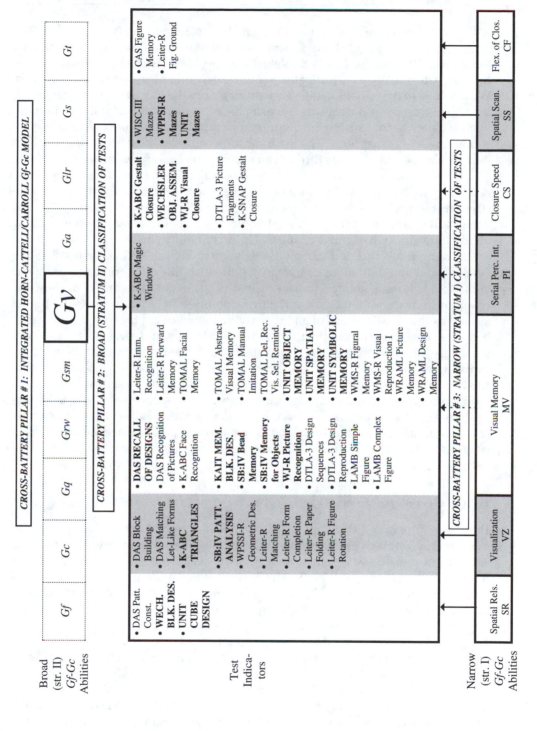

FIGURE 13–2 Translation of the Three *Gf-Gc* Cross-Battery Pillars into Practice

Finally, the bottom of Figure 13–2, labeled "Narrow (*str. I*) *Gf-Gc* Abilities," shows that the broad *Gv* ability subsumes many narrow abilities including Spatial Relations (SR), Visualization (VZ), Visual Memory (MV), Serial Perceptual Integration (PI), Closure Speed (CS), Spatial Scanning (SS), and Flexibility of Closure (CF). With regard to the major intelligence batteries, only the narrow abilities for which there are strong or moderate measures included in one or more of the eight intelligence batteries are listed in this figure (for a complete list of narrow abilities subsumed by *Gv* see Chapter 1). The test indicators were classified according to which narrow ability they measure through an expert consensus process (see Chapter 3). This classification process represents the third pillar of the cross-battery approach. Attending to the narrow ability classifications of tests will ensure appropriate *construct representation* as well as adherence to the second guiding principle of the cross-battery approach (i.e., include two or more qualitatively different narrow ability indicators when constructing *Gf-Gc* broad ability clusters).

In sum, the broad and narrow levels seen in Figure 13–2 correspond to the *Gf-Gc* model and definitions of human cognitive abilities presented in Figure 1–3 and Table 1–1, respectively. Similar schematic figures could be drawn to show the relations between all the broad and narrow abilities included in the *Gf-Gc* model as well as the classifications of all the individual subtests of the major intelligence batteries. However, rather than depict these relations and classifications in figures, this information has been translated into worksheets that can be used by practitioners to guide *Gf-Gc* cross-battery assessments. These worksheets together with a step-by-step approach to cross-battery assessment (presented below) provide a bridge between *Gf-Gc* theory and practice. The steps that follow will demonstrate how the *Gf-Gc* classifications of intelligence tests at the broad and narrow levels of ability can be translated into assessments that are more valid and comprehensive than those resulting from the administration of a single intelligence battery.

Gf-Gc *Cross-Battery Worksheets*

Prior to enumerating the steps of the cross-battery approach, it is necessary to describe the *Gf-Gc* cross-battery worksheets that were designed to facilitate this assessment practice. Seven cross-battery worksheets were constructed in all, one for each of the broad *Gf-Gc* abilities that is represented among the eight major intelligence tests included in the ITDR. These worksheets can be found in Appendix A. Each worksheet contains the following information: (1) the subtests of the major intelligence batteries that had either strong or moderate loadings on the respective broad *Gf-Gc* factor (these subtests are printed in bold/capital and bold/lowercase letters, respectively), (2) the subtests of the major intelligence batteries that were classified logically as measures of the respective broad *Gf-Gc* ability via an expert consensus process (these subtests are printed in regular lowercase type), and (3) the subtests of the special purpose batteries and tests that were classified logically as measures of the respective broad *Gf-Gc* ability (these subtests are also printed in regular lowercase type).

Additionally, each worksheet groups the subtests according to the narrow ability that they probably measure. For example, the *Gf* worksheet (see Appendix A or Figure 13–3) groups subtests according to those that measure either Induction (I), General Sequential Reasoning (RG), or Quantitative Reasoning (RQ)—three narrow abilities subsumed by *Gf*. It should be noted that the subtests were classified in the ITDR as "probable" and/or "possible" measures of narrow abilities (see Chapter 3 for details). Only "probable" classifications are reflected in the worksheets. When a subtest was classified as a probable measure of two different narrow abilities (subsumed by the same broad ability), it was grouped with other probable measures of one narrow ability and the other narrow ability was reported in parentheses next to the subtest. For example, a review of the *Gc* worksheet (see Appendix A or Figure 13–3) shows that the Wechsler Comprehension subtest is a probable measure of Language Development (LD) since it is grouped with other measures of LD on the worksheet. However, the Comprehension subtest was classified also as a probable measure of General Information (KO); therefore the code "KO" is printed in parentheses next to this subtest.

Finally, intelligence batteries that have adequate (or alternatively, inadequate) representation of the respective *Gf-Gc* broad ability are highlighted on each worksheet. Intelligence batteries that are characterized as having adequate representation of the respective *Gf-Gc* ability are those that include two or more qualitatively different test indicators of that broad ability. Conversely, intelligence batteries that are characterized as having inadequate representation of the respective *Gf-Gc* ability were found not to include two or more qualitatively different test indicators of that broad ability.

Worksheets were not constructed for *Gq* and *Grw*, two broad abilities specified in the integrated Cattell-Horn/Carroll *Gf-Gc* model, because these abilities are assessed best by comprehensive achievement (not intelligence) batteries (e.g., WIAT, WJ-R ACH). Also, a worksheet for the broad ability of *Gt* was not constructed because this ability (as it is defined currently in Chapter 1) is not measured by any of the major intelligence batteries. *Gt* is assessed best by reaction time (RT) paradigms, many of which are computer-administered (Vernon, 1990). Thus, in order to assess the 10 broad *Gf-Gc* abilities in the *Gf-Gc* model, tests other than the standard intelligence and special purpose batteries included in the ITDR would need to be administered. However, when the cross-battery approach presented here is used together with a comprehensive achievement battery, adequate coverage of 9 of the 10 broad cognitive abilities specified in contemporary *Gf-Gc* theory and research can be achieved (leaving only *Gt* unassessed). The *Gf-Gc* cross-battery worksheets are used in the next section to guide cross-battery assessments.

A Wechsler-Based Cross-Battery Case Example

A psychoeducational evaluation that employed cross-battery assessment was conducted recently by one of our colleagues and will be used here to demonstrate the various steps of the cross-battery approach. Following is a brief summary of the individual who was evaluated using cross-battery procedures.

Identifying Information

Name of Child: J.J.
Chronological Age: 9 years, 7 months
Grade: Fourth
Evaluation Dates: 4/17/97, 4/20/97
Language: English

Reason for Referral

J.J. was referred by his mother, a fourth-grade teacher, to a university-based center for psychological services due to reported difficulty with reading skills, particularly reading comprehension. According to his mother, J.J. can decode words, but this skill is not automatic and his reading lacks fluency. This description of J.J.'s reading skills was corroborated by his past and present classroom teachers. J.J.'s mother has been tutoring him in reading 1 hour each day for the past year. She requested a psychoeducational evaluation to determine whether he has a learning disability that underlies his slow academic performance in reading.

Background Information

J.J. lives with his biological mother, stepfather, and two sisters (ages 10 and 4). His mother has a 4-year college education, while his biological father and stepfather each have 2 years of college education. English is the language of J.J.'s household. J.J.'s mother reported an uneventful pregnancy. Developmental milestones were achieved within normal limits. J.J. was said to be healthy and his medical history is unremarkable. J.J.'s biological father reportedly may have dyslexia but has never sought an evaluation and has therefore never been formally diagnosed.

Tests Administered

- Wechsler Intelligence Scale for Children—Third Edition (WISC-III), selected subtests
- Woodcock-Johnson Psycho-Educational Battery—Revised, Tests of Cognitive Ability and Tests of Achievement, selected subtests

Behavioral Observations

J.J. was cooperative throughout the evaluation sessions. Although he appeared to put forth his best effort on all tasks, he seemed to especially enjoy tasks that included figural-abstract stimuli. At times J.J. had difficulty articulating his thoughts and needed to be queried to facilitate a response. On a task involving drawing shapes, J.J. worked slowly and deliberately. While engaged in this task he stated that he did not like drawing or being timed.

J.J.'s evaluator (hereafter referred to as Examiner A) completed a comprehensive assessment of his cognitive abilities, as enumerated below.

A Step-by-Step Approach to Gf-Gc *Cross-Battery Assessment*

Step 1: Begin with the Most Appropriate Intelligence Battery for Your Purpose.   For practical reasons, it is likely that practitioners will begin with a familiar intelligence battery. However, depending on the purpose of the assessment, the ideal strategy (according to the cross-battery guiding principles), would be to examine the *Gf-Gc* worksheets (in Appendix A) or Table 13–1 and begin with a battery that provides the most comprehensive coverage of *Gf-Gc* abilities (e.g., DAS, WJ-R) or coverage of abilities that are considered necessary to assess in light of referral concerns (see Chapter 14). By doing so, practitioners would reduce the number of tests minimally needed to augment the selected battery sufficiently. For J.J., Examiner A opted to use the battery with which he is most familiar, namely, the WISC-III. The selected battery can be considered to be the *core* battery around which a *Gf-Gc* cross-battery assessment is designed.

Once a core battery is selected, it is necessary to consider whether a full-scale score is needed. Many state and professional classification systems (e.g., AAMR mental retardation guidelines; Jacobson & Mulick, 1996) require the use of a full-scale "IQ." For example, full-scale scores are used regularly in formulas designed to aid decision making in the diagnosis of learning disabilities and developmental delays. The cross-battery approach does not yield a full-scale score. If a complete intelligence battery must be administered to obtain a full-scale score, then cross-battery assessment will increase testing time (since subtests that do not meet the cross-battery guiding principles will have to be administered), perhaps by as much as 30–40 minutes depending on the core battery preference of the practitioner. If formal criteria and regulations do not necessitate the use of a complete battery to obtain a full-scale score or if a global estimate of intelligence is not necessary to obtain, then *cross-battery testing time will probably remain equivalent to single-battery testing time.* Since Examiner A was not constrained by formal guidelines and was most interested in understanding J.J.'s *intracognitive* strengths and weaknesses, he did not find it necessary to obtain a WISC-III Full Scale score.

Before proceeding to Step 2, it is necessary to place the importance of a global intelligence score in perspective. Theoretical debates about *g* aside (see Chapter 1), proponents of *g* maintain that due to its undeniable importance in predicting a wide variety of academic and occupational outcomes (see Chapter 2), intelligence tests should provide a single full-scale or composite score that conceptually represents general intelligence. Why then doesn't the *Gf-Gc* cross-battery approach to intellectual assessment described here include procedures for calculating an average standard score composite across *Gf-Gc* abilities?

First, although a general intelligence factor undeniably accounts for the majority of the variance of academic and occupational success, its relevance for intervention is limited. For example, recent research that investigated the relations between *g* and seven *Gf-Gc* specific abilities and general and specific reading achievement (McGrew, Flanagan, et al., 1997) found that *Ga* abilities were strongly related to reading above and beyond the explanation provided by *g*. Although the effect of *g* was larger than that for *Ga*, recent research (e.g., Felton & Pepper, 1995; McGuiness et al., 1995; Wagner et al., 1994) has shown that intervention directed at specific *Ga* abilities can improve reading performance. Conversely, attempts to modify general intellectual ability have not resulted in longstanding changes (Gustafsson & Undheim, 1996), with the available research suggesting that specific abilities may be most amenable to modification (Carroll, 1993a). Thus, it is our belief that the probability of developing successful interventions lies not at the apex of the hierarchy of cognitive abilities (i.e., stratum III—*g*), but at lower levels (viz., stratum I and II *Gf-Gc* abilities).

Second, a global composite intelligence test score is at odds with the underlying *Gf-Gc* cross-battery philosophy. The cross-battery approach is expressly designed to improve the usefulness of intelligence test interpretation through the delineation of an individual's broad *Gf-Gc*–ability strengths and weaknesses. This point has been cogently articulated by many prominent psychological assessment spokespersons.

According to Kaufman (1990),

> the individual tested makes an unspoken plea to the examiner not to summarize his or her intelligence in a single, cold, number; the goal...should be to respond to that plea by identifying hypothesized strengths and weaknesses that extend well beyond the limited information provided by the FS-IQ, and that will conceivably lead to practical recommendations that help answer the referral questions. (p. 422)

Kaufman's comments are echoed by Lezak (1995), who, when discussing the Wechsler Full-Scale IQ score in her neuropsychological assessment text, stated that

> average scores on a WIS battery provide just about as much information as do averaged scores on a school report. There is no question about the performance of students with a four-point average: they can only have had an A in each subject. Nor is there any question about individual grades obtained by students with a zero grade point average. Excluding the extremes, however, it is impossible to predict a student's performance in any subject from the grade point average alone. In the same way, it is impossible to predict specific disabilities and areas of cognitive competency or disfunction from the averaged ability test scores. For these reasons, test data reported in IQ scores have not been presented in this book. (p. 691)

The *Gf-Gc* cross-battery approach does not include procedures for the calculation of a global cross-battery IQ for the reasons just mentioned. Although we recognize the substantial and undeniable empirical evidence that demonstrates that general ability (or *g*) is "among the most dominant and enduring factors, both causal and corollary, associated with scholastic and occupational success; environmental adaptation; physical propensity and morbidity; and scientific, cultural, and political acumen" (McDermott, Fantuzzo, & Glutting, 1990, p. 291), we believe that the *Gf-Gc* cross-battery approach uncovers the individual skills and abilities that are more diagnostic of learning and problem-solving processes than a global IQ score. Therefore, we believe that the *Gf-Gc* approach represents a "best practices" approach to intellectual assessment and concur with Lezak's (1995) position:

> It has been suggested that examiners retain IQ scores in their reports to conform to the current requirements of...various other administrative agencies.... [T]his is not merely a case of the tail wagging the dog but an example of how outdated practices may be perpetuated even when their invalidity and potential harmfulness has been demonstrated. Clinicians have a responsibility not only to maintain the highest—and most current—practice standards, but to communicate these to the consumer agencies. If every clinician who understands the problems inherent in labeling people with IQ scores ceased using them, then agencies would soon cease asking for them. (p. 691)

Step 2: Identify the *Gf-Gc* Abilities That Are Represented Adequately on the Core Battery.   This may be achieved by reviewing the *Gf-Gc* cross-battery worksheets in Appendix A. As stated previously, each worksheet lists the batteries for which there is adequate (and alternatively, inadequate) representation of the respective *Gf-Gc* construct. Examiner A reviewed the worksheets and found that *Gc*, *Gv*, and *Gs* are represented adequately on the WISC-III. If it is necessary to administer the full-core intelligence battery (to obtain a full-scale score), then all the test indicators of the abilities that are adequately represented on the battery will probably need to be administered. However, if a full-scale score is not needed (as in Examiner A's situation), then begin by identifying which subtests will be administered within the *Gf-Gc* domains that are represented adequately on the battery, since in some cases more than two qualitatively different indicators may represent a broad ability.

Examiner A reviewed the *Gc* worksheet and found that four WISC-III subtests (i.e., Comprehension, Similarities, Vocabulary, Information) are strong measures of *Gc* (i.e., they are printed in bold, uppercase letters). Based on the guiding principle that a minimum of two qualitatively different indicators are needed to represent a broad ability, Examiner A selected the Vocabulary (a measure of Language Development [LD] and Lexical Knowledge [VL]) and Information (a measure of General Information [KO]) subtests for inclusion in his battery. Although Examiner A could just as well have combined Information (KO) and Similarities (LD) to represent *Gc*, the Vocabulary test was selected given the significant relation that has been documented between the narrow ability of Lexical Knowledge (which is measured by Vocabulary tests) and reading achievement (Aaron, 1995; Joshi, 1995). This decision illustrates the need for examiners to select tests within the context of specific referral concerns (see Chapter 14 for further discussion).

Similarly, Examiner A selected Block Design (Spatial Relations—SR) and Object Assembly (Closure Speed—CS) from the *Gv* worksheet, and Symbol Search (Perceptual Speed—P) and Coding (Rate-of-Test-Taking—R9) from the *Gs* worksheet to represent the other broad target abilities. To this point, Examiner A's battery consists of six subtests that provide adequate representation of three *Gf-Gc* abilities (i.e., *Gc*, *Gv*, and *Gs*).

Step 3: Identify the *Gf-Gc* Abilities That Are Unrepresented and Underrepresented on the Core Battery and Determine the Subtests That Will Be Used to Approximate or Ensure Adequate Representation of These Abilities.   Identification of *Gf-Gc* abilities that are either not represented or underrepresented on a given intelligence battery can be achieved by either reviewing the *Gf-Gc* cross-battery worksheets in Appendix A or by locating the core battery in Table 13–1 and recording the abilities that are listed in the last two columns. Examiner A located the WISC-III in Table 13–1 and found that the abilities of *Gf*, *Ga*, and *Glr* are not represented on (i.e., not measured by) this battery.

Keeping in mind that a small number of batteries should be used (preferably two) whenever possible (following the third guiding principle of the cross-battery approach), Examiner A reviewed the *Gf*, *Ga*, and *Glr* cross-battery worksheets and found that the WISC-III could be supplemented best by using the WJ-R battery. For example, the WJ-R includes two strong, qualitatively different indicators of *Gf* (i.e., Concept Formation—a measure of Induction [I], and Analysis-Synthesis—a measure of General Sequential Reasoning [RG]). Likewise, the WJ-R includes two strong measures of *Ga*. However, both *Ga* test indicators are measures of Phonetic Coding (PC). Since no other measures of *Ga* (other than tests of PC) were identified (for a person of this age) on any of the intelligence batteries or special purpose tests or batteries included in the ITDR, it is important to remember to interpret the *Ga* cluster as a measure of the narrow ability of PC rather than the broad ability of *Ga*.

The WJ-R also includes two strong measures of *Glr*. However both subtests measure Associative Memory (MA). Unlike the situation that occurred with *Ga* (in which no additional test indicators could be administered to *broaden* the ability cluster to include indicators of *Ga* that were qualitatively different than PC), the examiner has some choices with respect to *Glr*. For example, Examiner A could administer the two strong measures of MA from the WJ-R that would yield an MA, rather than *Glr*, cluster. Alternatively, Examiner A could administer a logically classified test of Free Recall Memory (M6) from a special purpose battery (e.g., TOMAL; see Chapter 12) in addition to an empirically classified (strong) measure of MA from the WJ-R, which together would yield a *broad Glr* cluster. However, given that *Glr* was not highlighted a priori as an area of concern with respect to J.J.'s classroom performance and that the relationship between the *Glr* abilities for which measures are available (i.e., MA, MM, M6) and reading achievement is non-significant for an individual of J.J.'s age (see Chapter 2), Examiner A decided to use only empirically strong measures of *Glr* (following the first guiding principle) and supplement the WISC-III with WJ-R tests only, thus keeping the number of batteries used in cross-battery assessment to a minimum (following the third guiding principle).

As was the case with *Ga*, since the two tests that will be administered in the domain of *Glr* (i.e., Memory for Names and Visual-Auditory Memory) are both measures of MA, it is most appropriate to interpret the cluster yielded by these tests as representing the narrow ability of MA rather than the broad ability of *Glr*. To this point, Examiner A has 12 subtests in his battery—6 WISC-III subtests, identified in Step 2 to represent aspects of *Gc*, *Gv*, and *Gs*, and 6 WJ-R subtests, identified in this step to represent aspects of *Gf*, *Ga*, and *Glr*.

In addition to the abilities that are not represented on the WISC-III, Table 13–1 revealed that *Gq* and *Gsm* are underrepresented on this battery. Since *Gq* is assessed best by a comprehensive academic achievement battery (e.g., WIAT) and since mathematics achievement was not a specific referral concern for J.J., it was not considered further in the design of J.J.'s *Gf-Gc* cross-battery assessment. *Gsm* is underrepresented on the WISC-III because this battery includes only one narrow ability indicator (i.e., Digit Span) of this broad ability. However, as discussed in Chapter 1, *Gsm* subsumes only two narrow abilities, namely Memory Span (MS) and Learning Abilities. Since Learning Abilities are not well defined in the cognitive abilities literature (Carroll, 1993a), there is no indication (or evidence) that any intelligence subtests measure these abilities. Thus, *Gsm* is defined mainly by tests of MS.

However, there is some uncertainty in the literature regarding the breadth of narrow abilities that are subsumed by *Gsm*. Specifically, it is not clear whether Visual Memory (MV) abilities are subsumed by the broad ability of *Gsm* or *Gv* (e.g., Carroll, 1993). To accommodate this uncertainty, the *Gsm* worksheet includes space for visual memory tests. Thus, an examiner could supplement an MS test with an MV test to obtain a broad *Gsm* cluster. If this approach is taken, then measures of MV should not be included as indicators of *Gv*. Examiner A chose to conduct an assessment that was consistent with the integrated Cattell-Horn/Carroll *Gf-Gc* model presented in Chapter 1 and therefore opted to administer another MS test indicator of *Gsm*, namely the Memory for Words test of the WJ-R. Like the cognitive domains of *Ga* and *Glr*, the cluster yielded by the two *Gsm* tests (i.e., WISC-III Digit Span and WJ-R Memory for Words) is interpreted most appropriately as a measure of the narrow ability of MS rather than as the broad ability of *Gsm*. The fact that broad (stratum II) *Gf-Gc* clusters cannot be constructed for all broad abilities specified in the *Gf-Gc* model highlights the limitations of intelligence instrumentation with respect to diversity of abilities measured and adherence to contemporary theory.

Step 4: Administer the Core Battery Identified in Step 1 and Supplemental Tests Identified in Steps 2 and 3. Table 13–2 depicts the tests that were selected by Examiner A to be administered in J.J.'s cross-battery assessment. As can be seen in this table, two tests will be administered for each of seven *Gf-Gc* abilities. Representing each ability by two subtests (rather than one) will increase the reliability of the obtained cluster scores. It is also evident from the information presented in Table 13–2 that not all *Gf-Gc* abilities could be represented by two strong (or moderate) *and* qualitatively different indicators. For example, although *Ga* is represented by two strong test indicators, these tests measure the same narrow ability of PC. Since no other qualitatively different indicators were available (for a person of J.J.'s age) among the major intelligence and special purpose tests and bat-

TABLE 13–2   AWISC-III–Based *Gf-Gc* Cross-Battery Example

Gf	Gc	MS-Gsm	Gv	PC-Ga	MA-Glr	Gs
ANALYSIS-SYNTHESIS (RG)	INFORMATION (K0)	DIGIT SPAN (MS)	BLOCK DESIGN (SR)	INCOMPLETE WORDS (PC)	VISUAL-AUDITORY LEARNING (MA)	CODING (R9)
CONCEPT FORMATION (I)	VOCABULARY (VL)	MEMORY FOR WORDS (MS)	OBJECT ASSEMBLY (CS)	SOUND BLENDING (PC)	MEMORY FOR NAMES (MA)	Symbol Search (P)

Note: The subtest names in italics are from the WISC-III (the core battery). Subtests not in italics are from the WJ-R (the supplemental battery). Tests printed in uppercase/bold letters are strong measures as defined empirically. Tests printed in lowercase/no bold are logically classified measures that were defined through an expert consensus process.

Gf-Gc symbols that are preceded by narrow ability codes (e.g., MS-*Gsm*) indicate that two qualitatively similar (rather than different) narrow ability measures were used to form a cluster. In such instances, interpretation needs to reflect the narrow rather than broad *Gf-Gc* ability.

In this case study, two norm samples (WISC-III and WJ-R) were "crossed" and 14 tests were administered (seven each from the WISC-III and WJ-R). If the complete WISC-III had been administered in order to obtain a full-scale IQ score, 5 additional tests (viz., Similarities, Comprehension, Arithmetic, Picture Arrangement, and Picture Completion) would have been administered. This would have resulted in a total of 19 tests being administered.

teries that were published at the time this book was being prepared, it was not possible to construct a broad *Ga* ability cluster. Therefore, this ability is labeled "PC-*Ga*" in Table 13–2 to connote that the cluster represents a narrow (stratum I) rather than broad (stratum II) *Gf-Gc* ability.

Of the seven cognitive clusters that will be yielded by this cross-battery assessment, three warrant narrow ability interpretations (i.e., MS-*Gsm*, PC-*Ga*, and MA-*Glr*). In some cases certain *Gf-Gc* abilities could have been represented more broadly (e.g., *Glr*), but not without some costs. For example, an empirically strong measure of MA could have been supplemented with a logically classified measure of M6 (e.g., Recall of Objects from the DAS), resulting in a broad *Glr* cluster. However, less confidence is associated with clusters that are derived using logically classified as opposed to empirically classified tests. Furthermore, if Examiner A chose to construct a broad *Glr* cluster by combining empirically and logically classified tests, he would have had to cross more than two batteries, potentially introducing more measurement error to the assessment. Thus, as mentioned in the previous step, the potential costs associated with administering a measure of M6 were unnecessary.

Finally, Table 13–2 shows that in order to adhere closely to the guiding principles of the cross-battery approach, a seven-test WISC-III battery needed to be supplemented with tests from other batteries. In this case a seven-test WJ-R battery was chosen. This combination of tests provided the most psychometrically and theoretically defensible set of *Gf-Gc* test indicators. Moreover, this cross-battery assessment provides information about three *Gf-Gc* abilities not currently assessed by the WISC-III (i.e., *Gf*, PC-*Ga*, and MA-*Glr*) and yields a more reliable and valid measure of MS-*Gsm*, an ability currently underrepresented on the WISC-III. Also noteworthy is that the increase in test administration time associated with the

WISC-III/WJ-R cross-battery assessment was negligible. That is, a 14-test battery was administered (i.e., 7 WISC-III plus 7 WJ-R tests) instead of the more typical 13-test battery (i.e., the WISC-III). However, in the current example, if Examiner A needed a WISC-III Full Scale score (e.g., for the reasons stated in Step 1), then administration time would have increased considerably due to the need to administer 5 additional WISC-III subtests that were not necessary to include in the cross-battery assessment presented here.

It is important to note that Table 13–2 depicts only one of numerous cross-battery combinations that may result as a function of the core battery selected and/or the nature of the referral concerns. The WISC-III/WJ-R combination presented here likely represents one of the most practical unions of tests in light of the frequency with which the Wechsler scales are used and the diversity of *Gf-Gc* measures included on the WJ-R. Although it is beyond the scope of this book to present every possible combination of intelligence batteries, the reader can be certain that other combinations of tests that are derived following the above-mentioned cross-battery guiding principles and steps will yield equally valid and useful broad *Gf-Gc* clusters. Also, the various decisions made by Examiner A illustrate the idea that *the Gf-Gc cross-battery approach should not be considered as a rigid "cookbook" approach to intellectual assessment.* Rather, the design of each cross-battery assessment reflects an attempt to construct the most technically sound assessment within the confines of practical constraints (e.g., time and tests available to the examiner) and the specific referral concerns for an individual.

Step 5: Complete the *Gf-Gc* Cross-Battery Worksheets. Examiner A next records subtest standard scores on the worksheets in the column marked "SS" and follows the directions printed on the worksheet for recording narrow and broad ability standard score averages. Several issues are noteworthy with respect to recording standard scores. First, if a subtest score is on a standard score scale that does not have a mean of 100 and a standard deviation of 15, then the score must be converted to a score that is consistent with this metric. *A Percentile Rank and Standard Score Conversion* Table is included in Appendix B for this purpose. Second, while most intelligence batteries have *age-based* norms, the WJ-R has both age- and grade-based norms. Therefore, when the WJ-R is used, it is important to ensure that the standard scores are derived from age-based norms to allow for comparability with other batteries.

Third, the WJ-R yields *extended standard scores* (i.e., < 40 and > 160) (McGrew et al., 1991). Although this is a unique and positive feature of the WJ-R, it can be problematic when combining or comparing the WJ-R standard scores with standard scores from other tests used in cross-battery assessments. The standard scores for most intelligence batteries or special purpose tests represent *normalized standard scores* that are based on an area transformation of the raw score distribution. Very low or high normalized standard scores are typically calculated via extrapolation. As a result, low and high extrapolated scores are not based on "real" subjects (Woodcock, 1989). This problem is addressed typically by specifying a "cut off" score at both the top and bottom of the standard score scale. For example, the

WISC-III norm tables include standard scores that range from 40 to 160 (Wechsler, 1991). In contrast, the WJ-R standard scores are not extrapolated. They are based on the *linear transformation* of *W* scores that utilize two unique standard deviations that produce the observed 10th and 90th percentiles in the distribution. As a result, the WJ-R standard scores can range from 1 to 200 (Woodcock, 1989).

Thus, combining extreme WJ-R standard scores (i.e., < 40 and > 160) with standard scores from other tests that are constrained within a certain range (e.g., 40 to 160 inclusive) could potentially result in misleading cluster averages. Therefore, it is necessary to employ a method for reporting WJ-R standard scores that "emulate" those computed via more traditional methods. Following the logic of Woodcock (1989), whenever a WJ-R standard score (or a score from any test) is below 40, a value of 40 should be recorded on the appropriate *Gf-Gc* worksheet. Likewise, whenever a WJ-R standard score (or a score from any test) exceeds 160, a score of 160 should be recorded.

Keeping these standard score issues in mind, Examiner A began by recording the standard scores for the WJ-R Analysis-Synthesis (SS = 126) and Concept Formation (SS = 108) tests on the *Gf* cross-battery worksheet (see Figure 13–3). Since the WJ-R test scores are based on a mean of 100 and standard deviation of 15, these scores were recorded directly in the far right column. Next, Examiner A followed the three-step set of directions within each narrow ability section represented on the worksheet. That is, he summed the standard score columns within the narrow ability domains of Induction (I) and General Sequential Reasoning (RG) and divided this value by the number of subtests administered in the respective narrow ability areas (i.e., one subtest for each area) to obtain the respective *narrow ability averages*. Since only one subtest was administered within each of two narrow abilities subsumed by *Gf*, the narrow ability averages for I and RG are 108 and 126, respectively. Figure 13–3 also shows that shaded lines lead from the rows in which the narrow ability averages are recorded to a box labeled "Sum of Narrow Ability Averages." Examiner A recorded the *sum* of the narrow ability averages (i.e., 126 for Analysis-Synthesis + 108 for Concept Formation = 234) and the *number of narrow ability averages* reported on the worksheet (i.e., 2) in this box. Next, Examiner A recorded the score of 117 (i.e., 234/2 = 117) in the box at the farmost right side of the worksheet. (Note that averages that result in fractions of one-half or more are rounded up to the nearest whole number.) The final step that must be carried out on this *Gf* cross-battery worksheet (Figure 13–3) is to indicate whether this cluster score of 117 should be interpreted as a broad or narrow estimate of ability.

A cluster score would be considered a *broad* estimate of ability if it was derived by summing the standard scores of at least two test indicators of qualitatively *different* narrow abilities subsumed by the broad ability. As can be seen in Figure 13–3, the cluster average was computed by summing the standard scores of two test indicators of different narrow abilities subsumed by *Gf* (i.e., Analysis-Synthesis [a measure of RG] and Concept Formation [a measure of I]). Therefore, Examiner A placed a checkmark next to the word "Broad" on the *Gf* worksheet (see Figure 13–3) and recorded the broad (stratum II) code "*Gf*" in the parentheses adjacent to the word "Broad." Conversely, if the cluster average was derived by summing the

FLUID INTELLIGENCE (*Gf*) CROSS-BATTERY WORKSHEET

(McGrew & Flanagan, 1998)

Name: J.J
Age: 9 years 7 months
Grade: 4th
Examiner: A
Date of Evaluation: 1-18-97

Battery or Test	Age	*Gf* Narrow Abilities Tests	SS*	SS (100±15)
Induction (I)				
DAS	6-17	**MATRICES**		
DAS	2-5	Picture Similarities		
KAIT	11-85+	**MYSTERY CODES**		
SB:IV	7-24	**MATRICES**		
WAIS-III	16-89	Matrix Reasoning		
WJ-R	4-85+	**CONCEPT FORMATION**		108
CAS	5-17	Nonverbal Matrices		
CTONI	6-18	Geometric Sequences (RG)		
DTLA-3	6-17	**SYMBOLIC RELATIONS**		
K-BIT	4-90	Matrices		
KSNAP	11-85	Four-Letter Words		
Leiter-R	2-6	Classification		
Leiter-R	5-18+	Design Analogies		
Leiter-R	2-18+	Repeated Patterns		
Leiter-R	2-18+	Sequential Order		
MAT	5-17	Matrix Analogies (RG)		
Raven's	5-18+	Ravens Progressive Matrices		
TONI-3	5-85	Test of Nonverbal Intelligence-3rd Ed		
UNIT	5-17	**ANALOGIC REASONING**		
Other				
		1. Sum of column		108
		2. Divide by number of tests		1
		3. **Induction** average		108

Intelligence Batteries with adequate *Gf* representation
• DAS KAIT SB:IV WJ-R

Intelligence Batteries with inadequate *Gf* representation
• K-ABC WAIS-III WISC-III WPPSI-R

General Sequential Reasoning (RG)

Battery or Test	Age	Tests	SS*	SS
KAIT	11-85+	**LOGICAL STEPS**		
WJ-R	4-85+	**ANALYSIS-SYNTHESIS**		126
Leiter-R	2-10	Picture Context		
Leiter-R	6-18+	Visual Coding		
UNIT	5-17	**Cube Design**		
Other				
		1. Sum of column		126
		2. Divide by number of tests		1
		3. **General Sequential Reasoning** average		126

Quantitative Reasoning (RQ)

Battery or Test	Age	Tests	SS*	SS
DAS	6-17	**SEQ & QUANT REASONING (I)**		
SB:IV	12-24	**EQUATION BUILDING**		
SB:IV	7-24	Number series		
Other				
		1. Sum of column		
		2. Divide by number of tests		
		3. **Quantitative Reasoning** average		

Cluster Average **

Sum/No of Narrow Ability Averages: 234/2

√ Broad (Gf)
___ Narrow (___)

117

FIGURE 13–3   *Gf* Cross-Battery Worksheet

Tests in bold/uppercase letters are strong measures as defined empirically; bold/lowercase are moderate measures as defined empirically; regular face/lowercase measures were classified logically. In the case of tests with two "probable" narrow ability classifications the second classification is reported in parentheses. Only "probable" test classifications are included on the worksheet (not "possible"). Tests that were classified either empirically or logically as mixed measures are not included on the worksheet.

* If a test score is on a standard score scale other than 100 ±15, record the score in the column marked by an asterisk (*). Then refer to the *Percentile Rank and Standard Score Conversion Table* (Appendix B) to convert the score to the scale of 100 ±15. Record the new score in the next column.

** If the cluster includes two or more qualitatively different *Gf* indicators, then place a checkmark (✓) next to the word "Broad" and record "*Gf*" in the parentheses. If the cluster includes indicators from only one narrow ability subsumed by *Gf*, then place a checkmark (✓) next to the word "Narrow" and record the respective narrow ability code in the parentheses (i.e., I, RG, or RQ).

standard scores of two or more test indicators of only one narrow ability subsumed by the broad ability (e.g., two or more measures of RG), then this average would be interpreted most appropriately as representing a narrow (stratum I) ability (i.e., RG), rather than a broad (stratum II) ability (i.e., *Gf*). In this instance the examiner would place a checkmark next to the word "Narrow" and record the narrow (stratum I) code "RG" or "RG-*Gf*" in the parentheses adjacent to the word "Narrow." Examiner A completed worksheets for the remaining six *Gf-Gc* abilities that were assessed in this cross-battery evaluation (see Figure 13–4 through Figure 13–9).

Step 6: Transfer *Gf-Gc* Narrow Ability Test Indicator Standard Scores and Cluster Averages from the *Gf-Gc* Cross-Battery Worksheets to the *Gf-Gc* Profile.   A profile for plotting *Gf-Gc* narrow ability test indicator standard scores and cluster averages from the cross-battery worksheets can be found in Appendix C. The *Gf-Gc* profile includes a place for plotting the broad (or narrow) cluster averages from each of seven *Gf-Gc* worksheets and allows room for plotting the standard scores (based on a mean of 100 and standard deviation of 15) for up to four narrow ability test indicators from each worksheet. The cluster averages are plotted on the *thick bars* in the profile and standard scores for the narrow ability test indicators are plotted on the *thin bars*. The profile contains a total of seven *sets of bars* (i.e., one thick and four thin in each set)—one set for plotting the scores reported on each of seven *Gf-Gc* worksheets. A set of standard scores runs across the outside top of each thick bar on the profile.

The first step is to transfer all the cluster averages and subtest standard scores from the seven *Gf-Gc* worksheets to the appropriate places on the profile. Examiner A first recorded all the cluster averages (by placing a vertical hashmark on the thick bars corresponding to the standard score averages), making sure to indicate whether the average represented a "Broad" or "Narrow" ability (a critical component for test interpretation). As on the worksheets, this was achieved by placing a checkmark next to the word "Broad" or "Narrow" and recording the *Gf-Gc* ability code in the parentheses adjacent to the appropriate descriptor. Next, the standard scores of the two subtests that composed each cluster average were recorded directly below their respective *Gf-Gc* cluster averages. The *Gf-Gc* codes corresponding to the narrow ability classifications of these subtests also were recorded in the parentheses adjacent to the subtest names. Thus, a total of 21 scores (i.e., 7 cluster averages and 14 narrow ability test indicator standard scores) and their corresponding *Gf-Gc* ability codes were recorded by Examiner A on a profile for J.J.

The next step is to shade in the *confidence band* for each *Gf-Gc* score that was recorded on the profile, as shown in Figure 13–10. Confidence bands for cluster averages and narrow ability test indicator standard scores correspond to 1 standard error of measurement (SEM). Confidence bands represent the region in which an individual's true score on a test will likely fall. The confidence bands in Figure 13–10 extend from a point 1 SEM below J.J.'s obtained scores to a point 1 SEM above J.J.'s obtained scores. The SEM estimates for all cross-battery cluster averages and subtest standard scores were set at ±5 and ±7 (representing the average [median] *Gf-Gc* cluster and subtest SEM across all age ranges in the WJ-R norm

CRYSTALLIZED INTELLIGENCE (Gc) CROSS-BATTERY WORKSHEET

(McGrew & Flanagan, 1998)

Name: J.J
Age: 9 years 7 months
Grade: 4th
Examiner: A
Date of Evaluation: 1-18-97

Battery or Test	Age	Gc Narrow Abilities Tests	SS*	SS (100±15)
Language Development (LD)				
DAS	6-17	**SIMILARITIES**		
DAS	2-5	Verbal Comprehension (LS)		
SB:IV	12-24	**VERBAL RELATIONS**		
SB:IV	2-24	**Comprehension (K0)**		
SB:IV	2-14	**Absurdities**		
WECH	3-89	**COMPREHENSION (K0)**		
WECH	3-89	**SIMILARITIES**		
DTLA-3	6-17	Word Opposites		
DTLA-3	6-17	Story Construction		
Other				
		1. Sum of column		
		2. Divide by number of tests		
		3. **Language Development** average		
Lexical Knowledge (VL)				
DAS	6-17	**WORD DEFINITIONS (LD)**		
DAS	2-5	Naming Vocabulary (LD)		
SB:IV	2-24	**VOCABULARY (LD)**		
WECH	3-89	**VOCABULARY (LD)**	8	90
WJ-R	4-85+	**ORAL VOCABULARY (LD)**		
WJ-R	2-85+	**PICTURE VOCABULARY (K0)**		
EVT	2-85+	Expressive Vocabulary Test (LD)		
K-BIT	4-90	Expressive Vocabulary (K0, LD)		
PPVT-3	2-85	Peab. Pic. Voc. Test-3rd Ed (K0,LD)		
Other				
		1. Sum of column		90
		2. Divide by number of tests		1
		3. **Lexical Knowledge** average		90
Listening Ability (LS)				
WJ-R	4-85+	**LISTENING COMP (LD)**		
Other				
		1. Sum of column		
		2. Divide by number of tests		
		3. **Listening Ability** average		
General Information (K0)				
WECH	3-89	**INFORMATION**	10	100
DTLA-3	6-17	Basic Information		
Other				
		1. Sum of column		100
		2. Divide by number of tests		1
		3. **General Information** average		100
Information About Culture (K2)				
KAIT	11-85+	**FAMOUS FACES**		
Other				
		1. Sum of column		
		2. Divide by number of tests		
		3. **Information About Culture** average		

Intelligence Batteries with adequate Gc representation
• DAS SB:IV WAIS-III
WISC-III WPPSI-R WJ-R

Intelligence Batteries with inadequate Gc representation
• KAIT K-ABC ***

Sum/No of Narrow Ability Averages

190/2

Cluster Average *

√ Broad (Gc)
__ Narrow (___)

95

FIGURE 13–4 *Gc* Cross-Battery Worksheet

Tests in bold/uppercase letters are strong measures as defined empirically; bold/lowercase are moderate measures as defined empirically; regular face/lowercase measures were classified logically. In the case of tests with two "probable" narrow ability classifications the second classification is reported in parentheses. Only "probable" test classifications are included on the worksheet (not "possible"). Tests that were classified either empirically or logically as mixed measures are not included on the worksheet.

* If a test score is on a standard score scale other than 100 ±15, record the score in the column marked by an asterisk (*). Then refer to the *Percentile Rank and Standard Score Conversion Table* (Appendix B) to convert the score to the scale of 100 ±15. Record the new score in the next column.

** If the cluster includes two or more qualitatively different *Gc* indicators, then place a checkmark (✓) next to the word "Broad" and record "*Gc*" in the parentheses. If the cluster includes indicators from only one narrow ability subsumed by *Gc*, then place a checkmark (✓) next to the word "Narrow" and record the respective narrow ability code in the parentheses (i.e., LD, VL, LS, K0, or K2).

***The K-ABC Achievement Test provides qualitatively different indicators of *Gc*.

VISUAL PROCESSING (*Gv*) CROSS-BATTERY WORKSHEET

(1 of 2)

(McGrew & Flanagan, 1998)

Name: J.J
Age: 9 years 7 months
Grade: 4th
Examiner: A
Date of Evaluation: 1-18-97

Battery or Test	Age	*Gv* Narrow Abilities Tests	SS*	SS (100±15)
Spatial Relations (SR)				
DAS	3-17	Pattern Construction		
K-ABC	4-12	**TRIANGLES**		
SB:IV	2-24	**PATTERN ANALYSIS**		
WECH	3-89	**BLOCK DESIGN**	12	110
Leiter-R	11-18+	Figure Rotation (VZ)		
UNIT	5-17	Cube Design (VZ)		
Other				
		1. Sum of column		110
		2. Divide by number of tests		1
		3. **Spatial Relations** average		110
Visualization (VZ)				
DAS	2-3	Block Building		
DAS	4-5	Matching Letter-like Forms		
WPPSI-R	3-7	Geometric Designs (P2)		
Leiter-R	2-10	Matching		
Leiter-R	2-18+	Form Completion (SR)		
Leiter-R	11-18+	Paper Folding		
Other				
		1. Sum of column		
		2. Divide by number of tests		
		3. **Visualization** average		
Visual Memory (MV)				
DAS	6-17	**RECALL OF DESIGNS**		
DAS	3-7	Recognition of Pictures		
K-ABC	2-4	Face Recognition		
KAIT	11-85+	**MEM. FOR BLOCK DESIGNS**		
SB:IV	2-24	**Bead Memory**		
SB:IV	7-24	**Memory for Objects**		
WJ-R	4-85+	**Picture Recogniton**		
DTLA-3	6-17	Design Sequences		
DTLA-3	6-17	Design Reproduction		
LAMB	20-60	Simple Figure		
LAMB	20-60	Complex Figure		
Leiter-R	4-10	Immediate Recognition		
Leiter-R	2-18+	Forward Memory		
TOMAL	5-19	Facial Memory		
TOMAL	5-19	Abstract Visual Memory		
TOMAL	5-19	Manual Imitation		
TOMAL	5-19	Del Rec: Visual Sel. Reminding		
UNIT	5-17	**OBJECT MEMORY**		
UNIT	5-17	**SPATIAL MEMORY**		
UNIT	5-17	**SYMBOLIC MEMORY**		
WMS-R	16-74	Figural Memory		
WMS-R	16-74	Visual Reproduction I		
WRAML	5-17	Picture Memory		
WRAML	5-17	Design Memory		
Other				
		1. Sum of column		
		2. Divide by number of tests		
		3. **Visual Memory** average		

Intelligence Batteries with adequate *Gv* representation
• DAS K-ABC SB:IV WAIS-III
  WISC-III WPPSI-R WJ-R

Intelligence Batteries with inadequate *Gv* representation
• KAIT

(cont'd next page)

FIGURE 13–5   *Gv* Cross-Battery Worksheet

Tests in bold/uppercase letters are strong measures as defined empirically; bold/lowercase are moderate measures as defined empirically; regular face/lowercase measures were classified logically. In the case of tests with two "probable" narrow ability classifications the second classification is reported in parentheses. Only "probable" test classifications are included on the worksheet (not "possible"). Tests that were classified either empirically or logically as mixed measures are not included on the worksheet.

(cont'd prior page)

Battery or Test	Age	Gv Narrow Abilities Tests	SS*	SS (100±15)
Closure Speed (CS)				
K-ABC	2-12	**Gestalt Closure**		
WECH	3-89	**OBJECT ASSEMBLY**	13	115
WJ-R	2-85+	**Visual Closure**		
DTLA-3	6-17	Picture Fragments		
K-SNAP	11-85	Gestalt Closure		
Other				
		1. Sum of column		115
		2. Divide by number of tests		1
		3. **Closure Speed** average		115
Spatial Scanning (SS)				
WISC-III	6-16	Mazes		
WPPSI-R	3-7	**Mazes**		
UNIT	5-17	**Mazes**		
Other				
		1. Sum of column		
		2. Divide by number of tests		
		3. **Spatial Scanning** average		
Flexibility of Closure (CF)				
CAS	5-17	Figure Memory (MV)		
Leiter-R	2-18+	Figure Ground		
Other				
		1. Sum of column		
		2. Divide by number of tests		
		3. **Flexibility of Closure** average		
Serial Perceptual Integration (PI)				
K-ABC	2-4	Magic Window		
Other				
		1. Sum of column		
		2. Divide by number of tests		
		3. **Serial Perceptual Integration** average		

Sum/No of Narrow Ability Averages

225/2

Cluster Average **

√ Broad (Gv)
___ Narrow (___)

113

* If a test score is on a standard score scale other than 100 ±15, record the score in the column marked by an asterisk (*). Then refer to the *Percentile Rank and Standard Score Conversion Table* (Appendix B) to convert the score to the scale of 100 ±15. Record the new score in the next column.

** If the cluster includes two or more qualitatively different *Gv* indicators, then place a checkmark (✓) next to the word "Broad" and record "*Gv*" in the parentheses. If the cluster includes indicators from only one narrow ability subsumed by *Gv*, then place a checkmark (✓) next to the word "Narrow" and record the respective narrow ability code in the parentheses (i.e., SR, VZ, MV, CS, SS, CF, or PI).

(McGrew & Flanagan, 1998)

Name:	J.J
Age:	9 years 7 months
Grade:	4th
Examiner:	A
Date of Evaluation:	1-18-97

Battery or Test	Age	*Gsm* Narrow Abilities Tests	SS*	SS (100±15)
Memory Span (MS)				
DAS	3-17	Recall of Digits		
K-ABC	2-12	**NUMBER RECALL**		
K-ABC	4-12	**WORD ORDER**		
SB:IV	7-24	**MEMORY FOR DIGITS**		
WAIS-III	16-89	**DIGIT SPAN**		
WAIS-III	16-89	Letter-Number Sequencing		
WISC-III	6-16	**DIGIT SPAN**	10	100
WPPSI-R	3-7	Sentences		
WJ-R	4-85+	**MEMORY FOR WORDS**		95
CAS	5-17	Word Series		
DTLA-3	6-17	Word Sequences		
K-SNAP	11-85	Number Recall		
LAMB	20-60	Digit Span		
LAMB	20-60	Supraspan Digit		
TOMAL	5-19	Digits Forward		
TOMAL	5-19	Letters Forward		
WMS-R	16-74	Digit Span		
WRAML	5-17	Number/Letter Memory		
		1. Sum of column		195
		2. Divide by number of tests		2
		3. **Memory Span** average		98

Intelligence Batteries with adequate *Gsm* representation

Intelligence Batteries with inadequate *Gsm* representation
• DAS K-ABC KAIT SB:IV
WAIS-III WISC-III WPPSI-R WJ-R

Battery or Test	Age	*Gsm* Narrow Abilities Tests		
Visual Memory (MV)				
DAS	6-17	**RECALL OF DESIGNS**		
DAS	3-7	Recognition of Pictures		
K-ABC	2-4	Face Recognition		
KAIT	11-85+	**MEM. FOR BLOCK DESIGNS**		
SB:IV	2-24	**Bead Memory**		
SB:IV	7-24	**Memory for Objects**		
WJ-R	4-85+	**Picture Recogniton**		
DTLA-3	6-17	Design Sequences		
DTLA-3	6-17	Design Reproduction		
LAMB	20-60	Simple Figure		
LAMB	20-60	Complex Figure		
Leiter-R	4-10	Immediate Recognition		
Leiter-R	2-18+	Forward Memory		
TOMAL	5-19	Facial Memory		
TOMAL	5-19	Abstract Visual Memory		
TOMAL	5-19	Manual Imitation		
TOMAL	5-19	Del Rec: Visual Sel. Reminding		
UNIT	5-17	**OBJECT MEMORY**		
UNIT	5-17	**SPATIAL MEMORY**		
UNIT	5-17	**SYMBOLIC MEMORY**		
WMS-R	16-74	Figural Memory		
WMS-R	16-74	Visual Reproduction I		
WRAML	5-17	Picture Memory		
WRAML	5-17	Design Memory		
		1. Sum of column		
		2. Divide by number of tests		
		3. **Visual Memory** average		

	Sum/No of Narrow Ability Averages	Cluster Average **
		__ Broad (____)
		√ Narrow (MS)
	98/1	98

FIGURE 13–6 *Gsm* Cross-Battery Worksheet

Tests in bold/uppercase letters are strong measures as defined empirically; bold/lowercase are moderate measures as defined empirically; regular face/lowercase measures were classified logically. In the case of tests with two "probable" narrow ability classifications the second classification is reported in parentheses. Only "probable" test classifications are included on the worksheet (not "possible"). Tests that were classified either empirically or logically as mixed measures are not included on the worksheet.

* If a test score is on a standard score scale other than 100 ±15, record the score in the column marked by an asterisk (*). Then refer to the *Percentile Rank and Standard Score Conversion Table* (Appendix B) to convert the score to the scale of 100 ±15. Record the new score in the next column.

** If the cluster includes two or more qualitatively different *Gsm* indicators, then place a checkmark (✓) next to the word "Broad" and record "*Gsm*" in the parentheses. If the cluster includes indicators from only one narrow ability subsumed by *Gsm*, then place a checkmark (✓) next to the word "Narrow" and record the respective narrow ability code in the parentheses (i.e., MS, or MV).

LONG-TERM RETRIEVAL (*Glr*) CROSS-BATTERY WORKSHEET

(McGrew & Flanagan, 1998)

Name: J.J
Age: 9 years 7 months
Grade: 4th
Examiner: A
Date of Evaluation: 1-18-97

Battery or Test	Age	*Glr* Narrow Abilities Tests	SS*	SS (100±15)
Associative Memory (MA)				
KAIT	11-85+	**REBUS LEARNING**		
KAIT	11-85+	**REBUS DELAYED RECALL**		
WJ-R	2-85+	**MEMORY FOR NAMES**		86
WJ-R	4-85+	**VISUAL AUDITORY LEARNING**		81
WJ-R	4-85+	**DEL REC: MEM FOR NAMES**		
WJ-R	4-85+	**Del Rec: Visual-Auditory Learning**		
LAMB	20-60	Word Pairs (FI)		
Leiter-R	4-10	Delayed Recognition		
Leiter-R	2-18+	Associated Pairs (MM)		
Leiter-R	6-18+	Delayed Pairs (MM)		
TOMAL	5-19	Paired Recall		
WMS-R	16-74	Visual Paired Associates I		
WMS-R	16-74	Verbal Paired Associates I		
WMS-R	16-74	Visual Paired Associates II		
WMS-R	16-74	Verbal Paired Associates II		
WRAML	5-17	Sound Symbol		
Other				
		1. Sum of column		167
		2. Divide by number of tests		2
		3. **Associative Memory** average		84
Free Recall Memory (M6)				
DAS	4-17	Recall of Objects		
LAMB	20-60	Wordlist (MA)		
TOMAL	5-19	Word Selective Reminding		
TOMAL	5-19	Del Rec: Word Selective Reminding		
WRAML	5-17	Verbal Learning		
Other				
		1. Sum of column		
		2. Divide by number of tests		
		3. **Free Recall Memory** average		
Meaningful Memory (MM)				
WMS-R	16-74	Logical Memory I		
Other				
		1. Sum of column		
		2. Divide by number of tests		
		3. **Meaningful Memory** average		

Intelligence Batteries with adequate *Glr* representation

Intelligence Batteries with inadequate *Glr* representation
• DAS K-ABC KAIT SB:IV WAIS-III WISC-II, WPPSI-R, WJ-R

Sum/No of Narrow Ability Averages: 84/1

Cluster Average **
__ Broad (___)
√ Narrow (MA)
84

FIGURE 13–7 *Glr* Cross-Battery Worksheet

Tests in bold/uppercase letters are strong measures as defined empirically; bold/lowercase are moderate measures as defined empirically; regular face/lowercase measures were classified logically. In the case of tests with two "probable" narrow ability classifications the second classification is reported in parentheses. Only "probable" test classifications are included on the worksheet (not "possible"). Tests that were classified either empirically or logically as mixed measures are not included on the worksheet.

* If a test score is on a standard score scale other than 100 ±15, record the score in the column marked by an asterisk (*). Then refer to the *Percentile Rank and Standard Score Conversion Table* (Appendix B) to convert the score to the scale of 100 ±15. Record the new score in the next column.

** If the cluster includes two or more qualitatively different *Glr* indicators, then place a checkmark (✓) next to the word "Broad" and record "*Glr*" in the parentheses. If the cluster includes indicators from only one narrow ability subsumed by *Glr*, then place a checkmark (✓) next to the word "Narrow" and record the respective narrow ability code in the parentheses (i.e., MA, M6, or MM).

AUDITORY PROCESSING (*Ga*) CROSS-BATTERY WORKSHEET

(McGrew & Flanagan, 1998)

Name: J.J
Age: 9 years 7 months
Grade: 4th
Examiner: A
Date of Evaluation: 1-18-97

Battery or Test	Age	*Ga* Narrow Abilities Tests	SS*	SS (100±15)
		Phonetic Coding (PC)		
WJ-R	2-85+	**INCOMPLETE WORDS**		60
WJ-R	4-85+	**SOUND BLENDING**		72
TOPA	5-8	Test of Phonological Awareness		
Other				
		1. Sum of column		132
		2. Divide by number of tests		2
		3. **Phonetic Coding** average		66

Intelligence Batteries with adequate *Ga* representation

Intelligence Batteries with inadequate *Ga* representation
• DAS K-ABC KAIT SB:IV WAIS-III
  WISC-III WPPSI-R WJ-R

_____ ( )

1. Sum of column
2. Divide by number of tests
3. _____ average

_____ ( )

1. Sum of column
2. Divide by number of tests
3. _____ average

Sum/No of Narrow Ability Averages	Cluster Average **
	__ Broad ( )
	√ Narrow (PC)
66/1	66

FIGURE 13–8 *Ga* Cross-Battery Worksheet

Tests in bold/uppercase letters are strong measures as defined empirically; bold/lowercase are moderate measures as defined empirically; regular face/lowercase measures were classified logically. In the case of tests with two "probable" narrow ability classifications the second classification is reported in parentheses. Only "probable" test classifications are included on the worksheet (not "possible"). Tests that were classified either empirically or logically as mixed measures are not included on the worksheet.

* If a test score is on a standard score scale other than 100 ±15, record the score in the column marked by an asterisk (*). Then refer to the *Percentile Rank and Standard Score Conversion Table* (Appendix B) to convert the score to the scale of 100 ±15. Record the new score in the next column.

** If the cluster includes two or more qualitatively different *Ga* indicators, then place a checkmark (✓) next to the word "Broad" and record "*Ga*" in the parentheses. If the cluster includes indicators from only one narrow ability subsumed by *Ga*, then place a checkmark (✓) next to the word "Narrow" and record the respective narrow ability code in the parentheses.

PROCESSING SPEED (*Gs*) CROSS-BATTERY WORKSHEET

(McGrew & Flanagan, 1998)

Name: _J.J_
Age: _9 years 7 months_
Grade: _4th_
Examiner: _A_
Date of Evaluation: _1-18-97_

Battery or Test	Age	*Gs* Narrow Abilities Tests	SS*	SS (100±15)
Perceptual Speed (P)				
WAIS-III	16-89	Symbol Search (R9)		
WISC-III	6-16	Symbol Search (R9)	10	100
WJ-R	4-85+	**VISUAL MATCHING (R9)**		
WJ-R	4-85+	**CROSS OUT**		
CAS	5-17	Matching Numbers (R9)		
CAS	5-17	Receptive Attention (R4)		
Leiter-R	2-18+	Attention Sustained (R9)		
Other				
		1. Sum of column		100
		2. Divide by number of tests		1
		3. **Perceptual Speed** Average		100
Rate -of-test-taking (R9)				
WAIS-III	16-74	**DIGIT SYMBOL-CODING**		
WISC-III	6-16	**CODING**	4	70
WPPSI-R	3-7	Animal Pegs		
CAS	5-17	Planned Codes		
Other				
		1. Sum of column		70
		2. Divide by number of tests		1
		3. **Rate-of-test-taking** average		70
Mental Comparison Speed (R7)				
DAS	6-17	Speed of Information Processing		
CAS	5-17	Number Detection (R9)		
Other				
		1. Sum of column		
		2. Divide by number of tests		
		3. **Mental Comparison Speed** average		

Intelligence Batteries with adequate *Gs* representation
WAIS-III WISC-III

Intelligence Batteries with inadequate *Gs* representation
DAS K-ABC KAIT SB:IV
WPPSI-R WJ-R

Sum/No of Narrow Ability Averages: 170/2

Cluster Average **
√ Broad (Gs)
__ Narrow (___)

85

FIGURE 13–9   *Gs* Cross-Battery Worksheet

Tests in bold/uppercase letters are strong measures as defined empirically; bold/lowercase are moderate measures as defined empirically; regular face/lowercase measures were classified logically. In the case of tests with two "probable" narrow ability classifications the second classification is reported in parentheses. Only "probable" test classifications are included on the worksheet (not "possible"). Tests that were classified either empirically or logically as mixed measures are not included on the worksheet.

* If a test score is on a standard score scale other than 100 ±15, record the score in the column marked by an asterisk (*). Then refer to the *Percentile Rank and Standard Score Conversion Table* (Appendix B) to convert the score to the scale of 100 ±15. Record the new score in the next column.

** If the cluster includes two or more qualitatively different *Gs* indicators, then place a checkmark (✓) next to the word "Broad" and record "*Gs*" in the parentheses. If the cluster includes indicators from only one narrow ability subsumed by *Gs*, then place a checkmark (✓) next to the word "Narrow" and record the respective narrow ability code in the parentheses (i.e., P, R9, or R7).

sample, respectively).[3] The confidence bands that were constructed for the *Gf-Gc* ability scores (based on ±1 SEM) are also called *68% confidence bands* because they represent the standard score range in which an individual's true score falls two out of three times. Doubling the confidence bands or making them twice as wide (i.e., ±2 SEM) would increase one's degree of confidence from 68% to 95%, representing the standard score range in which an individual's true score falls 19 out of 20 times. The purpose of reporting confidence bands is to demonstrate the degree of precision (or imprecision) that is present in the *Gf-Gc* scores. Examining a test score on a profile as a confidence band (as opposed to a single or exact score) is usually preferred (Woodcock & Mather, 1989, 1990).

Examiner A shaded in the confidence bands for all the *Gf-Gc* standard scores reported on the profile. For example, the confidence band for J.J.'s broad *Gf* cluster score (i.e., 117 ±5) ranged from 112 (i.e., 117 − 5) to 122 (i.e., 117 + 5). Examiner A made vertical hashmarks through the standard scores of 112 and 122 on the *Gf* bar on the profile and shaded in the area between them. The completed *Gf-Gc* profile (see Figure 13–10) graphically displays J.J.'s level of ability. It provides a meaningful basis for making the necessary *Gf-Gc* ability comparisons to evaluate cognitive functioning (e.g., inter- and intra-individual strengths and weaknesses). Procedures for interpreting scores that are plotted on the *Gf-Gc* profile are presented in the next chapter.

Conclusions

Through a series of *Gf-Gc* cross-battery principles and steps, this chapter demonstrated how practitioners can augment any intelligence battery to measure more effectively the full range of broad cognitive abilities according to contemporary *Gf-Gc* theory and research. The foundational sources of information upon which the *Gf-Gc* cross-battery approach was built (viz., the classification of the major intelligence batteries according to *Gf-Gc* theory) provide a means to construct sys-

---

[3] Given the large number of individual tests that can be used in *Gf-Gc* cross-battery assessments, it is not practical to calculate and report the composite reliability and SEM estimates for every possible combination of tests. Since the WJ-R *Gf-Gc* broad ability clusters are based on *Gf-Gc* theory (the foundation of cross-battery assessment) and are derived from two-test combinations (like the clusters in cross-battery assessments), the *Gf-Gc* cluster SEMs reported in the *WJ-R Technical Manual* (McGrew et al., 1991) were used to estimate a SEM value for the broad *Gf-Gc* cross-battery clusters. Likewise, it is not practical to report all published SEMs for all individual tests that might be interpreted in cross-battery assessments. The SEMs reported across the 21 WJ-R cognitive tests across all age ranges were reviewed to identify a reasonable SEM estimate that could be used as a general "rule-of-thumb" for all individual tests used in cross-battery assessments. Furthermore, the respective subtest and composite SEMs reported for other intelligence batteries (e.g., WISC-III) were reviewed to ensure that these SEM rules-of-thumb values were reasonable approximate values across a variety of instruments.

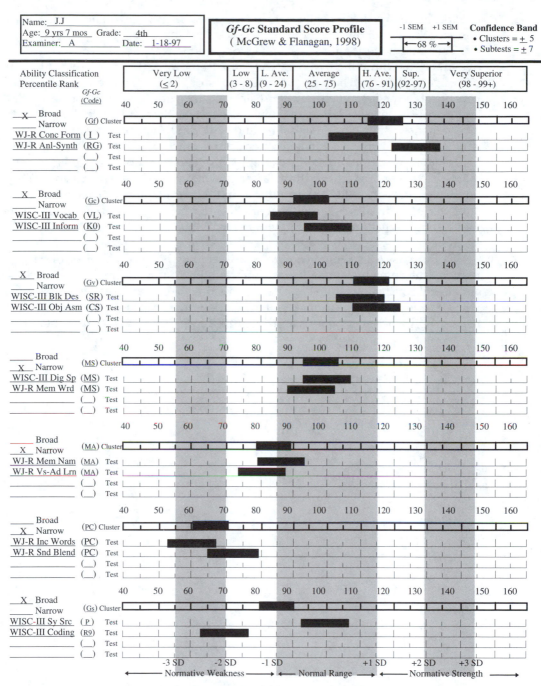

FIGURE 13–10 *Gf-Gc* **Cross-Battery Profile**

tematically more theoretically driven, comprehensive, and valid measures of human cognitive abilities.

The cross-battery approach in effect operationalizes the "universe" of cognitive functions within the psychometric *Gf-Gc* framework (i.e., the "table of human cognitive abilities"). The *Gf-Gc* classifications of all intelligence tests presented here brings stronger content and construct validity evidence to the assessment and interpretation process. Although intelligence tests of the future will likely be more comprehensive than current measures and provide stronger content and construct validity, it is unrealistic from an economic and practical standpoint to develop a battery that operationalizes fully contemporary *Gf-Gc* theory. Thus, it is probable that *Gf-Gc*–organized cross-battery factor analyses will become increasingly more important in establishing the validity of intelligence batteries. Thereafter, *Gf-Gc* cross-battery procedures can aid practitioners in the selective measurement of cognitive abilities that are important with regard to the presenting problem(s) of the examinee.

In the past a lack of theoretical clarity of intelligence batteries often confounded interpretation and adversely affected the examiner's ability to draw clear and useful conclusions from the data. Conducting *Gf-Gc* cross-battery assessments will allow practitioners to make interpretations that can be supported by both research evidence and theory. Guidelines for interpreting *Gf-Gc* cross-battery data are presented in Chapter 14.

Gf-Gc *Cross-Battery Interpretation and Selective Cross-Battery Assessment*

Referral Concerns and the Needs of Culturally and Linguistically Diverse Populations

> *Knowledge of theory is important above and beyond research findings as theory allows the clinician to do a better job of conceptualizing a child's score.*
> —KAMPHAUS, 1993, p. 44

> *The instruments of cognitive assessment, therefore, must be supplemented with careful preparation and regard for the complexities of the evaluative process and the LEP population.*
> —HOLTZMAN & WILKINSON, 1991, p. 251

The purpose of this chapter is to provide general guidelines for interpreting *Gf-Gc* cross-battery data. In addition, guidelines for conducting *Gf-Gc* selective cross-battery assessments will be offered as they pertain to reading and mathematics referral concerns and assessment of individuals from culturally and linguistically diverse populations.

Interpreting Gf-Gc *Cross-Battery Data*

Two common methods of intelligence test interpretation are inter-individual and intra-individual analysis (e.g., Kamphaus, 1993; Kaufman, 1979, 1994; Sattler, 1988). These methods will be described briefly and procedures will be offered for conducting both inter- and intra-individual analyses with *Gf-Gc* cross-battery data. Particular attention will be given to the way in which the *Gf-Gc* cross-battery approach circumvents some of the most salient limitations of traditional intra-individual subtest analysis. Due to space limitations, this section will present only *guidelines* for making *Gf-Gc* cross-battery interpretations, rather than a more global, comprehensive, and integrative approach to test interpretation. The guidelines presented here may be carried out effectively within the context of the scientific, practical, and well-conceived interpretive approaches of Kaufman (1994) and Kamphaus (1993).

Inter-Individual Analysis of Gf-Gc *Cross-Battery Data*

The information provided from an *inter*-individual analysis is *population-relative* and reveals *between*-individual differences as determined by normative score comparisons. That is, normative scores provide information about an individual's ability compared to his or her same-age peers (norm group) (e.g., Woodcock, 1994). Notably, an individual's normative score for one ability is not dependent upon his or her scores on other abilities. Inter-individual analysis is utilized mainly to interpret global and scale (or cluster) performance (e.g., Full Scale IQ, Verbal IQ, Performance IQ, etc.) and aid in making diagnostic, classification, and educational placement decisions.

The treatment of scores in cross-battery assessment, however, is a more complex task than in single-battery assessment because there are *different sources* of test scores in the former approach. In a typical intellectual assessment the majority (or all) of the evaluation is conducted with one battery, such as the WISC-III. Within this battery the subtest scores are on the same scale and standardized on the same population, allowing direct comparisons between scores. Since there is no single intelligence battery that adequately assesses all the broad *Gf-Gc* abilities in contemporary psychometric theory (hence the development of the cross-battery approach), scores yielded by cross-battery assessments, taken together, represent an unsystematic aggregate of standardized tests. That is, cross-battery assessments employ tests that were developed at different times, in different places, on different samples, with different scoring procedures, and for different purposes (Lezak, 1976, 1995). Thus, cross-battery assessments yield test scores that are on different scales, and a cross-battery norm group does not exist.

In order to make the comparisons necessary to understand cognitive functioning within the context of the *Gf-Gc* structure of abilities using cross-battery data, it was necessary to (1) convert all scores to a common metric and (2) identify a normative standard to which test scores could be compared. As directed in Step 5 of the cross-battery approach (see Chapter 13), all standard scores from cross-battery assessments were converted to a common metric having a mean of 100 and standard deviation of 15 (using the Standard Score Conversion Table in Appendix B). The next step is to compare these scores to a *normative standard* (in lieu of a cross-battery norm group). The most useful standard statistically and the one that likely addresses adequately the reality of having to cross batteries (and in effect norm groups) to conduct more comprehensive and theoretically meaningful assessments is the *normal probability curve.*

The normal probability curve "has very practical applications for comparing and evaluating psychological data in that the position of any test score on a standard deviation unit scale, in itself, defines the proportion of people taking the test who will obtain scores above or below a given score" (Lezak, 1976, p. 123). A description of *Gf-Gc* ability scores with respect to the normal probability curve is presented in Table 14–1 (e.g., percent of cases under portions of the normal curve). This table also provides commonly used "classification categories" (e.g., Low Average, Average, High Average, etc.) that correspond to different standard score and percentile rank ranges. The information in this table offers a way to describe and evaluate *Gf-Gc* cross-battery data. Note that most of this information can also be found on the *Gf-Gc* Standard Score Profile (Appendix C). The interpretation guidelines presented here should be followed after all *Gf-Gc* cross-battery data have been transferred from the *Gf-Gc* worksheets (Appendix A) to the profile and plotted (as directed in Chapter 13). These guidelines will be presented and discussed within the context of J.J.'s *Gf-Gc* cross-battery evaluation (see Wechsler-based case example in Chapter 13 and assessment results in Appendix D).

TABLE 14–1   Description and Evaluation of *Gf-Gc* Ability Scores

Description of Performance			Evaluation of Performance
Standard Score Range	Percentile Rank Range	*Gf-Gc* Ability Classification	
≥131	98–99+	Very Superior	Normative Strength
121–130	92–97	Superior	(16 % of the population)
111–120	76–91	High Average	(+1 *standard deviation:* SS = 115)
90–110	25–75	Average	Normal Range (68 % of the population)
80–89	9–24	Low Average	(−1 *standard deviation:* SS = 85)
70–79	3–8	Low	Normative Weakness
≤ 69	≤ 2	Very Low	(16 % of the population)

Note: Gf-Gc ability classifications correspond to those used to describe performance on the WJ-R (Woodcock & Mather, 1989, 1990).

Guideline 1: Evaluate Performance to Decide Whether Additional Measures Are Necessary

Careful evaluation of performance on one battery or portion thereof allows the practitioner to determine the need to administer more measures to test hypotheses about cognitive strengths and/or weaknesses or differences in *Gf-Gc* abilities. Interpretations and diagnostic conclusions should not be made based on a single test score outlier, regardless of the extent to which it deviates from all other scores. Because unreliability or chance alone may account for a single outlying score (see Atkinson, 1991; Lezak, 1995), assessment should be regarded as an "iterative" process. For example, when two or more narrow abilities within broad ability domains differ significantly, then another iteration (i.e., additional assessment) is necessary to determine whether this difference is an anomalous or irrelevant finding (Kamphaus, 1993).

***Following the* Gf-Gc *Interpretation Flowchart*.**   Evaluator A reviewed J.J.'s *Gf-Gc* cross-battery performance, which was recorded previously on the *Gf-Gc* profile in Figure 13–10. In order to determine whether additional measures should be administered (i.e., whether another iteration was warranted), Examiner A followed the interpretation flowchart presented in Figure 14–1. According to this chart, Examiner A needs to determine whether J.J.'s performance on narrow ability test indicators is uniform within broad and/or narrow *Gf-Gc* clusters. The evaluation of whether a true difference exists between two *Gf-Gc* scores in cross-battery assessments is based on whether the two respective confidence bands associated with these scores overlap (see Chapter 13 for a discussion of confidence bands used in cross-battery assessment). Following the procedures outlined for the WJ-R (McGrew et al., 1991), which take into account the reliability of the difference score, the following two guidelines should be used to evaluate differences between *Gf-Gc* confidence bands in cross-battery assessments.

First, if the confidence bands for any two test scores or clusters touch or overlap, the practitioner should assume that no significant difference exists between the examinee's true scores for the abilities being compared. Second, if the confidence bands for any two tests or clusters do not touch or overlap, then the practitioner should assume that a possible significant difference exists between the examinee's true scores for the abilities that are being compared (McGrew et al., 1991). According to McGrew and colleagues (1991), when the second, "nonoverlap" guideline is used, a practitioner can be 84% confident that a true difference in scores exists. This level of confidence was deemed to be appropriate for the clinical nature of the comparisons that are made in *Gf-Gc* cross-battery assessments.

Examiner A examined the confidence bands of J.J.'s narrow ability test indicator (i.e., subtest) scores within *Gf-Gc* domains (see Figure 13–10) to determine whether they overlapped. He found that the narrow ability test indicator bands overlapped within all *Gf-Gc* domains except *Gf* and *Gs*. Since the confidence bands overlapped for the respective tests that combined to yield the *Gc*, *Gv*, *Gs*, MA-*Glr*, MS-*Gsm*, and PC-*Ga* clusters, Examiner A assumed that J.J.'s performance was uniform within these *Gf-Gc* domains (see Figure 14–1). However, since the narrow

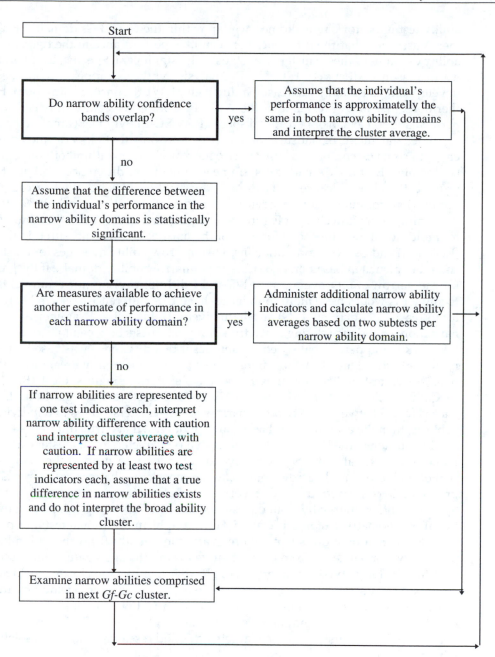

FIGURE 14–1 *Gf-Gc* **Cross-Battery Interpretation Flowchart**

NOTE: Bold rectangles indicate decision points.

ability test indicator bands did not overlap within the *Gf* and *Gs* domains, Examiner A assumed that the difference between J.J.'s performance in the two narrow ability domains of these clusters was statistically significant. Specifically, J.J.'s ability to reason deductively (RG; WJ-R Analysis-Synthesis) appears to be better developed than his ability to reason inductively (I; WJ-R Concept Formation). Furthermore, J.J.'s rate of test taking (R9; WISC-III Coding) is significantly below his performance on a task of perceptual speed (P; WISC-III Symbol Search).

Since statements of statistical probability imply only that J.J. performed differently, to some extent, on measures of two narrow abilities within both the *Gf* and *Gs* domains, Examiner A had to determine whether these differences had practical or educational significance in terms of understanding J.J.'s behavior or drawing implications for instruction or service delivery (Mather & Woodcock, 1989, 1990). According to the flowchart in Figure 14–1, ideally Examiner A should administer four additional measures, one for each of the narrow abilities measured in the *Gf* (RG and I) and *Gs* (R9 and P) domains. Then narrow ability averages (or clusters) could be calculated based on two subtests per narrow ability domain. If the bands for the narrow ability averages for RG and I did not overlap, for example, then Examiner A would have more confidence that a true difference exists in J.J.'s ability to reason deductively (RG) and inductively (I). Likewise, Examiner A would have more confidence stating that a true difference exists between J.J.'s rate of test taking (R9) and perceptual speed (P) abilities if this difference was based on narrow ability averages of two (or more) scores per narrow ability area, rather than one. A two-test ability cluster is more reliable than a single subtest (Bracken, McCallum, & Crain, 1993; McGrew et al., 1991). Therefore, if a significant difference is found between two two-test narrow ability clusters versus two individual subtests, then the examiner can have more confidence that a true difference exists.

In addition to the increase in reliability that is characteristic of clusters (as compared to individual subtests), there is validity evidence to support the interpretation of both broad and narrow ability *clusters*, since cross-battery assessments are grounded in contemporary *Gf-Gc* theory and research. It should be noted that this approach differs markedly from the "shared abilities" approach inherent in traditional psychometric test interpretation. For example, in traditional test interpretation, when two or more subtest scores vary consistently from the individual's average performance (or from the normative mean), the aggregate of these scores (i.e., the cluster) is typically interpreted. However, unlike the clusters yielded by cross-battery assessments, many of the shared abilities clusters yielded by traditional assessments lack validity evidence (Kamphaus, 1993). Because cross-battery clusters are constructed and interpreted within the context of *Gf-Gc* theory, interpretation of these clusters is based largely on sound research rather than solely on clinical acumen.

In situations in which statistically significant differences exist between narrow ability averages (based on two or more subtests per narrow ability area) the broad ability cluster (i.e., the aggregate of narrow ability test scores) should not be interpreted, as it is a misleading estimate of the broad ability. For instance, in the previous example, because the confidence bands corresponding to the RG and I narrow ability averages did not overlap, the broad *Gf* ability cluster should not be interpreted. Fluid Intelligence (*Gf*) in this instance would be described most accurately in terms of performance in the different narrow ability domains subsumed by *Gf* (i.e., RG and I).

The Decision-Making Process.   After reviewing J.J.'s profile (Figure 13–10), Examiner A made some decisions that deviated slightly from the steps suggested in the flowchart. With regard to *Gf*, Examiner A noted that J.J. performed within the Average range of ability on the measure of Inductive reasoning (I; WJ-R Concept Formation = 108 ±7) and in the Superior range of ability on the measure of General Sequential (or deductive) Reasoning (RG; WJ-R Analysis-Synthesis = 126 ±7). Although the confidence bands for these scores do not overlap, suggesting a statistically significant difference, Examiner A chose not to administer additional measures of I and RG, for three primary reasons.

First, a review of the WJ-R ITDR pages (see Chapter 11) showed that the Analysis-Synthesis and Concept Formation tests are highly reliable for an individual of J.J.'s age. Therefore, Examiner A is confident that J.J.'s obtained scores on these measures portray reliable estimates of his ability. Second, J.J.'s performance on the Analysis-Synthesis test suggests a normative strength, and his performance on the Concept Formation test was well within the normal range of ability (see Table 14–1). Together, these results suggest that tasks requiring fluid reasoning do not present difficulties for J.J. Third, a review of the cognitive abilities and achievement literature (see Chapter 2) demonstrates that *Gf* abilities are most strongly related to *mathematics* achievement. Results of J.J.'s performance on tests of math calculation and applied problems (as measured by the WJ-R Tests of Achievement) show that he is functioning in the Average range of ability in mathematics compared to same-age peers (see Appendix D). Also, the referral concerns of J.J.'s mother were not related to J.J.'s math performance (see Chapter 13). For these reasons, Examiner A did not believe that the difference displayed between J.J.'s inductive and general sequential (deductive) reasoning abilities had practical significance in terms of drawing implications for instruction or service delivery and therefore it was not necessary to administer additional measures of fluid reasoning.

With regard to *Gs*, Examiner A noted that J.J. performed within the Average range of ability on the measure of Perceptual Speed (WISC-III Symbol Search = 100 ±7) and at the juncture of the Low and Very Low range of ability on the Rate-of-Test-Taking task (WISC-III Coding = 70 ±7). The latter score is 2 standard deviations below the mean and therefore represents a normative weakness.[1]

Since Symbol Search and Coding measure related aspects of the broad ability of *Gs*, it is unusual to observe a significant disparity in performance on these subtests. However, observations of J.J.'s performance while taking the Coding subtest, in particular, help to explain this disparity. Specifically, J.J. stated that he did not

---

[1] Typically, a score that is ≥ 1 SD above or below the mean is considered a normative strength or weakness, respectively.

like drawing shapes or being timed. His lack of interest, and perhaps motivation, while taking the Coding test likely affected his performance adversely. Although these noncognitive or *individual/situational* factors (see ITDR) could be used fairly confidently to explain the difference in performance between the Symbol Search and Coding subtests, Examiner A wanted at least one additional piece of data to support his interpretation of J.J.'s performance in the *Gs* domain (see Kamphaus, 1993).

The Next Iteration.   Examiner A reviewed the *Gs* worksheet (see Appendix A) and decided to administer the WJ-R Visual Matching test. Since Visual Matching was classified as a probable measure of both Rate-of-Test-Taking (R9) and Perceptual Speed (P), Examiner A reasoned that it was not necessary to potentially introduce additional measurement error into the cross-battery assessment by selecting a test from a *third* battery. However, it is important to note that the WISC-III Coding and Symbol Search tests as well as the WJ-R Visual Matching test are not highly reliable for an individual of J.J.'s age (see ITDR, chapters 9 and 11, respectively).[2] Therefore, the Speed of Information Processing test on the DAS, for example, may have been a better test to administer to J.J. because it is highly reliable (see ITDR, Chapter 4). Nevertheless, as already stated, the reliability of cluster scores is higher than that of individual subtests. For example, the WISC-III Speed of Processing Index (i.e., Coding + Symbol Search) has a reliability coefficient of .85 (i.e., *medium* according to ITDR criteria) for individuals of J.J.'s age (Wechsler, 1991). Examiner A's decision-making process demonstrates that it is not always easy to determine which tests represent the most practical *and* psychometrically sound measures to use as supplements to "core" intelligence batteries.

With regard to the WJ-R Visual Matching test, according to Examiner A, J.J. appeared focused while taking this test and earned a score of 91 ±7 (Average). Examiner A recalculated the *Gs* cluster with J.J.'s Visual Matching score (i.e., with all three narrow ability indicators of *Gs*) and with Symbol Search and Visual Matching only. He obtained *Gs* clusters of 83 ±5 (Low Average) and 96 ±5 (Average), respectively. Based on these results, Examiner A concluded that J.J.'s performance on Speed of Processing tests (viz., perceptual speed) is Average, particularly when he is motivated and interested in the task at hand.

Guideline 2: Use the Normal Probability Curve to Draw Conclusions

After following the steps outlined in the flowchart in Figure 14–1 and administering one additional measure, Examiner A used the characteristics of the normal probability curve to draw conclusions about J.J.'s *Gf-Gc* cross-battery performance. J.J.'s profile of scores can be found in Figure 14–2. This figure is identical to Figure 13–10, with one exception. Figure 14–2 includes the WJ-R Visual Matching test as well as the recalculated *Gs* cluster based on the aggregate of Symbol Search and

---

[2] It is important to recognize that test-retest (not internal consistency) reliability coefficients are reported for speeded tests. As a result, the reliability coefficients for speeded tests are typically considered to be "lower bound" estimates of reliability.

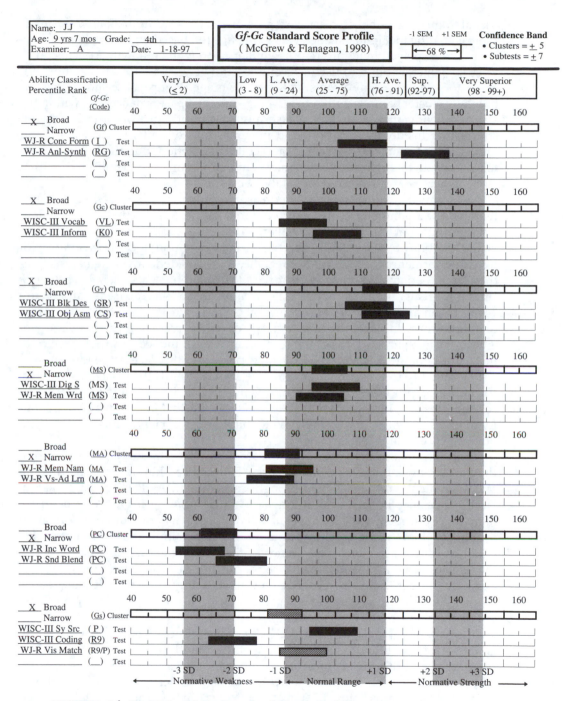

FIGURE 14–2 J.J.'s *Gf-Gc* Standard Score Profile

Visual Matching only, as discussed previously (this additional test/cluster is represented by the lighter shaded bars in the figure). Based on J.J.'s pattern of performance displayed in Figure 14–2, Examiner A drew the following conclusions.

J.J.'s general ability to use his acquired knowledge and accumulated experiences to solve everyday problems (Gc) is Average. Figure 14–2 shows that his broad Gc cluster bar falls within the Average range of performance (i.e., within the standard score range of 90–110). Specifically, his performance on Gc tasks demonstrates that his ability to absorb and integrate the concepts, ideas, values, and knowledge of mainstream United States culture (as reflected in the WISC-III) and to reason with this culturally based information is within normal limits (i.e., within ±1 *SD* where 68% of the population falls; see Table 14–1).

J.J. seems to demonstrate a greater reasoning capacity when solving problems that involve unfamiliar (or novel) information and procedures that are dependent not upon cultural knowledge but, rather, on adaptive and abstract reasoning (Gf). While his ability to reason inductively (Concept Formation) is commensurate with his Gc performance (i.e., Average), his ability to reason deductively (Analysis-Synthesis) is Superior. His performance on the latter task represents a *normative strength* since it is greater than 1 SD above the normative mean (see Table 14–1 and Figure 14–2). Taken together, J.J.'s performance on Gc and Gf tasks suggests that he ought to adapt, learn, and perform at an average or above average level in a variety of environments, particularly academic (see Chapter 2). Indeed, his performance in most academic areas is within the average range of ability (see Appendix D).

J.J.'s ability to analyze and synthesize visual stimuli (Gv) is High Average. Visualization processes may aid memory and assist with reasoning and problem solving (Kosslyn, 1985; cf. Hessler, 1993). It is possible that J.J.'s above average ability to process information visually led to increased proficiency in performance in other Gf-Gc domains (e.g., Gf).

Contrary to J.J.'s performance in the areas on Gc, Gf, and Gv, he performed in the Low Average range of ability on tasks that required him to store information and then fluently retrieve it later through association (MA-Glr). It appears that J.J. lacks proficiency in retrieving information by associating it with events, ideas, names, or concepts. While J.J. appears to have a sufficient amount of information available to him (Gc) and is able to hold information in immediate awareness long enough to either use, transform, or encode it (Gsm, Average), the manner in which the information is arranged or organized at the time of encoding for memory storage may be inefficient, thereby resulting in difficulty retrieving it later (Horn, 1989). J.J.'s difficulty with retrieving previously learned information may interfere with academic activities (e.g., reading).

Perhaps the greatest hindrance to J.J.'s academic success in the area of reading is his Very Low ability to analyze and synthesize auditory stimuli (PC-Ga). J.J.'s performance in this area represents a significant *normative weakness* (i.e., performance was between 2 and 3 SDs below the normative mean). Less than 2% of people will obtain scores below J.J.'s PC-Ga cluster score (see Table 14–1). Moreover, his performance in this area is approximately 1.5 to 2 SDs below his performance in all other Gf-Gc domains, indicating that it is significantly below his performance in all other areas.[3]

According to Horn (1989), auditory processing, which includes "phonological awareness"(Wagner, 1986), is "a facility for 'chunking' streams of sounds, keeping these chunks in awareness, and anticipating an auditory form that can develop out of such streams" (p. 84; cf. Hessler, 1993). There is a strong possibility that J.J.'s lack of proficiency in auditory processing has had a detrimental effect on the development of sound–symbol relationships. His performance on the WJ-R Letter-Word Identification (SS = 82) and Word Attack (SS = 70) tests demonstrated that his word recognition skills are not automatic. As a result, reading comprehension (i.e., WJ-R Passage Comprehension) appears to have been affected adversely (SS = 80) because the attention and cognitive resources that must be utilized to decode words detracted from the resources that were available for comprehension (Hessler, 1993). Furthermore, since it is likely that auditory processing "has both a causal and reciprocal relationship with reading" (Hessler, 1993, p. 69), diminished opportunities for success in reading reduce the capacity for developing auditory processing ability and, in turn, future success in reading (Felton & Pepper, 1995; McGuiness et al., 1995; Wagner et al., 1994).

Finally, J.J.'s speed of information processing (*Gs*), although estimated in the Average range of ability after eliminating the detrimental effects of noncognitive factors (e.g., lack of interest and motivation), may facilitate or inhibit cognitive performance depending on his level of attention, concentration, and interest in the task at hand. According to Woodcock (1993), "[s]low *Gs* ... probably would exert a limiting influence during complex task processing ... and would produce inefficiency and a longer time between initiation and completion of a complex task" (p. 88). In light of J.J.'s variability in performance on *Gs* tasks, it is possible that, at times, slow *Gs* may have inhibited his performance while engaged in *Glr* tasks. "The more quickly the relevant information can be searched for, retrieved, and applied to the problem at hand, the more likely it is that other information will not have been lost because of decay" (Vernon & Mori, 1990, p. 67). Likewise, J.J.'s lack of fluency and automaticity in the reading process may be exacerbated by slow *Gs*, as mediated by noncognitive factors (e.g., concentration, motivation).

Impressions and Recommendations.   Overall, J.J.'s pattern of cognitive performance is consistent with his level of reading skills. That is, the information on the relations between *Gf-Gc* abilities and reading achievement presented in Chapter 2 implicates *Ga* and, to a lesser extent, *Glr* (mainly Naming Facility—NA) in the reading decoding and comprehension process. Clear associations have been found between reading achievement and the ability to analyze and interpret sounds in words (e.g., McGrew et al., 1997). According to Stanovich, Cunningham, and Feeman (1984), phonological awareness predicted reading skill independent of general verbal comprehension ability (cf. Mather, 1991). Difficulty with reading nonsense words phonically, such as on the WJ-R Word Attack test, is characteristic of students with learning disabilities. For example, Kochnower, Richardson, and

---

[3] Typically, differences of 2 SDs or more are considered significant, whereas differences of 1–2 SDs suggest a trend (cf. Lezak, 1976).

DiBenedetto (1983) found that a deficiency in the ability to read phonically both regular and nonsense words interferes with reading vocabulary development and is a causal factor of reading disability. J.J.'s performance on the WJ-R tests of PC-*Ga* as well as the Letter-Word Identification and Word Attack tests suggests an auditory cognitive processing deficit that significantly limits his ability to achieve in reading at a level commensurate with same-age peers.

Based on J.J.'s performance, Examiner A recommended that he receive training in phonemic segmentation and sound blending, since this type of phonological awareness training has been shown to benefit the development of reading in elementary school children (e.g., Felton & Pepper, 1995; McGuiness et al., 1995; Wagner, Torgesen, & Rashotte, 1994; Velutino & Scanlon, 1982). Also, given J.J.'s above average performance in visual processing, Examiner A recommended that visual outlines and graphic organizers (as well as other visual learning strategies) be provided for J.J. during tasks that involve listening (Mather, 1991).

Although the link between reading and MA-*Glr* is not strong (see Chapter 2), children with learning disabilities have been reported to experience difficulty on tasks that require the linking of verbal labels with visual information (MA-*Glr*), similar to the Memory for Names and Visual-Auditory tests of the WJ-R (Mather, 1991). For example, Swanson (1986) found that on tasks that required pictures to be paired with an associated name, skilled readers performed much better than disabled readers. Likewise, Kavale (1982) found a significant correlation between reading achievement and performance on tasks that involve visual–auditory integration. It is possible that J.J.'s below average performance on associative memory tasks might contribute to his difficulty in reading. Therefore, Examiner A made the following additional recommendations for J.J.: (1) Sequence materials from simple to more complex and provide intensive review, repetition, and overlearning at each step; (2) provide frequent opportunities to practice and review, providing systematic review within a few hours of learning and reviewing previous information in each lesson; and (3) provide mnemonic aids or strategies for retention, such as the use of verbal mediation or rehearsal (e.g., saying the information to be remembered while looking at it) (cf. Mather, 1991).

The information obtained from J.J.'s *Gf-Gc* cross-battery assessment was consistent with information from J.J.'s mother, his classroom teacher, other school officials, and other members of Examiner A's staff. Together, this corroborative information provided the necessary data to develop interventions in the area of reading that would be appropriate to implement in J.J.'s regular education settings. Ongoing evaluation of the effectiveness of these interventions would provide the basis for discussing special education eligibility.

Cautions in Gf-Gc Cross-Battery Interpretation of Cluster Scores

It is important to understand the purpose of cross-battery assessment in terms of the utility of the scores yielded by this approach. The purpose of cross-battery assessment is to identify normative (and/or intra-individual) strengths and weaknesses among multiple broad *Gf-Gc* abilities that, by and large, define the structure of intelligence. Through the use of principles of cognitive psychology, the cross-battery approach attempts to measure a broader range of skills and abilities that are predictive or diagnostic of learning and problem-solving processes than those measured by a single battery (see Embretson, 1996). As a result, the cross-battery approach yields *seven Gf-Gc* cluster scores. However, because some of these scores are averages of subtests from two or more different batteries, caution must be used in the interpretation process.

Although the standard scores for individual subtests may be interpreted to reflect an individual's relative level of performance in a reference (norm) group, this is not the case for many of the cluster average scores computed in cross-battery assessments. As stated above, the *Gf-Gc* cluster average standard scores calculated and plotted for cross-battery assessments cannot be interpreted as if they represent actual cluster scores that were normed on a single norm group. Furthermore, *Gf-Gc* cluster average standard scores should not be interpreted as precise values that can be used to make critical decisions about individuals according to *formal criteria* (e.g., *Gf-Gc* clusters should not be used in formulas for identifying learning disabilities).

In addition to the problem of different norm groups (for tests that are combined from different batteries), the major reason why *Gf-Gc* cluster average standard scores should not be interpreted as actual normed standard scores is that *actual normed cluster scores are not always equal to the average of the individual standard scores that they comprise* (McGrew, 1994). For example, McGrew (1994) presents the case of an individual who obtained WISC-R subtest scaled scores of 4 (2 SDs below the mean) on all 10 individual WISC-R tests. When this performance was converted to the standard score scale with a mean of 100 and standard deviation of 15, the subtest scores were all 70. The average of these standard scores was 70. However, the obtained WISC-R Full Scale score (using the WISC-R norm tables) was 59, a score that is 11 points lower than the average of the subtest standard scores.

The failure of a normed cluster score to equal the arithmetic average of the individual tests that make up the cluster is related directly to the magnitude of the intercorrelations and number of tests in the cluster (Paik & Nebenzahl, 1987). The lower the intercorrelations between the tests that contribute to a cluster score, the more extreme will be the difference between a cluster score that is "normed" and a cluster score that is based on the arithmetic average of tests. The only time that a cluster standard score will equal the average of the individual tests that make up the cluster is when all the subtests of the cluster are correlated perfectly (see Paik & Nebenzahl, 1987, for details).

Thus, the *Gf-Gc* cross-battery clusters should be used to guide interpretation. These cluster scores, when interpreted with their corresponding confidence bands, will provide useful information about where an individual is functioning relative to a normative standard (i.e., the normal probability curve) and relative to his or her own average performance. The information yielded by the *Gf-Gc* cross-battery clusters can aid in making diagnostic and classification decisions when it is corroborated by at least two other sources of data (Kamphaus, 1993). The *clinical meaningfulness* of *Gf-Gc* cross-battery data will increase as a function of the extent to which they are integrated with other quantitative and qualitative information and interpreted within the context of relevant *Gf-Gc* theory and research.

Intra-Individual Analysis of Gf-Gc Cross-Battery Data

In contrast to inter-individual analysis, information from an *intra*-individual analysis (or ipsative analysis) is *person-relative* and reveals *within*-individual differences as determined by ipsative score comparisons. In general, ipsative interpretation is the process of generating strength and weakness hypotheses about cognitive abilities based on an analysis of an individual's subtest scores that deviate significantly (either in a positive or negative direction) from the average (mean) of all the subtest scores on the intelligence battery. Thus, the scaling of an ipsative score of a particular ability attribute is dependent upon the scores of every other ability attribute. Ipsative analysis, or the "Kaufman Psychometric Approach" (Kamphaus, et al. 1997), has been applied most frequently to the Wechsler batteries (Kaufman, 1979, 1990, 1994). This method is one of the most popular approaches to test interpretation and has been advanced as an alternative to global assessment of cognitive functioning. Ipsative analysis rests on the assumption that uncovering an individual's pattern of relative strengths and weaknesses across a variety of specific cognitive functions or ability traits provides a more valid and viable basis from which to develop remedial strategies and plan interventions than do global measures of ability (e.g., global IQ). This emphasis on within- rather than between-individual comparisons holds intuitive appeal because it is commonly believed that only through the discovery of person-relative patterns of differential abilities can interventions be tailored to meet the unique needs of an individual. Despite its popularity and intuitive appeal, ipsative analysis has significant limitations, which have led to considerable criticism (see Flanagan, Andrews, & Genshaft, 1997; McDermott, Watkins, et al., in press; McDermott & Glutting, in press; McDermott, et al., 1992).

Limitations of Ipsative Analysis

As reported in McDermott, Fantuzzo, and Glutting (1990) and summarized by Flanagan and colleagues (1997), the major weaknesses of ipsative analysis include the following:

> (1) [I]psative scores have no construct validity, (2) ipsative scores have near zero (and typically negative) intercorrelations, (3) ipsative scores are not stable over time, (4) the properties of ipsative scores (e.g., their sum equals zero) make any attempt at remediation a "no win" situation, (5) ipsative scores have poor predictive validity, and (6) ipsative scores do not carry any additional information that is not already provided by normative scores. (Flanagan et al., 1997, p. 468)

The major problem with ipsative score interpretation is that it is assumed that the ability constructs that underlie subtests are the same before and after ipsatization. However, "ipsatization automatically removes from a person's scores all common variance associated with Spearman's *g*" (McDermott, Fantuzzo, & Glutting, 1990, p. 293).

Because the common variance is most often the largest, most robust score variability for subtests of intelligence batteries, when it is removed, only residual variance is left, which includes unique variance (or invalidity) and error variance (or unreliability). Thus, the reliable variance that remains (viz., uniqueness or specificity) following ipsatization of subtests does not reflect the construct originally purported to underlie the respective subtests. This reality significantly confounds interpretation.

We agree with McDermott and Glutting's well-reasoned and empirically supported arguments against the practice of subtest-level interpretation (or ipsative analysis) for the reasons cited above (see also McGrew, Flanagan, et al., 1997). There is no question that the procedure is inherently flawed. However, although we (and many others) have recommended to our students and colleagues that they de-emphasize or eliminate subtest-level interpretation, the practice continues and will probably be commonplace for years to come. Therefore, the question that we address in this section is whether the traditional practice of ipsative analysis can be improved upon, despite its inherent flaws. Based on the theory and measurement concepts that we have presented in this text, we believe that *some* of the limitations of the ipsative approach to interpretation can be circumvented. Specifically, we believe that ipsative interpretations that are made following the analysis of *Gf-Gc* cross-battery *clusters* are better supported theoretically and psychometrically than those that are made based on subtest scores. A brief explanation for our position follows.

First, the "just say no to subtest analysis" admonition of McDermott and Glutting was based largely on research conducted with tests that represent outdated conceptualizations of intelligence (viz., the Wechslers). The Wechsler scales, for example, do not adequately measure several *Gf-Gc* abilities, including *Gf*, *Glr*, and *Ga*. As described in Chapter 1, the Wechsler batteries were not developed according to an empirically supported theory of intelligence—they are largely atheoretical. Thus, most ipsative test interpretation practice and research have not benefited from being grounded in a well-validated structure of human cognitive abilities (McGrew, Flanagan, et al., 1997).

As a result of this theory-measurement gap, we argued elsewhere that

the failure to find that specific abilities add anything to the prediction of achievement beyond that already provided by a *g* score from the Wechsler's may be a *correct* interpretation for the set of constructs measured by the Wechsler batteries, but may be a *premature generalization* to apply to all intelligence batteries . . . Before the interpretation of specific abilities on intelligence tests is declared legally dead, the *g*/specific ability research needs to be reexamined in light of current theory and with instruments or combinations of instruments that provide a more accurate and complete measurement of most *Gf-Gc* abilities. (McGrew, Flanagan, et al., 1997, p. 13).

Based on a series of studies that examined the relationship between both *g* and multiple *Gf-Gc* specific abilities (i.e., *Gf, Gc, Gv, Ga, Gs, Glr, Gsm*) and general and specific reading and math skills (Flanagan et al., 1997; McGrew, Flanagan, et al., 1997; McGrew, Vanderwood, et al., 1997), it was suggested that *both general and specific* cognitive abilities are important in understanding reading and math achievement (see Chapter 2 for a summary).[4]

Although these results need to be replicated, they demonstrate that the *g*/specific abilities issue, although complex, is not dead and deserves a reexamination within the context of *Gf-Gc* theory using sound research methodology and applied measurement (McGrew, Flanagan, et al., 1997). The *Gf-Gc* cross-battery approach presented in this text is grounded in contemporary theory and research and is based on sound measurement principles—conditions that greatly improve the practitioner's ability to draw clear and useful conclusions from the data (Kamphaus, 1993; Kamphaus et al., 1997; Keith, 1988).

Second, in addition to being theory-based, the *Gf-Gc* cross-battery approach significantly improves upon the reliability and validity of the cognitive indicators used in ipsative interpretation. For example, traditional ipsative approaches have used individual subtest scores as the "raw material" for interpretation. As a result, the data of ipsative interpretation often have been based on measures with relatively weak reliability. For example, the WISC-III Picture Completion, Coding, Picture Arrangement, Object Assembly, Comprehension, Arithmetic, Symbol Search, and Mazes subtests have *low* reliability (i.e., coefficients < .80) for 9–11 year olds (see ITDR, Chapter 9). In contrast, it is known from reliability theory that combinations of tests (i.e., composites or clusters) are more reliable than the individual tests comprised in the cluster. For example, for 12-year-olds the WJ-R *Gs* tests of Visual Matching and Cross Out have reported reliability coefficients of .87 (medium) and .77 (low), respectively (McGrew et al., 1991). The reliability coefficient of the WJ-R Processing Speed cluster that is based on the combination of these two measures of *Gs* is .90 (high) at age 12. Because cross-battery interpretation is based on cluster (not subtest) performance, the reliabilities of the estimates of cognitive abilities (i.e., the clusters) in this approach are typically higher than the reliabilities corresponding to the estimates of cognitive abilities (i.e., the subtests) in the traditional approach.

Third, when a set of subtests (e.g., all Wechsler Verbal tests) is ipsatized, the common variance (i.e., the variance shared by all the verbal tests) or *g* is removed. As stated above, the reliable variance that is left in each subtest (i.e., specificity) is then interpreted. Thus, ipsative interpretation is based typically on the *smallest* portion of the test's reliable variance. Conversely, when the *Gf-Gc* cross-battery clusters are ipsatized, the variance that is common to all clusters (i.e., *Gf, Gc, Gv, Ga*, etc.) is removed. However, the variance that is shared by the two subtests that combine to yield the respective clusters remains. Therefore, when clusters that rep-

---

[4] "Specific" abilities here are the *broad* (stratum II) *Gf-Gc* constructs of *Gf, Gc, Gv*, etc., which were represented in these studies by two or more strong test indicators. The term "specific" rather than "broad" is used in these studies to maintain consistency with the terminology of traditional *g*/specific ability research.

resent stratum II abilities are ipsatized (as opposed to subtests that represent stratum I abilities), proportionally more reliable variance remains. Cluster-level analysis shifts the focus of interpretation away from individual subtests. We believe that intra-individual interpretations of cognitive abilities that are operationally defined by the reliable common variance shared by at least two strong indicators of each broad *Gf-Gc* ability represent a more promising practice than individual subtest analysis.

Finally, the *Gf-Gc* cross-battery clusters are more valid than the individual subtests used in traditional ipsative interpretation. This is because they are composed of two strong and qualitatively different indicators of the respective *Gf-Gc* abilities. The cross-battery approach was designed to improve upon the validity of the *Gf-Gc* constructs that are measured in any given assessment through the reduction of *construct-irrelevant variance* and better *construct representation* (following the first and second guiding principles of the cross-battery approach, respectively) (see Chapter 13). Moreover, a large body of research on the relations between the *Gf-Gc* constructs (which are represented by the *Gf-Gc* cross-battery clusters) and numerous outcome criteria (see Chapter 2) provides a network of validity evidence that enriches and informs the interpretive process. The corresponding validity evidence available to support subtest-level interpretation does not approach that which is available to support *Gf-Gc* cluster-level interpretation.

In sum, the traditional approach to ipsative interpretation of intelligence batteries (viz., the Wechslers) has been found (correctly, we believe) to be seriously flawed. The traditional subtest-based ipsative approach has been limited by the lack of a comprehensive and empirically supported theoretical framework to guide interpretation and a reliance on individual subtests, many of which have low reliability and inadequate validity support. The *Gf-Gc* cross-battery ipsative approach (described briefly below) overcomes some of the fundamental flaws of the traditional method of intra-cognitive interpretation through the use of more reliable and valid indicators of cognitive ability constructs that are grounded in an empirically supported model of the structure of intelligence (i.e., *Gf-Gc* theory).

Notwithstanding, because a high degree of variation across tasks and item types is typical in the normal population, intra-individual differences alone are not sufficient grounds for making diagnostic, classification, or treatment decisions (Reschly & Grimes, 1995). When significant intra-individual differences are found using *Gf-Gc* cross-battery data, they should be corroborated by other sources of data. *In the absence of supporting evidence*, intra-individual differences, although statistically significant, cannot be considered unusual, unique, or clinically meaningful.

Guidelines for Conducting an Intra-Individual Analysis with Gf-Gc Cross-Battery Data

The brief set of steps that follow will be presented using J.J.'s *Gf-Gc* cluster scores. The information derived from following these steps is presented in Table 14–2. The first step in conducting an intra-individual analysis is to sum the individual's *Gf-Gc* cluster averages and divide by the total number of averages to obtain the individual's average level of performance across all seven *Gf-Gc* clusters (i.e., the *overall Gf-Gc* cluster average, or the average of the averages). Examiner A obtained an overall *Gf-Gc* cluster average of 94 by summing J.J.'s *Gf-Gc* cluster standard score averages (sum = 658), reported in column 2 of Table 14–2, and dividing by the total number of cluster averages (i.e., 7). J.J.'s overall *Gf-Gc* cluster average of 94 (658/7 = 94) is reported in column 3 of Table 14–2.

Step 2 requires that the examiner obtain *difference scores* by subtracting the overall *Gf-Gc* cluster average (column 3 in Table 14–2) from the individual *Gf-Gc* cluster averages (located in column 2). J.J.'s difference scores are reported in column four of Table 14–2. Note that either a "+" or "–" sign precedes the values reported in column 4 to indicate either a positive or negative difference, respectively, between the *Gf-Gc* individual cluster scores and the overall cluster score. The third step is to determine whether the absolute value of any of the difference scores is of sufficient magnitude to suggest that the respective *Gf-Gc* ability be considered a significant (relatively speaking) intra-individual strength or weakness for the examinee.

Since it is contrary to our understanding of human behavior to expect an individual's abilities to be developed uniformly, a criterion must be specified to identify those *Gf-Gc* clusters that vary *significantly* from the individual's overall *Gf-Gc* cluster average. A criterion of ±15 was chosen to represent significant intra-individual strengths and weaknesses in *Gf-Gc* cross-battery assessments because it is similar to the intra-individual analysis procedures advocated for other intelligence batteries. For example, Wechsler subtest scores that differ by 1 standard deviation or more (i.e., ≥ ±3, based on a subtest scaled score scale having a mean of 10 and a standard deviation of 3) from the average (mean) subtest scaled score are considered as possible strengths and weaknesses (Kaufman, 1979, 1990). The ±15 standard score criterion is of similar magnitude to this Wechsler-based rule of thumb. That is, all standard scores in *Gf-Gc* cross-battery assessments are converted to a scale having a mean of 100 and a standard deviation of 15. Thus, any individual

TABLE 14–2   Intra-Individual Analysis Results of J. J.'s *Gf-Gc* **Cross-Battery Evaluation**

Gf-Gc Cluster	Cluster Standard Score Average	Overall *Gf-Gc* Cluster Average	Difference Score	Strength or Weakness
Gf	117	94	+23	Strength
Gc	95	94	+1	
Gv	113	94	+19	Strength
MS-*Gsm*	98	94	+4	
MA-*Glr*	84	94	–10	
PC-*Ga*	66	94	–28	Weakness
Gs	85	94	–9	

Note: The overall *Gf-Gc* cluster average is calculated by adding the seven individual cluster averages together (sum = 658) and dividing by the total number of cluster averages (i.e., 7). Thus, 658/7 = 94. Strength = difference score of ≥ +15. Weakness = difference score of ≥ –15.

Gf-Gc cluster standard score averages that differ from the overall standard score average by ±15 (i.e., ≥ 1 standard deviation above or below the mean) can be considered as *possible* intra-individual strengths or weaknesses, respectively.

Examiner A reviewed the absolute value of J.J.'s difference scores located in column 4 of Table 14–2. He found that three difference scores exceeded the criterion value of 15, namely those associated with *Gf*, *Gv*, and PC-*Ga*. The difference scores for *Gf* and *Gv* were positive; therefore, they were identified as significant intra-cognitive *strengths* for J.J. (see column 5 of Table 14–2). Conversely, the difference score for PC-*Ga* was negative and therefore was recorded in column 5 as a significant *weakness*.

Once significant intra-individual cognitive strengths and weaknesses have been identified, the findings must be translated into clinically meaningful descriptions of cognitive functioning (see Kaufman, 1994; Kamphaus, 1993; McGrew, 1994; Sattler, 1988, for a discussion). The goal of intra-individual analysis is to identify those tasks that the individual is most adept at handling (reasoning and visual processing tasks in the case of J.J.) and use them to aid in planning instructional programs (e.g., in reading) that incorporate those strengths. It is important to keep in mind that patterns of intra-individual strengths and weaknesses are of limited utility diagnostically. That is, there is little research evidence to support making diagnostic decisions from profile analysis (Glutting, McDermott, & Konold, 1997; Kamphaus, 1993; Kamphaus et al., 1997; McDermott, et al., 1992; Watkins & Kush, 1994).

Intra-individual analysis may be used as a supplement to inter-individual analysis with the common goal being to uncover clues about an individual's abilities that may clarify the functional nature of learning problems and lead to more appropriate recommendations for clinical treatment, educational remediation, or vocational placement. In the case of J.J., the information provided by the intra-individual analysis did not uncover any additional clues not already discovered by the inter-individual analysis (discussed previously).

Until empirical evidence is available to support the practice of intra-individual analysis, we recommend that it be de-emphasized in the interpretive process or that it be used in conjunction with inter-individual analysis to aid in understanding the unique learning and problem-solving processes of the individual. Since there is no agreed-upon litmus test for diagnosing learning problems, some combination of resourcefulness, clinical experience, current theoretical and empirical research (chapters 1 and 2), and knowledge of quantitative and qualitative characteristics of a great many cognitive ability tests (ITDR) must guide the practitioner through the interpretation of an individual's performance on *Gf-Gc* cross-battery assessments.

Addressing Referral Concerns: An Example of Selective Cross-Battery Assessment

"A prerequisite for effective assessment is the ability to plan assessment strategies and to choose tests to meet specific needs" (Sattler, 1988, p. 7). *Gf-Gc* cross-battery assessments, like traditional assessments, should be designed to address specific referral concerns. Responding to *every* referral with a "knee-jerk" canned intelligence battery or a "complete" *Gf-Gc* cross-battery assessment (as described in Chapter 13) is inconsistent with "best practices" in intellectual assessment. Best practices "require careful judgments about *when* intellectual assessment instruments are used, *how* they are used, the selection, administration, and interpretation of tests, and efforts to protect children and youth from misuses and misconceptions" (Reschly & Grimes, 1990). A *selective Gf-Gc* cross-battery approach, which we believe to be consistent with best practices, is outlined briefly below.

Selective cross-battery assessment is the process of using cross-battery guidelines and principles to tailor a unique *Gf-Gc*–organized assessment battery to address the specific concerns or questions of a referral. The goal of the following section is not to anticipate and describe every possible selective cross-battery scenario in response to the myriad of possible referral concerns. Rather, a "mode of thinking" or general philosophy of designing cross-battery assessments is presented in terms of the case study of J.J. Based on the reason for referral and knowledge of the relations between *Gf-Gc* abilities and achievement or outcome criteria, practitioners should be able to tailor cross-battery assessments that are time-efficient and, more importantly, likely to provide information that will result in more focused and referral-relevant recommendations.

Selective Cross-Battery Assessment: The Case of J.J.

As presented in Chapter 13, J.J. was referred by his mother due to reported difficulty with reading, particularly comprehension. Although he is reported to be able to decode words, these skills are not automatic and his reading lacks fluency. (See Chapter 13 for additional background information.) As previously described, Examiner A chose to conduct a "complete" or comprehensive *Gf-Gc* cross-battery assessment. That is, J.J.'s cross-battery assessment was designed to provide for measurement in seven broad *Gf-Gc* domains. Given that J.J. had never been evaluated previously for his reading difficulties, the decision to conduct a complete cross-battery assessment was appropriate. However, Examiner A could have conducted a selective cross-battery approach designed to measure mainly those abilities that are closely associated with the academic skill in which J.J. was reported to demonstrate a weakness (i.e., reading). If Examiner A was to begin anew with an understanding of the purpose and benefits of *Gf-Gc* selective cross-battery assessment, the following decisions with respect to choosing measures for inclusion in J.J.'s assessment battery might have ensued.

The outcome-criterion evidence presented in Chapter 2 should serve as the starting point for the design of school achievement–related (viz., reading and mathematics) *Gf-Gc* cross-battery assessments. If Examiner A had reviewed the outcome-criterion evidence summarized in Chapter 2, he would have discovered that all *Gf-Gc* abilities "are not created equal" in all contexts. For example, in the reading research reviewed, *Gv* abilities displayed no significant relation with reading achievement. In contrast, *Ga* abilities were found to be particularly important for the development of reading skills during the elementary school years. These findings suggest that *Ga* abilities should be featured prominently in all reading referrals during the early school years. In contrast, the largely negative *Gv* findings raise questions about the value of spending significant time (often as much as half of an intelligence battery like the Wechsler batteries) assessing *Gv* abilities for most reading-related referrals. A review of the information in Chapter 2 would have directed Examiner A to include measures of *Ga* in J.J.'s assessment and, most likely, not to include measures of *Gv*.

To facilitate the design of selective achievement-related cross-battery assessments, the main findings presented for reading and mathematics achievement in Chapter 2 are summarized in Table 14–3. Table 14–3, together with the more detailed discussion in Chapter 2, can be used to identify *Gf-Gc* abilities that should receive consideration in the design of selective cross-battery assessments.

If Examiner A had consulted Table 14–3, he probably would have (or should have) decided to include measures of *Gc*, *Ga*, and *Gs* abilities in J.J.'s assessment. Also the mention of J.J.'s nonfluent reading and problems in the automatic decoding of words would have directed Examiner A to the domains of *Ga* and *Gs*. Additionally, although not a key ability for early reading skill development, the mention of reading comprehension problems for J.J. would have suggested the need to measure *Gf* abilities. The abilities of *Gc*, *Ga*, *Gs*, and *Gf*, then, would be the most likely *minimum* cross-battery assessment for J.J. This minimum battery would have successfully identified J.J.'s most significant and potentially diagnostically important *Ga* weakness (see prior interpretation in this chapter).

In the absence of concerns about poor functioning on tasks that require the use of visual processing abilities (e.g., artwork, direction finding, performance on constructional tasks), *Gv* tests could have been eliminated from J.J.'s assessment. The decision to not measure *Gv* abilities would have resulted in a savings of time, time that might have been reallocated to more in-depth assessment in other domains more closely associated with reading achievement.

The decision of whether to include measures of *Gsm* and/or *Glr* abilities in J.J.'s assessment illustrates the case-by-case nature of selective cross-battery design. As presented in Chapter 2 and Table 14–3, Memory Span (MS-*Gsm*) appears to be related to reading. However, an astute clinician could have conducted a detailed interview with J.J.'s teacher and mother to inquire about memory span performance in his natural environment. That is, if J.J. was reported to experience problems following oral directions, particularly when they are long and require the retention of a sequence of concepts, this would suggest that assessment of *Gsm* abilities is warranted. Conversely, if J.J. was reported to have little difficulty with such real-world memory span activities, then Examiner A could have decided not to include measures of *Gsm* in the assessment. Again, this decision could result in a more time-efficient and selectively focused assessment.

In the case of *Glr*, a review of Table 14–3 suggests that measures of Naming Facility (NA) should have been included in J.J.'s assessment (either in addition to or in lieu of Associative Memory [MA] tests) due to their importance in reading during the elementary school years. However, a review of the *Glr* cross-battery worksheet (Appendix A) reveals that no measures of naming facility are present in any of the major intelligence batteries. Furthermore, the reading research summarized in Table 14–3 does not suggest strongly the need to administer measures of Associative Memory (MA), which are included on a small number of intelligence batteries. So, what could Examiner A have done?

TABLE 14–3   Summary of Significant Relations Between *Gf-Gc* Abilities and Reading and Mathematics Achievement

Gf-Gc Ability	Reading Achievement	Mathematics Achievement
Gf	Inductive (I) and general sequential (RG) reasoning abilities play a moderate role in reading comprehension.	**Inductive (I) and general sequential (RG) reasoning abilities are consistently very important at all ages.**
Gc	**Language development (LD), lexical knowledge (VL), and listening ability (LS) are important at all ages. These abilities become increasingly more important with age.**	**Language development (LD), lexical knowledge (VL), and listening ability (LS) are important at all ages. These abilities become increasingly more important with age.**
Gsm	Memory span (MS) is important especially when evaluated **within the context of working memory.**	Memory span (MS) is important especially when evaluated **within the context of working memory.**
Gv		May be important primarily for higher-level or advanced mathematics (e.g., geometry, calculus).
Ga	**Phonetic coding (PC) or "phonological awareness/processing" is very important during the elementary school years.**	
Glr	**Naming facility (NA) or "rapid automatic naming" is very important during the elementary school years.** Associative memory (MA) abilities may be somewhat important at select ages (e.g., age 6).	
Gs	**Perceptual speed (P) abilities are important during all school years, particularly the elementary school years.**	**Perceptual speed (P) abilities are important during all school years, particularly the elementary school years.**

Note: This table represents a summary of research presented in Chapter 2. The absence of comments for a particular *Gf-Gc* ability and achievement area (e.g., *Ga* and mathematics) indicates that the research reviewed either did not report any significant relations between the respective *Gf-Gc* ability and the achievement area or, if significant findings were reported, they were weak and were for only a limited number of studies. Comments in bold represent the *Gf-Gc* abilities that showed the strongest and most consistent relations with the respective achievement domain.

First, although Associative Memory (MA) is not consistently and significantly related to reading, it still may have made sense to include a measure of MA in J.J.'s selective cross-battery assessment, particularly one that employs a rebus reading testing format. For example, by consulting the *Glr* cross-battery worksheet (Appendix A) and the test descriptions in the ITDR for the associative memory tests listed on this worksheet, Examiner A could have decided to administer the WJ-R Visual-Auditory Learning Test, a task that simulates the learning-to-read process. The rationale for administering this test would be two-fold. First, the inclusion of at least one MA-*Glr* indicator would serve as a kind of "*Glr* thermometer." That is, the WJ-R Visual-Auditory Learning test would sample at least one aspect of *Glr*. If the resultant score was very low, this would indicate the need for further assessment (or another iteration) in the domain of *Glr*, a process that could be guided by consulting the *Glr* worksheet (Figure 13–7) for additional tests. Second, given that J.J. was described as experiencing problems with reading fluency and basic reading decoding, the direct observation of J.J. on a task that simulates the beginning reading process might provide rich clinical insights into his problems with reading (see McGrew, 1986, 1994, for a discussion of the clinical information that may be derived from such a test).

Another *Glr* option that Examiner A could have pursued would have been to seek out supplemental, special purpose measures of naming facility or rapid automatic naming (see Chapter 12). A review of Table 12–1 reveals that the CAS includes a test (i.e., Expressive Attention) that may measure this ability. No other tests of this ability are listed. However, new tests are always forthcoming. During the preparation of this book, standardization of the *Comprehensive Test of Phonological Processes* (Wagner & Torgesen, in press) was underway. In the data collection version of this battery, four different rapid naming tests were included. Although neither of these two tests was available at the time of J.J.'s referral, this analysis demonstrates how the ITDR pages and Chapter 12 can be used to design *Gf-Gc* cross-battery assessments tailored to individual referrals.

Selective Cross-Battery Assessment: General Guidelines

As can be seen from the brief discussion of a possible selective cross-battery assessment for J.J., each individual referral, by definition, is concerned with the unique circumstances of people with individual needs and concerns. In essence, the decision-making process that ensues during the design and implementation of *Gf-Gc* selective cross-battery assessments is analogous to Kamphaus's (1993) "iterative process" of test interpretation. According to Kamphaus, "[t]est interpretation is something like detective work, where the clinician follows clues and develops leads until eventually a clear picture of a crime emerges" (p. 166). In *Gf-Gc* selective cross-battery assessments, after initial design decisions are made, the results of the assessment, as well as the practitioner's careful observation of the examinee during the assessment, will provide additional information that will, in turn, result in further assessment (e.g., more in-depth *Ga* assessment for J.J.). This iterative process will continue until findings are substantiated with corroborating evidence and a complete understanding of the individual's cognitive strengths and/or weaknesses emerges.

Since an iterative process captures best the "mode of thinking" that underlies *Gf-Gc* selective cross-battery assessments, it is difficult to operationalize a set of formalized steps or procedures for designing these assessments. Therefore, the following guidelines are offered to aid practitioners in developing and implementing selective cross-battery assessments. First, selective cross-battery assessments should adhere to the same principles that guided the more complete *Gf-Gc* cross-battery assessment approach that was described in Chapter 13.

Second, the research literature on the relations between *Gf-Gc* abilities and achievement and/or other outcome-criterion variables should play a significant role in the selection of the *Gf-Gc* domains that will be assessed initially. Selective cross-battery assessments are only as good as the practitioner who designs and conducts them. A working knowledge of *Gf-Gc* achievement and outcome-criterion research and important areas of psychology (e.g., cognition, learning, etc.), together with intimate familiarity with the characteristics of assessment tools (the ITDR), is necessary to design appropriate *Gf-Gc* cross-battery assessments.

Third, selective cross-battery assessment should be conceived of as an iterative decision-making and assessment process. Initial assessments produce information that, in turn, may result in decisions to assess further as well as refine the assessment process. Whenever possible, practitioners should make maximum use of other sources of information (e.g., cumulative educational records, case histories, prior assessment results, parent and teacher comments) to aid in determining which *Gf-Gc* abilities should be assessed, as well as which abilities may not need to be assessed.

Fourth, selective cross-battery assessments should not be pursued simply to save the practitioner time. Rather, the time saved by either not assessing or by reducing the assessment coverage in a given *Gf-Gc* domain can be reallocated to more focused intellectual assessment activities (e.g., more in-depth assessment of narrow *Gf-Gc* abilities in a given domain) or to other types of assessment (e.g., classroom observation, criterion-referenced) in other important domains that are relevant to the referral (e.g., self-concept). In short, *selective cross-battery assessments should have a purpose*. The nature of the specific referral concerns should drive the design of the assessment. Tests to be included should be selected in direct proportion to their potential relevance to the presenting referral concerns.

In conclusion, the iterative process in intellectual assessment and interpretation described by Kamphaus (1993) and inherent in the *Gf-Gc* cross-battery approach is useful when unexpected findings emerge. The ITDR section of this book provides an arsenal of cognitive ability tests from which to choose measures for subsequent iterations in the assessment process. Since all cognitive ability tests included in the ITDR were classified (empirically and/or logically) according to *Gf-Gc* theory, practitioners have the added benefit of grounding their selective assessments and interpretations within the context of current theory and research.

Selective Cross-Battery Assessments: Guidelines for Culturally and Linguistically Diverse Populations

One of the most difficult tasks facing psychologists today is assessment of the cognitive capabilities of individuals from culturally and linguistically diverse populations. Failure to accurately distinguish normal, culturally based variation in behavior, first (L1) and second (L2) language acquisition, acculturation, and cognitive development from true disabilities has led to overrepresentation of individuals from diverse populations in special education and other remedial programs (Cervantes, 1988). Because such placement has been demonstrated to have significant negative effects on children's learning, social, and psychological development (Dunn, 1968; Hobbs, 1975; Jones, 1972), it is imperative that psychologists incorporate systematic assessment methods appropriate for culturally and linguistically diverse populations.

For the purposes of this chapter, the phrase *culturally diverse* is used to describe individuals whose personal and familial cultural experiences and knowledge differ from mainstream U.S. culture (Flanagan & Halsell Miranda, 1995). The phrase *linguistically diverse* is defined here as representing the continuum of individuals who are non–native English speakers including those who are monolingual speakers of a language other than English with varying levels of proficiency, dual-language learners with varying levels of L1 and L2 proficiency (often referred to as Limited English Proficient [LEP]), and those who are proficient in both L1 and L2 (true bilinguals). According to the U.S. Department of Education, *LEP* refers to individuals who (1) were born in a country other than the United States and whose native language is not English, or (2) originated from environments in which English is not the dominant language spoken. Generally speaking, individuals who are described as LEP tend to be dominant (more fluent or comfortable) in their native language; however, they may not be highly proficient in that language. Proficiency in L1 does not guarantee proficiency in L2, and these individuals tend to be considerably less proficient in English. Individuals who develop levels of proficiency in two languages may be described as *bilingual*, or dual-language learners, though again, their proficiency in either language may be high, low, or any combination thereof. It is important to appreciate that, by itself, the term *bilingual* does not necessarily imply any particular level of proficiency, comfort, or skill with the languages spoken. For a more detailed description of LEP and bilingual populations, see Lopez (1997) and Valdés and Figueroa (1994).

The assessment of culturally and linguistically diverse students is a concern, particularly within the field of school psychology, because many psychologists are ill-prepared to meet the unique needs of the growing number of students from diverse backgrounds who are entering the public school systems. For example, in the 1980s the number of LEP students increased two and a half times faster than regular school enrollment (McLeod, 1994; cf. Ochoa et al., 1996). According to Lopez (1997), "the nation's linguistic diversity is reflected in our school systems where educators often work with significant numbers of children from LEP and bilingual backgrounds. In New York City, for example, there are individual schools in which more than 50 languages and dialects are spoken by the student population" (p. 503).

Future projections reinforce the need for psychologists to be competent in serving diverse populations. It is estimated that by the year 2000, 38% of the U.S. population under the age of 18 will be non-Anglo whites and nonwhites (Research and Policy Committee of the Committee for Economic Development, 1987), and by the year 2030 the number of Latino children, African American children, and children of other races will increase by 5.5, 2.6, and 1.5 million, respectively, while the number of white, non-Latino children will decrease by 6.2 million from the 1985 figure (Children's Defense Fund, 1989) (cf. Flanagan & Halsell Miranda, 1995). As a result of the increasing linguistic and cultural diversity of the United States, the number of multilingual and multicultural individuals in need of services is on the rise; yet the number of appropriately trained (and sufficiently bilingual) psychologists available to work with these individuals does not appear to have risen proportionately (see Flanagan & Halsell Miranda, 1995). In the absence of prior training in bilingual, cross-cultural assessment, in general, and prior experience in working with diverse populations, in particular, many psychologists will increasingly find themselves confronted with the challenge of assessing individuals whose cultural and linguistic backgrounds differ markedly from their own and from the mainstream culture and language of the United States.

In recognition of the growing diversity of the population of the United States, the American Psychological Association (APA) called for psychologists to acknowledge the influences of language and culture on behavior and to consider those factors when working with diverse groups in its *Guidelines for Providers of Psychological Services to Ethnic, Linguistic, and Culturally Diverse Populations* (1990). These guidelines also encouraged psychologists to consider the validity of the methods and procedures used to assess minority groups and to make interpretations of resultant psychological data within the context of the linguistic and cultural characteristics of the individual (cf. Lopez, 1997). However, it appears that the degree of knowledge and level of skill necessary to accomplish these ideals are not automatically or routinely acquired through formal education in pre-service psychology training programs (Cook-Morales, Ortiz, & Ortiz, 1994). This situation is compounded by the fact that few national or state standards exist that define basic competencies for a "bilingual" psychologist. Mere possession of the capacity to communicate in an individual's native language does not ensure appropriate, nondiscriminatory assessment of that individual. Traditional assessment practices and all their inherent biases can be quite easily replicated in any number of languages. The lack of trained psychologists and shortage of qualified bilingual psychologists leads directly to a variety of difficulties in the assessment process. According to Ysseldyke (1979), these problem areas include referral, instrument selection, instrument administration, instrument interpretation, and decision making. It is the potential bias created by instrument selection that is the primary focus of this section.

Well-intentioned but untrained and inexperienced psychologists have often adopted the use of assessment batteries that may be inappropriate or of limited utility in understanding the intellectual functioning of culturally and linguistically diverse individuals (Flanagan & Halsell Miranda, 1995; Lopez, 1997; Ochoa, Powell, & Robles-Pina, 1996). For example, the most commonly used instruments with culturally and linguistically diverse students include a Wechsler test (administered in English), the Bender, Draw A Person, and Leiter (see Ochoa, Powell, & Robles-Pina, 1996). This battery of tests is problematic for use with these populations for a variety of reasons (e.g., inadequate psychometric properties, inappropriate norms and comparison groups, unidimensional assessments, linguistic and cultural confounds, etc.) (see Lopez, 1997; McCallum & Bracken, 1997, for a discussion). Although psychologists typically use a combination of tests to assess linguistically and culturally diverse populations because "...no single instrument is a panacea for the complex problem of conducting cognitive assessment...fairly and equitably" in these groups (Holtzman & Wilkinson, 1991, p. 251; cf. Ochoa, Powell, & Robles-Pina, 1996), their selection of instruments is typically unsystematic—reflecting a lack of understanding of crucial issues in bilingual, cross-cultural assessment. While we recognize that substantive integration of the principles of *Gf-Gc* cross-battery assessment into a comprehensive bilingual, cross-cultural, nondiscriminatory assessment framework is well beyond the scope and purpose of this chapter, nevertheless, we believe we can offer general guidelines that complement such practices and can assist in identifying more culturally and linguistically fair tests of intelligence and cognitive ability. Accordingly, what follows is a discussion of the major cultural and linguistic factors that influence the selection of measures for use with diverse populations within the context of *Gf-Gc* theory and cross-battery assessment.

Considering Cultural and Linguistic Influences on Cognitive Ability Test Performance

As much as practitioners, trainers, and scholars subscribe to the philosophy that well-standardized and psychometrically sound instruments can be an important and valuable component of assessment, the changing demographics of the United States mandate that the influences of cultural and linguistic factors on test performance be considered as equally important (Dana, 1993). Table 14–4 provides a matrix of cognitive ability tests organized according to three important test characteristics: (1) stratum I and stratum II abilities measured according to *Gf-Gc* theory; (2) degree of cultural content; and (3) degree of linguistic demands. Each of these test characteristics represents a broad facet of bilingual, cross-cultural assessment. Taken together, they provide information about specific cognitive ability tests that may aid in compiling a selective set of measures that may be more valid for use with culturally and linguistically diverse populations than the typical psychoeducational battery. Following is a brief description of the characteristics of cognitive ability tests that are included in Table 14–4.

TABLE 14–4   Degree of Cultural Content and Linguistic Demand on Cognitive Ability Tests

Battery	Age	Subtest	Gf-Gc Ability
		Cultural Content LOW/Linguistic Demand LOW	
CTONI	6–18	Geometric Sequences	*Gf* (I, RG)
LEITER-R	5–18+	Design Analogies	*Gf* (I)
LEITER-R	2–18+	Repeated Patterns	*Gf* (I)
LEITER-R	2–18+	Sequential Order	*Gf* (I)
LEITER-R	11–18+	Paper Folding	*Gv* (VZ)
LEITER-R	11–18+	Figure Rotation	*Gv* (VZ, SR)
UNIT	5–17	**CUBE DESIGN**	*Gf* (RG)
UNIT	5–17	**Mazes**	*Gv* (SS)
DAS	6–17	**MATRICES**	*Gf* (I)
DAS	6–17	**SEQUENTIAL & QUANTITATIVE REASONING**	*Gf* (I, RG)
DTLA-3	6–17	**Symbolic Relations**	*Gf* (I)
MAT	5–17	Matrix Analogies Test	*Gf* (I, RG)
Raven's	5–18+	Raven's Progressive Matrices	*Gf* (I)
TONI-3	5–17	Test of Nonverbal Intelligence—Third Edition	*Gf* (I)
DAS	3–17	Pattern Construction	*Gv* (SR)
DAS	2–3	Block Building	*Gv* (VZ)
DAS	4–5	Matching Letter-Like Forms	*Gv* (VZ)
DAS	6–17	**RECALL OF DESIGNS**	*Gv* (MV)
K-ABC	4–12	**TRIANGLES**	*Gv* (VZ, SR)
KAIT	11–85+	**MEMORY FOR BLOCK DESIGNS**	*Gv* (MV)
SB:IV	2–24	**PATTERN ANALYSIS**	*Gv* (VZ)
WPPSI-R	3–7	Geometric Design	*Gv* (VZ, P2)
WECHSLERS	3–74	**BLOCK DESIGN**	*Gv* (SR)
CAS	5–17	Figure Memory	*Gv* (CF, MV)
DTLA-3	6–17	Design Sequences	*Gv* (MV)
DTLA-3	6–17	Design Reproduction	*Gv* (MV)
TOMAL	5–19	Facial Memory	*Gv* (MV)
TOMAL	5–19	Abstract Visual Memory	*Gv* (MV)
TOMAL	5–19	Manual Imitation	*Gv* (MV)
TOMAL	5–19	Delayed Recall of Visual Selective Reminding	*Gv* (MV)
WMS-R	16–74	Visual Paired Associates II	*Glr* (MA)
		Cultural Content LOW/Linguistic Demand MODERATE	
CAS	5–17	Matching Numbers	*Gs* (P, R9)
CAS	5–17	Planned Codes	*Gs* (R9)
CAS	5–17	Number Detection	*Gs* (R7, R9)
DAS	3–17	Recall of Digits	*Gsm* (MS)
K-ABC	2–12	**NUMBER RECALL**	*Gsm* (MS)
SB:IV	7–24	**MEMORY FOR DIGITS**	*Gsm* (MS)
WAIS-III	16–89	**DIGIT SPAN**	*Gsm* (MS)
WISC-III	6–16	**DIGIT SPAN**	*Gsm* (MS)
K-SNAP	11–85	Number Recall	*Gsm* (MS)
LAMB	20–60	Digit Span	*Gsm* (MS)

TABLE 14–4 *Continued*

Battery	Age	Subtest	Gf-Gc Ability
TOMAL	5–19	Digits Forward	Gsm (MS)

Cultural Content LOW/Linguistic Demand MODERATE *Continued*

Battery	Age	Subtest	Gf-Gc Ability
TOMAL	5–19	Letters Forward	Gsm (MS)
WMS-R	16–74	Digit Span	Gsm (MS)
WRAML	5–17	Number/Letter Memory	Gsm (MS)
WJ-R	2–85+	**MEMORY FOR NAMES**	Glr (MA)
WJ-R	4–85+	**DELAYED RECALL—MEMORY FOR NAMES**	Glr (MA)
WRAML	5–17	Sound Symbol	Glr (MA)
DAS	6–17	Speed of Information Processing	Gs (R7)
DTLA-3	6–17	Word Sequences	Gsm (MS)
TOMAL	5–19	Word Selective Reminding	Glr (M6)
TOMAL	5–19	Delayed Recall of Word Selective Reminding	Glr (M6)
SB:IV	7–24	**MATRICES**	Gf (I)
SB:IV	2–24	**Bead Memory**	Gv (MV)
WISC-III	6–16	Mazes	Gv (SS)
WPPSI-R	3–7	**Mazes**	Gv (SS)
LAMB	20–60	Simple Figure	Gv (MV)
LAMB	20–60	Complex Figure	Gv (MV)
WMS-R	16–74	Figural Memory	Gv (MV)
WMS-R	16–74	Visual Reproduction I	Gv (MV)
WRAML	5–17	Design Memory	Gv (MV)
WMS-R	16–74	Visual Paired Associates I	Glr (MA)
WISC-III	6–16	Symbol Search	Gs (P, R9)
WAIS-III	16–89	**DIGIT SYMBOL—CODING**	Gs (R9)
WISC-III	6–16	**CODING**	Gs (R9)
WJ-R	4–85+	**VISUAL MATCHING**	Gs (P, R9)
WJ-R	4–85+	**CROSS OUT**	Gs (P)

Cultural Content LOW/Linguistic Demand HIGH

Battery	Age	Subtest	Gf-Gc Ability
SB:IV	7–24	Number Series	Gf (RQ)
WJ-R	4–85+	**CONCEPT FORMATION**	Gf (I)
WJ-R	4–85+	**ANALYSIS SYNTHESIS**	Gf (RG)
LAMB	20–60	Supraspan Digit	Gsm (MS)

Cultural Content MODERATE /Linguistic Demand LOW

Battery	Age	Subtest	Gf-Gc Ability
LEITER-R	6–18+	Visual Coding	Gf (RG)
LEITER-R	2–10	Matching	Gv (VZ)
LEITER-R	2–18+	Attention Sustained	Gs (P, R9)
DAS	2–5	Picture Similarities	Gf (I)
CAS	5–17	Geometric Sequences	Gf (I)
DAS	3–7	Recognition of Pictures	Gv (MV)
K-ABC	2–4	Face Recognition	Gv (MV)
SB:IV	7–89	**Memory for Objects**	Gv (MV)
WECHSLERS	3–74	**OBJECT ASSEMBLY**	Gv (CS)
WJ-R	4–85+	**Picture Recognition**	Gv (MV)

Continued

TABLE 14–4   *Continued*

Battery	Age	Subtest	*Gf-Gc* Ability
K-ABC	2–4	**WORD ORDER**	*Gsm* (MS)
CAS	5–17	Receptive Attention	*Gs* (P, R4)
K-ABC	2–4	Magic Window	*Gv* (PI)
K-ABC	2–12	**Gestalt Closure**	*Gv* (CS)
WJ-R	2–85+	**Visual Closure**	*Gv* (CS)
DAS	4–17	Recall of Objects	*Glr* (M6)
TOMAL	5–19	Paired Recall	*Glr* (MA)

		Cultural Content MODERATE/Linguistic Demand MODERATE	
CAS	5–17	Word Series	*Gsm* (MS)
KAIT	11–85+	**REBUS LEARNING**	*Glr* (MA)
KAIT	11–85+	**REBUS DELAYED RECALL**	*Glr* (MA)
WJ-R	4–85+	**VISUAL-AUDITORY LEARNING**	*Glr* (MA)
WJ-R	4–85+	**Delayed Recall—Visual Auditory Learning**	*Glr* (MA)
KAIT	11–85+	**MYSTERY CODES**	*Gf* (I)
K-SNAP	11–85	Four-letter Words	*Gf* (I)
WMS-R	16–74	Verbal Paired Associates I	*Glr* (MA)
WMS-R	16–74	Verbal Paired Associates II	*Glr* (MA)
WPPSI-R	3–7	Animal Pegs	*Gs* (R9)
KAIT	11–85+	**LOGICAL STEPS**	*Gf* (I)
LAMB	20–60	Word Pairs	*Glr* (MA, FI)
DAS	3–5	Early Number Concepts	*Gq* (A3, KM)
SB:IV	2–4	**QUANTITATIVE**	*Gq* (A3)
WECHSLERS	3–89	**ARITHMETIC**	*Gq* (A3)

		Cultural Content MODERATE/Linguistic Demand HIGH	
WJ-R	2–85+	**INCOMPLETE WORDS**	*Ga* (PC)
WJ-R	4–85+	**SOUND BLENDING**	*Ga* (PC)
TOPA	5–8	Test of Phonological Awareness	*Ga* (PC)
SB:IV	12–24	**EQUATION BUILDING**	*Gf* (RQ)
WPPSI-R	3–7	Sentences	*Gsm* (MS)
WJ-R	4–85+	**MEMORY FOR WORDS**	*Gsm* (MS)
WRAML	5–17	Verbal Learning	*Glr* ((M6)

		Cultural Content HIGH/Linguistic Demand LOW	
LEITER-R	2–6	Classification	*Gf* (I)
LEITER-R	2–10	Picture Context	*Gf* (RG)
UNIT	5–17	Analogic Reasoning	*Gf* (I)
LEITER-R	2–18+	Form Completion	*Gv* (VZ, SR)
LEITER-R	4–10	Immediate Recognition	*Gv* (MV)
LEITER-R	2–18+	Forward Memory	*Gv* (MV)
LEITER-R	2–18+	Figure Ground	*Gv* (CF)
LEITER-R	4–10	Delayed Recognition	*Glr* (MA)
LEITER-R	2–18+	Associated Pairs	*Glr* (MA, MM)
LEITER-R	6–18+	Delayed Pairs	*Glr* (MA, MM)
K-BIT	4–90	Matrices	*Gf* (I)

TABLE 14–4 *Continued*

Battery	Age	Subtest	*Gf-Gc* Ability
		Cultural Content HIGH/Linguistic Demand MODERATE	
DAS	2–5	Verbal Comprehension	*Gc* (LD, LS)
WRAML	5–17	Picture Memory	*Gv* (MV)
DAS	2–5	Naming Vocabulary	*Gc* (LD, VL)
KAIT	11–85+	**FAMOUS FACES**	*Gc* (K2)
WJ-R	4–85+	**ORAL VOCABULARY**	*Gc* (VL, LD)
WJ-R	4–85+	**PICTURE VOCABULARY**	*Gc* (VL, KO)
DTLA-3	6–17	Word Opposites	*Gc* (LD)
K-BIT	4–90	Expressive Vocabulary	*Gc* (VL, KO, LD)
DTLA-3	6–17	Picture Fragments	*Gv* (CS)
K-SNAP	11–85	Gestalt Closure	*Gv* (CS)
		Cultural Content HIGH/Linguistic Demand HIGH	
DAS	6–17	**SIMILARITIES**	*Gc* (LD)
DAS	6–17	**WORD DEFINITIONS**	*Gc* (VL, LD)
SB:IV	2–24	**VOCABULARY**	*Gc* (LD, VL)
SB:IV	2–14	**Absurdities**	*Gc* (LD)
WECHSLERS	3–89	**SIMILARITIES**	*Gc* (LD)
WECHSLERS	3–89	**VOCABULARY**	*Gc* (LD, VL)
WECHSLERS	3–89	**INFORMATION**	*Gc* (KO)
DTLA-3	6–17	Story Construction	*Gc* (LD)
DTLA-3	6–17	Basic Information	*Gc* (KO)
PPVT-3	2–85	Peabody Picture Vocabulary Test—Third Edition	*Gc* (VL, KO, LD)
WJ-R	4–85+	**LISTENING COMPREHENSION**	*Gc* (LS, LD)
EVT	2–85+	Expressive Vocabulary Test	*Gc* (VL, LD)
LAMB	20–60	Wordlist	*Glr* (M6, MA)
SB:IV	12–24	**VERBAL RELATIONS**	*Gc* (LD)
SB:IV	2–24	**Comprehension**	*Gc* (LD, KO)
WECHSLERS	3–74	**COMPREHENSION**	*Gc* (LD, KO)
WMS-R	16–74	Logical Memory I	*Glr* (MM)

Note: Tests in bold/uppercase are strong measures as defined empirically; bold/lowercase are moderate measures as defined empirically; no bold/lowercase are logical classifications. Probable narrow ability classifications are reported in parentheses. Only "probable" test classifications are included (not "possible"). Tests that were classified empirically or logically as *mixed measures* are not included. The test classification process is described in Chapter 3.

First, the cognitive ability tests included in Table 14–4 are classified according to the broad (stratum II) and narrow (stratum I) *Gf-Gc* abilities they measure. The tests listed in Table 14–4 are the same measures that are included in the seven *Gf-Gc* cross-battery worksheets in Appendix A (see Chapter 13 for a comprehensive discussion). Also, the way these tests are reported in Table 14–4 is consistent with the *Gf-Gc* cross-battery worksheets. For example, tests whose names are printed in bold/uppercase letters are those that were defined empirically as measuring the respective broad (and narrow) *Gf-Gc* abilities that are reported in the column to the right of the test names in Table 14–4. Also, like the cross-battery worksheets, Table 14–4 includes the name of the battery in which the subtest is included as well as the age range for which the subtest is appropriate. Classification along this dimension does not strictly represent an accommodation to an issue particular to cultural or linguistic diversity. Rather, it is intended to reflect once again that the basis of any valid assessment, including those conducted on diverse individuals, must first and foremost rest on the best available and most solid theoretical and empirical grounds.

The question remains, however, as to whether there is cross-cultural validity to the *Gf-Gc* model—or any other model of intelligence, for that matter. With respect to *Gf-Gc* theory, the specific constructs (represented by the abilities measured by intelligence batteries) have shown evidence of *cross-cultural validity* (see Chapter 2).[5] In particular, the *Gf-Gc* structure of intelligence was found to be invariant across different cultural and racial groups (see Carroll, 1993, for a review; Flanagan & McGrew, in press). Because different factor-analytic methods resulted in an invariant *Gf-Gc* structure across cultures, cross-cultural validity has been inferred (Dana, 1993). Such validity, however, rests upon the premise that cognitive abilities (i.e., those posited by *Gf-Gc* theory or another theory) have and retain universal dimensions. Do cultural inventions (e.g., science, statistics, intelligence, etc.) exist, are they defined, and are they valued in precisely the same way from one culture to the next?

In all likelihood, social behavior, patterns of communication, and perceptual and cognitive styles will all significantly influence how a particular culture construes the things we call intelligence and, consequently, how intelligence should or can be measured, if at all. Therefore, while it appears that *Gf-Gc* constructs can be validly measured in individuals from a particular culture (Loevinger, 1957; cf. Dana, 1993), interpretation of results from cognitive ability tests that measure these underlying *Gf-Gc* constructs (specifically because they were developed in the United States) needs to be accomplished with extreme caution. It should be noted that establishing *construct equivalence* (through cross-cultural factor-analytic studies) for a test designed for the dominant culture (e.g., the U.S. population) is only one means of transforming the instrument into a measure that is thought to be more appropriate for other specific cultural populations (Dana, 1993; Helms, 1997).

---

[5] It should be noted that this body of research is limited. However, the evidence that does exist supports the invariance of the *Gf-Gc* structure of intelligence across gender, ethnic, and racial groups (Carroll, 1993).

Although construct equivalence is considered *most* important (Dana, 1993), other types of equivalence not addressed here are also important to consider (e.g., functional equivalence, metric or scale equivalence, etc.); the reader is referred to Dana (1993), Helms (1997), and Valdés and Figueroa (1994) for a comprehensive discussion.

Second, the cognitive ability tests included in Table 14–4 are classified according to their "degree of cultural content," that is, the degree to which their subtests require specific knowledge of and experience with mainstream U.S. culture. As discussed in Chapter 3, performance on all intelligence batteries reflects, at least in part, the extent to which examinees are familiar with the social mores and conventions of the culture in which the battery was developed and normed. Given that the vast majority of tests used by psychologists in the United States were developed and normed in the United States, including those found in the ITDR, it is reasonable to conclude that the content of such tests will necessarily reflect native anthropological content as well as the culturally bound conceptualizations of intelligence of the test developers themselves.

Exposure to mainstream U.S. culture (or lack thereof) has been identified as the crucial element in the cultural bias of U.S. IQ tests, one that can influence (in some instances, dramatically) an individual's performance on measures of cognitive abilities (Valdés & Figueroa, 1994). It is important to note that tests of cognitive ability do not demonstrate cultural bias when culture is viewed as a unitary construct intended merely to differentiate one group of people from another. This is because tests of cognitive ability measure quite well the degree to which someone has been able to acquire and readily access culturally specific information across virtually the entire age-based developmental spectrum. This process of acculturation remains invariant whether it is being learned natively by itself, simultaneously with another culture, or otherwise (Figueroa, 1983). Rather, cultural bias exists in the anthropological content unique to a given culture inherent in the structure and design of tests that assume equivalent levels of acculturation across the variables of age or grade for individuals from other cultures. In order for such bias to be controlled, it must be recognized that tests of intelligence and cognitive ability developed and normed in the United States will likely measure a lower range of ability in diverse individuals because they fail to sample "cultural content that is part of the cognitive repertoire and processes available to the bicultural individual" (Valdés & Figueroa, 1994, p. 99). Therefore, two important and interrelated pieces of information must be known in order to better validate the assessment and interpretive process: the individual's level of acculturation and the culturally specific requirements of any given test or subtest. Mercer (1979), Valdés and Figueroa (1994), and others have addressed the few studies reported in the literature that attempt to measure the former issue. Our focus is on the latter, and Table 14–4 assists in that endeavor.

The cognitive ability tests included in the ITDR were evaluated in terms of emphasis on process, content, and nature of response (see Chapter 3 for details). It was reasoned that tests that are more process-dominant (as opposed to product-dominant); contain abstract or novel stimuli (as opposed to culture-specific stimuli); and require simple, less culturally bound communicative responding (e.g., affirmative head nods, pointing) (see McCallum & Bracken, 1997) might yield scores that are less affected by an individual's level of exposure to mainstream U.S. culture (Jensen, 1974; Valdés & Figueroa, 1994). Since these three characteristics (i.e., process-product dominance, nature of test stimuli, response requirements) represent continuous rather than dichotomous test features, we classified cognitive ability tests as either "high," "moderate," or "low" with respect to their degree of cultural content.

Since the degree of cultural content classifications were reported in the ITDR for the major intelligence batteries, this information was simply repeated in Table 14–4. However, it was necessary to review the subtests of the 17 special purpose batteries and tests (included in Chapter 12) according to underlying process, nature of test stimuli, and response requirements in order to provide similar classifications for these measures for inclusion in Table 14–4. Thus, although the ITDR includes these classifications only for the major intelligence batteries, Table 14–4 includes them for the special purpose tests as well. As can be seen in Table 14–4, tests that reflect a low degree of cultural content are reported first, whereas tests that were rated as having a high degree of cultural content are reported in the far right column. As noted previously, a given individual's relative standing on the acculturation continuum directly influences test performance; low levels of acculturation tend to equate to test performance that is below developmentally appropriate expectations and higher levels of acculturation generally lead to test performance that is closer to or fully consistent with developmentally appropriate expectations. Therefore, careful selection and use of tests of cognitive ability can serve to reduce the distance between an individual's familiarity with mainstream culture and the cultural demands of the test. Age- or grade-related expectations of test performance can then be adjusted accordingly, thereby offering a fairer, less biased, and more valid interpretation of an individual's true functioning and potential.

Third, the cognitive ability tests included in Table 14–4 were classified according to their respective "degree of linguistic demand." In order to classify tests on this dimension, we considered two particular factors. First, tests were evaluated and classified as to the extent to which they require expressive and receptive language skills on the part of the assessor in order to be properly administered. Some tests have lengthy, verbose instructions (e.g., WISC/WAIS Block Design subtest, WJ-R Analysis-Synthesis subtest), whereas others may be given using only gestures or minimal language (e.g., CTONI, Leiter-R, UNIT). In addition, tests were evaluated on the basis of the level of language proficiency required by the examinee in order to comprehend the assessor's instructions and provide an appropriate response. Responses on some tests require considerable expressive language skills (e.g., WISC/WAIS Vocabulary and Comprehension subtests), while others can be accomplished without a word (e.g., WJ-R Visual Matching and Cross Out subtests). Final classification was based on joint consideration of both factors using a three-dimensional categorization system that reflects the continuous nature of these variables (low, moderate, and high). These categories are presented along side the cultural content categories and are arranged in order of increasing language demands.

The linguistic barrier to reliable test performance seems obvious enough, but it remains a poorly understood factor. Consistent with previous discussion, Valdés and Figueroa (1994) assert that "empirically established difficulty levels in psychometric tests are not altered by cultural differences. Neither are they because of proficiencies in the societal language" (p. 101). Language proficiency follows an experientially based developmental course every bit as invariant as that for acculturation. It is a lack of concurrence between constructs measured through distinct channels (i.e., verbal and nonverbal) that creates bias. There are few scientific studies in the literature that have utilized this model of analysis; nevertheless, they are uniformly consistent in their findings: Incidental linguistic learning is not measured equally by tasks that are linguistic rather than perceptual (Jensen, 1974, 1976). These results provide minimal but powerful evidence that intelligence and cognitive ability tests that carry high linguistic demands (e.g., vocabulary tests) may be biased against individuals who are dual-language learners. There is also evidence that bilinguals might best be viewed as completely distinct linguistic entities (Grosjean, 1989) who possess unique mental processing characteristics (Valdés & Figueroa, 1994). Until such conceptualizations of the bilingual mind are further researched and disseminated in the literature, nondiscriminatory assessment must continue to include, at the very least, data on two closely related factors: the individual's level of language proficiency in which they were assessed and the degree or level of linguistic demand contained in that test.

Cummins (1984) has defined two types of *language proficiency*, Basic Interpersonal Communicative Skills (BICS) and Cognitive/Academic Language Proficiency (CALP). BICS represents conversational proficiency and develops during informal and interactive learning. It is used to secure basic interpersonal needs including communication with family and peers as well as with others in a variety of socially related situations (Hessler, 1993; Lopez, 1997). CALP is an advanced level of language proficiency and is necessary for success in school-related learning. It "includes conceptual level knowledge, reasoning and abstractions associated with academic learning and performance" (Hessler, 1993, p. 88). Native speakers as well as dual-language learners first acquire BICS in approximately 2 to 3 years and, given an appropriate environmental context (e.g., solid formal instruction, adequate familial support, and proper language models), develop CALP in approximately 5 to 7 years.

Before assessing individuals with multilingual backgrounds, a measure of native (L1) and English (L2) language proficiency should be administered. According to Lopez (1997), "[t]he level of proficiency should be established in each of the two languages using measures that tap both expressive and receptive skills across context-embedded, interpersonal situations (i.e., BICS) as well as context-reduced, academic conditions (i.e., CALP)" (p. 507). There are a number of informal measures of English and Spanish language proficiency, including questionnaires of language background, observations, and language samples (Ramirez, 1990; cf. Lopez, 1997), as well as formal measures (e.g., Woodcock, 1991; Woodcock & Munoz-Sandoval, 1993, 1996). However, formal language proficiency measures in other languages are not readily available (Hamayan & Damico, 1991; Lopez, 1997). Language proficiency data are used in many different ways and for various purposes in bilingual assessment including gauging the appropriateness of a normative comparison group, evaluating the need for test adaptations or modifications, determining the language or languages that will be used during evaluation, and guiding appropriate interpretation of results.

While there are tests available that aid in the collection of information related to language proficiency, there are no existing guides to assist in determining the extent of language required by various tests of intelligence and cognitive ability. Table 14–4 represents an initial attempt to provide this information and makes it readily accessible for practitioners engaged in the process of assessment of diverse individuals. In these situations, knowledge of the degree of a test's linguistic demand may be particularly useful in the assessment and interpretation process. Assessors must be cautious, however, not to assume that even complete reduction of the verbal or oral language requirements of a particular test automatically eliminates linguistic bias. In many cases the assessment of culturally and linguistically diverse populations relies heavily upon the use of "nonverbal intelligence" tests. Although this approach to assessment can assist in developing more linguistically fair results for these populations (e.g., McCallum & Bracken, 1997), the interpretation of abilities measured by "nonverbal" tests or clusters can be misleading for two primary reasons.

First, the use of the term "nonverbal intelligence" suggests that these types of tests measure a theoretical construct called *nonverbal intelligence*. As discussed in Chapter 1, no theoretical model within the psychometric tradition (e.g., *Gf-Gc* theory) has identified a narrow or broad nonverbal ability or intelligence construct (see Carroll, 1993; Kamphaus, 1993). A review of the *Gf-Gc* ability classifications of tests (see Table 14–4) that make up the so-called nonverbal batteries, as well as tests that are interpreted often as measures of nonverbal abilities, provides support for the position that "the word 'nonverbal' simply describes a methodology for assessing the same general intelligence that has been of interest to psychologists since the early part of the century" (Kamphaus, 1993, p. 323). For example, as can be seen from a review of Table 14–4, most of these "nonverbal" tests appear to measure primarily *Gf* and *Gv* and, to a lesser extent, *Gs* and *Glr* (and not *nonverbal intelligence*). Moreover, nonverbal tests and batteries appear to measure a relatively limited range of cognitive abilities and/or may be characterized by redundancy in measurement of certain abilities (e.g., the Lieter-R includes four measures of *Gf*-I).

The second reason why interpretation of nonverbal tests or clusters may be hazardous is because it is sometimes assumed that language does not influence or only minimally influences performance on these measures. Very often nonverbal tests, although not requiring oral expressive language per se, demand a high level of nonverbal *receptive* language skill for optimal performance (e.g., WISC/WAIS Block Design subtest). There are, in fact, tests that can be administered entirely through the use of gestures or pantomime (e.g., CTONI, Leiter-R, UNIT) that effectively eliminate most if not all oral language requirements. However, test performance under such administration conditions is still largely contingent upon the examiner's ability to clearly and correctly convey the nature of a given task and its expected response—as well as the examinee's ability to comprehend that communication and accurately re-convey an acceptable response to the examiner. While "nonverbal" tests appear to require little in the way of oral language proficiency, they nevertheless remain dependent upon communication between individuals and their ability to interact effectively in a nonverbal manner. The influence of language on task performance, therefore, cannot be presumed to operate solely within the verbal domain.

Use of the test classifications presented in Table 14–4 can assist in constructing cognitive ability test batteries and in making more appropriate interpretations of performance, whether administered verbally or nonverbally. For example, an individual's performance on the Leiter-R Design Analogies, Repeated Patterns, and Sequential Order tests (all measures of *Gf*-I) would be interpreted as reflecting an aspect of Fluid Intelligence (i.e., Induction) that is assessed via a nonverbal method (i.e., pantomime), not as reflecting the individual's nonverbal intelligence. The nonverbal method of assessment allows individuals to express certain *Gf-Gc* abilities using visual, concrete, manipulative stimuli. Nonverbal assessment *methods* should not be confused with the *Gf-Gc constructs* that are measured by such methods, and neither should they be thought of as being independent of the influence of language on task performance. Much as an individual's standing on the acculturation spectrum directly influences test performance, so too does an individual's level of language proficiency directly influence test performance (Figueroa, Delgado, & Ruiz, 1984). Once again, careful, deliberate selection and use of tests of cognitive ability that have lower linguistic demands can reduce the distance between an individual's familiarity and proficiency with the English language and the inherent language demands of the test. When combined with other relevant information, interpretation of test performance with individuals for whom English is not the native language can be made less biased, yielding a more valid representation of ability and potential.

To summarize, the classifications of cognitive ability tests according to "Degree of Cultural Content" and "Degree of Linguistic Demand" reported in Table 14–4 are by no means definitive or necessarily based on the most appropriate criteria. They are clearly *subjective* and were derived primarily from a combination of recognized issues found in the literature as well as our own judgments and are insufficient, by themselves, to establish a comprehensive basis for assessment of diverse individuals. They are intended only to supplement the assessment process by guiding test selection that may more appropriately meet the needs of culturally and linguistically diverse populations within the context of a broader, defensible system of bilingual, nondiscriminatory, cross-cultural assessment (cf. Dana, 1993; Hamayan & Damico, 1991; Valdés & Figueroa, 1994). They may also serve as a starting point for both researchers and practitioners to begin establishing empirically supportable standards of practice. Research is necessary to provide an objective basis for understanding the cultural and linguistic demands on cognitive ability test performance. The classifications presented in Table 14–4 may provide the necessary framework for conducting such research. Their limitations notwithstanding, these classifications offer one method by which decisions about culturally fair assessment can be made on a systematic and logical basis. Used in conjunction with other information relevant to appropriate cross-cultural assessment (e.g., level of acculturation, language proficiency, socio-economic status, academic history, developmental data, etc.), these classifications should prove to be of practical value in decreasing bias in both test selection and interpretation.

Designing an Assessment: A Brief Case Example

The purpose of this section is to demonstrate how to design a cognitive assessment battery for individuals with varying levels of acculturation and English language proficiency using the descriptions of cognitive ability tests provided in Table 14–4 as a guide. There are numerous ways in which the information in Table 14–4 can be used to construct a battery of cognitive ability tests for multicultural-multilingual populations. As in the general cross-battery approach, a set of tests collected for a particular purpose, with consideration of the relevant cultural and linguistic factors, might provide more valid assessment data than those offered by a single intelligence battery. Cognitive batteries developed from the information in Table 14–4 will differ as a function of the unique language competencies and cultural experiences of the examinee as well as the nature of the referral concerns. The case of Marta, presented here, demonstrates only one of several cognitive ability test combinations that can be used to more effectively meet the needs of children and adults from diverse backgrounds.

Examiner B is a monolingual, English-speaking school psychologist asked to evaluate a 9-year-old, fourth-grade, bilingual student, Marta, who was referred by her classroom teacher because her academic performance was below expectations. After conducting a thorough review of Marta's school records, Examiner B interviewed Marta's teacher, who reported that Marta was achieving 2 to 3 years below the levels in reading and writing skills seen in her age- and grade-equivalent peers who possess similar cultural and linguistic backgrounds. Examiner B obtained several work samples and concurred that Marta's skills in reading and writing were below expectations, even when compared to other children in her class whose bicultural and bilingual experiences closely match hers. According to the teacher, Marta is well behaved, cooperative, and pleasant and has many friends. She reportedly communicates only in English at school, although this is likely due to the fact that she has not received primary language instruction and because the structure of the curriculum provides little opportunity for formal and social interaction with Spanish-speaking peers. Examiner B conducted several classroom and playground behavioral observations and determined that Marta was receiving appropriate instruction and that she had clear opportunities for advancing her learning. The behaviors that Examiner B observed corroborated those reported by Marta's classroom teacher.

Examiner B then arranged a home interview with Marta's mother, who speaks only Spanish and understands very little English, through the assistance of an interpreter. From an extensive review of Marta's linguistic, academic, and developmental history, Examiner B learned that Marta and her family (i.e., mother, father, and older brother, age 10) moved to the United States from Puerto Rico 5 years ago. Marta's mother graduated from high school but her father dropped out in fifth grade to go to work and help his family economically. Marta's mother is not employed outside the home; her father works as a cook in a local chain restaurant. They currently reside in a large Puerto Rican community in New York City and are actively involved in a variety of specific Puerto Rican cultural activities with friends and neighbors in the area. Marta's mother reported that Marta speaks only Spanish at home and speaks mostly Spanish in the community and with her neighborhood friends. Marta spoke very little English prior to moving to the United States, where she has been receiving instruction in English as a Second Language (ESL) since kindergarten. She has never received any formal instruction in Spanish. Marta's brother receives mostly B's and C's in school and has never been referred for academic difficulties. Marta's medical history is unremarkable for severe trauma, illness, or injury, although she was subject to occasional ear infections as a toddler. Moreover, Marta's mother reported that Marta "talked late," at about 36 months, but that she seemed to "catch up" later, during her kindergarten year.

The facts that Marta has not received primary language instruction, that she is at best only moderately acculturated to the mainstream at this point, and that her level of English language proficiency is probably between an advanced stage of BICS and emerging CALP suggest that her academic achievement may be more a reflection of these inhibiting factors than a disability. Alternatively, because Marta's performance in the classroom does not appear to be commensurate to that of her peers who share similar cultural and linguistic experiences, coupled with the fact that she was reported to be slightly delayed in language development, and given that her brother (1 year older) appears to be having reasonable success in school, the existence of a disability cannot be readily dismissed. Such is the nature of bilingual, cross-cultural assessment—the myriad variables involved rarely paint a clear picture. In this case, Examiner B's decision to move ahead with obtaining an estimate of Marta's cognitive capabilities in order to determine whether she is performing academically at a level that is consistent with her potential is, therefore, neither right nor wrong. It is simply a judgment guided by experience and based upon the available information that provides partial but reasonable support for that decision.

Acknowledging a lack of bilingual ability, Examiner B recognized that assessment in Marta's native language, Spanish, could only be accomplished through the use of an interpreter, a questionable practice that tends to introduce more confounds than it alleviates (Valdés & Figueroa, 1994). However, because the school could not provide a properly trained interpreter, Examiner B was limited to English language assessment only. After an informal interaction and brief interview with Marta, Examiner B noted that Marta communicated well in English, indicating that she was at least at the BICS level of proficiency. In order to obtain more formal data about her proficiency in English, Examiner B next administered the tests that make up the Oral Language cluster on the WJ-R, since this cluster assesses the higher-level conceptual and reasoning aspects of oral communication (i.e., CALP) (see Hessler, 1993).

Marta obtained an Oral Language cluster standard score range of 65–75 (1st–5th percentile), indicating that her level of CALP, particularly the semantic and syntactic components of English language, is well below average when compared to other individuals her age who were included in the standardization sample. Even when compared to the collected local norms for this cluster, Marta's score (5th–16th percentile) remained significantly below what would be expected of her, given her cultural and linguistic background. Given the fact that the Oral Language cluster contains many narrow-ability test indicators of *Gc* (e.g., lexical knowledge, listening ability, language development) and that *Gc* is an important predictor of reading and writing achievement (see Chapter 2 and Table 14–3), Examiner B's comparisons provided preliminary evidence consistent with Marta's below average classroom performance in these academic domains. However, since the tests in the Oral Language cluster are strongly influenced by cultural, linguistic, and other environmental experiences (see *Environmental/Background* variables in the ITDR, Chapter 11), it is probable that the limited exposure that Marta has had to mainstream societal culture inhibited her performance to some extent. Furthermore, the limitations and bias associated with tests containing high language demands (e.g., overemphasis on discrete aspects of language) suggest caution in interpretation (Lopez, 1997; Olmedo, 1981).

Examiner B hypothesized that because of noted cultural and linguistic factors, Marta's actual level of CALP would be higher if measured in Spanish rather than English, as it might better sample the range of her cultural knowledge, skills, and cognitive processes. With this option unavailable due to the aforementioned reasons, Examiner B examined the specific linguistic demands of the cognitive ability tests she selected for administration as well as their degree of cultural content in order to determine the extent to which performance on these measures was likely to be affected. To begin, Examiner B reviewed Table 14–3 to assist her in determining which cognitive abilities are important to assess in light of Marta's reported academic difficulties and then used Table 14–4 to guide her in constructing a cognitive assessment battery of select tests that would provide a fairer representation and estimate of her cognitive capabilities. Examiner B could have chosen merely to select "nonverbal intelligence" tests in order to reduce linguistic bias as much as possible. However, as described previously, the interpretation of the abilities that are measured by many "nonverbal" tests or clusters can be quite confusing, are often much less defensible, and do not necessarily provide more valid assessment data (McCallum & Bracken, 1997).

After reviewing Table 14–3, Examiner B concluded that measures of *Gf*, *Ga*, *Glr*, and *Gs* ought to be administered, as these *Gf-Gc* abilities appear to be most closely associated with reading achievement. Likewise, *Gf*, *Ga*, and *Gs* are important in predicting basic writing skills, and *Gf* and *Ga* also have been found to predict written expression (McGrew, 1994; McGrew & Knopik, 1993). (An estimate of *Gc*, which is also an important predictor of reading and writing achievement, had already been obtained from the WJ-R Oral Language cluster.) Note that, in spite of the inherent limitations of a monolingual approach and with recognition of the potential biases, Examiner B chose to proceed this way because it would allow her to make interpretations that are well grounded in contemporary theory and research encompassing both the science of intelligence and bilingual, cross-cultural assessment.

Because none of the comprehensive tests of intelligence found in Table 14–4 include reliable indicators of *all* of the *Gf-Gc* abilities that Examiner B identified as necessary to assess in light of Marta's academic difficulties (i.e., *Gf, Ga, Glr, Gs*), Examiner B needed to "cross" batteries to assess these abilities. In addition, she needed to construct a battery of tests that could assess Marta's abilities in a way that incorporated both reduced cultural content and minimal language demands.

Examiner B began by reviewing the tests listed first in Table 14–4, since these measures have the lowest comparative language demands and are also considered to have a relatively low degree of cultural content. However, in addition to considering cultural and linguistic factors, Examiner B attempted to adhere to the *Gf-Gc* cross-battery guiding principles in the battery construction decision-making process to allow for a psychometrically and theoretically defensible assessment. That is, she attempted to use a small number of batteries, include two or more qualitatively different indicators of each broad *Gf-Gc* ability, and select tests of *Gf-Gc* abilities that were empirically (rather than logically) classified. Examiner B's task of building a battery of tests to measure Marta's cognitive capabilities reflected a delicate and practical balance between (1) representing the breadth of *Gf-Gc* abilities that were found to be strongly related to the academic achievement areas in which Marta demonstrated difficulty, (2) selecting tests that were classified as having a low degree of cultural content and low language demands, and (3) identifying the most empirically strong measures of all important *Gf-Gc* abilities while keeping the number of tasks and batteries to a minimum.

Careful consideration of the abovementioned factors led Examiner B to utilize a selective DAS/WJ-R cross-battery approach to assessing Marta's cognitive capabilities. The specific tests that Examiner B selected are presented in Table 14–5. As can be seen from the information presented in this table, Examiner B selected a total of 10 cognitive ability subtests, 4 from the DAS and 6 from the WJ-R. Nearly all of the tests selected were defined empirically as strong measures of their respective underlying *Gf-Gc* constructs. Among the tests that were selected, those that measure *Gf* and *Gs* abilities appear to be least influenced by cultural factors (with varying levels of linguistic demand); tests of *Ga* ability appear to have the highest level of both cultural content and language demands (see Table 14–5). The scores yielded from this DAS/WJ-R battery of tests can be combined into *broad Gf, Gs*, and *Glr* clusters and a *narrow* PC-*Ga* cluster. The *Gf-Gc* Standard Score Profile (Appendix C) can be used for plotting selective cross-battery test scores and clusters and to aid in interpretation.

Compared to all other tests included in the DAS/WJ-R cross-battery, Marta's performance on *Ga* tests is likely to be affected the most by her current level of acculturation and English language proficiency (Table 14–5). Therefore, if her *Ga* performance differs significantly from her estimated level of ability in all other domains, it is imperative that Examiner B arrange to have Marta's language skills assessed more thoroughly (in both English *and* Spanish) before drawing conclu-

TABLE 14–5   Marta's *Gf-Gc* Cross-Battery Assessment

Degree of Linguistic Demand	Degree of Cultural Content					Gf-Gc Ability
	Low		Moderate			
	Battery	Subtest	Battery	Subtest		
Low	DAS DAS	**MATRICES** **SEQUENTIAL &** **QUANTITATIVE** **REASONING**				Gf (I) Gf (RG,I)
			DAS	Recall of Objects		Glr (M6)
Moderate	DAS WJ-R	Speed of Information Processing **MEMORY FOR NAMES**				Gs (R7) Glr (MA)
			WJ-R	**VISUAL-AUDITORY** **LEARNING**		Glr (MA)
High	WJ-R WJ-R	**VISUAL MATCHING** **CROSS OUT**				Gs (P,R9) Gs (R9)
			WJ-R WJ-R	**SOUND BLENDING** **INCOMPLETE** **WORDS**		Ga (PC) Ga (PC)

Note: Tests in bold/uppercase letters are strong measures as defined empirically; no bold/lowercase are logical classifications. Probable narrow ability classifications are reported in parentheses. Classifications are explained in detail in Chapter 3 of the text.

sions about cognitive performance in this domain or making educational programming decisions. Ideally, comprehensive assessment of language is conducted concurrently with cognitive assessment in cases where individuals present with dual-language learning backgrounds. However, such practice is dependent upon the availability of a trained and certified *bilingual* speech-language specialist, which, unfortunately, is rarely the case. When combined and evaluated in context with all other collected assessment data, the results of Marta's performance on the DAS/WJ-R cross-battery tests will determine the steps that follow (e.g., Is additional assessment or another iteration in any cognitive domain warranted? Is it necessary to gather additional data from other sources to corroborate findings? Should other professionals be consulted?).

Without question, the decision-making process within a bilingual, cross-cultural framework is complex and difficult. Not only must psychologists account for a wide variety of variables not ordinarily addressed in mainstream assessments, they must also gather information that spans the traditional boundaries of various disciplines. This makes the process extremely intimidating and discourages even those with the best of intentions when there is little time for learning and even less for assessment. While not a complete solution to this dilemma, with proper planning and a systematic approach the average psychologist should be able to complement any method of practice with diverse populations if care is taken to examine and use the information outlined in Table 14–4. Well-reasoned use of the selective cross-battery approach may actually lead to greater efficiency in the use of precious resources in assessment, including time and effort, while still achieving both a reduction in potential bias and a probable increase in test scores and interpretive validity.

Conclusions

This chapter offered guidelines for interpreting *Gf-Gc* cross-battery data. The procedures demonstrate how inter- and intra-cognitive analyses of individual cognitive ability *clusters* can provide diagnostic and prescriptive information that may be more useful in developing treatment and intervention plans than a traditional full-scale or composite IQ. Guidelines were also offered for conducting *selective Gf-Gc* cross-battery assessments that may be more informative and useful for addressing reading and math referrals than the administration of any single intelligence battery.

Because selective *Gf-Gc* cross-battery assessments are supported by a body of research on the relations between *Gf-Gc* abilities and academic achievement, they (1) ensure that those abilities that are most closely associated with academic referrals are well represented in the assessment, and (2) significantly reduce or eliminate the evaluation of abilities that are not related to the achievement skill(s) in question. For these reasons, selective cross-battery assessments are more likely to provide adequate measurement of cognitive abilities and processes that underlie specific academic learning disabilities than measurement by a single intelligence battery and may be particularly useful in triennial and special education evaluations.

Finally, this chapter offered an initial, but defensible, framework for selecting cognitive ability tests that may provide fairer and perhaps more valid assessment of the cognitive capabilities of culturally and linguistically diverse individuals. This was achieved through classification of all cognitive ability tests included on the major intelligence batteries (and a variety of special purpose tests) according to: (1) the underlying *Gf-Gc* ability measured by each test; (2) the extent to which the test requires acculturation, or acquired culturally based knowledge, and (3) the level of language needed in order to properly administer as well as to comprehend and respond appropriately in accordance with the test's standardized procedures. We readily acknowledge that the treatment of the issues of bilingual, cross-cultural assessment presented here is rather limited. However, because the approach to conducting cognitive ability assessments of multicultural and multilingual populations offered in this chapter is grounded in contemporary theory and research, and due to the fact that it is sensitive to cultural and linguistic influences on test performance, it is believed to offer a substantially more appropriate means of assessing the cognitive abilities of individuals from diverse groups than does the use of a single intelligence battery. The validity of such practice and its underlying assumptions awaits empirical support.

Investigations of the diagnostic and treatment validity of the *Gf-Gc* cross-battery approach presented in this section of the text *are* a much needed and viable avenue for future research. Decades of Wechsler-based research have shown that "it is impossible to predict specific disabilities and areas of cognitive competency or dysfunction from the averaged ability test scores" (i.e., IQs) (Lezak, 1995); *Gf-Gc* cross-battery data may prove to yield more clinically meaningful and diagnostically relevant information than IQ scores.

In an attempt to uphold the highest standards in the use and interpretation of intelligence tests, Reschly (1995) formulated a "Surgeon General's Warning" that could be included in test reports or attached to test protocols that were likely to be reviewed by other school officials, professionals, and members of the multidisciplinary team (including parents). Reschly's warning was designed to "protect children and youth from unwarranted inferences about their intellectual abilities ..." (p. 771). We agree with Reschly's "warning" and offer the following similar statement, or "Psychologist General's Warning" for users of the *Gf-Gc* cross-battery approach:

> The Gf-Gc *cross-battery approach, although designed to provide for measurement of a broad range of human cognitive abilities, only measures a portion of the competencies involved in intellectual functioning. The* Gf-Gc *cross-battery cluster standard scores yield only estimates of likely educational and/or occupational success and reflect, to a greater or lesser extent, the degree to which individuals have mastered important facts, concepts, and problem-solving strategies inherent in mainstream U.S. culture. Because* Gf-Gc *clusters derived from cross-battery assessments may be made up of a combination of tests from two or more batteries, these scores should always be reported with the recommended confidence bands and should not be used in formulas for making special education placement decisions. The information yielded by the* Gf-Gc *cross-battery clusters is most useful within the context of a broader assessment of skills and abilities and can aid in making important diagnostic or treatment decisions when it is supported by corroborating evidence.*

Gf-Gc Cross-Battery Worksheets

Note: The following information pertains to all *Gf-Gc Cross-Battery Worksheets* included in this Appendix.

Tests in bold/uppercase letters are strong measures as defined empirically; bold/lower case are moderate measures as defined empirically; regular face/lowercase measures were classified logically. In the case of tests with two "probable" narrow ability classifications the second classification is reported in parentheses. Only "probable" test classifications are included on the worksheet (not "possible"). Tests that were classified either empirically or logically as mixed measures are not included on the worksheet.

*If a test score is on standard score scale other than 100±15, record the score in the column marked by an asterisk. Then refer to the *Standard Score Conversion Table* (Appendix B) to convert the score to the scale of 100±15. Record the new score in the next column.

**If the cluster includes two or more qualitatively different broad *Gf-Gc* indicators, then place a (✓) next to the word "Broad" and record the appropriate *Gf-Gc* code in the parentheses. If the cluster includes indicators from only one narrow ability subsumed by the broad *Gf-Gc* ability, then place a (✓) next to the word "Narrow" and record the respective narrow ability code in the parentheses.

*** The K-ABC Achievement Test provides qualitatively different indicators of *Gc*.

FLUID INTELLIGENCE (*Gf*) CROSS-BATTERY WORKSHEET

(McGrew & Flanagan, 1998)

Name:
Age:
Grade:
Date of Evaluation:

Battery or Test	Age	*Gf* Narrow Abilities Tests	SS*	SS (100±15)
Induction (I)				
DAS	6-17	**MATRICES**		
DAS	2-5	Picture Similarities		
KAIT	11-85+	**MYSTERY CODES**		
SB:IV	7-24	**MATRICES**		
WAIS-III	16-89	Matrix Reasoning		
WJ-R	4-85+	**CONCEPT FORMATION**		
CAS	5-17	Nonverbal Matrices		
CTONI	6-18	Geometric Sequences (RG)		
DTLA-3	6-17	**SYMBOLIC RELATIONS**		
K-BIT	4-90	Matrices		
KSNAP	11-85	Four-Letter Words		
Leiter-R	2-6	Classification		
Leiter-R	5-18+	Design Analogies		
Leiter-R	2-18+	Repeated Patterns		
Leiter-R	2-18+	Sequential Order		
MAT	5-17	Matrix Analogies (RG)		
Raven's	5-18+	Ravens Progressive Matrices		
TONI-3	5-85	Test of Nonverbal Intelligence-3rd Ed		
UNIT	5-17	**ANALOGIC REASONING**		
Other				
		1. Sum of column		
		2. Divide by number of tests		
		3. **Induction** average		

Intelligence Batteries with adequate *Gf* representation
• DAS KAIT SB:IV WJ-R

Intelligence Batteries with inadequate *Gf* representation
• K-ABC WAIS-III WISC-III WPPSI-R

Battery or Test	Age	**General Sequential Reasoning (RG)**		
KAIT	11-85+	**LOGICAL STEPS**		
WJ-R	4-85+	**ANALYSIS-SYNTHESIS**		
Leiter-R	2-10	Picture Context		
Leiter-R	6-18+	Visual Coding		
UNIT	5-17	**CUBE DESIGN**		
Other				
		1. Sum of column		
		2. Divide by number of tests		
		3. **General Sequential Reasoning** average		

Battery or Test	Age	**Quantitative Reasoning (RQ)**		
DAS	6-17	**SEQ & QUANT REASONING (I)**		
SB:IV	12-24	**EQUATION BUILDING**		
SB:IV	7-24	Number series		
Other				
		1. Sum of column		
		2. Divide by number of tests		
		3. **Quantitative Reasoning** average		

Sum/No of Narrow Ability Averages

**Cluster Average ** **

— Broad (__)
— Narrow (__)

CRYSTALLIZED INTELLIGENCE (*Gc*) CROSS-BATTERY WORKSHEET

(McGrew & Flanagan, 1998)

Name:_____
Age:_____
Grade:_____
Examiner:_____
Date of Evaluation:_____

Intelligence Batteries with adequate *Gc* representation
• DAS SB:IV WAIS-III WISC-III WPPSI-R WJ-R

Intelligence Batteries with inadequate *Gc* representation
• KAIT K-ABC ***

Battery or Test	Age	*Gc* Narrow Abilities Tests	SS*	SS (100±15)
Language Development (LD)				
DAS	6-17	**SIMILARITIES**		
DAS	2-5	Verbal Comprehension (LS)		
SB:IV	12-24	**VERBAL RELATIONS**		
SB:IV	2-24	**Comprehension (K0)**		
SB:IV	2-14	**Absurdities**		
WECH	3-89	**COMPREHENSION (K0)**		
WECH	3-89	**SIMILARITIES**		
DTLA-3	6-17	Word Opposites		
DTLA-3	6-17	Story Construction		
Other				
		1. Sum of column		
		2. Divide by number of tests		
		3. **Language Development** average		
Lexical Knowledge (VL)				
DAS	6-17	**WORD DEFINITIONS (LD)**		
DAS	2-5	Naming Vocabulary (LD)		
SB:IV	2-24	**VOCABULARY (LD)**		
WECH	3-89	**VOCABULARY (LD)**		
WJ-R	4-85+	**ORAL VOCABULARY (LD)**		
WJ-R	2-85+	**PICTURE VOCABULARY (K0)**		
EVT	2-85+	Expressive Vocabulary Test (LD)		
K-BIT	4-90	Expressive Vocabulary (K0, LD)		
PPVT-3	2-85	Peab. Pic. Voc. Test-3rd Ed (K0,LD)		
Other				
		1. Sum of column		
		2. Divide by number of tests		
		3. **Lexical Knowledge** average		
Listening Ability (LS)				
WJ-R	4-85+	**LISTENING COMP (LD)**		
Other				
		1. Sum of column		
		2. Divide by number of tests		
		3. **Listening Ability** average		
General Information (K0)				
WECH	3-89	**INFORMATION**		
DTLA-3	6-17	Basic Information		
Other				
		1. Sum of column		
		2. Divide by number of tests		
		3. **General Information** average		
Information About Culture (K2)				
KAIT	11-85+	**FAMOUS FACES**		
Other				
		1. Sum of column		
		2. Divide by number of tests		
		3. **Information About Culture** average		

Sum/No of Narrow Ability Averages

Cluster Average *
__ Broad (___)
__ Narrow (___)

VISUAL PROCESSING (*Gv*) CROSS-BATTERY WORKSHEET

(1 of 2)

(McGrew & Flanagan, 1998)

Name:_____
Age: _____
Grade:_____
Examiner:_____
Date of Evaluation: _____

Battery or Test	Age	*Gv* Narrow Abilities Tests	SS*	SS (100±15)
Spatial Relations (SR)				
DAS	3-17	Pattern Construction		
K-ABC	4-12	**TRIANGLES**		
SB:IV	2-24	**PATTERN ANALYSIS**		
WECH	3-89	**BLOCK DESIGN**		
Leiter-R	11-18+	Figure Rotation (VZ)		
UNIT	5-17	Cube Design (VZ)		
Other				
		1. Sum of column		
		2. Divide by number of tests		
		3. **Spatial Relations** average		
Visualization (VZ)				
DAS	2-3	Block Building		
DAS	4-5	Matching Letter-like Forms		
WPPSI-R	3-7	Geometric Designs (P2)		
Leiter-R	2-10	Matching		
Leiter-R	2-18+	Form Completion (SR)		
Leiter-R	11-18+	Paper Folding		
Other				
		1. Sum of column		
		2. Divide by number of tests		
		3. **Visualization** average		
Visual Memory (MV)				
DAS	6-17	**RECALL OF DESIGNS**		
DAS	3-7	Recognition of Pictures		
K-ABC	2-4	Face Recognition		
KAIT	11-85+	**MEM. FOR BLOCK DESIGNS**		
SB:IV	2-24	**Bead Memory**		
SB:IV	7-24	**Memory for Objects**		
WJ-R	4-85+	**Picture Recogniton**		
DTLA-3	6-17	Design Sequences		
DTLA-3	6-17	Design Reproduction		
LAMB	20-60	Simple Figure		
LAMB	20-60	Complex Figure		
Leiter-R	4-10	Immediate Recognition		
Leiter-R	2-18+	Forward Memory		
TOMAL	5-19	Facial Memory		
TOMAL	5-19	Abstract Visual Memory		
TOMAL	5-19	Manual Imitation		
TOMAL	5-19	Del Rec: Visual Sel. Reminding		
UNIT	5-17	**OBJECT MEMORY**		
UNIT	5-17	**SPATIAL MEMORY**		
UNIT	5-17	**SYMBOLIC MEMORY**		
WMS-R	16-74	Figural Memory		
WMS-R	16-74	Visual Reproduction I		
WRAML	5-17	Picture Memory		
WRAML	5-17	Design Memory		
Other				
		1. Sum of column		
		2. Divide by number of tests		
		3. **Visual Memory** average		

Intelligence Batteries with adequate *Gv* representation
• DAS K-ABC SB:IV WAIS-III WISC-III WPPSI-R WJ-R

Intelligence Batteries with inadequate *Gv* representation
• KAIT

(cont'd next page)

VISUAL PROCESSING (*Gv*) CROSS-BATTERY WORKSHEET

(McGrew & Flanagan, 1998)

(2 of 2)

(cont'd prior page)

Battery or Test	Age	*Gv* Narrow Abilities Tests	SS*	SS (100±15)
Closure Speed (CS)				
K-ABC	2-12	**Gestalt Closure**		
WECH	3-89	**OBJECT ASSEMBLY**		
WJ-R	2-85+	**Visual Closure**		
DTLA-3	6-17	Picture Fragments		
K-SNAP	11-85	Gestalt Closure		
Other				
		1. Sum of column		
		2. Divide by number of tests		
		3. **Closure Speed** average		
Spatial Scanning (SS)				
WISC-III	6-16	Mazes		
WPPSI-R	3-7	**Mazes**		
UNIT	5-17	**Mazes**		
Other				
		1. Sum of column		
		2. Divide by number of tests		
		3. **Spatial Scanning** average		
Flexibility of Closure (CF)				
CAS	5-17	Figure Memory (MV)		
Leiter-R	2-18+	Figure Ground		
Other				
		1. Sum of column		
		2. Divide by number of tests		
		3. **Flexibility of Closure** average		
Serial Perceptual Integration (PI)				
K-ABC	2-4	Magic Window		
Other				
		1. Sum of column		
		2. Divide by number of tests		
		3. **Serial Perceptual Integration** average		

Sum/No of Narrow Ability Averages

Cluster Average **

__ Broad (___)
__ Narrow (___)

SHORT-TERM MEMORY (*Gsm*) CROSS-BATTERY WORKSHEET

(McGrew & Flanagan, 1998)

Battery or Test	Age	*Gsm* Narrow Abilities Tests	SS*	SS (100±15)
		Memory Span (MS)		
DAS	3-17	Recall of Digits		
K-ABC	2-12	**NUMBER RECALL**		
K-ABC	4-12	**WORD ORDER**		
SB:IV	7-24	**MEMORY FOR DIGITS**		
WAIS-III	16-89	**DIGIT SPAN**		
WAIS-III	16-89	Letter-Number Sequencing		
WISC-III	6-16	**DIGIT SPAN**		
WPPSI-R	3-7	Sentences		
WJ-R	4-85+	**MEMORY FOR WORDS**		
CAS	5-17	Word Series		
DTLA-3	6-17	Word Sequences		
K-SNAP	11-85	Number Recall		
LAMB	20-60	Digit Span		
LAMB	20-60	Supraspan Digit		
TOMAL	5-19	Digits Forward		
TOMAL	5-19	Letters Forward		
WMS-R	16-74	Digit Span		
WRAML	5-17	Number/Letter Memory		
		1. Sum of column		
		2. Divide by number of tests		
		3. **Memory Span** average		
		Visual Memory (MV)		
DAS	6-17	**RECALL OF DESIGNS**		
DAS	3-7	Recognition of Pictures		
K-ABC	2-4	Face Recognition		
KAIT	11-85+	**MEM. FOR BLOCK DESIGNS**		
SB:IV	2-24	**Bead Memory**		
SB:IV	7-24	**Memory for Objects**		
WJ-R	4-85+	**Picture Recogniton**		
DTLA-3	6-17	Design Sequences		
DTLA-3	6-17	Design Reproduction		
LAMB	20-60	Simple Figure		
LAMB	20-60	Complex Figure		
Leiter-R	4-10	Immediate Recognition		
Leiter-R	2-18+	Forward Memory		
TOMAL	5-19	Facial Memory		
TOMAL	5-19	Abstract Visual Memory		
TOMAL	5-19	Manual Imitation		
TOMAL	5-19	Del Rec: Visual Sel. Reminding		
UNIT	5-17	**OBJECT MEMORY**		
UNIT	5-17	**SPATIAL MEMORY**		
UNIT	5-17	**SYMBOLIC MEMORY**		
WMS-R	16-74	Figural Memory		
WMS-R	16-74	Visual Reproduction I		
WRAML	5-17	Picture Memory		
WRAML	5-17	Design Memory		
		1. Sum of column		
		2. Divide by number of tests		
		3. **Visual Memory** average		

Name:_____
Age: _____
Grade:_____
Examiner:_____
Date of Evaluation: _____

Intelligence Batteries with adequate *Gsm* representation

Intelligence Batteries with inadequate *Gsm* representation
• DAS K-ABC KAIT SB:IV
WAIS-III WISC-III WPPSI-R WJ-R

Sum/No of Narrow Ability Averages

Cluster Average **

__ Broad (___)
__Narrow (___)

LONG-TERM RETRIEVAL (*Glr*) CROSS-BATTERY WORKSHEET

(McGrew & Flanagan, 1998)

Battery or Test	Age	*Glr* Narrow Abilities Tests	SS*	SS (100±15)
Associative Memory (MA)				
KAIT	11-85+	**REBUS LEARNING**		
KAIT	11-85+	**REBUS DELAYED RECALL**		
WJ-R	2-85+	**MEMORY FOR NAMES**		
WJ-R	4-85+	**VISUAL AUDITORY LEARNING**		
WJ-R	4-85+	**DEL REC: MEM FOR NAMES**		
WJ-R	4-85+	**Del Rec: Visual-Auditory Learning**		
LAMB	20-60	Word Pairs (FI)		
Leiter-R	4-10	Delayed Recognition		
Leiter-R	2-18+	Associated Pairs (MM)		
Leiter-R	6-18+	Delayed Pairs (MM)		
TOMAL	5-19	Paired Recall		
WMS-R	16-74	Visual Paired Associates I		
WMS-R	16-74	Verbal Paired Associates I		
WMS-R	16-74	Visual Paired Associates II		
WMS-R	16-74	Verbal Paired Associates II		
WRAML	5-17	Sound Symbol		
Other				
		1. Sum of column		
		2. Divide by number of tests		
		3. **Associative Memory** average		
Free Recall Memory (M6)				
DAS	4-17	Recall of Objects		
LAMB	20-60	Wordlist (MA)		
TOMAL	5-19	Word Selective Reminding		
TOMAL	5-19	Del Rec: Word Selective Reminding		
WRAML	5-17	Verbal Learning		
Other				
		1. Sum of column		
		2. Divide by number of tests		
		3. **Free Recall Memory** average		
Meaningful Memory (MM)				
WMS-R	16-74	Logical Memory I		
Other				
		1. Sum of column		
		2. Divide by number of tests		
		3. **Meaningful Memory** average		

Name:_____
Age: _____
Grade:_____
Examiner:_____
Date of Evaluation: _____

Intelligence Batteries with adequate *Glr* representation

Intelligence Batteries with inadequate *Glr* representation
• DAS K-ABC KAIT SB:IV WAIS-III WISC-II, WPPSI-R, WJ-R

Sum/No of Narrow Ability Averages

Cluster Average *

__ Broad (___)
__ Narrow (___)

AUDITORY PROCESSING (*Ga*) CROSS-BATTERY WORKSHEET

(McGrew & Flanagan, 1998)

Battery or Test	Age	*Ga* Narrow Abilities Tests	SS*	SS (100±15)
		Phonetic Coding (PC)		
WJ-R	2-85+	**INCOMPLETE WORDS**		
WJ-R	4-85+	**SOUND BLENDING**		
TOPA	5-8	Test of Phonological Awareness		
Other				
		1. Sum of column		
		2. Divide by number of tests		
		3. **Phonetic Coding** average		

_____(   )

		1. Sum of column		
		2. Divide by number of tests		
		3. _____ average		

_____(   )

		1. Sum of column		
		2. Divide by number of tests		
		3. _____ average		

Name:_____
Age: _____
Grade:_____
Examiner:_____
Date of Evaluation: _____

Intelligence Batteries with adequate *Ga* representation

Intelligence Batteries with inadequate *Ga* representation
• DAS K-ABC KAIT SB:IV WAIS-III
   WISC-III WPPSI-R WJ-R

Sum/No of Narrow Ability Averages

Cluster Average *

__ Broad (___)
__ Narrow (___)

PROCESSING SPEED (*Gs*) CROSS-BATTERY WORKSHEET

(McGrew & Flanagan, 1998)

Name:_____
Age: _____
Grade:_____
Examiner:_____
Date of Evaluation: _____

Battery or Test	Age	*Gs* Narrow Abilities Tests	SS*	SS (100±15)
Perceptual Speed (P)				
WAIS-III	16-89	Symbol Search (R9)		
WISC-III	6-16	Symbol Search (R9)		
WJ-R	4-85+	**VISUAL MATCHING (R9)**		
WJ-R	4-85+	**CROSS OUT**		
CAS	5-17	Matching Numbers (R9)		
CAS	5-17	Receptive Attention (R4)		
Leiter-R	2-18+	Attention Sustained (R9)		
Other				
		1. Sum of column		
		2. Divide by number of tests		
		3. **Perceptual Speed** Average		
Rate -of-test-taking (R9)				
WAIS-III	16-89	**DIGIT SYMBOL-CODING**		
WISC-III	6-16	**CODING**		
WPPSI-R	3-7	Animal Pegs		
CAS	5-17	Planned Codes		
Other				
		1. Sum of column		
		2. Divide by number of tests		
		3. **Rate-of-test-taking** average		
Mental Comparison Speed (R7)				
DAS	6-17	Speed of Information Processing		
CAS	5-17	Number Detection (R9)		
Other				
		1. Sum of column		
		2. Divide by number of tests		
		3. **Mental Comparison Speed** average		

Intelligence Batteries with adequate *Gs* representation
WAIS-III WISC-III

Intelligence Batteries with inadequate *Gs* representation
DAS K-ABC KAIT SB:IV
WPPSI-R WJ-R

Sum/No of Narrow Ability Averages

Cluster Average **

__ Broad (___)
__ Narrow (___)

Percentile Rank and Standard Score Conversion Table

Percentile Rank	Standard Score			
	WJ-R	DAS	SB:IV	Wechslers K-ABC KAIT
	(M = 100; SD = 15)	(M = 50; SD = 10)	(M = 50; SD = 8)	(M = 10; SD = 3)
99.99	160	90	82	
99.99	159	89		
99.99	158	89	81	
99.99	157	88		
99.99	156	87	80	
99.99	155	87		
99.99	154	86	79	
99.98	153	85		
99.98	153	85	78	
99.97	152	85		
99.96	151	84	77	
99.95	150	83		
99.94	149	83	76	
99.93	148	82		
99.93	147	81	75	
99.89	146	81		
99.87	145	80	74	19
99.84	144	79		
99.80	143	79	73	
99.75	142	78		
99.70	141	77	72	
99.64	140	77		18
99.57	139	76	71	
99	138	75		
99	138	75	70	
99	137	75		
99	136	74	69	
99	135	73		17
99	134	73	68	
99	133	72		
98	132	71	67	
98	131	71		
98	130	70	66	16
97	129	69		
97	128	69	65	
97	127	68		
96	126	67	64	

Percentile Rank	Standard Score			
	WJ-R	DAS	SB:IV	Wechslers K-ABC KAIT
	(M = 100; SD = 15)	(M = 50; SD = 10)	(M = 50; SD = 8)	(M = 10; SD = 3)
95	125	67		15
95	124	66	63	
94	123	65		
93	123	65	62	
92	122	65		
92	121	64	61	
91	120	63		14
89	119	63	60	
88	118	62		
87	117	61	59	
86	116	61		
84	115	60	58	13
83	114	59		
81	113	59	57	
79	112	58		
77	111	57	56	
75	110	57		12
73	109	56	55	
71	108	55		
69	108	55	54	
67	107	55		
65	106	54	53	
65	105	53		11
62	104	53	52	
57	103	52		
55	102	51	51	
52	101	51		
50	100	50	50	10
48	99	49		
45	98	49	49	
43	97	48		
40	96	47	48	
38	95	47		9
35	94	46	47	
33	93	45		
31	93	45	46	
29	92	45		
27	91	44	45	

Percentile Rank	Standard Score			
	WJ-R	DAS	SB:IV	Wechslers K-ABC KAIT
	(M = 100; SD = 15)	(M = 50; SD = 10)	(M = 50; SD = 8)	(M = 10; SD = 3)
25	90	43		8
23	89	43	44	
21	88	42		
19	87	41	43	
17	86	41		
16	85	40	42	7
14	84	39		
13	83	39	41	
12	82	38		
11	81	37	40	
9	80	37		6
8	79	36	39	
8	78	35		
7	78	35	38	
6	77	35		
5	76	34	37	
5	75	33		5
4	74	33	36	
3	76	32		
3	72	31	35	
3	71	31		
2	70	30	34	4
2	69	29		
2	68	29	33	
1	67	28		
1	66	27	32	
1	65	27		3
1	64	26	31	
1	63	25		
1	63	25	30	
1	62	25		
.49	61	24	29	
.36	60	23		2
.30	59	23	28	
.25	58	22		
.20	57	21	27	
.16	56	21		

Percentile Rank	Standard Score			
	WJ-R	DAS	SB:IV	Wechslers K-ABC KAIT
	(M = 100; SD = 15)	(M = 50; SD = 10)	(M = 50; SD = 8)	(M = 10; SD = 3)
.16	55	20	26	1
.11	54	19		
.09	53	19	25	
.07	52	18		
.06	51	17	24	
.05	50	17		
.04	49	16	23	
.03	48	15		
.02	48	15	22	
.02	47	15		
.01	46	14	21	
.01	45	13		
.01	44	13	20	
.01	43	12		
.01	42	11	19	
.01	41	11		
.01	40	10	18	

Gf-Gc Standard
Score Profile

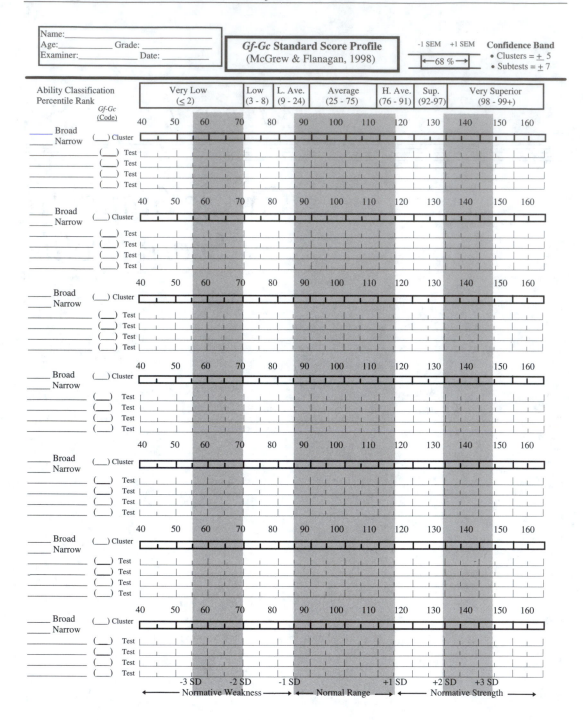

Case Study Test Scores for J.J.

WISC-III
Information = 100
Vocabulary = 90
Coding = 70
Symbol Search = 100
Digit Span = 100
Block Design = 110
Object Assembly = 115

WJ-R COG
Analysis-Synthesis = 126
Concept Formation = 108
Memory for Names = 86
Visual-Auditory Learning = 81
Visual Matching = 91
Memory for Words = 95
Incomplete Words = 60
Sound Blending = 72

WJ-R ACH
Letter-Word Identification = 82
Word Attach = 70
Passage Comprehension = 80
Calculation = 105
Applied Problems = 115
Dictation = 91
Writing Samples = 95

References

Aaron, P. G. (1995). Differential diagnosis of reading disabilities. *School Psychology Review, 24* (3), 345–360.

Ackerman, P. L., & Heggestad, E. D. (1997). Intelligence, personality, and interests: Evidence for overlapping traits. *Psychological Bulletin, 121* (2), 219–245.

Adkins, D. C., & Kuder, G. F. (1940). The relation of primary mental abilities to activity preferences. *Psychometrika, 5,* 251–262.

Alfonso, V. C., & Flanagan, D. P. (in press). Cognitive assessment of preschoolers. In E. V. Nuttall (Ed.), *Assessing and screening preschoolers: Psychological and educational dimensions.* Boston: Allyn and Bacon.

American Psychological Association (1985). *Standards for educational and psychological testing.* Washington, DC: Author.

American Psychological Association (1990). *Guidelines for providers of psychological services to ethnic, linguistic, and culturally diverse populations.* Washington, DC: Author.

Anastasi, A., & Urbina, S. (1997). *Psychological testing* (7th ed.). Upper Saddle River, NJ: Prentice-Hall.

Anderson, J. R. (1985). *Cognitive psychology and its implications* (2d ed.). New York: Freeman.

Anokhin, P. K. (1969). Cybernetics and the integrative activity of the brain. In M. Cole & I. Maltzman (Eds.), *A handbook of contemporary Soviet psychology* (pp. 830–856). New York: Basic Books.

Armour-Thomas, E. (1992). Intellectual assessment of children from culturally diverse backgrounds. *School Psychology Review, 21,* 552–565.

Atkinson, L. (1991). On WAIS-R difference scores in the standardization sample. *Psychological Assessment, 3,* 292–294.

Badian, N. A. (1988). A prediction of good and poor reading before kindergarten entry: A nine-year follow-up. *Journal of Learning Disabilities, 21* (2), 98–103, 123.

Baker, L. A., Decker, S. N., & DeFries, J. C. (1984). Cognitive abilities in reading-disabled children: A longitudinal study. *Journal of Child Psychology & Psychiatry & Allied Disciplines, 25* (1), 111–117.

Barona, M. S., & Barona, A. (1991). The assessment of culturally and linguistically different preschoolers. *Early Childhood Research Quarterly, 6,* 363–376.

Berninger, V. W. (1990). Multiple orthographic codes: Key to alternative instructional methodologies for developing the orthographic-phonological connections underlying word identification. *School Psychology Review, 19* (4), 518–533.

Bishop, A. J. (1980). Spatial abilities and mathematics education: A review. *Educational Studies in Mathematics, 11,* 257–269.

Boehm, A. E. (1991). Assessment of basic relational concepts. In B. Bracken (Ed.), *The psychoeducational assessment of preschool children* (2d ed.) (pp. 86–106). Boston: Allyn and Bacon.

Bogen, J. E. (1969). The other side of the brain. Parts I, II, and III. *Bulletin of the Los Angeles Neurological Society, 34,* 73–105, 135–162, 191–203.

Bouchard, T. J., Jr. (1984, July 20). [Review of the book *Frames of mind: The theory of multiple intelligences*]. *American Journal of Orthopsychiatry, 54,* 506–508.

Bowey, J. A., Cain, M. T., & Ryan, S. M. (1992). A reading-level design study of phonological skills underlying fourth-grade children's word reading difficulties. *Child Development, 63,* 999–1011.

Bowey, J. A., & Patel, R. K. (1988). Metalinguistic ability and early reading achievement. *Applied Psycholinguistics, 9,* 367–383.

Boyle, G. J. (1991). Does item homogeneity indicate internal consistency of item redundancy in psychometric scales? *Personality and Individual Differences, 12* (3), 291–294.

Bracken, B. A. (1984). *Bracken Basic Concept Scale.* Columbus, OH: Merrill.

Bracken, B. A. (1986). Incidence of basic concepts in the directions of five commonly used American tests of intelligence. *School Psychology International, 7,* 1–10.

Bracken, B. A. (1987). Limitations of preschool instruments and standards for minimal levels of technical adequacy. *Journal of Psychoeducational Assessment, 4,* 313–326.

Bracken, B. A., & Fagan, T. K. (Eds.) (1990). Intelligence: Theories and practice [Special Issue]. *Journal of Psychoeducational Assessment, 8* (3).

Bracken, B. A., & Howell, K. K. (1989). K-ABC subtest specificity recalculated. *Journal of School Psychology, 27,* 335–345.

Bracken, B. A., McCallum, R. S., & Crain, R. M. (1993). WISC-III subtest composite reliabilities and specificities: Interpretive aids. *Journal of Psychoeducational Assessment* [Monograph Series: WISC-III Monograph], 20–34.

Brady, S., Shankweiler, D., & Mann, V. (1983). Speech perception and memory coding in relation to reading ability. *Journal of Experimental Child Psychology, 35,* 345–367.

Briggs, S. R., & Cheek, J. M. (1986). The role of factor analysis in the development and evaluation of personality scales. Special Issue: Methodological developments in personality research. *Journal of Personality, 54* (1), 106–148.

Broadbent, D. E. (1958). *Perception and communication.* Oxford, England: Pergamon.

Brown, L., Sherbenou, R. J., & Johnsen, S. K. (1997). *Test of Nonverbal Intelligence—Third Edition.* Austin, TX: Pro-Ed.

Bryant, P. E., Bradley, L., Maclean, M., & Crossland, J. (1989). Nursery rhymes, phonological skills and reading. *Child Language, 16,* 407–428.

Burns, R. B. (1994, April). Surveying the cognitive domain. *Educational Researcher,* 35–37.

Burt, C. (1949). Alternative methods of factor analysis and their relations to Pearson's method of 'principal axes.' *British Journal of Psychology, Statistical Section, 2,* 98–121.

Byrne, B., & Fielding-Barnsley, R. (1995). Evaluation of a program to teach phonemic awareness to young children: A 2 and 3 year follow-up and a new preschool trial. *Journal of Educational Psychology, 87* (3), 488–503.

Campbell, D. P. (1971). *Handbook for the Strong Vocational Interest Blank.* Stanford, CA: Stanford University Press.

Carnine, L., Carnine, D., & Gersten, R. M. (1984). Analysis of oral reading errors made by economically disadvantaged students taught with a synthetic-phonics approach. *Reading Research Quarterly, 19* (3), 343–356.

Carroll, J. B. (1983). Studying individual differences in cognitive abilities: Through and beyond factor analysis. In R. F. Dillon (Ed.), *Individual differences in cognition* (vol. 1) (pp. 1–33). New York: Academic Press.

Carroll, J. B. (1989). Factor analysis since Spearman: Where do we stand? What do we know? In R. Kanfer, P. L. Ackerman, & R. Cudeck (Eds.), *Abilities, motivation, and methodology* (pp. 43–67). Hillside, NJ: Erlbaum.

Carroll, J. B. (1993a). *Human cognitive abilities: A survey of factor-analytic studies.* Cambridge, England: Cambridge University Press.

Carroll, J. B. (1993b). What abilities are measured by the WISC-III? *Journal of Psychoeducational Assessment* [Monograph Series: WISC-III Monograph], 134–143.

Carroll, J. B. (1995a). [Review of the book *Assess-*

ment of cognitive processes: The PASS theory of intelligence]. *Journal of Psychoeducational Assessment, 13*, 397–409.

Carroll, J. B. (1995b). On methodology in the study of cognitive abilities. *Multivariate Behavioral Research, 30* (3), 429–452.

Carroll, J. B. (1997). The three-stratum theory of cognitive abilities. In D. P. Flanagan, J. L. Genshaft, & P. L. Harrison (Eds.), *Contemporary intellectual assessment: Theories, tests, and issues* (pp. 122–130). New York: Guilford.

Carroll, J. B., & Maxwell, S. E. (1979). Individual differences in cognitive abilities. *Annual Review of Psychology, 30*, 603–640.

Cattell, R. B. (1941). Some theoretical issues in adult intelligence testing. *Psychological Bulletin, 38*, 592.

Cattell, R. B. (1957). *Personality and motivation structure and measurement.* New York: World Book.

Cervantes, H. T. (1988). Nondiscriminatory assessment and informal data gathering: The case of Gonzaldo L. In R. L. Jones (Ed.), *Psychoeducational assessment of minority group children: A casebook.* Berkeley, CA: Cobb & Henry.

Chen, J-Q., & Gardner, H. (1997). Alternative assessment from a multiple intelligences theoretical perspective. In D. P. Flanagan, J. L. Genshaft, & P. L. Harrison (Eds.), *Contemporary intellectual assessment: Theories, tests, and issues* (pp. 105–121). New York: Guilford.

Children's Defense Fund (1989). *A vision for America's children.* Washington, DC: Author.

Clarke, L. A., & Watson, D. (1995). Constructing validity: Basic issues in objective scale development. *Psychological Assessment, 7*, 309–319.

Cohen, J. (1959). The factorial structure of the WISC at ages 7-7, 10-6, and 13-6. *Journal of Consulting Psychology, 23*, 285–299.

Comrey, A. L. (1988). Factor-analytic methods of scale development in personality and clinical psychology. *Journal of Consulting and Clinical Psychology, 56* (5), 754–761.

Cook-Morales, V. J., Ortiz, S. O., & Ortiz, O. G. (1994). *Preliminary analysis: Survey of California school psychologists listed in the CASP multilingual directory.* Paper presented at the CASP Multicultural Affairs Committee Meeting and Workshop at the annual conference of the Cal-ifornia Association of School Psychologists, Long Beach, CA.

Cooney, J. B., & Swanson, L. H. (1990). Individual differences in memory for mathematical story problems: Memory span and problem perception. *Journal of Educational Psychology, 82* (3), 570–577.

Costa, P. T., Jr., & McCrae, R. R. (1992a). Four ways five factors are basic. *Personality and Individual Differences, 13*, 653–665.

Costa, P. T., Jr., & McCrae, R. R. (1992b). "Four ways five factors are *not* basic": Reply. *Personality and Individual Differences, 13*, 861–865.

Crocker, L., & Algina, J. (1986). *Introduction to classical and modern test theory.* New York: Holt, Rinehart, & Winston.

Cronbach, L. (1986). Signs of optimism for intelligence testing. *Educational Measurement: Issues and Practice, 5*, 23–24.

Cronbach, L. J., & Snow, R. E. (1977). *Aptitudes and instructional methods.* New York: Irvington.

Cummins, J. (1984). *Bilingualism and special education.* Clevedon, England: Multilingual Matters.

Cummins, J. C. (1984). *Bilingual and Special Education: Issues in Assessment and Pedagogy.* Austin, TX: Pro-Ed.

Dana, R. H. (1993). *Multicultural assessment perspectives for professional psychology.* Boston: Allyn and Bacon.

Daneman, M., & Carpenter, P. A. (1980). Individual differences in working memory and reading. *Journal of Verbal Learning and Verbal Behavior, 19*, 450–466.

Das, J. P., Kirby, J. R., & Jarman, R. F. (1979). *Simultaneous and successive cognitive processes.* New York: Academic Press.

Das, J. P., & Naglieri, J. A. (1997). *Cognitive assessment system.* Itasca, IL: Riverside.

Das, J. P., Naglieri, J. A., & Kirby, J. R. (1994). *Assessment of cognitive processes: The PASS theory of intelligence.* Needham Heights, MA: Allyn and Bacon.

Das, J. P., & Siu, I. (1982). Good and poor readers' word naming time, memory span, and story recall. *Journal of Experimental Education, 57* (2), 101–114.

Davidson, L., & Torff, B. (1994). Musical intelligence. In R. J. Sternberg (Ed.), *Encyclopedia of human intelligence* (pp. 744–746). New York: Macmillan.

Dawis, R. V. (1994). Occupations. In R. J. Sternberg (Ed.), *Encyclopedia of human intelligence* (pp. 781–785). New York: Macmillan.

Decker, S. N., & DeFries, J. C. (1980). Cognitive abilities in families with reading disabled children. *Journal of Learning Disabilities, 13* (9), 517–522.

Detterman, D. K. (1979). Detterman's laws of individual differences research. In R. J. Sternberg & D. K. Detterman (Eds.), *Human intelligence: Perspectives on its theory and measurement.* Norwood, NJ: Abbex.

Dixon, R. A., Kramer, D. A., & Baltes, P. B. (1985). Intelligence: A life-span developmental perspective. In B. B. Wolman (Ed.), *Handbook of intelligence: Theories, measurements, and applications* (pp. 301–350). New York: Wiley.

Dunn, L. (1968). Special education for the mildly retarded—Is much of it justifiable? *Exceptional Children, 35,* 5–22.

Dunn, L. M., Dunn, L. M., & Williams, K. T. (1997). *Peabody Picture Vocabulary Test—Third Edition.* Circle Pines, MN: American Guidance Service.

Eden, G. F., Stein, J. F., Wood, H. M., & Wood, F. B. (1996). Differences in visuospatial judgment in reading-disability and normal children. *Perceptual and Motor Skills, 82,* 155–177.

Eggen, P., & Kauchak, D. (1997). *Educational psychology: Windows on classrooms.* Upper Saddle River, NJ: Merrill.

Elliott, C. D. (1990a). *Differential Ability Scales.* San Antonio, TX: Psychological Corporation.

Elliott, C. D. (1990b). *The Differential Ability Scales: Introductory and technical handbook.* San Antonio, TX: Psychological Corporation.

Elliott, C. D. (1994, April). *The measurement of fluid intelligence: Comparison of the Wechsler scales with the DAS and the KAIT.* Paper presented at the annual National Association of School Psychologists (NASP) Convention, Seattle, WA.

Embretson, S. E. (1996). Cognitive design principles and the successful performer: A study on spatial ability. *Journal of Educational Measurement, 33* (1), 29–39.

Engle, R. W., Cantor, J., & Carullo, J. J. (1992). Individual differences in working memory and comprehension: Test of four hypotheses. *Journal of Experimental Psychology, 18* (5), 972–992.

Engle, R. W., Nations, J. K., & Cantor, J. (1990). Is "working memory capacity" just another name for word knowledge? *Journal of Educational Psychology, 82* (4), 799–804.

Esters, E. G., Ittenbach, R. F., & Han, K. (1997). Today's IQ tests: Are they really better than their historical predecessors? *School Psychology Review, 26,* 211–223.

Eysenck, H. J. (1991). Dimensions of personality: 16, 5 or 3? Criteria for a taxonomic paradigm. *Personality and Individual Differences, 12,* 773–790.

Eysenck, H. J. (1992). Four ways five factors are not basic. *Personality and Individual Differences, 13,* 667–673.

Farmer, M. F., & Klein, R. M. (1995). The evidence for a temporal processing deficit linked to dyslexia: A review. *Psychonomic Bulletin and Review, 2* (4), 460–493.

Felton, R. H., & Pepper, P. P. (1995). Early identification and intervention of phonological deficits in kindergarten and early elementary children at risk for reading disability. *School Psychology Review, 24,* 405–414.

Feuerstein, R., Feuerstein, R., & Gross, S. (1997). The Learning Potential Assessment Device. In D. P. Flanagan, J. L. Genshaft, & P. L. Harrison (Eds.), *Contempory intellectual assessment: Theories, tests, and issues* (pp. 297–313). NY: Guilford.

Feuerstein, R., Feuerstein, R., & Schur, Y. (1995). *The theory of structural cognitive modifiability.* Unpublished manuscript.

Figueroa, R. A. (1983). Test bias and Hispanic children. *Journal of Special Education, 17,* 431–440.

Figueroa, R. A., Delgado, G. L., & Ruiz, N. T. (1984). Assessment of Hispanic children: Implications for Hispanic hearing-impaired children. In G. L. Delgado (Ed.), *The Hispanic deaf: Issues and challenges for bilingual special education,* (pp. 124–153), Washington, DC: Galaudet College Press.

Flanagan, D. P., & Alfonso, V. C. (1994, May). *A critical review of intelligence tests for culturally diverse preschoolers.* Paper presented at the meeting of the New York State Psychological Association, Bolton Landing, New York.

Flanagan, D. P., & Alfonso, V. C. (1995). A critical review of the technical characteristics of new and recently revised intelligence tests for preschool children. *Journal of Psychoeducational Assessment, 13,* 66–90.

Flanagan, D. P., Alfonso, V. C., & Flanagan, R. (1994). A review of the Kaufman Adolescent and Adult Intelligence Test: An advancement in cognitive assessment? *School Psychology Review, 23,* 512–525.

Flanagan, D. P., Alfonso, V. C., Kaminer, T., & Rader, D. E. (1995). Incidence of basic concepts in the directions of new and revised American intelligence tests for preschool children. *School Psychology International, 16,* 345–364.

Flanagan, D. P., Andrews, T. J., & Genshaft, J. L. (1997). The functional utility of intelligence tests with special education populations. In D. P. Flanagan, J. L. Genshaft, & P. L. Harrison (Eds.), *Contemporary intellectual assessment: Theories, tests, and issues* (pp. 457–483). New York: Guilford.

Flanagan, D. P., & Genshaft, J. L. (1997). Guest editors' comments: Mini-series on issues related to the use and interpretation of intelligence testing in the schools. *School Psychology Review, 26,* 146–149.

Flanagan, D. P., Genshaft, J. L., & Harrison, P. L. (Eds.). (1997). *Contemporary intellectual assessment: Theories, tests, and issues.* New York: Guilford Press.

Flanagan, D. P., Keith, T. Z., McGrew, K. S., & Vanderwood, M. L. (1997). *Is g all there is? An investigation of the relationship between Gf-Gc specific cognitive abilities and math achievement in individuals from grades 1 through 12.* Manuscript in preparation.

Flanagan, D. P., & McGrew, K. S. (1995, March). *Will you evolve or become extinct? Interpreting intelligence tests from modern Gf-Gc theory.* Paper presented at the meeting of the National Association of School Psychologists, Chicago.

Flanagan, D. P., & McGrew, K. S. (1997). A cross-battery approach to assessing and interpreting cognitive abilities: Narrowing the gap between practice and cognitive science. In D. P. Flanagan, J. L. Genshaft, & P. L. Harrison (Eds.), *Contemporary intellectual assessment: Theories, tests, and issues* (pp. 314–325). New York: Guilford.

Flanagan, D. P., & McGrew, K. S. (in press). Interpreting intelligence tests from contemporary

Gf-Gc theory: Joint confirmatory factor analysis of the WJ-R and KAIT in a non-White sample. *Journal of School Psychology.*

Flanagan, D. P., & Miranda, A. H. (1995). Working with culturally different families. In A. Thomas & J. Grimes (Eds.), *Best practices in school psychology—III* (pp. 1039–1060). Washington, DC: National Association of School Psychologists.

French, J. L., & Hale, R. L. (1990). A history of the development of psychological and educational testing. In C. R. Reynolds & R. W. Kamphaus (Eds.), *Handbook of psychological and educational assessment of children: Intelligence and achievement* (pp. 3–28). New York: Guilford.

French, J. W., Ekstrom, R. B., & Price, L. A (1963). *Manual and kit of reference tests for cognitive factors.* Princeton, NJ: Educational Testing Service.

Friedman, L. (1995). The space factor in mathematics: Gender differences. *Review of Educational Research, 65* (1), 22–50.

Gagné, E. D. (1985). *The cognitive psychology of school learning.* Boston: Little, Brown.

Gardner, H. (1983). *Frames of mind: The theory of multiple intelligences.* New York: Basic Books.

Gardner, H. (1993). *Frames of mind: The theory of multiple intelligences* (10th-anniversary ed.). New York: Basic Books.

Gardner, H. (1994). Multiple intelligences theory. In R. J. Sternberg (Ed.), *Encyclopedia of human intelligence* (pp. 740–742). New York: Macmillan.

Geary, D. C. (1993). Mathematical disabilities: Cognitive, neuropsychological, and genetic components. *Psychological Bulletin, 114* (2), 345–362.

Ghiselli, E. E. (1966). *The validity of occupational aptitude tests.* New York: Wiley.

Glutting, J. J., & Kaplan, D. (1990). Stanford-Binet Intelligence Scale, Fourth Edition: Making the case for reasonable interpretations. In C. R. Reynolds & R. W. Kamphaus (Eds.), *Handbook of psychological and educational assessment of children: Intelligence and achievement* (pp. 277–296). New York: Guilford.

Glutting, J. J., McDermott, P. A., & Konold, T. R. (1997). Ontology, structure, and diagnostic benefits of a normative subtest taxonomy from the WISC-III standardization sample. In D. P. Flanagan, J. L. Genshaft, & P. L. Harrison (Eds.), *Contemporary intellectual assessment: Theories, tests, and issues* (pp. 349–372). New York: Guilford.

Glutting, J. J., McDermott, P. A., Watkins, M. M., Kush, J. C., & Konold, T. R. (1997). The base rate problem and its consequences for interpreting children's ability profiles. *School Psychology Review, 26,* 176–188.

Greenspan, S., & Driscoll, J. (1997). The role of intelligence in a broad model of personal competence. In D. P. Flanagan, J. L. Genshaft, & P. L. Harrison (Eds.), *Contemporary intellectual assessment: Theories, tests, and issues* (pp. 131–150). New York: Guilford.

Griswold, P. C., Gelzheiser, L. M., & Shepherd, M. J. (1987). Does a production deficiency hypothesis account for vocabulary learning among adolescents with learning disabilities? *Journal of Learning Disabilities, 20* (10), 620–626.

Grosjean, F. (1989). Neurolinguists beware! The bilingual is not two monolinguals in one person. *Brain and Language, 36,* 3–15.

Guilford, J. P. (1954). *Psychometric methods* (2d ed.). New York: McGraw-Hill.

Gustafsson, J. E. (1984). A unifying model for the structure of intellectual abilities. *Intelligence, 8,* 179–203.

Gustafsson, J. E. (1988). Hierarchical models of individual differences in cognitive abilities. In R. J. Sternberg (Ed.), *Advances in the psychology of human intelligence* (vol. 4) (pp. 35–71). Hillsdale, NJ: Erlbaum.

Gustafsson, J. E. (1989). Broad and narrow abilities in research on learning and instruction. In R. Kanfer, P. L. Ackerman, & R. Cudeck (Eds.), *Abilities, motivation, and methodology: The Minnesota Symposium on Learning and Individual Differences* (pp. 203–237). Hillside, NJ: Erlbaum.

Gustafsson, J. E. (1994). General intelligence. In R. J. Sternberg (Ed.), *Encyclopedia of human intelligence* (pp. 469–475). New York: Macmillan.

Gustafsson, J. E., & Undheim, J. O. (1996). Individual differences in cognitive functions. In D. C. Berliner & R. C. Calfee (Eds.), *Handbook of educational psychology* (pp. 186–242). New York: Macmillan Library Reference USA.

Gutkin, T. B., Reynolds, C. R., & Galvin, G. A. (1984). Factor analysis of the Wechsler Adult Intelligence Scale—Revised (WAIS-R): An examination of the standardization sample. *Journal of School Psychology, 22,* 83–93.

Hakistan, A. R., & Bennet, R. W. (1977). Validity studies using the Comprehensive Ability Scale (CAB): I. Academic achievement criteria. *Educational and Psychological Measurement, 37,* 425–437.

Hakistan, A. R., & Cattell, R. B. (1978). Higher stratum ability structure on a basis of twenty primary abilities. *Journal of Educational Psychology, 70,* 657–659.

Hale, R. L. (1981). Concurrent validity of the WISC-R factor scores. *Journal of School Psychology, 19* (3), 274–278.

Hamayan, E. V., & Damico, J. S. (1991). Developing and using a second language. In E. V. Hamayan & J. S. Damico (Eds.), *Limiting bias in the assessment of bilingual students* (pp. 39–75). Austin: Pro-Ed.

Hammill, D. D., Brown, L., & Bryant, B. R. (1992). *A consumer's guide to tests in print* (2d ed.). Austin, TX: Pro-Ed.

Hammill, D. D., & Bryant, B. R. (1991). *Detroit Tests of Learning Aptitude—3.* Austin, TX: Pro-Ed.

Hammill, D. D., Pearson, N. A., & Wiederholt, J. L. (1996). *Comprehensive Test of Nonverbal Intelligence.* Austin, TX: Pro-Ed.

Hansen, J.-I. C., & Betsworth, D. G. (1994). Vocational abilities. In R. J. Sternberg (Ed.), *Encyclopedia of human intelligence* (pp. 1117–1122). New York: Macmillan.

Harrison, P. L., Flanagan, D. P., & Genshaft, J. L. (1997). An integration and synthesis of contemporary theories, tests, and issues in the field of intellectual assessment. In D. P. Flanagan, J. L. Genshaft, & P. L. Harrison (Eds.), *Contemporary intellectual assessment: Theories, tests, and issues* (pp. 533–562). New York: Guilford.

Harrison, P. L., Kaufman, A. S., Hickman, J. A., & Kaufman, N. L. (1988). A survey of tests used for adult assessment. *Journal of Psychoeducational Assessment, 6,* 188–198.

Helms, J. E. (1997). The triple quandary of race, culture, and social class in standardized cognitive ability testing. In D. P. Flanagan, J. L. Genshaft, & P. L. Harrison (Eds.), *Contemporary intellec-*

tual assessment: Theories, tests, and issues (pp. 517–532). New York: Guilford.

Hessler, G. (1993). *Use and interpretation of the Woodcock-Johnson Psycho-Educational Battery—Revised*. Chicago: Riverside.

Hitch, G. J. (1978). The role of short-term working memory in mental arithmetic. *Cognitive Psychology, 10*, 302–323.

Hobbs, N. (1975). *The futures of children*. San Francisco: Jossey-Bass.

Holland, J. L. (1973). *Making vocational choices: A theory of careers*. Englewood Cliffs, NJ: Prentice-Hall.

Holtzman, W. H., & Wilkinson, C. Y. (1991). Assessment of cognitive ability. In E. V. Hamayan & J. S. Damico (Eds.), *Limiting bias in the assessment of bilingual students* (pp. 247–280). Austin, TX: Pro-Ed.

Horn, J. L. (1965). *Fluid and crystallized intelligence: A factor analytic and developmental study of the structure among primary mental abilities*. Unpublished doctoral dissertation, University of Illinois, Champaign.

Horn, J. L. (1968). Organization of abilities and the development of intelligence. *Psychological Review, 75*, 242–259.

Horn, J. L. (1976). Human abilities: A review of research and theory in the early 1970s. *Annual Review of Psychology, 27*, 437–485.

Horn, J. L. (1982). The theory of fluid and crystallized intelligence in relation to learning and adult development. In F. I. M. Craik & S. Trehub (Eds.), *Aging and cognitive processes* (pp. 237–278). New York: Plenum.

Horn, J. L. (1985). Remodeling old theories of intelligence: *Gf-Gc* theory. In B. B. Wolman (Ed.), *Handbook of intelligence* (pp. 267–300). New York: Wiley.

Horn, J. L. (1988). Thinking about human abilities. In J. R. Nesselroade & R. B. Cattell (Eds.), *Handbook of multivariate psychology* (rev. ed.) (pp. 645–685). New York: Academic Press.

Horn, J. L. (1989). Cognitive diversity: A framework for learning. In P. L. Ackerman, R. J. Sternberg, & R. Glaser (Eds.), *Learning and individual differences: Advances in theory and research* (pp. 61–114). New York: Freeman.

Horn, J. L. (1991). Measurement of intellectual capabilities: A review of theory. In K. S. McGrew, J. K. Werder, & R. W. Woodcock, *Woodcock-Johnson technical manual* (pp. 197–232). Chicago: Riverside.

Horn, J. L. (1994). Theory of fluid and crystallized intelligence. In R. J. Sternberg (Ed.), *Encyclopedia of human intelligence* (pp. 443–451). New York: Macmillan.

Horn, J. L., & Cattell, R. B. (1967). Age differences in fluid and crystallized intelligence. *Acta Psychologica, 26*, 107–129.

Horn, J. L., & Noll, J. (1997). Human cognitive capabilities: *Gf-Gc* theory. In D. P. Flanagan, J. L. Genshaft, & P. L. Harrison (Eds.), *Contemporary intellectual assessment: Theories, tests, and issues* (pp. 53–91). New York: Guilford.

Humphreys, L. G. (1992). Commentary: What both critics and users of ability tests need to know. *Psychological Science, 3*, 271–274.

Hunt, E. (1990). A modern arsenal for mental assessment. *Educational Psychologist, 25* (3 & 4), 223–241.

Hunt, E., & Lansman, M. (1986). Unified model of attention and problem solving. *Psychological Review, 93*, 446–461.

Institute for Scientific Information (1992). *Current Contents on Diskette*. Philadelphia: Author.

Ittenbach, R. F., Esters, I. G., & Wainer, H. (1997). The history of test development. In D. P. Flanagan, J. L. Genshaft, & P. L. Harrison (Eds.), *Contemporary intellectual assessment: Theories, tests, and issues* (pp. 17–31). New York: Guilford.

Iverson, L. L. (1979). The chemistry of the brain. *Scientific American, 241*, 134–149.

Jackson, N. E., Donaldson, G. W., & Cleland, L. N. (1988). The structure of precocious reading ability. *Journal of Educational Psychology, 80* (2), 234–243.

Jacobson, J. W., & Mulick, J. A. (Eds.) (1996). *Manual of diagnosis and professional practice in mental retardation*. Washington, DC: American Psychological Association.

Jensen, A. R. (1974). How biased are culture-loaded tests? *Genetic Psychology Monographs, 90*, 185–244.

Jensen, A. R. (1976). Construct validity and test bias. *Phi Delta Kappan, 58*, 340–346.

Jensen, A. R. (1984). Test validity: *g* versus the specificity doctrine. *Journal of Social and Biological Structures, 7*, 93–118.

Jensen, A. R. (1992). Understanding *g* in terms of information processing. *Educational Psychology Review, 4,* 271–308.

Jensen, A. R. (1997, July). *What we know and don't know about the g factor.* Keynote address delivered at the bi-annual convention of the International Society for the Study of Individual Differences. Aarhus, Denmark.

Jensen, A. R., & Weng, L. -J. (1994). What is a good *g*? *Intelligence, 18,* 231–258.

Jones, R. (1972). Labels and stigma in special education. *Exceptional Children, 38,* 553–546.

Jones, R. L. (1988). *Psychoeducational assessment of minority group children: A casebook.* Berkeley, CA: Cobb & Henry.

Joshi, R. M. (1995). Assessing reading and spelling skills. *School Psychology Review, 24* (3), 361–375.

Just, M. A., & Carpenter, P. A. (1992). A capacity theory of comprehension: Individual differences in working memory. *Psychological Review, 99* (1), 122–149.

Kail, R. (1991). Developmental changes in speed of processing during childhood and adolescence. *Psychological Bulletin, 109,* 490–501.

Kamphaus, R. W. (1990). K-ABC theory in historical and current contexts. *Journal of Psychoeducational Assessment, 8,* 356–368.

Kamphaus, R. W. (1993). *Clinical assessment of children's intelligence.* Boston: Allyn and Bacon.

Kamphaus, R. W., Petoskey, M. D., & Morgan, A. W. (1997). A history of test intelligence interpretation. In D. P. Flanagan, J. L. Genshaft, & P. L. Harrison (Eds.), *Contemporary intellectual assessment: Theories, tests, and issues* (pp. 32–51). New York: Guilford.

Kamphaus, R. W., & Reynolds, C. R. (1984). Development and structure of the Kaufman Assessment Battery for Children (K-ABC). *Journal of Special Education, 18* (3), 213–228.

Kaufman, A. S. (1978). The importance of basic concepts in individual assessment of preschool children. *Journal of School Psychology, 16,* 207–211.

Kaufman, A. S. (1979). *Intelligent testing with the WISC-R.* New York: Wiley.

Kaufman, A. S. (1984). K-ABC and controversy. *Journal of Special Education, 18* (3), 409–444.

Kaufman, A. S. (1990a). *Assessing adolescent and adult intelligence.* Boston: Allyn and Bacon.

Kaufman, A. S. (1990b). The WPPSI-R: You can't judge a test by its colors. *Journal of School Psychology, 28,* 387–394.

Kaufman, A. S. (1994). *Intelligent testing with the WISC-III.* New York: Wiley.

Kaufman, A. S., & Kaufman, N. L. (1983). *Kaufman Assessment Battery for Children.* Circle Pines, MN: American Guidance Service.

Kaufman, A. S., & Kaufman, N. L. (1990). *Kaufman Brief Intelligence Test.* Circle Pines, MN: American Guidance Service.

Kaufman, A. S., & Kaufman, N. L. (1993). *The Kaufman Adolescent and Adult Intelligence Test.* Circle Pines, MN: American Guidance Service.

Kaufman, A. S., & Kaufman, N. L. (1994). *Kaufman Short Neuropsychological Assessment Procedure.* Circle Pines, MN: American Guidance Service.

Kavale, K. A. (1982). Meta-analysis of the relationship between visual perceptual skills and reading achievement. *Journal of Learning Disabilities, 15* (1), 42–51.

Keith, T. (1988). Research methods in school psychology: An overview. *School Psychology Review, 17,* 502–520.

Keith, T. Z. (1990). Confirmatory and hierarchical confirmatory analysis of the Differential Ability Scales. *Journal of Psychoeducational Assessment, 8,* 391–405.

Keith, T. Z. (1994). Intelligence is important, intelligence is complex. *School Psychology Quarterly, 9,* 209–221.

Keith, T. Z. (1997). Using confirmatory factor analysis to aid in understanding the constructs measured by intelligence tests. In D. P. Flanagan, J. L. Genshaft, & P. L. Harrison, (Eds.), *Contemporary intellectual assessment: Theories, tests, and issues* (pp. 373–402). New York: Guilford.

Kintsch, W. (1988). The role of knowledge in discourse comprehension: A construction-integration model. *Psychological Review, 95* (2), 163–182.

Kirby, J. R., & Becker, L. D. (1986). Cognitive components of reading problems in arithmetic. *RASE: Remedial and Special Education, 9* (5), 7–15, 27.

Kochnower, J., Richardson, E., & DiBenedetto, B. (1983). A comparison of the phonic decoding ability of normal and learning disabled children. *Journal of Learning Disabilities, 16,* 348–351.

Kosslyn, S. M. (1985). Mental imagery ability. In R. J. Sternberg (Ed.), *Human abilities: An information processing approach* (pp. 151–172). New York: Freeman.

Kranzler, J. H., & Weng, L. (1995). Factor structure of the PASS cognitive tasks: A reexamination of Naglieri et al. (1991). *Journal of School Psychology, 33,* 143–157.

LaBuda, M. C., & DeFries, J. C. (1988). Cognitive abilities in children with reading disabilities and controls: A follow-up study. *Journal of Learning Disabilities, 21* (9), 562–566.

Leather, C. V., & Henry, L. A. (1994). Working memory span and phonological awareness tasks as predictors of early reading ability. *Journal of Experimental Child Psychology, 58,* 88–111.

Lemaire, P., Abdi, H., & Fayol, M. (1996). The role of working memory resources in simple cognitive arithmetic. *European Journal of Cognitive Psychology, 8* (1), 73–103.

Lezak, M. D. (1976). *Neuropsychological assessment.* New York: Oxford University Press.

Lezak, M. D. (1995). *Neuropsychological assessment* (3d ed.). New York: Oxford University Press.

Lidz, C. S. (Ed.) (1987). *Dynamic assessment: An interactional approach to evaluation of learning potential.* New York: Guilford.

Lidz, C. S. (1991). *Practitioner's guide to dynamic assessment.* New York: Guilford.

Lidz, C. S. (1997). Dynamic assessment approaches. In D. P. Flanagan, J. L. Genshaft, & P. L. Harrison (Eds.), *Contemporary intellectual assessment: Theories, tests, and issues* (pp. 281–296). New York: Guilford.

Loevinger, J. (1954). The attenuation paradox in test theory. *Psychological Bulletin, 51,* 493–504.

Loevinger, J. (1957). Objective tests as instruments of psychological theory. *Psychological Reports, 3,* 635–694.

Logie, R. (1996). The seven ages of working memory. In J. Richardson, R. Engle, L. Hasher, R. Logie, E. Stoltzfus, & R. Zacks (Eds.), *Working memory and human cognition* (pp. 31–65). New York: Oxford University Press.

Lohman, D. F. (1989). Human intelligence: An introduction to advances in theory and research. *Review of Educational Research, 59* (4), 333–373.

Lohman, D. F. (1994). Spatial ability. In R. J. Sternberg (Ed.), *Encyclopedia of human intelligence* (pp. 1000–1007). New York: Macmillan.

Lopez, E. C. (1997). The cognitive assessment of limited English proficient and bilingual children. In D. P. Flanagan, J. L. Genshaft, & P. L. Harrison (Eds.), *Contemporary intellectual assessment: Theories, tests, and issues* (pp. 506–516). New York: Guilford.

Lord, F., & Novick, M. (1968). *Statistical theories of mental test scores.* Reading, MA: Addison-Wesley.

Lubinski, D., & Benbow, C. P. (1995). An opportunity for empiricism. *Contemporary Psychology, 40* (10), 935–940.

Luria, A. R. (1966). *Human brain and psychological processes.* New York: Harper & Row.

Luria, A. R. (1970). The functional organization of the brain. *Scientific American, 222,* 66–78.

Luria, A. R. (1973). *The working brain: An introduction to neuropsychology.* New York: Basic Books.

Luria, A. R. (1976). *Cognitive development: Its cultural and social foundations.* Cambridge, MA: Harvard University Press.

Luria, A. R. (1980). *Higher cortical functions in man* (2d ed., rev. & expanded). New York: Basic Books.

Luria, A. R. (1982). *Language and cognition.* New York: Wiley.

Lyon, G. R. (1995). Toward a definition of dyslexia. *Annals of Dyslexia, 45,* 3–27.

MacDonald, G. W., & Cornwall, A. (1995). The relationship between phonological awareness and reading and spelling achievement eleven years later. *Journal of Learning Disabilities, 28* (8), 523–527.

Mackintosh, N. J. (1986). The biology of intelligence? *British Journal of Psychology, 77,* 1–18.

Manger, T., & Eikeland, O. -J. (1996). Relationship between boys' and girls' nonverbal ability and mathematical achievement. *School Psychology International, 17,* 71–80.

Mann, V. A., & Liberman, I. Y. (1984). Phonological awareness and verbal short-term memory. *Journal of Learning Disabilities, 10,* 592–599.

Marjoribanks, K. (1976). Academic achievement, intelligence and creativity: A regression surface analysis. *Multivariate Behavioral Research, 11* (1), 105–118.

Matarrazzo, J. D. (1990). Psychological assessment versus psychological testing: Validation from Binet to the school, clinic, and courtroom. *American Psychologist, 45*, 999–1017.

Mather, N. (1991). *An instructional guide to the Woodcock-Johnson Psycho-Educational Battery— Revised.* Brandon, VT: Clinical Psychology.

Mayer, R. E. (1994). Reasoning, Inductive. In R. J. Sternberg (Ed.), *Encyclopedia of human intelligence* (pp. 935–938). New York: Macmillan.

McArdle, J. J., & Prescott, C. A. (1997). Contemporary models for the biometric genetic analysis of intellectual abilities. In D. P. Flanagan, J. L. Genshaft, & P. L. Harrison (Eds.), *Contemporary intellectual assessment: Theories, tests, and issues* (pp. 403–436). New York: Guilford.

McBride-Chang, C. (1995). Phonological processing, speech perception, and reading disability: An integrative review. *Educational Psychologist, 30* (3), 109–121.

McCallum, R. S., & Bracken, B. A. (1997). The Universal Nonverbal Intelligence Test. In D. P. Flanagan, J. L. Genshaft, & P. L. Harrison (Eds.), *Contemporary intellectual assessment: Theories, tests, and issues* (pp. 268–280). New York: Guilford.

McCallum, R. S., & Bracken, B. A. (in press). *Universal Nonverbal Intelligence Test.* Chicago: Riverside.

McDermott, P. A., Fantuzzo, J. W., & Glutting, J. J. (1990). Just say no to subtest analysis: A critique on Wechsler theory and practice. *Journal of Psychoeducational Assessment, 8*, 290–302.

McDermott, P. A., Fantuzzo, J. W., Glutting, J. J., Watkins, M. W., & Baggaley, R. A. (1992). Illusions of meaning in the ipsative assessment of children's ability. *Journal of Special Education, 25*, 504–526.

McDermott, P. A., & Glutting, J. J. (1997). Informing stylistic learning behavior, disposition, and achievement through ability subtests—Or, more illusions of meaning? *School Psychology Review, 26*, 163–175.

McGhee, R. L. (1993). Fluid and crystallized intelligence: Confirmatory factor analysis of the Differential Abilities Scale, Detroit Tests of Learning Aptitude–3, and Woodcock-Johnson Psycho-Educational Assessment Battery— Revised. *Journal of Psychoeducational Assessment* [Monograph Series: Woodcock-Johnson Psycho-Educational Battery—Revised], 20–38.

McGrew, K. S. (1984). Normative-based guides for subtest profile interpretation of the Woodcock-Johnson Tests of Cognitive Ability. *Journal of Psychoeducational Assessment, 2*, 325–332.

McGrew, K. S. (1986). *Clinical interpretation of the Woodcock-Johnson Tests of Cognitive Ability.* Orlando, FL: Grune and Stratton.

McGrew, K. S. (1993). The relationship between the WJ-R *Gf-Gc* cognitive clusters and reading achievement across the lifespan. *Journal of Psychoeducational Assessment* [Monograph Series: WJ-R Monograph], 39–53.

McGrew, K. S. (1994). *Clinical interpretation of the Woodcock-Johnson Tests of Cognitive Ability— Revised.* Boston: Allyn and Bacon.

McGrew, K. S. (1995, March). *Intelligence is a "many splendored" thing: Implications of theories of multiple intelligences.* Presentation at the meeting of the National Association of School Psychologists, Chicago.

McGrew, K. S. (1997). Analysis of the major intelligence batteries according to a proposed comprehensive *Gf-Gc* framework. In D. P. Flanagan, J. L. Genshaft, & P. L. Harrison (Eds.), *Contemporary intellectual assessment: Theories, tests, and issues* (151–180). New York: Guilford.

McGrew, K. S., & Flanagan, D. P. (1996). The Wechsler Performance Scale debate: Fluid intelligence (*Gf*) or visual processing (*Gv*)? *Communiqué, 24* (6), 14–16.

McGrew, K. S., & Flanagan, D. P. (1997). [Investigation of differences between Horn's and Carroll's *Gf-Gc* models of the strcture of intelligence]. Unpublished raw data.

McGrew, K. S., Flanagan, D. P., Keith, T. Z., & Vanderwood, M. (1997). Beyond *g*: The impact of *Gf-Gc* specific cognitive abilities research on the future use and interpretation of intelligence tests in the schools. *School Psychology Review, 26*, 189–210.

McGrew, K. S., & Hessler, G. L. (1995). The relationship between the WJ-R *Gf-Gc* cognitive clusters and mathematics achievement across the life-span. *Journal of Psychoeducational Assessment, 13*, 21–38.

McGrew, K. S., & Knopik, S. N. (1993). The relationship between the WJ-R *Gf-Gc* cognitive clusters and writing achievement across the lifespan. *School Psychology Review, 22,* 687–695.

McGrew, K. S., & Knopik, S. N. (1996). The relationship between intra-cognitive scatter on the Woodcock-Johnson Psycho-Educational Battery—Revised and school achievement. *Journal of School Psychology, 34,* 351–364.

McGrew, K. S., & Murphy, S. R. (1995). Uniqueness and general factor characteristics of the Woodcock-Johnson Tests of Cognitive Ability. *Journal of Psychoeducational Assessment, 2,* 141–148.

McGrew, K. S., & Pehl, J. (1988). Prediction of future achievement by the Woodcock-Johnson Psycho-Educational Battery and the WISC-R. *Journal of School Psychology, 26,* 275–281.

McGrew, K. S., Untiedt, S. A., & Flanagan, D. P. (1996). General factor and uniqueness characteristics of the Kaufman Adolescent and Adult Intelligence Scale (KAIT). *Journal of Psychoeducational Assessment, 14,* 208–219.

McGrew, K. S., Vanderwood, M., Flanagan, D., & Keith, T. (1997). *Stuck on g? Gf-Gc specific cognitive abilities and their relationship to reading achievement from grades 1 through 12.* Manuscript in preparation.

McGrew, K. S., Werder, J. K., & Woodcock, R. W. (1991). *Woodcock-Johnson Psycho-Educational Battery—Revised technical manual.* Chicago: Riverside.

McGrew, K. S. & Wrightson, W. (1997). The calculation of new and improved WISC-III reliability, uniqueness, and general factor characteristics information through the use of data smoothing procedures. *Psychology in the Schools, 34* (3), 181–195.

McGue, M., & Bouchard, T. J. Jr. (1989). Genetic and environmental determinants of information processing and special mental abilities: A twin analysis. In R. J. Sternberg (Ed.), *Advances in the psychology of human intelligence* (vol. 5) (pp. 7–45). Hillsdale, NJ: Erlbaum.

McGuiness, D., McGuiness, C., & Donohue, J. (1995). Phonological training and the alphabet principle: Evidence for reciprocal causality. *Reading Research Quarterly, 30* (4), 830–852.

McLeod, B. (1994). Introduction. In B. McLeod (Ed.), *Language and learning: Educating linguistically diverse students* (pp. xiii–xxii). Albany, NY: State University of New York Press.

McNemar, Q. (1964). Lost: Our intelligence? Why? *American Psychologist, 19,* 871–882.

Mercer, J. R. (1979). *System of Multicultural Pluralistic Assessment.* New York: The Psychological Corporation.

Messick, S. (1992). Multiple intelligences or multi-level intelligence? Selective emphasis on distinctive properties of hierarchy: On Gardner's *Frames of Mind* and Sternberg's *Beyond IQ* in the context of theory and research on the structure of human abilities. *Psychological Inquiry, 3* (4), 365–384.

Messick, S. (1995). Validity of psychological assessment: Validation of inferences from persons' responses and performances as scientific inquiry into score meaning. *American Psychologist, 50,* 741–749.

Naglieri, J. A. (1985). *Matrix Analogies Test.* San Antonio, TX: Psychological Corporation.

Naglieri, J. A. (1997). Planning, attention, simultaneous, and successive theory and the cognitive assessment system: A new theory-based measure of intelligence. In D. P. Flanagan, J. L. Genshaft, & P. L. Harrison (Eds.), *Contemporary intellectual assessment: Theories, tests, and issues* (pp. 247–267). New York: Guilford.

Naglieri, J. A., & Das, J. P. (1990). Planning, attention, simultaneous, and successive (PASS) cognitive processes as a model for intelligence. *Journal of Psychoeducational Assessment, 8,* 303–337.

Näslund, J. C., & Schneider, W. (1996). Kindergarten letter knowledge, phonological skills, and memory processes: Relative effects on early literacy. *Journal of Experimental Child Psychology, 62,* 30–59.

Neisser, U., Boodoo, G., Bouchard, T. J., Boykin, A. W., Brody, N., Ceci, S. J., Halpern, D. F., Loehlin, J. C., Perloff, R., Sternberg, R. J., & Urbina, S. (1996). Intelligence: Knowns and unknowns. *American Psychologist, 51,* 77–101.

Nettelbeck, T. (1994). Speediness. In R. J. Sternberg (Ed.), *Encyclopedia of human intelligence* (pp. 1014–1019). New York: Macmillan.

New York City Public Schools (1993). *Answers to frequently asked questions about limited English proficient (LEP) students and bilingual ESL programs: Facts and figures, 1992–1993.* New York: Author.

Newland, T. E. (1971). Psychological assessment of exceptional children and youth. In W. Cruickshank (Ed.), *Psychology of exceptional children and youth* (pp. 115–172). Englewood Cliffs, NJ: Prentice-Hall.

Nunnally, J. S. (1978). *Psychometric theories*. New York: McGraw-Hill.

Ochoa, S. H., Powell, M. P., & Robles-Pina, R. (1996). School psychologists' assessment practices with bilingual and limited-English-proficient students. *Journal of Psychoeducational Assessment, 14*, 250–275.

Olmedo, E. S. (1981). Testing linguistic minorities. *American Psychologist, 36*, 1078–1085.

Paik, M., & Nebenzahl, E. (1987). The overall percentile rank versus the individual percentile ranks. *American Statistician, 41*, 136–138.

Petrill, S. A., Plomin, R., McClearn, G. E., Smith, D. L., Vignetti, S., Chorney, M. J., Chorney, K., Thompson, L. A., Detterman, D. K., Benbow, C., Lubinski, D., Daniels, J., Owen, M. J., & McGuffin, P. (1996). DNA markers associated with general and specific cognitive abilities. *Intelligence, 23*, 191–203.

Plomin, R., DeFries, J. C., & McClearn, G. E. (1980). *Behavioral genetics*. San Francisco: Freeman.

Plomin, R., DeFries, J. C., & McClearn, G. E. (1990). *Behavioral genetics: A primer* (2d ed.). New York: Freeman.

Plomin, R., & Lochlin, J. C. (1989). Direct and indirect IQ heritability estimates: A puzzle. *Behavior Genetics, 19* (3), 331–342.

Prohovnik, I. (1980). *Mapping brainwork*. Malmo, Sweden: CWK Gleerup.

Ramirez, A.G. (1990). Prospectives on language proficiency assessment. In A. Barona & E. E. Garcia (Eds.), *Children at risk: Poverty, minority status, and other issues in educational equity* (pp. 305–323). Washington, DC: National Association of School Psychologists.

Rasanen, P., & Ahonen, T. (1995). Arithmetic disabilities with and without reading difficulties: A comparison of arithmetic errors. *Developmental Neuropsychology, 11* (3), 275–295.

Raven, J. C. (1938). *Progressive matrices: A perceptual test of intelligence*. San Antonio, TX: Psychological Corporation.

Reed, M. T., & McCallum, S. (1995). Construct validity of the Universal Nonverbal Intelligence Test (UNIT). *Psychology in the Schools, 32*, 277–290.

Reitan, R. M., & Wolfson, B. (1985). *The Halstead-Reitan Neuropsychological Test Battery: Theory and clinical interpretation*. Tuscon, AZ: Neuropsychology Press.

Reschly, D. J. (1990). Found: Our intelligences: What do they mean? *Journal of Psychoeducational Assessment, 8*, 259–267.

Reschly, D. J., & Grimes, J. P. (1990). Best practices in intellectual assessment. In A. Thomas & J. Grimes (Eds.), *Best practices in school psychology—II* (pp. 425–439). Washington, DC: National Association of School Psychologists.

Reschly, D. J., & Grimes, J. P. (1995). Best practices in intellectual assessment.

Research and Policy Committee of the Committee for Economic Development. (1987). *Children in need—Investment strategies for the educationally disadvantaged*. New York: Author.

Reynolds, C. R., & Bigler, E. D. (1994). *Test of Memory and Learning*. Austin, TX: Pro-Ed.

Reynolds, C. R., & Kamphaus, R. W. (Eds.) (1990). *Handbook of psychological and educational assessment of children: Intelligence and achievement*. New York: Guilford.

Reynolds, C. R., Kamphaus, R. W., & Rosenthal, B. (1988). Factor analysis of the Stanford-Binet Fourth Edition for ages 2 through 23. *Measurement and Evaluation in Counseling and Development, 21*, 52–63.

Reynolds, C. R., & Kaufman, A. S. (1990). Assessment of children's intelligence with the Wechsler Intelligence Scale for Children—Revised (WISC-R). In C. R. Reynolds & R. W. Kamphaus, *Handbook of psychological and educational assessment of children: Intelligence and achievement* (pp. 127–165). New York: Guilford.

Richardson, J. (1996). Evolving concepts of working memory. In J. Richardson, R. Engle, L. Hasher, R. Logie, E. Stoltzfus, & R. Zacks (Eds.), *Working memory and human cognition* (pp. 3–30). New York: Oxford University Press.

Rogoff, B., & Chavajay, P. (1995). What's become of research on the cultural basis of cognitive development? *American Psychologist, 50, 859*–877.

Roid, G. H., & Gyurke, J. (1991). General-factor and specific variance in the WPPSI-R. *Journal of Psychoeducational Assessment, 9*, 209–223.

Roid, G. H., & Miller, L. J. (1997). *The Leiter International Performance Scale—Revised Edition*. Wood Dale, IL: Stoelting.

Salvia, J., & Ysseldyke, J. (1991). *Assessment in special*

and remedial education (5th ed.). Boston: Houghton-Mifflin.

Santos, O. B. (1989). Language skills and cognitive processes related to poor reading comprehension performance. *Journal of Learning Disabilities, 22,* 131–133.

Sattler, J. M. (1988). *Assessment of children's intelligence and special abilities* (2d ed.). San Diego, CA: Sattler.

Sattler, J. (1992). *Assessment of children* (rev. 3d ed.). San Diego, CA: Sattler.

Scarr, S. (1985). An author's frame of mind: Review of *Frames of mind: The theory of multiple intelligences. New ideas in psychology, 3,* 95–100.

Scarr, S., & Carter-Saltzman, L. (1982). Genetics and intelligence. In R. J. Sternberg (Ed.), *Handbook of human intelligence* (pp. 792–896). Cambridge, England: Cambridge University Press.

Schaie, K. W. (1979). The primary mental abilities in adulthood: An exploration in the development of psychometric intelligence. In P. B. Baltes & O. G. Brim, Jr. (Eds.), *Life-span development and behavior* (vol. 2) (pp. 67–115). New York: Academic Press.

Schaie, K. W. (Ed.) (1983). *Longitudinal studies of adult psychological development.* New York: Guilford.

Schaie, K. W. (1994). The course of adult intellectual development. *American Psychologist, 49,* 304–314.

Schmidt, J. P., & Tombaugh, T. (1995). *Learning and Memory Battery.* North Tonawanda, NY: Multi-Health Systems.

Shankweiler, D., Liberman, I. Y., Mark, L. S., Fowler, C. A., & Fischer, F. W. (1979). Human learning and memory. *Journal of Experimental Psychology, 5* (6), 531–545.

Shaw, S. E., Swerdlik, M. E., & Laurent, J. (1993). Review of the WISC-III [WISC-III Monograph]. *Journal of Psychoeducational Assessment,* 151–160.

Sheslow, D., & Adams, W. (1990). *Wide Range Assessment of Memory and Learning.* Wilmington, NC: Wide Range.

Silverstein, A. (1976). Variance components in the subtests of the WISC-R. *Psychological Reports, 39,* 1109–1110.

Snider, V. E. (1989). Reading comprehension performance of adolescents with learning disabilities. *Learning Disability Quarterly, 12* (2), 87–96.

Snider, V. E., & Tarver, S. G. (1987). The effect of early reading failure on acquisition of knowledge among students with learning disabilities. *Journal of Learning Disabilities, 20* (6), 351–356, 373.

Snow, R. E. (1985). [Review of *Frames of mind: The theory of multiple intelligences*]. *American Journal of Education, 85,* 109–112.

Snow, R. E. (1986). Individual diffferences and the design of educational programs. *American Psychologist, 41,* 1029–1039.

Snow, R. E. (1989). Aptitude–treatment interaction as a framework for research on individual differences in learning. In P. L. Ackerman, R. J. Sternberg, & R. Glaser (Eds.), *Learning and individual differences: Advances in theory and research* (pp. 13–59). New York: Freeman.

Snow, R. E. (1991). The concept of aptitude. In R. E. Snow & D. E. Wiley (Eds.), *Improving inquiring in social science* (pp. 249–284). Hillsdale, NJ: Erlbaum.

Snow, R. E. (1992). Aptitude theory: Yesterday, today, and tomorrow. *Educational Psychologist, 27,* 5–32.

Snow, R. E., Corno, L. & Jackson, D. (1996). Individual differences in affective and conative functions. In D. C. Berliner & R. C. Colfee (Eds.), *Handbook of educational psychology.* New York: Macmillan Library Reference USA.

Snow, R. E., & Swanson, J. (1992). Instructional psychology: Aptitude, adaptation, and assessment. *Annual Review of Psychology, 43,* 583–626.

Spearman, C. E. (1904). "General intelligence," objectively determined and measured. *American Journal of Psychiatry, 15,* 201–293.

Spearman, C. E. (1927). *The abilities of man.* London: Macmillan.

Sperry, R. W. (1968). Hemisphere deconnection and unity in conscious awareness. *American Psychologist, 23,* 723–733.

Sperry, R. W. (1974). Lateral specialization in the surgically separated hemispheres. In F. O. Schmitt & F. G. Worden (Eds.), *The neurosciences: Third study program.* Cambridge, MA: MIT Press.

Stahl, S. A., & Murray, B. A. (1994). Defining phonological awareness and its relationship to early reading. *Journal of Educational Psychology, 86* (2), 221–234.

Stankov, L. (1994). Auditory abilities. In R. J. Sternberg (Ed.), *Encyclopedia of human intelligence* (pp. 157–162). New York: Macmillan.

Stanovich, K. F., Cunningham, A. F., & Cramer, B. B. (1984). Assessing phonological awareness in kindergarten children: Issues of task comparability. *Journal of Experimental Child Psychology, 38*, 175–190.

Stanovich, K. E., Cunningham, A. E., & Feeman, D. J. (1984). Intelligence, cognitive skills, and early reading progress. *Reading Research Quarterly, 19*, 278–303.

Sternberg, R. J. (1985). *Beyond IQ: A triarchic theory of human intelligence.* New York: Cambridge University Press.

Sternberg, R. J. (1986). Intelligence, wisdom, and creativity: Three is better than one. *Educational Psychologist, 21* (3), 175–190.

Sternberg, R. J. (1992). Ability tests, measurements, and markets. *Journal of Educational Psychology, 84*, 134–140.

Sternberg, R. J. (1993). Rocky's back again: A review of the WISC-III. *Journal of Psychoeducational Assessment* [WISC-III Monograph], 161–164.

Sternberg, R. J. (1994). A triarchic model for teaching and assessing students in general psychology. *General Psychologist, 30* (2), 42–48.

Sternberg, R. J. (1997). The triarchic theory of intelligence. In D. P. Flanagan, J. L. Genshaft, & P. L. Harrison (Eds.), *Contemporary intellectual assessment: Theories, tests, and issues* (pp. 92–104). New York: Guilford.

Stevenson, H. W., Parker, T., Wilkinson, A., Hegion, A., & Fish, E. (1976). Longitudinal study of individual differences in cognitive development and scholastic achievement. *Journal of Educational Psychology, 68* (4), 377–400.

Stinnett, T. A., Havey, J. M., & Oehler-Stinnett, J. (1994). Current test usage by practicing school psychologists: A national survey. *Journal of Psychoeducational Assessment, 12*, 331–350.

Stone, B. J. (1992). Joint confirmatory factor analyses of the DAS and WISC-R. *Journal of School Psychology, 30*, 185–195.

Stone, B., & Brady, S. (1995). Evidence for phonological processing deficits in less-skilled readers. *Annals of Dyslexia, 45*, 51–78.

Swanson, H. L. (1982). Verbal short-term memory encoding of learning disabled, deaf, and normal readers. *Learning Disabilities Quarterly, 5*, 21–28.

Swanson, H. L. (1986). Learning disabled readers' verbal coding difficulties: A problem of storage or retrieval? *Learning Disabilities Research, 1*, 73–82.

Swanson, H. L. (1996). Individual and age-related differences in children's working memory. *Memory and Cognition, 24* (1), 70–82.

Swanson, H. L., & Berninger, V. W. (1995). The role of working memory in skilled and less skilled readers' comprehension. *Intelligence, 21*, 83–108.

Taylor, L. C., Brown, F. G., & Michael, W. B. (1976). The validity of cognitive, affective, and demographic variables in the prediction of achievement in high school algebra and geometry: Implications for the definition of mathematical aptitude. *Educational and Psychological Measurement, 36*, 971–982.

Taylor, T. R. (1994). A review of three approaches to cognitive assessment, and a proposed integrated approach based on a unifying theoretical framework. *South African Journal of Psychology, 24* (4), 183–193.

Tellegen, A. (1982). *Brief manual for the Multidimensional Personality Questionnaire (MPQ).* Minneapolis, MN: Author.

Tellegen, A. T., & Waller, N. G. (in press). Exploring personality through test construction: Development of the Multidimensional Personality Questionnaire. In S. R. Briggs & J. M. Cheek (Eds.), *Personality measures: Development and evaluation* (vol. 1). Greenwich, CT: JAI Press.

Terman, L. M. (1916). *The measurement of intelligence: An explanation of and a complete guide for the use of the Stanford revision and extension of the Binet-Simon intelligence scale.* Boston: Houghton Mifflin.

Terman, L. M., & Merrill, M. A. (1937). *Measuring intelligence:* Boston: Houghton Mifflin.

Terman, L. M., & Merrill, M. A. (1960). *Stanford-Binet Intelligence Scale: Manual for the third revision form L-M.* Boston: Houghton Mifflin.

Terman, L. M., & Merrill, M. A. (1972). *Stanford-Binet Intelligence Scale: 1972 norms edition.* Boston: Houghton Mifflin.

Thorndike, R. M. (1997). The early history of intelligence testing. In D. P. Flanagan, J. L. Genshaft, & P. L. Harrison (Eds.), *Contemporary intellectual assessment: Theories, tests, and issues* (pp. 3–16). New York: Guilford.

Thorndike, R. L., Hagen, E. P., & Sattler, J. M. (1986). *Stanford-Binet Intelligence Scale: Guide for administering and scoring the Fourth Edition.* Chicago: Riverside.

Thorndike, R. M., & Lohman, D. F. (1990). *A century of ability testing.* Chicago: Riverside.

Thurstone, L. L. (1938). Primary mental abilities. *Psychometric Monographs* (1).

Thurstone, L. L. (1947). *Multiple factor analysis: A development and expansion of the vectors of mind.* Chicago: University of Chicago Press.

Thurstone, L. L., & Thurstone, T. G. (1941). Factorial studies of intelligence: *Psychometric Monographs*, No. 2.

Torgesen, J. K. (1988). Studies of children with learning disabilities who perform poorly on memory-span tasks. *Journal of Learning Disabilities, 21* (10), 605–612.

Torgesen, J. K., & Bryant, B. R. (1994). *Test of Phonological Awareness.* Austin, TX: Pro-Ed.

Torgesen, J. K., Wagner, R. K., & Rashotte, C. A. (1994). Longitudinal studies of phonological processing and reading. *Journal of Learning Disabilities, 27* (5), 276–286.

Travers, J. F., Elliott, S. N., & Kratochwill, T. R. (1993). *Educational psychology: Effective teaching, effective learning.* Madison, WI: WCB Brown & Benchmark.

Turner, M. L., & Engle, R. W. (1989). Is working memory capacity task dependent? *Journal of Memory and Language, 28,* 127–154.

Undheim, J. O., & Gustafsson, J. E. (1987). The hierarchical organization of cognitive abilities: Restoring general intelligence through the use of linear structural relations (LISREL). *Multivariate Behavioral Research, 22,* 149–171.

Valdés, G., & Figueroa, R. A. (1994). *Bilingualism and testing: A special case of bias.* Norwood, NJ: Ablex Publishing.

Vandenberg, S. G., & Vogler, G. P. (1985). Genetic determinants of intelligence. In B. B. Wolman (Ed.), *Handbook of intelligence: Theories, measurements, and applications* (pp. 3–57). New York: Wiley.

Vellutino, F. R., & Scanlon, D. M. (1982). Verbal processing in poor and normal readers. In C. Brainerd & M. Pressley (Eds.), *Verbal processing in children: Progress in cognitive development research* (pp. 189–264). Chicago: University of Chicago Press.

Vernon, P. A. (1990). An overview of chronometric measures of intelligence. *School Psychology Review, 19* (4), 399–410.

Vernon, P. A., & Mori, M. (1990). Physiological approaches to the assessment of intelligence. In C. R. Reynolds & R. W. Kamphaus (Eds.), *Handbook of psychological and educational assessment: Intelligence and achievement* (pp. 389–402). New York: Guilford.

Vernon, P. E. (1961). *The structure of human abilities* (2d ed.). London: Methuen.

Vernon, P. E., Jackson, D. N., & Messick, S. (1988). Cultural influences on patterns of abilities in North America. In S. H. Irvine & J. W. Berry (Eds.), *Human abilities in cultural context* (pp. 208–231). New York: Cambridge University Press.

Vygotsky, L. S. (1978). *Mind in society: The development of higher psychological processes* (M. Cole, V. John-Steiner, S. Scribner, & E. Souberman, Eds.). Cambridge, MA: Harvard University Press.

Vygotsky, L. S. (1986). *Thought and language* (A. Kozulin, Ed.). Cambridge, MA: MIT Press.

Wagner, R. K. (1986). Phonological processing abilities and reading: Implications for disabled readers. *Journal of Learning Disabilities, 19,* 623–630.

Wagner, R. K., & Torgesen, J. K. (1987). The nature of phonological processing and its causal role in the acquisition of reading skills. *Psychological Bulletins, 101* (2), 192–212.

Wagner, R. K., Torgesen, J. K., Laughton, P., Simmons, K., & Rashotte, C. A. (1993). Development of young readers' phonological processing abilities. *Journal of Educational Psychology, 85* (1), 83–103.

Wagner, R. K., Torgesen, J. K., & Rashotte, C. A. (1994). Development of reading related phonological processing abilities: New evidence of bidirectional causality from a latent variable longitudinal study. *Developmental Psychology, 30* (1), 73–87.

Watkins, M. W., & Kush, J. C. (1994). Wechsler subtest analysis: The right way, the wrong way, or no way? *School Psychology Review, 23,* 640–651.

Webster, R. E. (1979). Visual and aural short-term memory capacity deficits in mathematics disabled students. *Journal of Educational Research, 72* (5), 277–283.

Wechsler, D. (1949). *Manual for the Wechsler Intelligence Scale For Children*. San Antonio, TX: Psychological Corporation.

Wechsler, D. (1955). *Manual for the Wechsler Adult Intelligence Scale*. New York: Psychological Corporation.

Wechsler, D. (1967). *Manual for the Wechsler Preschool and Primary Scale of Intelligence*. San Antonio, TX: Psychological Corporation.

Wechsler, D. (1974). *Manual for the Wechsler Intelligence Scale for Children—Revised*. San Antonio, TX: Psychological Corporation.

Wechsler, D. (1981). *Wechsler Adult Intelligence Scale—Revised*. San Antonio, TX: Psychological Corporation.

Wechsler, D. (1987). *Wechsler Memory Scale—Revised*. San Antonio, TX: Psychological Corporation.

Wechsler, D. (1989). *Wechsler Preschool and Primary Scale of Intelligence—Revised*. San Antonio, TX: Psychological Corporation.

Wechsler, D. (1991). *Wechsler Intelligence Scale for Children—Third Edition*. San Antonio, TX: Psychological Corporation.

Wechsler, D. (1997). *Manual for the Wechsler Adult Intelligence Scale—Third Edition*. San Antonio, TX: Psychological Corporation.

Williams, K. T. (1997). *Expressive Vocabulary Test*. Circle Pines, MN: American Guidance Service.

Wilson, M. S., & Reschly, D. J. (1996). Assessment in school psychology training and practice. *School Psychology Review, 25,* 9–23.

Wolf, M. (1991). Naming-speed and reading: The contribution of the cognitive neurosciences. *Reading Research Quarterly, 26* (2), 123–141.

Woodcock, R. (1989). *Emulation of the WISC-R type standard scores for users of the WJ-R*. Unpublished manuscript.

Woodcock, R. W. (1990). Theoretical foundations of the WJ-R measures of cognitive ability. *Journal of Psychoeducational Assessment, 8,* 231–258.

Woodcock, R. W. (1991). *Woodcock Language Proficiency Battery—Revised* (English form). Chicago: Riverside.

Woodcock, R. W. (1993). An information processing view of Gf-Gc theory. *Journal of Psychoeducational Assessment* [Monograph Series: WJ-R Monograph], 80–102.

Woodcock, R. W. (1994). Measures of fluid and crystallized intelligence. In R. J. Sternberg (Ed.), *The encyclopedia of intelligence* (pp. 452–456). New York: Macmillan.

Woodcock, R. W. (1997). The Woodcock-Johnson Tests of Cognitive Ability—Revised. In D. P. Flanagan, J. L. Genshaft, & P. L. Harrison (Eds.), *Contemporary intellectual assessment: Theories, tests, and issues* (pp. 230–246). New York: Guilford.

Woodcock, R. W., & Johnson, M. B. (1977). *Woodcock-Johnson Psycho-Educational Battery*. Chicago: Riverside.

Woodcock, R. W., & Johnson, M. B. (1989). *Woodcock-Johnson Psycho-Educational Battery—revised*. Chicago: Riverside.

Woodcock, R. W., & Mather, N. (1989/1990). WJ-R Tests of Cognitive Ability—Standard and Supplemental Batteries: Examiner's manual. In R. W. Woodcock & M. B. Johnson, *Woodcock-Johnson Psycho-Educational Battery—Revised*. Chicago: Riverside.

Woodcock, R. W., & Munoz-Sandoval, A. F. (1993). An IRT approach to cross-language test equating and interpretation. *European Journal of Psychological Assessment, 9,* 233–241.

Woodcock, R. W., & Munoz-Sandoval, A. F. (1996). *Bateria Woodcock-Munoz Pruebas de Habilidad Cognoscitiva—Revisada*. Chicago: Riverside.

Yopp, H. K. (1988). The validity and reliability of phonemic awareness tests. *Reading Research Quarterly, 23* (2), 159–177.

Ysseldyke, J. (1990). Goodness of fit of the Woodcock-Johnson Psycho-Educational Battery—Revised to the Horn-Cattell *Gf-Gc* theory. *Journal of Psychoeducational Assessment, 8,* 268–275.

Ysseldyke, J. E. (1979). Issues in psycho-educational assessment. In G. D. Phye, & D. Reschly (Eds.), *School psychology: Methods and role*. New York: Academic Press.

Yuill, N., Oakhill, J., & Parking, A. (1989). Working memory, comprehension ability and the resolution of text anomaly. *British Journal of Psychology, 80,* 351–361.

Zachary, R. A. (1990). Wechsler's intelligence scales: Theoretical and practical considerations. *Journal of Psychoeducational Assessment, 8,* 276–289.

Zwick, W. R., & Velicer, W. F. (1986). Comparison of five rules for determining the number of components to retain. *Psychological Bulletin, 99* (3), 432–442.

Index